Critique and the Care of the Self

Critique and the Care of the Self
The Economy of Truth and Government in Michel Foucault's Late Work

Karl Katz Lydén

Södertörns högskola

Subject: Philosophy
Research Area: Critical and Cultural Theory
School: School of Culture and Education
Baltic and East European Graduate School

Södertörns högskola
(Södertörn University)
The Library
SE-141 89 Huddinge
www.sh.se/publications
© Karl Katz Lydén

Cover: Jonathan Robson
Graphic form: Per Lindblom & Jonathan Robson

Stockholm 2024

Södertörn Doctoral Dissertations 229
ISSN 1652–7399

ISBN 978-91-89504-80-6 (print)
ISBN 978-91-89504-81-3 (digital)

Abstract

This thesis engages Michel Foucault's late work on ancient philosophy in relation to his earlier investigations of modern forms of government and events in his political present. Beginning with a reinterpretation of the function of style in Foucault's oeuvre, it demonstrates that the ancient notion of the care of the self – the style of existence – unfolds as a critical project. The thesis considers Foucault's last three lecture courses at the Collège de France: *The Hermeneutics of the Subject* (1982), *The Government of Self and Others* (1983), and *The Courage of the Truth* (1984). It shows that what is at stake in the ancient notions of truth-telling and the technologies of the self is not reducible to an ethical, individual subject in Greco-Roman antiquity, but rather something that bears on Foucault's previous critical work on modern forms of subjection, on his notion of critique, and on political, collective subjects in the present.

No previous study has treated this relation between Foucault's notion of the care of the self and his theory of critique. And while shorter attempts have noted their *conceptual* common basis in "virtue" and "government," this thesis opens new perspectives. Through a formal analogy to Kant's critical project, it proposes a model of three Foucauldian kinds of critique: the historical-philosophical practice of theoretical work, truth-telling in the political field, and the individual or collective "art of not being governed like that." Moving between the theoretical work and lesser discussed materials – specifically Foucault's engagement with the Polish trade union *Solidarność* and the French labor union CFDT – important continuities are identified. It is demonstrated that Foucault understands critique, the care of the self, and collective movements in his own time, not only by the same conceptual framework of government, virtue, and truth, but also as non-discursive forms or practices in which means and ends merge. This is significant in relation to Foucault's definition of modern economic government in his lecture course on neoliberalism, *The Birth of Biopolitics* (1979): a government guided by an equally non-discursive "veridiction of the market." Building on these continuities in Foucault's oeuvre, it is concluded that the ancient notions of truth-telling and of the style of existence offer significant tools in the art of not being governed like that: as collective configurations of critique in the present.

Keywords: Foucault, Critique, Care of the self, Governmentality, Socialist Governmentality, Neoliberalism, Means and ends, Self-finalization, Parrēsia, Parrhesia, Truth-telling, Veridiction of the market, *Solidarność*, labor unions, CFDT, Style, Performativity, Montage.

Abstract (på svenska)
Titel: Kritik och omsorgen om sig: sanningssägandets och regerandets ekonomi
i Michel Foucaults sena verk

Denna avhandling tar upp Michel Foucaults sena verk om antik filosofi i relation
till hans tidigare undersökningar av det moderna regerandet och händelser i hans
politiska samtid. Utifrån en omtolkning av stilens funktion i Foucaults arbeten
visas här att den antika idén om omsorgen om sig – levnadsstilen – hos Foucault
läggs fram som ett kritiskt projekt. Avhandlingen tar upp Foucaults tre sista
föreläsningsserier vid Collège de France: *Subjektets hermeneutik* (1982),
Styrandet av sig själv och andra (1983), och *Modet till sanning* (1984). Den visar
att det subjektsbegrepp som introduceras i den grekisk-romerska antikens läror
om sanningssägande och självteknologier inte kan reduceras till ett etiskt,
individuellt subjekt begränsat till sin egen historiska situation, utan står i relation
till Foucaults tidigare kritiska verk om moderna former av "subjektion" eller
underkastelse (*asujettissement*), hans kritikbegrepp och hans diskussioner om
politiska kollektiva begrepp i samtiden. Ingen längre studie har behandlat denna
relation mellan Foucaults begrepp om omsorgen om sig och hans definition av
kritik. Medan kortare forskningsbidrag har noterat deras begreppsliga gemensamma nämnare i "dygd" och "regerande" öppnar denna avhandling nya perspektiv. Med en formell analogi med Kants kritiska projekt föreslås här en modell
av tre foucauldianska typer av kritik: det teoretiska arbetets historisk-filosofiska
praktik, sanningssägandet inom det politiska fältet och den individuella och
kollektiva "konsten att inte låta sig styras på ett visst sätt". Genom att undersöka
både de teoretiska arbetena och mindre uppmärksammat material – som
Foucaults engagemang i *Solidarność* och den franska fackföreningen CFDT – kan
viktiga kontinuiteter uppmärksammas. Här visas att Foucault förstår kritik,
omsorgen om sig och kollektiva rörelser i sin egen samtid inte bara genom ett
och samma begreppsliga ramverk av regerande, dygd och sanning, utan också
som icke-diskursiva former eller praktiker i vilka mål och medel sammanfaller.
Detta är viktigt med avseende på Foucaults definition av modernt ekonomiskt
regerande i föreläsningarna om nyliberalism, *Biopolitikens födelse* (1979): ett
regerande grundat på "marknadens veridiktion". Utifrån dessa kontinuiteter
dras slutsatsen att de antika idéerna om sanningssägande och levnadsstilen
erbjuder avgörande verktyg för konsten att inte låta sig styras på ett viss sätt: som
kollektiva konfigurationer av kritik i samtiden.

Nyckelord: Foucault, kritik, omsorgen om sig, regerande, socialistisk regerings-
konst, nyliberalism, medel och mål, parrēsia, parrhesia, sanningssägande, marknadens veridiktion, *Solidarność*, fackföreningar, CFDT, stil, performativitet,
montage.

Still from *Passageraren* (*The Passenger*), directed by Eric M Nilsson (1966).

The philosopher must say quite simply what there is. [...] He is just the man of the day and of the moment: passing, closer than anyone to what is passing.

Michel Foucault, 1966.*

* "[L]e philosophe doit dire tout simplement ce qu'il y a. […] Il est seulement l'homme du jour et du moment: passager, plus près que personne du passage." Michel Foucault, *Le discours philosophique* (Paris: Seuil/Gallimard, 2023), 17.

Contents

Introduction

How can Michel Foucault's late work on ancient philosophy and its notions of the care of the self and *parrēsia*, a form of speaking the truth, be related to the present? This thesis will demonstrate that Foucault's extended investigations into Greco-Roman antiquity in the 1980s – which many have considered as an ethical turn, a turn away from the intensely political nature of his works on the prison and asylum – are developed in formal and conceptual continuity with his definition of critique, his analyses of modern government, and in relation to events and movements in his political present. The care of the self must be understood as a critical project. The thesis will also show that Foucault's late work – despite the great thematic, methodological, and stylistic differences – does not break with the earlier work, and that the notion of the subject that can constitute itself in a certain practice of truth is not a deviation from, or somehow incompatible with, the earlier work and its notion of the subject as an effect of power/ knowledge relations. On the contrary, the subject that constitutes itself in the technologies of the self is described as the first node in the reversibility of power relations and governmentality.

In the summer of 1983, Foucault planned to write a book with the title "La tête des socialistes". It was conceived in relation to the discussions surrounding the intellectuals' support or rather non-support of Mitterand's socialist government and was to be comprised of a series of interviews with Didier Eribon. The aim was to analyze the "successive failures of Left governments in France," indicating a lack of a proper governmentality of the Left. The question to be considered was the possibility of "governing in a different way" – something that Foucault had touched upon already in his lecture courses *"Society Must Be Defended"* and *The Birth of Biopolitics* at Collège de France. The project, however, was abandoned at an early stage: according to Eribon, with his work on *The History of Sexuality* once again running smoothly, Foucault deemed it too complex and time-consuming.

As an aborted and marginal project, it may seem insignificant for what will be the principal focus in this thesis here. But as we shall see, the problem of "governing in a different way" articulates rather well some of the questions that Foucault is concerned with during this time. This will be discussed in the following chapters: the Greek notion of *epimeleia heautou*, i.e. the care of the self, which is also defined as a government of the self; the truth-telling of the public speaker in the democratic assembly and the political advisor of the Prince in the city-state, and lastly "the art of not being governed like that," as defined in Foucault's 1978 "What is Critique?" But above all, the plan to write a book on Left governmentality can serve to remind us of the importance of what Foucault defined, in the recently published book manuscript *Le discours philosophique* from 1966, as the very task of philosophy: the diagnostic of the present.[1] And if we needed reminding of this then it is because most often, Foucault undertakes this diagnostic of the present by investigating the past.

Before we go any further, something must be said of what we have fixed as the object of study. What constitutes Foucault's late work? The editors of the recent anthology *The Late Foucault*, give an interesting answer: not only is the late work something very different today than 20 years ago, with the numerous posthumous publications of tape-recorded material and manuscripts, it is still growing with new publications being added all the time. Thus the late work is a *changing* body of works.[2] Against such a Heraclitean view of the growing Foucauldian oeuvre, one can object that there remain decisive points within this open-ended process. For a long time, when heirs and publishers still abided by Foucault's will ("No posthumous publications"), the late work consisted of the last two volumes of *The History of Sexuality* published in 1984, along with articles, shorter texts and interviews. Today, all of Foucault's annual lecture courses at Collège de France have been published – giving us a marvelous overview of his work in the making – as well as the fourth volume of *The History of Sexuality, The Confessions of the Flesh*; whatever is added after this is unlikely to be of the same importance.

This expansion has in recent years led to a considerable reevaluation of Foucault's work. Perhaps the most important and interesting part concerns the work on antiquity, of which the sheer amount – of fourteen lecture courses at Collège de France, six are devoted to ancient material – may change our image of Foucault: "quantitatively speaking, he is a scholar of antiquity."[3]

---

[1] Michel Foucault, *Le discours philosophique* (Paris: Seuil/Gallimard, 2023), 17.

[2] *The Late Foucault*, eds. Marta Faustino and Gianfranco Ferraro, (London: Bloomsbury, 2020),

[3] Foucault's courses at Collège de France stretched from 1970–71 to 1983–84, with a sabbatical in 1976–77. Considering the "almost three thousand pages that deal with ancient material, which thus constitutes the largest part of his research [...] the former common picture of Foucault, which also formed the basis for part of the criticism directed against him that he focuses too much on the "classical era," that is, the 17th and 18th centuries, and in a predominantly French material, must thus be revised: quantitatively speaking, he is a scholar of antiquity." See Sven-Olov Wallenstein,

Perhaps that depends on how one is counting, but it is indisputable that Foucault's engagement with the Classic, Roman, and Hellenistic periods is substantial and merits study. What may have garnered more attention outside the specialized circles, however, is a much publicized anthology entitled *Foucault and Neoliberalism*, in which the authors set out to demonstrate that his late work "functioned to legitimate a neoliberal common sense,"[4] being of an "eminently conservative character."[5] While some of the volume's contributions may not engage very much with Foucault's work, and while the editor's suggestion that Foucault was seduced by neoliberalism[6] has been characterized as "a mixture of old news and falsification,"[7] the anthology can be interesting to recall simply because the following work will make the exact opposite assessment. What shall be demonstrated in the coming chapters is that Foucault, in his work on topics like Stoic and Epicurean ethics, Periclean discourses, and Cynic truth-telling, was very much concerned with the possibility of forming an *other* life. And if we understand this research in relation to some of his other theoretical and practical engagements in present events during this period, it provides us with the outlines of a political subjectivity that is highly incongruent with any "neoliberal common sense."

If this answers the question of *what* this thesis will try to do, we shall, before turning to *how*, say something about *why*. Why do we ask this question of Foucault's late work? Apart from hoping that it may prove useful in our lives, it is of interest because there is something of a riddle to it. The late work was cut short by Foucault's untimely death. The late work is unfinished, incomplete, a collection of lecture notes that at times seem like fragments moving somewhat haphazardly between this and that concept, this and that theme or problem in this or that ancient school of philosophy. And even

---

"Introduktion," in *Foucault och Antiken*, eds. Sven-Olov Wallenstein and Johan Sehlberg (Hägersten: Tankekraft, 2017), 9.

[4] Daniel Zamora, "Introduction," in *Foucault and Neoliberalism*, eds. Daniel Zamora and Michael C. Behrent (Cambridge, UK: Polity Press 2015), 4.

[5] Jean-Loup Amselle, "Michel Foucault and the Spiritualization of Philosophy," in *Foucault and Neoliberalism*, 159.

[6] Daniel Zamora, "Introduction," 3.

[7] Colin Gordon, *Foucault News*, January 2015. https://foucaultnews.files.wordpress.com/2015/01/colin-gordon-2015.pdf (January 9, 2017). "The old news is that Foucault was not a Marxist or a supporter of any existing model of revolutionary socialism, and was hostile to the USSR and the political influence of the French Communist Party. The falsification is the claim that Foucault 'endorsed' or 'embraced' some or all forms of liberalism and neoliberalism." (Colin Gordon worked with Foucault on several occasions, and is the editor of *The Foucault Effect* which introduced Foucault's concept of governmentality to a larger audience. See *The Foucault Effect*, eds. Graham Burchell, Colin Gordon, Peter Miller [Chicago: The University of Chicago Press, 1991].)

when it seems to be proceeding in a loosely ordered genealogy of Western subjectivity, it remains open-ended and without solid conclusions. One could imagine that something unfinished is possible to finish, and one could be drawn to this possibility. But the fact is that the late work was unfinished long before Foucault's death. To understand why we are inquiring into his late work, it is important to know that Foucault, at the height of his career, stopped writing books.

The Long Silence

In 1976, Foucault published *The Will to Knowledge*, the first volume of *The History of Sexuality*. This short but pivotal book in Foucault's overall body of work develops questions that Foucault had opened at earlier points,[8] and it anticipates the work to come – as well as the work that would not come. It is here, with the focus on the confessing subject, that Foucault begins his work on the subject as being constituted by speaking the truth of itself; an idea which informs the very last things Foucault wrote. And it is here he announces the future work that was never written. When *Histoire de la sexualité* came out in France in 1976, its back page listed five more titles; of these, none were published.[9] In fact, this plan of a six-volume work marks the starting point of a long period of unpublished books – during which at least another three books were announced but never realized.[10] Not until eight

---

[8] The project of writing a history of sexuality was announced already in *L'Archéologie de Savoir*, to form another great history along with the history of madness in *History of Madness* from 1961 and *The Birth of the Clinic* from 1963. Published just a year after *Discipline and Punish*, *The Will to Knowledge* extends the analysis of power in terms of power-knowledge relations, and further develops the idea that power must be understood as productive, as opposed to simply repressive. But rather than describing how the disciplinary organization and the "diagram" of the military camp function as models in the shaping of the prison, the casern, the school, and the hospital, the workings of power are now thematized primarily as confession, and in terms of truth. Ever since the Middle Ages, truthful confession has become a central procedure of individualization by power: "Western man has become a confessing animal." See Michel Foucault, *The History of Sexuality Volume 1: An Introduction.*, trans. R. Hurley (New York: Pantheon Books 1978), 58–59.

[9] Listed as upcoming titles were: 2 *La Chair et le corps* (The Flesh and the Body) 3 *La Croisade des enfants* (The Childrens's Crusade) 4 *La Femme, la mère et l'hystérique* (The Woman, The Mother, and The Hysteric) 5 *Les* Pervers (The Perverse) 6 *Population et races* (Population and races). At least two were drafted: *Les Pervers* and *La Chair et le corps*. For further early but still relevant discussion on this matter, see: *Space, Knowledge and Power: Foucault and Geography*, eds. Jeremy W. Crampton and Stuart Elden, (Hampshire/Burlington: Ashgate 2007), 68. For an an updated account, see Frédéric Gros, "Avertissement," in Michel Foucault, *Les aveux de la chair* (Paris: Gallimard, 2018).

[10] In his preparations for the *The Hermeneutics of the Subject*, Foucault was planning to use the material for a book entitled "The Care of the Self" (further discussed in chapter 2); in 1983 he planned to write a white paper with Pierre Bourdieu on how the Left government failed being Left (further

years after the initial plan was drafted, in 1984, two entirely new titles were published as volumes two and three: *The Use of Pleasures* and *The Care of the Self*. In addition to these, a fourth volume entitled *The Confessions of the Flesh* was published posthumously in 2018. It was announced in a press release drafted by Foucault in June 1984, but the work still needed editing and was left incomplete: Foucault died on June 25th in the Salpêtrière hospital in Paris.

This "lengthy silence,"[11] as Didier Eribon would call it in his biography of Foucault, harbors quite a few contradictions. First of all, it was only "silent" with regard to the absence of published books. As before, Foucault wrote a large amount of shorter texts and essays, taught his courses at Collège de France, as he had done since 1970, and intervened in the social and political questions of his time. He also started teaching more regularly at Berkeley in California (while at the same time leaving his longtime workplace at the *Bibliotheque nationale* for the much smaller *Bibliotheque de Saulchoir*), and in 1978, Foucault embarked on a journalistic endeavor for *Corriere della Sera*, covering the nascent Islamic revolution in Iran.[12]

Second, the intellectual and political landscape of the late 1970s was changing rapidly in France. For Foucault, his most consistent political work of the early 1970s came to an end after the *Groupe d'information sur les prisons* (GIP) was dissolved, an organization he had helped found with his partner Daniel Defert. The organization strived to disseminate information about the conditions in French prisons and had close ties to the French Maoist group *Gauche Prolétarienne* (GP). Foucault now mobilized in solidarity with the Vietnamese Boat People, the dissidents of the Soviet Union, and the Polish labor union *Solidarność*. These engagements are often regarded as part of a shift in Foucault's political stances, sometimes in relation to the fallout with Deleuze over the "Croissant Affair,"[13] and the liaison with the New Philosophers – a group of former Maoists who vehemently turned against Marx and Marxism in a grand attack on all "totalitarianism." Since much has been made of this link, and since his late work at times has been understood in light of it, a few things can be noted.

---

discussed in chapter 3); finally the already mentioned "La Tête des socialistes" was projected around the same time.

[11] Didier Eribon, *Foucault*, trans. Betsy Wing, (Cambridge: Harvard University Press, 1991), 343.

[12] David Macey, *The Lives of Michel Foucault* (London: Vintage 1994), 407–411.

[13] The "Croissant Affair" was a debate in France about extradition or political asylum for the West German lawyer Klaus Croissant, one of the defense attorneys for the *Rote Armee Fraktion*. While both Foucault and Deleuze supported his appeal for political asylum, Foucault refused to sign the petition circulated by Deleuze's longtime collaborator Guattari, because of how it adopted RAF's terminology, referring to West Germany as a "fascist" state.

There was indeed a mutual benevolence: more consistently from *les nouveaux philosophes*, but also from Foucault, who in an appreciative book review of Glucksmann made it clear that he did not share Deleuze's assessment of the New Philosophers as "TV buffoons" working with grand but hollow concepts like Law, Power, Rebellion, etc.[14] On the other hand he continued to refer to (and not to refer to)[15] Marx in what Balibar has called a lifelong and "genuine struggle with Marx, [which] can be viewed as one of the driving forces of his productiveness."[16] It therefore seems important, in this regard, to acknowledge the futility of trying to identify Foucault with any given political position, and even more so, of trying to build an analysis of it. Foucault repeatedly refused to be inscribed within certain ideological and political discourses. This becomes evident in two interviews given in 1977. When interviewed by Bernard-Henri Lévy in *Le Nouvel Observateur*, he describes his analysis of sexuality in terms of Marx's analysis of capitalism's inherent immiseration of the worker, and refutes Lévy's dismissal of the "marxist vulgate and neo-leftism of the May 1968 slogan 'Sous les pavés, la plage,'" by quoting Jacques Rancière's (leftist) critique of the "leftist doxa".[17] But some months later, in an interview with Rancière for the latter's journal *Révoltes Logiques*, Foucault immediately distances himself from his interlocutor and rehearses his appreciation of Glucksmann for not trying to save a true socialism from the pseudo-socialism that produced the Gulag.[18] More than simple gestures of defiance, these refusals of politically programmatic discourses testify to Foucault's consistent efforts to let his work be defined on its own terms. This does not seem to increase the likelihood that Foucault was "seduced" by key ideas of neoliberalism; in any case the following chapters will not be concerned with Foucault's political belonging. It will instead try to make use of his work.

Third, a certain confusion arises from Foucault's conflicting announcements of upcoming work and what he actually went on to do. In the beginning of 1976, in the second lecture of *"Society Must Be Defended,"* Foucault

---

[14] Gilles Deleuze, "À propos des nouveaux philosophes et d'un problème plus général" *Minuit* 24 (1977). https://archive.org/details/1977G.DeleuzeAProposDesNouveauxPhilosophes (January 9, 2017).

[15] Foucault mentions in an interview his habit of quoting and discussing Marx without references, see: Michel Foucault, Entretien sur la prison: le livre et sa méthode (1975), in *Dits et écrits I, 1954–1975*, eds. Daniel Defert and François Ewald, Collab. Jacques Lagrange (Paris: Gallimard, 2001), 1620–1621.

[16] Étienne Balibar, "Foucault and Marx: The question of nominalism," in *Michel Foucault Philosopher*, trans. T. Armstrong, (Hertfordshire: Harvester 1992), 39.

[17] Michel Foucault, "Non à sexe roi," *Dits et écrits II 1976–1988*, ed. Daniel Defert and François Ewald, Collab. Jacques Lagrange (Paris: Gallimard 2001), No. 200, 265.

[18] Michel Foucault, "Pouvoirs et stratégies," *Dits et écrits II 1976–1988*, No. 218, 418.

is very clear: "Until now, or for roughly the last five years, it has been disciplines; for the next five years, it will be war, struggle, the army."[19] Later in the same year he completes *The Will to Know*, outlining a completely different project with the remaining five volumes of *The History of sexuality*, to be written with the frequency of one per year. And then, after a sabbatical year in 1977, in the subsequent lectures at Collège de France, published as *Security, Territory, Population*, he ends up doing neither, but goes on to study the population as an emerging political problem, pastoral power, and the emergence of the police as backgrounds to the governmentality of modernity. This, to a certain degree, is work he continues in 1979 with *The Birth of Biopolitics*. As a partial explanation – but also further complication – of these matters, one must take into account what is stated by Daniel Defert, namely, that the series of unpublished books was a deliberate act. Following a frustrated negotiation with the publishing house Gallimard, Foucault signed a five-year exclusivity agreement in 1975 deciding that "his next book would be of very small format (which was *The Will to Know*) and that there would be no other books for five years (which many interpreted as a crisis in his thought)."[20] While this may explain why there were no books between 1976 and 1980, it does not account for the continued absence after that.

Thus, it is not entirely clear that Foucault knows where he is heading in 1978 when he scraps two already conflicting five-year plans for a third project. But what he actually does, through the comparison of Greek and Roman Christian relations of truth and government in the fourth lecture that year, is to introduce the problem that will occupy him during the 1980s and that we will discuss here, in relation to truth-telling, subjectivity, and *parrēsia*. Ultimately it is the problem of government, and the government of oneself and others.[21] All the while, the silence of unpublished books continues.

—

[19] Michel Foucault, *"Society Must Be Defended": Lectures at Collège de France 1975–1976*, trans. D. Macey (New York: Picador 2003), 23.

[20] "1976, December. Publication of *The Will to Know*, first volume of *The History of Sexuality*. [...] The book is presented as an introduction to a history of sexuality in six volumes, but the author confides that he has no intention to write them. [...] Also, in 1975, Foucault had asked the publishing house Gallimard to forward 200.000 francs to [the director] René Allio to direct *Pierre Rivière*. The publisher's laywer had Foucault, who had no more obligations, sign a five year exclusivity agreement. Foucault then decided that his next book would be of very small format (which was *The Will to Know*) and that there would be no other books for five years (which many interpreted as a crisis in his thought)." Daniel Defert, "Chronologie," in *Dits et écrits I, 1954–1975*, eds. Daniel Defert and François Ewald, Collab. Jacques Lagrange (Paris: Gallimard, 2001), 68.

[21] Foucault establishes a link between "the art of government" during the 16th century practices developed in antiquity: "I think that the general problem of 'government' suddenly breaks out in the sixteenth century with respect to many different problems at the same time and in completely different aspects. There is the problem of the government of oneself, for example. The sixteenth century

Stakes of Philosophical and Political Subjectivity

This thesis is born from the desire to grasp Foucault's late work. On the one hand, as we have seen, the late work can be understood as a kind of potentiality, an ever-receding horizon, as something unfinished in relation to the (unanswerable) long silence of unwritten books. On the other hand, it can be understood as deeply engaged with its own present, and as such, possible to work out in its further implications.

To do this, we have to say something about the relation to the earlier (which includes the early to mid-) work. Not with the intention of accounting for the diverse earlier works such, nor under the illusion of making a kind of balance sheet between early and late. Rather, it is about articulating what kind of reading of the early to mid-works lies at the basis of investigating Foucault's late work – because the former very much determines our understanding of the latter. It is thus about giving an account of the reading of Foucault's earlier writings I am guilty of. A far more able reader than me, Louis Althusser, in the process of distinguishing between late and early work of Marx, had to ask the question: what is it to read? That, along with another question of his – what is the unicity or singular traits of this work? – forms the ground for chapter one. The reading accounted for therein will serve as the ground and motivation for the investigation undertaken in the following chapters.

Our very first hypothesis will hold that the play of contradictions, which can be identified in Foucault's early and mid-work – on the level of style and form, articulating real, social and historical contradictions – remains in the late work, only somewhere under its calm surface, where we cannot see it. And that is why, when we first encounter the notion of *epimeleia heautou* or the care of the self in the 1982 lectures *The Hermeneutics of the Subject*, we stress the importance of how Foucault defines the care of the self in terms of liberation and critique, that is, as a process whereby the subject breaks with what "enslaves" it. An important aspect here is Foucault's insistence that the care of the self (described also in related terms as the aesthetics of the self, the art of life, style of life, form of life, etc.) is not primarily an individual practice: it requires at least another person (to speak the truth), or a communal setting. Nor is it an aristocratic privilege. We learn, for example, of popular, "working-class" Epicurean communities. A further example of particular

---

return to Stoicism revolves around this reactualization of the problem of how to govern oneself." See Michel Foucault, *Security, Territory, Population: Lectures at Collège de France 1977–1978*, trans. G. Burchell, (Hampshire/New York: Palgrave/Macmillan 2007), 88.

interest (and a certain ambiguity, as we shall see) in this context is the *Therapeutae* who, in their communal garden outside Alexandria, were comprised of both women and men. This feature is extremely rare given women's non-status in political and philosophical life during antiquity; a status of absence and invisibility that is not discussed by Foucault and that will remain largely unaddressed in the following chapters, but that does not by necessity (nor by intention), as we shall see, exclude non-male perspectives. The *Therapeutae*, interestingly, also denied private property, and opposed slavery. These variously popular, gender-mixed, poor, and mostly urban communities are interesting in that they contradict the Spartan maxim of *skholē*, the free time of the free citizen, as a condition for caring for oneself or developing an art of life. It is perhaps in light of this that we can understand what Gayatri Chakravorty Spivak said about *The Courage of the Truth*, Foucault's subsequent lecture course on the Cynics: "This is a text without women." But then added: "I can live with that."[22] Meaning that nothing necessarily restricts these ancient technologies of the self (or Foucault's use of them) to any particularly privileged group, or any preexisting subject. On the contrary, as is shown by Agamben,[23] there is no proper Foucauldian subject, but only a process of subjectivation. And as is shown in Foucault's discussion of "revolutionary subjectivity," the development of a care of the self and a common art of life seems inherent to social and political struggle.

What we see here is the notion of a subject that constitutes itself in a kind of emancipatory, critical project articulated in a certain practice of truth. This forms an important counterpoint and addition to the notion of subjectivity developed in his earlier, published work. While Foucault previously had described the subject as an effect of power/knowledge relations and of subjugation[24] – which made some accuse him of ensnaring subjectivity in an all-encompassing mesh of discursive and coercive relations – a new side appears with his studies of practices of the self in Greco-Roman antiquity. Indeed, when at one point in the lectures Foucault discusses his overarching

---

[22] This comment was made in a seminar on Foucault's late work at Columbia University. On the same occasion Spivak also mentioned a certain eurocentrism on Foucault's part; while this study will remain within Foucault's Greco-Roman perspective, for a recent problematization of it, see Avram Alpert, *Global Origins of the Modern Self* (Albany: SUNY Press, 2019). For Spivak's comments, see Gayatri Chakravorty Spivak, "Additional Thoughts," Columbia University, accessed April 11, 2024, https://blogs.law.columbia.edu/foucault1313/2016/04/14/gayatri-chakravorty-spivak-additional-thoughts/.

[23] Agamben, *The Use of Bodies*, trans. Adam Kotsko (Stanford: Stanford University Press, 2015), 101.

[24] This is how we can understand Foucault when he says that the soul is not a substance, but "the effect and instrument of a political anatomy." See Michel Foucault, *Discipline and Punish: The Birth of the Prison*, trans. Alan Sheridan (New York: Vintage Books 1995), 30.

purposes, he states that the reflection on power relations and govern-mentality in their possible "reversibility" cannot avoid passing through the element of the subject's relation to itself. Drawn to its very limit, the question for us then becomes: can Foucault's account of what has been perceived as operating merely on an individuated and ethical level in antiquity in some way pertain to collective, political subjects in the present? Foucault provides us with no direct answer. In the following year's lectures, *The Government of Self and Others*, Foucault turns to examine the notion of *parrēsia*, and inves-tigates how this form of frank speech or truth-telling functions in the political field. Here he discusses the role of the public speaker and the philosopher approaching an autocratic ruler as political advisor. While, as we shall see, these figures certainly are related to Foucault's and our own present, and while their practices can be considered in terms of critique, the subjectivity at stake is not collective, not even political; it is philosophical.

Yet there is one instance when collective political subjectivity and phi-losophical subjectivity coincide, or at least coexist, subsumed under the same concept: Foucault's notion of critique. In "What is Critique?," a lecture given in 1978 at the Society of Philosophy in Paris, Foucault defines critique as, on the one hand, the individual and collective "art of not being governed like that," which could take the form of insubordination or general revolt, and on the other, as theoretical work described as a "historical-philosophical practice," articulated along the lines of his own work. An important remark is made in "What is Critique?" that will appear in various forms throughout Foucault's late work: critique is always directed toward something, it is always a means for something other; yet it is a kind of virtue, and thus an end in itself. In *The Hermeneutics of the Subject*, for example, it is stated that in Hellenistic philosophy, the care of the self is an end in itself: it is *the* virtue. Here, Foucault explicitly appropriates Pierre Hadot's notion of philosophy as way of life: an idea that ancient philosophy was not only, as modern philosophy has increasingly come to be, concerned with questions of truth and knowledge, but always a specific spiritual project concerned with how to live one's life.[25] So what is changing in Foucault's late work is not only the description of the subject, but the very understanding of the function of philosophy. To his earlier definition of philosophy as a diagnostic of the present – which never ceased to animate his work; in these later lectures he calls it an "ontology of the

---

[25] Pierre Hadot, *Philosophy as a Way of Life: Spiritual Exercises from Socrates to Foucault*, trans. Michael Chase (Oxford: Blackwell Publishers Ltd, 1995), 265.

present" – it seems that in his late work on antiquity, Foucault adds a definition of philosophy as practice, defined by the art of life or the technologies of the self, and always as a practice of truth. And this is where the philosophical and collective political subjectivities coincide once more – in the subjectivation of truth, in a practice whose form is its own end.

Chapter Structure

The five chapters of this thesis are rather different from each other. The first sets out from the question of style and the stylistic shift that appears in Foucault's writings, analyzing the early to mid-style in order to grasp what is at stake in Foucault's late work. The second and third chapters are devoted to Foucault's engagement with ancient philosophy, specifically the notions of subjectivity and truth in his three last lecture courses at the Collège de France. The fourth chapter takes up the Foucauldian question of critique in a formal analogy with the Kantian three Critiques. The fifth chapter discusses Foucault's theoretical and practical engagements with contemporary forms of government and critique during his late period. In sum, this thesis forms a movement that begins with Foucault's major works, and then traces his thinking of antiquity, moves through Kant's question of the Enlightenment and Foucault's question of critique, and ends in the near present with Foucault's lectures on neoliberalism and his engagement in contemporary struggles. To establish continuities between these different levels and parts of Foucault's work, we employ something that could be described as a transversal hermeneutics. For example: from the performativity of style in Foucault's early and mid-works, a line is drawn to the performativity inherent in his proposal of a style of existence. Another example concerns the conceptual figure of merging means and ends, which we trace in its isomorphic reappearance in the definition of critique, the description of the care of the self, the analysis of Kant's calling for the enlightenment of the public in an Enlightenment publication, and in the form of a social movement. This makes it possible to grasp the inarticulate but important continuities across Foucault's work, and across the chapters of the thesis. We shall give a slightly more elaborate description of the chapters.

Chapter 1 forms a kind of prelude to the main investigation. As a point of departure, it takes the stylistic shift that appears with the late work, and proposes that the style of "fire and intoxication" in his early to mid-work – which we define as a play of internal tensions, breaks, and contradictions, and discuss in terms of montage and a particular kind of performative reading –

may disappear from the cool surface of the late work, but reappears on another level, for the reader to perform in what Foucault calls the style of life, the aesthetics of existence. This chapter gives an account of how our reading of the late work is grounded in and determined by the experience of reading the earlier work. In its analysis of early and mid-style, it can also serve as an introduction to the lesser known "found works" of Foucault, and as a reminder of certain aspects of Foucault's most well-known work.

Chapter 2 is devoted to the notion of the subject in Foucault's late work. More precisely, it concerns the subjectivity at stake in Foucault's discussion of *epimeleia heautou* or the care of the self in *The Hermeneutics of the Subject* from 1982. Here it is demonstrated to which degree Foucault advances this care of the self in terms of truth-telling, liberation, unlearning, and critique. In addition to this, it is shown that Foucault describes the care of the self in Hellenistic philosophy as an end in itself, in what he terms a "self-finalization" (an important concept for the thesis, and an instance of the figure of merging means and ends), and as a process to be practiced throughout life, in relation to study and knowledge in *mathēsis* and exercise in *askēsis*. This chapter also discusses some of the criticism that has been raised against the later Foucault, for instance Pierre Hadot's assessment that Foucault's understanding of these issues was purely aesthetic, and shows, with Agamben, Hadot's misconstrued notion of the subject in Foucault.

Chapter 3 investigates the theme of truth, *parrēsia*, and truth-telling in *The Government of Self and Others* from 1983 and *The Courage of the Truth* from 1984. In the first of these lecture courses (which is opened with a lecture on Kant's "What is Enlightenment?"), Foucault defines a political *parrēsia* practiced by the public speaker at the assembly, and a philosophical *parrēsia* practiced by the philosopher in the political sphere or as political advisor. In exchange with Marcelo Hoffman's analysis, it is argued that Foucault's interpretation of Plato's letters – describing Plato's encounter with the tyrant of Syracuse – must be seen in light of the crisis and conflict between the French Socialist government and the intellectuals at the time of the lecture course. The chapter ends with a critical reading of Cynics's position and potential in Foucault's late thought. Generally hailed by commentators as a figure of resistance, it is here demonstrated that the Cynics' acts of truth are not easily reconciled with other important elements of Foucault's late thought, i.e. what we have called the recurring figure of merging means and ends.

Chapter 4 is devoted to Foucault's question of critique: between the two definitions of critique Foucault gives in "What is Critique?," a third is added, giving us the very Kantian model of "Foucault's three critiques." While

Kant's critiques are individual theoretical works, providing systematic accounts of the application of reason, what is here called Foucault's three critiques can be regarded as possible fields of intervention. Since the first critique appropriates Foucault's definition of "historical-philosophical practice" (theoretical work), and the second concerns truth-telling in the political sphere, it is the third mode of critique, "the art of not being governed like that," that will be the subject of further investigation.

In chapter 5, the conditions and possibilities of this third critique are investigated in light of Foucault's engagement with three political phenomena of his own time: his analysis of neoliberalism in the lecture course *The Birth of Biopolitics* from 1979; his engagement in the Polish *Solidarność* movement; and his interaction with the French union CFDT. In operationalizing this third mode of critique we will see how the most central and already interconnected notions of his late thought can be activated: truth-telling and veridiction, the figure of merging means and ends, the production of a tension or contradiction, critique as virtue, and – to some extent – even the notion of a left governmentality.

Delineating the field of study

This study of Foucault's late work will focus on the most substantial development of the notions of care of the self and *parrēsia*, and will thus take Foucault's last three lecture courses at the Collège de France as its primary material: *The Hermeneutics of the Subject* from 1982; *The Government of Self and Others* from 1983, and *The Courage of the Truth* from 1984. For reasons of coherence and delimitation of the study, overlapping, partly overlapping, and similar lecture courses such as *Speaking the Truth about Oneself*[26] and *Wrong-Doing, Truth-Telling*[27] will be considered to a lesser extent.

While there are good reasons to argue that Foucault's late work is initiated before his work on antiquity, namely in the lecture course *Security, Territory, Population* from 1978 when he starts operating the shift from the conceptual pair power/knowledge toward that of government/truth, a detailed engagement with this material would stretch this thesis over too vast thematic divergences. And while the first two courses from the 1980s, *The Government of the Living* and *Subjectivity and Truth*, are devoted to

---

[26] Michel Foucault, *Speaking the Truth about Oneself: Lectures at Victoria University, Toronto, 1982* (Chicago: The University of Chicago Press, 2021).
[27] Michel Foucault, *Wrong-Doing, Truth-Telling: The Function of Avowal in Justice*, trans. Stephen W. Sawyer (Chicago: University of Chicago Press, 2014).

antiquity and partly to the same material as the subsequent courses, they are still largely inscribed in the "confessional regime" of obligatory truth-telling, as outlined in the first volume of *The History of Sexuality*, and therefore not immediately relevant to the questions here. The same applies to the recently published fourth volume of *The History of Sexuality*, *The Confessions of the Flesh*. As for Foucault's very first work on antiquity, the first Collège de France course *Lectures on the Will to know* from 1970, it is largely disregarded because of its methodological differences and its thematic distance to what is investigated here.

English translations are used throughout in the following work. When quoted from French or other languages, the translations are my own.

Previous Literature on Foucault's late Work

The literature on Foucault in general is immense. Moreover, the overarching themes of the late work discussed here have also been thoroughly studied, such as in the important interpretations of the care of the self offered by Edward McGushin, in his *Foucault's Askēsis*, or in the careful assessments of the later Foucault's theoretical trajectory presented by Stuart Elden, in his *Foucault's Last Decade*. However, when it comes to literature concerning the most central point of this thesis – i.e. the care of the self and *parrēsia* as possible forms of critique – there exist only shorter texts: e.g. Judith Butler's "What is Critique? An Essay on Foucault's Virtue," Laura Cremonesi's "La *parrēsia* et l'attitude critique,"[28] and Daniele Lorenzini's and Arnold I. Davidson's introduction to the French critical edition of "What is Critique?," which they published alongside "The Culture of the Self."[29] Compared to these shorter, more general observations, the study of Foucault's work on antiquity in relation to his notion of critique, presented in this thesis, will provide a more detailed analysis and, most importantly, pave new ground in at least three ways.

Noting with Butler and Cremonesi that the conceptual common basis of critique and the care of the self in virtue (Butler) and in government (Cremonesi), the analysis offered in this thesis also identifies a significant formal common basis. The formal commonality lies in how Foucault defines both critique and the care of the self as instances where means and ends

---

[28] Laura Cremonesi, "La parrēsia et l'attitude critique," in *Michel Foucault: éthique et verité, 1984*, eds. D. Lorenzini A. Revel, A. Sforzini (Paris: Vrin, 2013).

[29] Daniele Lorenzini and Arnold I. Davidson, "Introduction." in Qu'est-ce que la critique? suivi de La culture de soi, eds. Henri-Paul Fruchaud and Daniele Lorenzini (Paris: Vrin, 2015).

coincide. This significant aspect can now be traced as a recurring figure of thought in different parts of Foucault's late work and practice, such as the definition of *parrēsia*, the discussion of philosophy's "test of reality" (speaking its truth to power, like Plato before Dionysios), and the description of a social movement (*Solidarność*). Second, this allows us to draw a model of three modes of critique in Foucault. In comparison with Deleuze's[30] and Amy Allen's[31] use of the Kantian tripartite structure of critique in order to understand Foucault's work, the Foucauldian-Kantian analogue in this thesis draws on specific remarks made by Foucault himself, in offering critique as a mode of possible action: theoretical work, truth-telling in the political field, and the art of not being governed like that. Third, seizing on the unrecognized event that Foucault applies the notion of truth-telling to a labor union, pitting it against what he previously had defined as the "veridiction of the market," an entirely new proposal will be made: namely, a consideration of a non-verbal, non-discursive truth-telling based on action or force – which does not appear in the sphere of life itself like in the Cynic *parrēsia*, or in the embodiment of truth as transvaluation, which many have investigated[32] – that operates as a form of critique in the political-economic sphere, which could be defined through valorization, production and circulation.

Concerning the notion of the late Foucauldian subject as process, Giorgio Agamben[33] has made an important explication which is engaged with in chapter 2: added to Agamben's account is the description of, and relation to, the equally processual nature of the subject that appears in power/knowledge relations in Foucault's earlier work. Concerning the arguments in chapter 3 that Foucault's discussion of *parrēsia* must be understood in relation to the contemporary French political debate, and in chapter 5, regarding Foucault's relation to *Solidarność*, Marcelo Hoffman's *Foucault and Power* is a rare – as for the first argument, perhaps only – contribution in the field.[34] Largely in agreement with Hoffman's view on the French polemics and Foucault's *parrēsia*, the argument here lays greater emphasis on Foucault's probing approach; and to the existing descriptive accounts of Foucault and *Solidar-*

---

[30] Gilles Deleuze, *Foucault*, trans. Séan Hand (London/Minnesota: The University of Minnesota Press, 1988).

[31] Amy Allen, *The Politics of Our Selves: Power, Autonomy, and Gender in Contemporary Critical Theory* (New York: Columbia University Press, 2008).

[32] See for example Vanessa Lemm, "The Embodiment of Truth and the Politics of Community," in *The Government of Life: Foucault, Biopolitics, and Neoliberalism*, eds. Vanessa Lemm and Miguel Vatter (New York: Fordham University Press, 2014).

[33] Agamben, *The Use of Bodies*.

[34] Marcelo Hoffman, *Foucault and Power* (London/New York: Bloomsbury, 2015).

ność, chapter 5 adds a new perspective by identifying continuities with his philosophical work.

In addition to this, while the question of style in Foucault's work has been touched on by many, it has rarely, if ever, been properly analyzed. Therefore, the opening discussion of this thesis should form an original contribution in a number of ways: by discussing Foucault's three edited works *I, Pierre Riviére, having slaughtered my mother, my sister, and my brother, Herculine Barbin*, and *Disorderly Families* in terms of *objets trouvés*, found objects or found texts. Further, by considering Foucault's early to mid- style in terms of montage, through his particular use of archival material in his written work, i.e. his way of arranging contradicting "historical contents" against each other. And, lastly, by suggesting that this stylistic-critical play of contradiction that disappears from the written expression of the late work, actually reappears in the style of life and care of the self as a critical project.

A Work of the Practice of the Self

Beyond the academic undertaking and the ambition to contribute to existing research on Michel Foucault's later investigations into ancient thought, this thesis has been written in a continuous engagement and experimentation with the ideas they advance – in their therapeutic, aesthetic, as well as critical regards. It is my hope that some of its readers shall experience that pleasure too.

CHAPTER 1

A Prelude on Style, Form, Methodology

Fire and Intoxication

In order to prepare the following investigation into Foucault's late work, an investigation into how practices of truth-telling and the care of the self can be understood as forms of critique, we will start in what might be an unexpected end: the question of style and the well-known but little discussed stylistic shift appearing with Foucault's last publications. By paying attention to these formal and methodological conditions in Foucault's writing, the famous break of the late work will be cast in a new light, making important but less acknowledged continuities appear. This will structure our reading of the late work in a way that both reaches back to his earlier writings and underlines its relevance for our own present.

When the second and third volumes of the *History of Sexuality* appeared in 1984, one of the first things to strike the reader was the dramatic change of style. Eight years after Foucault's last published work, the introduction to *The Use of Pleasures* begins in a plain and direct manner, accounting for the theoretical transformations that have taken place: how the project has deviated from its original plan, how certain modifications have become necessary, and how it will be concluded. It has none of the theoretical boldness of the original introduction to the *History of Madness*,[1] none of the defiant playfulness of the foreword to *The Archaeology of Knowledge*,[2] none of the polemical fervor of the opening of *The Will to Know*.[3] The book's inves-

---

[1] This introduction, which Foucault would remove from subsequent editions, sets out how he intended to write not the history of psychiatric language, but an archaeology of what it had silenced: "A history not of psychiatry, but of madness itself, in all its vivacity, before it is captured by knowledge." See Michel Foucault, *History of Madness*, trans. Jonathan Murphy and Jean Khalfa (London/New York: Routledge, 2006), xxxii.

[2] Here Foucault inserts an imagined conversation and invents a labyrinth for himself into which he can venture and where he can open up underground passages. See Michel Foucault, *The Archaeology of Knowledge*, trans. A.M. Sheridan Smith (New York: Pantheon Books, 1972), 17.

[3] Here, Foucault turns all common assumptions on sexuality upside down: "For a long time, the story goes, we supported a Victorian regime, and we continue to be dominated by it even today. Thus the image of the imperial prude is emblazoned on our restrained, mute, and hypocritical sexuality." See

tigation into *chrēsis aphrodision* ("the use of pleasures" or what today may be called sexual practices) in Greek and Roman societies proceeds in a similar, non-confrontative vein, and – just like volumes three and four, the *The Care of the Self* and the posthumously published *Confessions of the Flesh* – it forms a narrative with little friction with the ancient sources it quotes, in a manner separating it from Foucault's earlier work.

Many have commented on this dramatic shift. Blanchot characterized Foucault's late style as "calm, at peace, without the passion that gives so many of his other texts their fire,"[4] while Deleuze called it "sober."[5] Foucault himself confirms this departure from his earlier, explosive style, as the result of a "rupture" occuring in 1975–76: "I completely abandoned this style insofar as I intended to write a history of the subject."[6] It seems safe to say that a consensus has been reached surrounding Foucault's stylistic shift. Even in the words of his most careful readers, his late work, in all its sobriety, is characterized by a certain absence or lack: an absence of passion and fire, or, even, intoxication. Strangely, however, the discussion generally ends there: with a short descriptive note on the transformation, without further analysis and conclusion. No questions of the theoretical implications are raised, no texts are subject to closer scrutiny, and to the extent that any possible reasons for the shift are considered, the most commonly identified cause seems to be the author's illness and – echoing other famous accounts on late style[7] – his approaching death. Yet one is likely mistaken to see the "calm" and peaceful expression of the late work merely as a sort of final reconciliation or, worse, to hail it as a natural serenity marked by the imminent passage into death. A less revering but perhaps more accurate comparative judgment of the last volumes of the *History of Sexuality* may recall Adorno's remark on how the maturity of late style is quite unlike that of ripe fruits: "Devoid of sweetness, bitter and spiny, they do not submit themselves to mere delectation."[8]

Michel Foucault, *The History of Sexuality: An Introduction. Volume 1 (The Will to Know)*, trans. Robert Hurley (New York: Vintage Books, 1990), 3.

[4] Maurice Blanchot, "Michel Foucault as I imagine him," in *Foucault/Blanchot*, (New York: Zone Books, 1987), 108.

[5] As quoted in Eribon, *Foucault*, 331.

[6] The full quote registers the archaeological, genealogical stakes in the early style: "I completely abandoned this style insofar as I intended to write a history of the subject, which would not be the same as one of an event produced a certain day, and of which it would be necessary to recount the genesis and outcome." See Michel Foucault, "Le retour de la morale", *Dits et écrits II, 1976–1988*, No 354, 1516.

[7] Edward Said, *On Late Style* (New York: Pantheon Books, 2006), 24.

[8] Theodor W. Adorno, "Late Style in Beethoven" in *Essays on Music*, trans. Susan H. Gillespie, (Berkeley: University of California Press, 2002), 564.

But the purpose here is obviously not to extend the line of brief observations of style in Foucault's late work, as if style were simply a matter of ornament or decorative effects on the surface of thought. Nor, on the other hand, is it to be understood as an expression of the author's psycho-physiological condition.[9] Indeed, such disregard of the formal singularity of Foucault's works, always handed over to the reader by means of a number of stylistic intensities, would be strange. On the contrary, if form and content are inseparable in Foucauldian methodology, one must consider the late work not just as something that happens to coincide with a change in form, style, and methodology, but as something that could to some extent be understood in light of this transformation. Now, it has already been suggested that the shift or change consists in an absence or lack. And if we accept this negative definition of the late style, it would be most reasonable to investigate in what such a lack would actually consist. Which means that we must ask: what is it that actually constitutes the fire and intoxication of the earlier works? What, precisely, is lacking in the later writings? Perhaps we must first specify "style" a bit further. The style of a writer is often defined merely in terms of tone, rhythm, flow, diction, etc. In *Raymond Roussel*, his only book on literature, Foucault himself defines literary style as the possibility "to say the same thing, but in other ways."[10] But just like Roussel's style became all the more fascinating to Foucault after he learned of the formal rigidity that "was behind it – the process, the machines, the mechanisms,"[11] Foucault's own style is very much defined by, and even inseparable from, form. And form here, as we shall see, will above all be understood as a particular citation, disposition, and use of archival sources. Proceeding in such a way, outlining a few elements that define Foucault's early and mid-style – the metaphors related to archaeology and periodization, a certain authorial self-reflexivity, the extensive use of archival material in a way that resembles a kind of montage practice (rendering the absurdity and historical contingency of Western power and knowledge relations, prompting us to be suspicious of their present configurations), for example – we will see that these stylistic features activate a play of contradictions that constitute a fundamental tension in Foucault's work. And we shall argue that

---

[9] For a recent collection of texts on Foucault's methodology (generally less interested with matters of style and form than theoretical kinship with other thinkers), see: *Continental Thought & Theory* Vol 3, Issue 4 Foucault's Method Today, 2022, for example David Pavón-Cuéllar, "Foucault's Marxism," *Continental Thought & Theory*, 327–345.

[10] Michel Foucault, *Raymond Roussel* (Paris: Gallimard, 1963), 25.

[11] Michel Foucault, "An Interview with Michel Foucault" in *Death and the Labyrinth: The World of Raymond Roussel*, trans. Charles Ruas (London/New York: Continuum, 2006), 174.

this tension is not simply absent or lacking in the style and form of the late work, but actually transposed to another register; that of practice, the stylization of life, and the aesthetics of existence. To make the hypothesis a bit more clear, we may say that the formal contradictions and performativity of the earlier works – in which Foucault's "historical-philosophical practice" unfolds simultaneously as a theoretical critique and as performative event on the part of the reader – reappears on another level in the late work: it is transposed from philosophical style to the style of life; from theoretical critique to critique as a way of life.

Found Texts

The point of departure for the following examination of the Foucauldian shift between earlier and late style is certainly not a very much studied or commented part of Foucault's oeuvre, but it may be the closest we get to anything like a *punctum Archimedis* in this regard: the series of works he did not even write himself.[12] We shall thus look at Foucault's *objets trouvés*, i.e. the different historical texts he edited and published as books during a period of ten years, which traverse the divide between earlier and late work: *I, Pierre Riviére, having slaughtered my mother, my sister, and my brother: A Case of Parricide in the 19th Century* (1972); *Herculine Barbin: Being the Recently Discovered Memoirs of a Nineteenth-Century French Hermaphrodite* (1978), and *Disorderly Families: Infamous Letters from the Bastille Archives* (co-edited with Arlette Farge, 1982). While these texts display many differences – both in terms of subject matter and the specific conditions under which they were first written, as well as how they were edited by Foucault and his collaborators – there are also some common traits that are significant with regards to Foucault's own written work, both early and late.

In *Pierre Rivière*, we find the 20-year old Rivière's apology and detailed description of how he murdered half of his family: in this idiosyncratic document from 1835, the farmer's son claims full responsibility for his crime, determined to demonstrate that he cannot be acquitted on grounds of insanity. Along with this *Memoir*, the book contains a rich dossier with medico-legal testimonies and judicial protocols, as well as a final section of *Notes* with theoretical reflections by Foucault and some of the persons listed as authors of this collective work, which emanated from a seminar at

---

[12] A rare example of attention to these works as unified by a common principle is found in: Philippe Artières, "Éditer" in *D´´après Foucault: Gestes, luttes, programmes*, ed. Philippe Artières, Mathieu Potte-Bonneville (Paris: Seuil, 2012), 121–139.

Collège de France.[13] Similarly, the more elaborate first-person account of *Herculine Barbin* – their childhood memories and change of legal sex as an adult, with ensuing suicide – is followed by a shorter dossier with medical reports, though with one important difference: it has only a minimal, italicized note by Foucault, in which he abstains from any commentary or theoretical contribution, as well as from "any exhaustive documentation."[14] In addition to these longer, personal 19th century documents, there are the more formal letters of the *Disorderly Families* – written by scribes for wives, parents, and husbands who want to request a *lettre de cachet* from the king, that is, a royal order to imprison an incorrigibly dangerous or depraved spouse, son or daughter.

What is common to these peculiar books, and what is interesting in relation to Foucault's written work, both early and late, can be summarized under three rubrics. First of all, these exhibits of individual lives provide an interesting prefiguration of Foucault's later interest in the technologies of the self and the ancient Greek notion of *bios*, of life as the lived experience of reflecting and working on itself, in a constitutive process of subjectivation. Second, they testify to Foucault's interest in what we may call the per-formativity of texts. These texts are themselves acts or actions: they go beyond the more isolated, enclosed or hermeneutically defined relation to the reader of most genres of writing to appear in books, and, as we shall see, they are inscribed in a completely different kind of causality. Third, their very status as found texts points to Foucault's other uses of found material in his earlier work: his extensive and particular clippings of archival material, which we shall discuss as a kind of montage practice.

Parallel Lives and Self-Writing

Pierre Rivière was published in 1972, around a decade before Foucault's lectures on the ancient technologies of the self and the individual subject that constitutes itself in a process of truth-telling. Yet both *Pierre Rivière* and *Herculine Barbin* from 1978 prefigure some of these themes. In 1982, for

---

[13] The work first appeared in the series *Collection Archives* edited by Pierre Nora and Jacques Revel as *Moi, Pierre Rivière, ayant égorgé ma mère, ma sœur et mon frère... Un cas de parricide au XIXe siècle présenté par Michel Foucault*. It is presented in the colophon as a collective work undertaken at the *Collège de France* by Blandine Barret-Kriegel, Gilbert Burlec-Torvic, Robert Castel, Jeanne Favret, Alexandre Fontana, Michel Foucault, Georgette Legée, Patricia Moulin, Jean-Pierre Peter, Philippe Riot, Maryvonne Saison. See *Moi, Pierre Rivière, ayant égorgé ma mère, ma sœur et mon frère... Un cas de parricide au XIXe siècle présenté par Michel Foucault* (Paris: Gallimard/Juillard, 1973), 8 (unpaginated).

[14] *Herculine Barbin dite Alexina B*, Présenté par Michel Foucault, (Paris: Gallimard, 1978), 131.

example, when Foucault takes up the notion of the care of the self, and the ascetic processes in which the subject constitutes itself in relation to truth, he discusses the practice of "self-writing," which he further develops in an essay with the same name. He writes: "As an element of self-training, writing has, to use an expression that one finds in Plutarch, an *ethopoietic* function: it is an agent of the transformation of truth into *ethos*."[15] These 19th century autobiographical accounts can of course not be fully understood in light of Plutarch's ancient notion of *ethopoiesis* or, for instance, Epictetus' instructions of writing for a meditative purpose; but as very particular forms of writing singled out for publication by Foucault, they display a similar entanglement of subjectivity and truth. In 1983, Foucault discusses the truth-telling of *parrēsia* during classical Greek antiquity whereby the speaker binds himself to the truth: "he binds himself both to the content of the statement and to the act of making it: I am the person who will have said this."[16] In their different ways, both Pierre Rivière and Herculine Barbin display a bold will to speak the truth about themselves, which unravels as chronological narrations of their whole lives. With regards to the centrality of the notion of life here, we should keep in mind that Foucault in his late work equals the Greek notion of *bios* with our modern notion of subjectivity,[17] and that he considers how Cynicism "makes life, existence, *bios*, what could be called an alethurgy, a manifestation of truth."[18] Most clear in this regard is perhaps *Herculine Barbin*, whose writer speaks it all, with a mixture of despair, resignation and accusation: "Forsaken, outlawed in the midst of my brothers! Ah! What am I saying! Have I the right to give that name to those who surround me? No, I do not. I am alone! My arrival in Paris marks the beginning of a new phase of my double and bizarre existence."[19] The book was published as the first – and only – title in a new book series to be edited by Foucault for the publisher Gallimard. The title of the series was *Les vies paralleles*, with reference to the parallelism of Plutarch's *Lives of the Noble Greeks and Romans*. But on the backside of the first French edition a brief text suggests that these lives are parallel in a wholly other sense than that of

---

[15] Michel Foucault, "Self-Writing" in *Essential Works, Ethics: Subjectivity and Truth*, trans. Robert Hurley (London/New York: Penguin Books, 1997), 207.

[16] Foucault, *The Government of Self and Others: Lectures at the Collège de France 1982–1983, trans.* Graham Burchell (Houndmills/New York: Palgrave Macmillan, 2010), 65.

[17] Foucault, *Subjectivity and Truth: Lectures at the Collège de France 1980–1981*, trans. Graham Burchell (London/New York: Palgrave Macmillan, 2017), 253.

[18] Foucault, *The Courage of the Truth (The Government of Self and Others II): Lectures at the Collège de France 1983–1984*, trans. Graham Burchell (Houndmills/New York: Palgrave Macmillan, 2011), 172.

[19] Michel Foucault, *Herculine Barbin*, trans. Richard McDougall (New York: Vintage Books, 2010), 98.

kinship, similitude, or analogy; lives that go on in parallel but infinitely separated from most of us: "lives that are so parallel that no one can make them meet."[20]

On the one hand, we have a life that is radically other, and that constitutes itself in this position of irreconcilable alterity, appearing to its protagonist as strange and commanding like an "impossible dream".[21] On the other hand, this life is proof of an outside we did not know existed: an opening or a possibility that can be understood both in terms of the notion of transgression, to which Foucault was drawn in his earlier works on literature, and the more systematic, processual, immanent work of the technologies of the self that he investigated in the late work. Regardless of how it is understood, *Herculine Barbin*'s account contains instances that, in the secret love affair at a boarding school for example, testify to and produce a transformation of sex and subjectivity: "In our deliciously intimate conversations she took pleasure in using the masculine qualifiers for me, qualifiers which would later suit my official status. '*Mon cher* Camille, I love you so much!!'"[22]

It thus seems that these strange and personal texts provide a kind of counterpoint to Foucault's own books on historical formations of internment, exclusion, and productive domination, where subjectivity appears as a mere effect of power-knowledge relations. To begin with, these "documents" are writings of a common, popular, non-scholarly origin.[23] In their own respective ways, they are also more or less literary or formalized self-expressions of what Foucault discusses elsewhere as the notion of abnormality: the relation between madness and crime, hermaphroditism, and the dangerous individual, as represented in official records.[24] Evidently, these texts are not products of scientific inquiry or erudition, they are not excerpts of legal articles or medical records of which Foucault makes such great use elsewhere:

---

[20] *Herculine Barbin dite Alexina B*, Présenté par Michel Foucault, Back Cover.

[21] Foucault, *Herculine Barbin*, 79.

[22] Foucault, *Herculine Barbin*, 58.

[23] In the methodological discussion of the *Archaeology of Knowledge*, Foucault explains that archaeology "does not treat discourse as *document*, as a sign of something else," but as monument, as positivity, as accumulation and formation of statements, while at the same time working out the very rules that guide these discourses. This describes Foucault's earlier work fairly well: how, in *The History of Madness*, exclusion and confinement of the 'insane' developed into psychiatric discourse, how *The Birth of the Clinic* records the modification of enunciative forms of medical discourse at the threshold between the 18th and the 19th centuries, and how *The Order of Things* investigates the common formation of concepts across General Grammar, Natural History, and the Analysis of Wealth. Opposed to this, however, we have Foucault's publication of found texts: this practice is evidently not part of this archaeology, but rather seems to grasp the specific texts precisely as "documents," even "as a sign of something else." See Foucault, *Archaeology of Knowledge*, 138.

[24] Michel Foucault, *Abnormal: Lectures at the Collège de France 1975–75*, 31–32., 34, 66–75.

on the contrary, they are, in a sense, testimonies of singular lived experiences opposed to those disciplinary, individualizing, and normative technologies of power that form our social institutions and that Foucault investigated so thoroughly in his other works, most notably *Discipline and Punish* and *The History of Sexuality*. It is striking that Foucault, during a period when he was accused of leaving no room for the agency of political subjects in what some understood to be an all-encompassing mesh of power-knowledge relations, presents the two lives of *Pierre Rivière* and *Herculine Barbin*, two written-down lived experiences that to some degree evade or even transgress the boundaries of family, law, and sexuality. In what can be regarded as a rare gesture of affirmation, the act of publication retroactively elevates these, so to speak, discursively impossible enunciations, inscribing them within a new, undetermined discourse, or in any case, in a new relation to the historical discursive formations from which they have been excluded.[25]

One can discuss and problematize much further the publication of these found texts in relation to Foucault's work on the technologies of power and domination as well as on the technologies of the self. While this is just a brief sketch of how the accounts evade or oppose legal and normative frameworks, one could also point to how these confessions reproduce and uphold such frameworks; not only in the editorial inclusion of legal and medical documents, but also in the texts themselves. It could also be argued that the highly formalized letters of *Disorderly Families*, often written by scribes in a predetermined standard and addressed to the King and the Lieutenant General of Police, must be read in opposition to the singular and striking expressions of *Pierre Rivière* and *Herculine Barbin*. In a "The Life of Infamous Men," a text written as a foreword to an unrealized anthology of *lettres de cachet*, Foucault even suggest that they ensured that "everyone could make use of the enormity of absolute power for themselves."[26] Far from *Pierre Rivière* and *Herculine Barbin*, the letters could thus be understood both in distinction to and as a development of the confessional regime, its "coercive transposition into discourse" and its regulative, normative production of moral behavior.[27] At the same time, Farge and Foucault introduce the letters as testimonies of the "passions of the common people" and documents that

---

[25] This is not to say that the accounts of Herculine Barbin or Pierre Rivière were "repressed" or silenced, but simply that they had no discernible place in any given discourse. See Foucault, *Archaeology of Knowledge*, 119.

[26] Michel Foucault, "The Life of Infamous Men" in *Michel Foucault: Power, Truth, Strategy*, eds. Meaghan Morris and Paul Patton (Sydney: Feral Publications, 1979), 85.

[27] Foucault, *History of Sexuality: An Introduction*, Vintage Books, 34.

"could offer a fascinating peek into the landscape of daily life for the lower classes in Paris during the era of the absolute monarchy."[28] Perhaps one could say that *Disorderly Families* – despite the letter-writing supplicants' invocation of order and their reiteration of the demarcation lines of exclusion and internment of deviant elements – offer glimpses, through the peephole of the letters, of the denounced parties and their ways of living, sometimes in misery, sometimes in what seems like defiant practices of freedom. One may think of one Madame Duchesne whose "dominant passions" of gluttony and wine have led her, according to her husband, to both sacrilege and crime: "Become faithless and lawless, nothing is sacred to her, she no longer knows any yoke of Religion, having trampled it under her feet, it is not astonishing that she cares naught for that of the household and that she respects no one."[29]

But such further problematization cannot be elaborated here. Instead, this side-glance thrown into the periphery of Foucault's work will simply suggest that these three books form a bridge between a few early and late Foucauldian themes. Extending over a long period, covering both sides of the stylistic shift, they articulate a subjectivity from positions strictly in opposition to the scholarly, regulatory, and official discourses on madness, criminality, and sexuality. To begin with, these "other lives" take place in a kind of semi-literary writing – in a degree zero of literature as Philippe Artières has noted[30] – somehow standing on the shoulders of Foucault's early texts on literature: the thinking from the outside, as Maurice Blachot put it, that is, the "extralinguistic" aspect of literature,[31] and the literary transgressions of Marquis de Sade and Georges Bataille. Such texts affirm both the limit and the limitlessness of a more general agency.[32] Indeed, Foucault describes the letters of internment as a strange theater, as "novellas" and as "life-poems," as looking toward Racine, and even as a

---

[28] Arlette Farge and Michel Foucault, *Disorderly Families: Infamous Letters from the Bastille Archives*, trans. Thomas Scott-Railton (Minnesota: University of Minnesota Press, 2016), 19.

[29] Farge and Foucault, *Disorderly Families*, 70.

[30] Philippe Artières, "Éditer," 126.

[31] This notion of the extralinguistic was developed by Foucault in material recently compiled and published in Michel Foucault, *Language, Madness and Desire: On Literature*, (Minneapolis: University of Minnesota Press, 2015). See also Azucena G. Blanco, "Foucault on Raymond Roussel: The Extralinguistic Outside of Literature," Theory, Culture & Society, Vol 40 Issue 1–2, 2020, https://doi-org.till.biblextern.sh.se/10.1177/0263276420950458.

[32] Michel Foucault, "Preface to Transgression" in *Language, Counter-Memory, Practice: Selected Essays and Interviews*, trans. Donald F. Bouchard and Sherry Simon (Ithaca, Cornell University Press, 1977), 35. For Sade, see also Michel Foucault, *La grande étrangère: à propos de litterature*, eds. Philippe Artières, Jean-François Bert, Mathieu Potte-Bonneville and Judith Revel (Paris, EHESS, 2013), 145–218.

meeting between literature and power: "Like characters of Céline wanting to make themselves heard at Versailles."[33] For the early Foucault, literature possesses a certain capacity. In opposition to the Cartesian *cogito* as the model of thinking that founds the subject, literature leads to language outside discourse, to "the outside in which the speaking subject disappears",[34] or, as Foucault puts it in *Raymond Roussel*, where "language has the strange power of splitting the speaking subject."[35] It seems that this other space provides the conditions of possibility for other forms of subjectivation: this may be the case in *Pierre Rivière* and *Herculine Barbin* as much as in, for example, Foucault's description of 19th century literature in *The Order of Things*, emerging as a contestation of philology, in the form of "the scandalous, the ugly, the impossible," manifesting "the power of naked speech."[36]

In addition to this relationship to Foucault's own considerations of literature, there is, as we have seen, a link pointing forward in time. As careful, confessional, and yet mercurial self-reflections of lived experiences, *Pierre Rivière* and *Herculine Barbin* prefigure some of the central concepts developed by Foucault during his last three lecture courses at the Collège de France: the *epimeleia heautou* (the care of the self) and *parrēsia* (truth-telling, frank speech), as well as the notions of an aesthetics of existence, of life as a manifestation of truth, or of the subject constituting itself as such through a practice of veridiction. These autobiographical accounts of hardship and endurance display a rather thorough "work on the self" of the kind Foucault discusses in relation to ancient philosophy, where "care" also means to meditate, to practice, to train, to exercise.[37] In this sense, they will strengthen our conviction that the care of the self must be understood as a critical project, where self-reflected operations of transformation amount to what Foucault would later call "practices of freedom."[38]

---

[33] Foucault, "The Life of Infamous Men," 76, 78, 88.

[34] Michel Foucault, "Maurice Blanchot: The Thought from the Outside," trans. Brian Massumi, in *Foucault/Blanchot* (New York: Zone Books, 1987), 13.

[35] Michel Foucault, *Death and the Labyrinth: The World of Raymond Roussel*, 62.

[36] Michel Foucault, *The Order of Things*, trans. Alan Sheridan (London/New York: Routledge, 1989/2005), 327.

[37] Foucault, *The Hermeneutics of the Subject*, 327.

[38] Michel Foucault, "L'éthique du souci de soi comme pratique de la liberté," in *Dits et écrits II, 1976–1988* (Paris: Gallimard, 2001), No 356, 1530.

Acts of Writing and Performativity of Texts

These three works, published between 1972 and 1982, testify to Foucault's interest in what we may call, for lack of better words, the performativity of texts.[39] They are themselves acts or actions: through their original purpose, they go beyond the hermeneutical relation between text and reader of most kinds of writing to appear in books, and the kinds of writing they may even resemble (e.g. literary pieces, works of description or chronicle, argumentative accounts, speculative pieces, etc). They are inscribed in a completely different kind of causality. In this regard, *Disorderly Families* is the most obvious example: the letters are composed with the aim of imprisoning a family member, and the supplicants "most humbly beseech" the Lieutenant General of Police to have so-and-so "locked up" or put on "bread and water;" requests that are generally granted.[40] Each of these epistolary appeals to the authorities is the first link in a well-defined chain of events, and in that sense they are not unlike performative statements. However, this performativity also applies to some extent to *Herculine Barbin* and *Pierre Rivière*. In *Herculine Barbin* we find the attempt to show through the written form the difficult and unrecounted experience of hermaphroditism, the illegal and historically erased sexual status of belonging to neither/both of the two legally recognized sexes. It is a precarious attempt to be true to the transgressive position of an intersex life, one that does not succumb to the rigidity of biological and legal dualisms. This is why Foucault – who in his *History of Sexuality* had already embarked on a critique of the confessional construction of sex and of sex as "the most speculative, the most ideal element" in the formation of bodies in their materiality, forces, and pleasures[41] – in his fore-

---

[39] When Foucault himself invokes the notions of performative acts or utterances of speech act theory, which he does on a number of occasions, he is careful to use inverted commas or mark a certain distance to a terminological and philosophical tradition which is not his: "a 'performative' act, as the British analysts call it," (*Archaeology of Knowledge*, 107.) or that "which has been called for some years now the performative utterance. [...] You are familiar with the extremely banal example: the chairman of the meeting sits down and says: 'The meeting is open'" (*The Government of Self and Others*, 61). In the following, we will use the term both in a preliminary way and in a more general sense than that of a strictly performative utterance like "'I name this ship the Queen Elizabeth.'" See J.L. Austin, *How to Do Things with Words* (Oxford: Clarendon Press, 1975), 5.

[40] One supplicant writes: "I reiterate that if this young man is given his freedom, the family will be dishonored entirely. The warden will be paid what he is owed, be so good as to inform him of this and that he is to have my brother live on bread and water." See Farge and Foucault, *Disorderly Families*, 174.

[41] On the contrary, sex is the most speculative, most ideal, and most internal element in a deployment of sexuality organized by power in its grip on bodies and their materiality, their forces, energies, sensations, and pleasures. Foucault, *The History of Sexuality: An Introduction. Volume 1 (The Will to Know)*, 155.

word to the English translation of *Herculine Barbin* discusses the text as "the happy limbo of non-identity"[42] (this is the object of Judith Butler's critique in *Gender Trouble,* an interesting echo of Derrida's famous remarks on *The History of Madness*).[43] Foucault seems to regard it as a courageous insistence upon that which the individual, understood as Alexina/Camille/Abel who are forced to change their legal sex, can no longer be, and that which the notion of sexuality, in the development of 19th century medicine, can no longer tolerate.

In *Pierre Rivière*, on the other hand, the wretched parricide writes his "memoir" in order to prove his sanity and thus be sentenced to death. The fact that the author had started writing it before committing the murder – he then decided to burn it, out of fear of anybody finding it before the actualization of his plans – is taken by Foucault, in his introduction, as an indication of a specific kind of causality, in which the text has "the purpose of leading on to the crime" and "to summon death."[44] In his own theoretical contribution – one of seven reflections on the memoir produced by members of the research seminar at the Collège de France – this aspect forms the main argument, and Foucault regards it as a "text which was neither confession nor defense, but rather a factor in the crime."[45] Rivière was the double author of a single deed, and the whole memoir takes on this performative function that both completes and goes beyond the crime. Rivière does not only write about what he considers to be his mother's wrong-doings, but also, with a strange beauty, about the weapons he makes for hunting birds, and for which he invents his own names (the caliben and the albalesters); about his repressed sexual desire and "horror for incest"; about his love of reading and reading every text he could find, his torture of animals, his attempt of being a preacher as a child, etc. In short, what he acknowledges as his "singularities."

---

[42] Michel Foucault, "Introduction," in *Herculine Barbin*, trans. Richard McDougall (New York: Vintage Books, 2010), XIII.

[43] Just as Derrida regards Foucault's attempt in *The History of Madness* to write a history of "madness itself," as something preceding its ordered representation in psychiatry, as the "maddest aspect of his project," Judith Butler writes that although Foucault "argues in *The History of Sexuality* that sexuality is coextensive with power, he fails to recognize the concrete relations of power that both construct and condemn Herculine's sexuality. Indeed, he appears to romanticize their world of pleasures as the "happy limbo of a non-identity" (xiii), a world that exceeds the categories of sex and of identity." See Jacques Derrida, "Cogito and The History of Madness" in *Writing and Difference*, trans. Alan Bass (London/New York: Routledge, 1978/2004), 40; see also Judith Butler, *Gender Trouble: Feminism and the Subversion of Identity* (London/New York: Routledge, 1990/1999), 120.

[44] Michel Foucault, ed., *I, Pierre Rivière, having slaughtered my mother, my sister, and my brother,* trans. Frank Jellinek (Lincoln/London: University of Nebraska Press, 1975) XI.

[45] Michel Foucault, ed., *I, Pierre Rivière, having slaughtered my mother, my sister, and my brother,* 201.

Yet ultimately, in Foucault's words, "the fact of killing and the fact of writing, the deeds done and the things narrated, coincided since they were elements of a like nature."[46] It thus seems that *Herculine Barbin* and *Pierre Rivière* fit the description in "The Life of Infamous Men:" "I insisted that these texts should always be in a relationship or rather in the greatest number of possible relationships with reality: not only that they refer to it, but that they perform in it; that they should play a part in the dramaturgy of the real."[47]

Found Texts as Philosophical Style

The performativity in these texts is not only interesting *per se*, but significant of a larger tendency with respect to the relation between text and reader in Foucault's work. In some sense, performativity is at the heart of Foucault's famous claim that his books are to function as a toolbox for his readers. But a stronger sense of performativity, of texts that *do* something, appears on another level, setting the reader to work within the reading, in a more direct way than the analogy of the toolbox (in which the doing is performed by the reader *after the reading*, after a process of hermeneutics, decision and application). To access this level, which contains something like the experience of reading, and to use these three documents presented and edited by Foucault as an Archimedean point with regards to the shift in his writing, style, and methodology, we must consider the unusual act of publishing these texts as books; the status of these texts as *objets trouvés* authored in the Foucauldian oeuvre. How many 20th century philosophers sought out, edited, and published historical texts by non-philosophers as books in their own right? One could probably think of a large number of historians, sociologists, writers, and poets – but almost no philosophers. There is Deleuze's publication of Sacher-Masoch's *Venus in Furs*, but the famous and short novella is supplied with a hundred pages long essay by Deleuze, shifting authorship away from the act of publication, back to the traditional productive domain of the philosopher's own theoretical writing. Foucault, on the other hand, is intent to minimize his own theoretical contributions, emphasizing the act of publication and its aspect of found material, opting for "the frugal lyricism of citation."[48] While he does not address so much this aspect of "found objects" or ready-mades in his own work (he does so with regards to works he takes

---

[46] Michel Foucault, ed., *I, Pierre Rivière, having slaughtered my mother, my sister, and my brother*, 200.
[47] Foucault, "The Life of Infamous Men," 77. The French original has "operate/*opèrent*" where the English translation has "perform." See Michel Foucault, "La vie des hommes infâmes" in *Dits et écrits II, 1976–1988*, No 198, 239–240.
[48] Foucault, "The Life of Infamous Men," 77.

interest in),[49] he nonetheless makes their nature apparent through his way of presenting and editorially framing the material. Firstly, all three texts are accompanied by a dossier of related historical documents, and in the case of *Pierre Rivière* and *Disorderly Families*, also by an introductory and commentative apparatus. Yet Foucault takes great care to preserve their status as documents and forms of writing in their own right; in terms of content, he affirms the beauty and astonishment that these texts produce as their main reason to be published, and in the case of *Pierre Rivière*, to keep the text from being dominated by its editorial framework, Foucault draws up certain limitations regarding any theoretical contribution.[50] In terms of formal-editorial choices, there are also a number of elements that put the original texts at the center of the publication. For example, the introductory and commentative text in all three books is italicized. In *Herculine Barbin*, Foucault lets the text itself, *Mes souvenirs* by Alexina/Camille, open the book without any kind of introduction, and he adds no theoretical reflection of his own (this abstention from commentary was apparently also his idea for *Disorderly Families*, before he was persuaded by co-editor Arlette Farge to add a framework of brief introductions to each section and an afterword that could tie the parts together into a whole). Unlike the other two works, which both form parts of the voluminous Gallimard/Juillard's series *Collections archives*, edited by Pierre Nora and Jacques Revel,[51] *Herculine Barbin* was published in a new Gallimard series to be edited by Foucault himself. Here, the formal-editorial decisions are even more revealing. In the French original, the book has a title, *Herculine Barbin dite Alexina B*, but no listed author: there is only the title of the series, *Les vies parallèles*, the publisher's name, and on the backside, the aforementioned text declaring the inverted

---

[49] In his early book on Raymond Roussel, Foucault is attentive to this aspect, later confirming his interest in Roussel's use of "found language". See Foucault, *Death and the Labyrinth: The World of Raymond Roussel*, 19, 179.

[50] For instance, Foucault and the other contributors decide "not to interpret it and not to subject it to any psychiatric or psychoanalytic commentary." See "Foreword" in *I, Pierre Rivière, having slaughtered my mother, my sister, and my brother*, trans. Frank Jellinek (Lincoln/London: University of Nebraska Press, 1975) XIII.

[51] In *Collections archives* each book was a "compilation of historical documents assembled and commented, devoted to one subject, event, or era," but compared to *Pierre Rivière*, other books contained more commentary and/or a firmer editorial authorship: Léon Poliakov's *Auschwitz*, for example, cites the correspondence between high ranking Nazi officials, concentration camp commanders and doctors, and Primo Levi, but the text unfolds like one larger narrative, much like most historical monographs, only with longer quotes; similarly Louis Bergeron's *Les Capitalistes en France* varies longer pieces of the author's writing with excerpts from diaries and public proclamations of French rentiers between 1780 and 1914. See Léon Poliakov, *Auschwitz* (Paris: Gallimard/Juillard, 1973) and Louis Bergeron's *Les Capitalistes en France* (Paris: Gallimard/Juillard, 1978).

Plutarchian parallelism of lives "plunged into an obscurity" where nothing of them is recounted. Indeed, this peculiar paratextual device[52] is undersigned by Foucault, which means that the only proper name on the front and back cover is Foucault's own, emphasizing its status as a found text and at the same time further affirming Foucault's authorship of the volume.

Having now grasped these works in their capacity as found texts, we can see how they relate to Foucault's earlier work. Because these strange, tormented and defiant writings do not only, as we have seen, constitute a kind of outside, externality, or counterpoint to Foucault's own work on the regularity of discourses, the constitutive exclusions of insanity and abnormality, and the spatialized, disciplinary power of surveillance. They do not only show us how these parallel lives form pockets of an unbending reflection on the self, of a fearless stating of the truth, which could be pointing either to a Bataillean "ruptured subjectivity and transgression,"[53] or to the sense that Foucault will later give to critique as the art of "not being governed like that,"[54] and thus further toward the late work on the ancient technologies of the self and truth-telling. In addition to this, they also, in the singular experience of reading that they offer – that is, in their own right as incandescent testimonies and their rare status as found texts somehow authored by a philosopher – reach back to and connect with Foucault's equally singular and emblematic use of archival material in much of his works prior to 1976. In *The History of Madness*, *The Birth of the Clinic*, and *Discipline and Punish*, Foucault's use of archival material, his employment of fragments of beauty of long-forgotten documents, is obviously not equal to presenting a found text in its totality, but it also exceeds, as we shall see, any traditional practice of quotation. Perhaps it can even be regarded as one of the components of fire and intoxication; an important component of that which seems to be lacking in the late, calm, and sober works.

Montage

The question of style in Foucault's early to mid-work may require several answers, some of which have been given and which we can mention, others toward which we can only gesture, and one in particular which we will try to develop a bit more. In an early essay on *The History of Madness*, Michel Serres

---

[52] Gérard Genette, *Paratexts: Thresholds of interpretation*, trans. Jane E. Lewin (Cambridge: Cambridge University Press, 1997), 37.
[53] Foucault, "Maurice Blanchot: The Thought from Outside," 18.
[54] Michel Foucault, "What is Critique?" in *Politics of Truth*, ed. Sylvère Lotringer, trans. Lysa Hochroth & Catherine Porter (Los Angeles: Semiotext(e), 1997/2007), 56–57.

analyzed the "geometrical structure" of Foucault's "language, writing, and style;"[55] later, Deleuze discussed the writing of *The Archaeology of Knowledge* and *Discipline and Punish* as a shift from that of an archivist to that of a cartographer; from the sayable to the visible.[56] Yet if one were to identify some overarching, most general, common traits of the early to mid-works, one could single out a few aspects as particularly important. First, the billows of periodization, or what Foucault calls epistemic breaks. This is not to say that the historical periodization or epistemic breaks inherent to Foucault's archeological project are themselves expressions of style, but that these scissions, along with the very notion of archaeology, seem to structure language and produce certain stylistic effects: spatial and other metaphors such as sedimentations, ruptures, cracks, layers, and densities. Second, a recurring and often highly formalized kind of reflexivity and self-reflexivity: the mirrors, the laughter that sets *The Order of Things* in motion, the fictive interview with himself in *The Archaeology of Knowledge*. Third, a particular use of archival material, a manner of letting the found texts speak for and among themselves. This list could surely be prolonged or adjusted, but at least it should be fairly uncontroversial and, arguably, limited to features that are distinctly Foucauldian (as opposed to stylistic features that can apply to other philosophers as well). Now, what all these answers to the question of style have in common, is that they suggest a *mise en scene* of certain internal tensions and oppositions, perhaps even a deployment of contradiction. Whether or not we see it in terms of geometry, Foucault arranges and opposes different elements against each other, "pitching diagrams against one another,"[57] letting these oppositions play out on a formal level for the reader to work out.

This preliminary characterization of Foucault's early style points toward a first answer to what, textually, constitutes the fire and intoxication of the early work or, in Gary Gutting's words, the "volcanic subtexts of mythological struggles [which] almost entirely disappear in favor of the cool exploration of alternative aesthetic forms of human existence" in the late work.[58] And if we take interest in this fiery expression that is said to disappear, if we

---

[55] Michel Serres, "La géométrie de l'incommuicable: la folie" in *Hermès 1. La communication* (Paris: Éditions de Minuit, 1969), 168.

[56] With regards to this development in Foucault's work, Deleuze provides a "triple definition of writing: to write is to struggle and resist; to write is to become; to write is to draw a map: 'I am a cartographer'." *See* Gilles Deleuze, *Foucault*, trans. Séan Hand (London/Minnesota: The University of Minnesota Press, 1988), 44.

[57] Deleuze, *Foucault*, 44.

[58] Gary Gutting, "Introduction" in *The Cambridge Companion to Foucault*, ed. Gary Gutting (New York: Cambridge University Priess, 2005), 24.

want to know in what it actually consists, it is precisely because we suspect that it doesn't disappear at all; rather, this tension or contradiction, as will be argued, is transferred to another register or level, which is that of life: the art of living, the style of existence. To demonstrate this, to formulate it as a hypothesis but not a study itself, we shall limit the discussion to one of these formal, stylistic and methodological traits, to which we were led already by the three books of *objets trouvés*: Foucault's use of found material; his singular practice of incorporating rare, archival material in his books, but also his unexpected use of artistic and literary works.

A few examples will remind us of this elaborated technique. In *Discipline and Punish*, we might recall the manner in which Foucault dates the completion of the carceral system not to the completion of the 1810 penal code, but to "that glorious day, unremarked and unrecorded when a child in Mettray remarked as he lay dying: 'What a pity I left the [penal] colony so soon'".[59] In *The Order of Things* we are confronted with the elegant analysis of Velázquez' painting *Las Meninas* as an image of Classical thought (with a photographic reproduction of the image itself included), and in the abundance of striking archival material in *Madness and Civilization* we can recall the centrifugation of melancholy in the horrifying "rotatory machine": "a perpendicular pillar is attached to both floor and ceiling; the sufferer is attached to a chair or a bed hung from a horizontal arm moving around the pillar; by means of a 'not very complicated system of gears' the machine is set for 'the degree of speed desired.'"[60] Even in *The Archaeology of Knowledge*, this formal, methodological, and often abstract discussion of archaeology and the formation of knowledge in which there is not a single footnote, Foucault manages – with a slight movement of his hand – to incorporate a rather specific and material kind of found text: "Let us look at the example again: the keyboard of a typewriter is not a statement; but the same series of letters, A, Z, E, R, T, listed in a typewriting manual, is the statement of the alphabetical order adopted by French typewriters."[61] This last quote is particularly interesting: not only can it serve as an example of Foucault's striking use of found material, it also invokes a certain performativity in that the quoted statement does what it says; further pointing back to the hand of the writer,

---

[59] Foucault is quoting an 1850s report by Belgian prison inspector Ducpétiaux. See Michel Foucault, *Discipline and Punish: The Birth of the Prison*, trans. A. Sheridan (New York: Vintage Books 1995), 293.

[60] Foucault quotes the English physician Mason Cox. *See:* Foucault, *Civilization and Madness*, 175 (or Foucault, *History of Madness*, 321).

[61] Foucault, *The Archaeology of Knowledge*, 86.

it forms a particular kind of self-reflexivity, and if it may not be a statement of periodization, it inscribes itself in certain historical and material conditions, i.e. the individual's mechanized mode of literary production.

In addition to these examples of the both rich and sudden impact of quoted texts and images within the body of Foucault's own text, there is another Foucauldian kind of employment of found material, which is one of juxtaposition, where the contradiction or opposition appears between the quoted objects more directly. One may think of the two doctors' journals in the *The Birth of the Clinic*: one who, in the middle of the 17th century, recounts the treatment of a hysteric with daylong baths, perpetuating the "old myths of nervous pathology," another who, less than a hundred years later, in accordance with modern science, "described the encephalic lesions of general paralysis for an era from which we have not yet emerged," thus introducing Foucault's critical investigation of the historical development of the medical gaze.[62] The procedure is brought to perfection in the opening pages of *Discipline and Punish*: first, without any introduction, the long torturous execution scene of Robert-François Damiens – convicted of regicide – that is not over until dusk has fallen and the fire of his torn limbs has turned into ashes, by which a dog finds the warmth to sleep. Then, in immediate succession, the regulating articles 17–28 from an institution for delinquents in Paris: "Art. 18. At the first drum-roll, the prisoners must rise and dress in silence, as the supervisor opens the cell doors."[63] With this grand shift in punitive practices, separated by a mere 80 years, Foucault situates his discussion of the historical development from the spectacle of sovereign power's capital punishment, to the disciplinary project of forming docile bodies.

It is apparent that Foucault's use of found material, found texts, and found objects produces contrasts, shocks, and tensions within his work. But it also produces connections, syntheses, and a specific work of interpretation on the part of the reader, which is not the same as the interpretive work regarding an exposition of logical arguments supported by textual references in the course of a text. For this reason, it is insufficient and inadequate to simply put things in the general terms of a quotation, of basing an argument on historical research or archival work. To better grasp this central feature in Foucault's way of writing – writing as a doubly creative practice that sets off different elements against each other, that produces a fundamental tension

---

[62] Foucault, *The Birth of the Clinic: An Archaeology of Medical Perception*, trans. A.M. Sheridan (London: Tavistock Publications Limited, 1973/1977).

[63] Foucault, *Discipline and Punish*, 5.

constitutive of the Foucauldian critique, to be resolved or perhaps rather performed by the reader themselves – we may think of it in very specific terms, namely in terms of montage. We may even take these terms in their most original sense: "And now we can say that it is precisely the *montage* principle, as distinguished from that of *representation*, which obliges spectators themselves to *create*[;] and the montage principle, by this means, achieves that great power of inner creative excitement in the *spectator*."[64] Foucault's style and method may be thought of as a montage-like practice: his singular use of found objects or documents in his texts is a strategic employment of an "untypical potentiality" in writing – just like Sergei Eisenstein "was preoccupied by a potentiality untypical in normal film construction and film composition."[65] This is not without significance: after all, the montage principle in general "if fully understood, passes far beyond the limits of splicing bits of film together," just like Foucault's use of archival material passes beyond mere quotation.[66] To define Foucault's work as a montage-like practice is above all to suggest that it produces a particular experience, a special kind of reading: like Eisenstein's montage "obliges spectators themselves to *create*," it is a critical poetics in which the *poiesis*, the creating or making (as separate from, but also entwined with understanding), lies with the reader to a higher degree than in other philosophical, let's say propositional-theoretical, writing.[67] This is not an ornamental effect or stylistic device in the service of mere pleasure of reading; on the contrary, Foucault's careful sampling of voices and documents is the driving force in his rewritings of the history of internments and exclusions, and can be understood in the light of what Georges Didi-Huberman says about Brecht's practice of montage: "one must show/demonstrate (a question of form) in order to show/demonstrate anew (a question of content, a question of struggle)."[68]

Just as Foucault's three books of found texts, *Pierre Rivière*, *Herculine Barbin*, and *Disorderly Families*, demand contextualization with his other

---

[64] Sergei Eisenstein, "Word and Image," *Film Sense*, ed. and trans. Jan Leyda (New York: Harcourt, Brace & World, 1942/1947), 35.

[65] Eisenstein, "Word and Image," 9.

[66] Eisenstein, "Word and Image," 36.

[67] While this formal aspect of *poiesis* or aesthetic experience of reading certainly sets Foucault apart from a general tradition of modern Western philosophy, something similar can be found in (often later) works by other French philosophers of his generation; think of Deleuze and Guattari's use of images and chapter titles in *A Thousand Plateaus*, or Derrida's parallel columns of text on Hegel and Genet in *Glas*.

[68] Georges Didi-Huberman, *Quand les images prennent position: L'Oeil de l'histoire, 1* (Paris: Les Éditions de Minuit, 2009), 112.

books and take on significance in relation to his written work, the remarkable arrangement or even dramatization of archival material within Foucault's written books obliges the reader to engage in certain operations of synthesis. In *The History of Madness*, for example, in the description of an English hospital, another text suddenly interjects, appearing like a door sign in Foucault's argument: "To enter here, inmates must be poor, judged to be manic, it must be less than a year since the onset of their disease, and they must not have been previously treated in another hospital for the mad. No imbeciles are admitted, nor are those who suffer from convulsions or venereal diseases, or who are senile, pregnant, or have smallpox."[69] In *Discipline and Punish*, in order to show how discipline unfolded through society, from the military camp through working-class housing estates, hospitals, asylums, prisons, and schools, not only in the spatial/architectural organization of these institutions but also in the infinite correction of all that does not conform to the set standards, Foucault lets the reader sense the vicinity of military and school: "The regulations for the Prussian infantry ordered that a soldier who had not correctly learnt to handle his rifle should be treated with the 'greatest severity'. Similarly, 'when a pupil has not retained the catechism from the previous day, he must be forced to learn it, without making any mistake, and repeat it the following day; either he will be forced to hear it standing or kneeling, his hands joined, or he will be given some other penance'."[70] This is one of the features that makes reading Foucault a singular and, indeed, performative experience. And this "frugal lyricism of citation" does have a way of driving the narrative and argument between the reader and writer that recalls classical montage works: think of what Alfred Döblin and John Dos Passos did to capture modernity in the 1920s and 1930s by including fragments of "Traffic Regulations" and "Newsreels" in their

---

[69] This quote is actually from Jacques-René Tenon's *Papiers sur les hopitaux*, and it serves to illustrate Foucault's thesis that insanity was separated from the general domain of unreason toward the end of the 18th century, but still kept in confinement. One may compare it to another, very different statement from about 50 years later, from Philippe Pinel's successor, the 19th century reformer Jean-Étienne Esquirol. Foucault warns against taking him as the liberator he professes to be, but quotes his description of the confinement of the insane, which almost take on Howl-like, Ginsbergesque notes: "I saw them naked and covered in rags, with nothing but straw to protect themselves from the damp cold of the stones on which they lay. I saw them badly fed and deprived of fresh air to breathe and water to quench their thirst, lacking even the basic necessities of life. They were in the charge of gaolers, and entirely at the mercy of their brutish ways. I saw them in cramped, dirty places, deprived of air and light, locked up in dens where men would hesitate to keep the wild animals that governments maintain at great cost in the capitals of Europe." See Foucault, *History of Madness*, 385, 48.

[70] Foucault is quoting the 1743 Prussian infantry regulation and, regarding the pupil and the catechism, Jean-Baptist de la Salle's *Conduite des écoles chrétiennes*. See Foucault, *Discipline and Punish*, 179.

novels.[71] However, this is not to say that Foucault is thinking of his own work in terms of montage, or that montage practices are particularly important to him; only that montage lets us grasp a particular aspect of the poetics, performativity, and formal contradictions of his early to mid-work. (With regards to the context that Foucault grows out of and considers important, there is on the one hand the literature in which he is theoretically interested, such as Bataille, Blanchot, Roussel, and Sade, as well as Alain Robbe-Grillet and some other of the *nouvau roman* authors from the 1950s; Foucault credits these, along with Beckett, for having lifted his student eyes above what he considered the too narrow French horizon of Marxism, phenomenology, and existentialism. On the other hand, Foucault is, as much as was everybody else, a part of the period – the long 1960s – that saw a widespread and general surge in documentary practices: experimental sociological writing and filmmaking, literary montage practices like Alexander Kluge's *The Battle*, and of course the cinematic works of the French New Wave; to some degree these two different kinds of context may have overlapped, for example in Alain Robbe-Grillet's subjection of language to visual description, or in works like *Last Year at Marienbad*. But no matter how well Foucault's way of structuring archival material may be understood in light of classical montage practices – think of the detail in the juxtaposition that opens *Discipline and Punish*, how the aforementioned execution scene and the Delinquency house rules are mounted with the shift from dusk to dawn, from the stakes burning into the night and the dog sleeping nearby to the prisoners waking up by a drumroll – there is one major problem with this analogy: the problem of dialectics. This is not the place to inquire seriously into the relation between Foucault's work and dialectics, but the issue cannot be left unaddressed. Because montage, on the one hand, is the modern artistic and aesthetic strategy most intimately linked with the notion of dialectics. This has been the case from its very inception: in Eisenstein's inference, nature and the world's events form a dialectical process; the projection of this process into abstract thinking is what results in philosophy or dialectical materialism, and the further projection of this into concrete creation and form-giving is what is called art, of which cinema and cinematic contradiction – the dialectical interplay of meanings and images in montage – is regarded as the highest form.[72] Foucault, on the other hand, is known to be a lifelong anti-dialectician: from

---

[71] Alfred Döblin, *Berlin Alexanderplatz*, trans. Michael Hofmann (London/New York: Penguin Books, 2019), 150–151; John Dos Passos, *U.S.A.* (London/New York: Penguin Books, 2001), 83.
[72] Sergei Eisenstein, "A Dialectic Approach to Film Form," *Film Form*, ed. and trans. Jan Leyda (New York: Harcourt, Brace & World, 1949/1977), 45.

his 1963 "Preface to Transgression," where he considers the possibilities to "awaken us from the confused sleep of dialectics" to the 1979 lectures on *The Birth of Biopolitics* in which he rejects a simplistic "dialectical logic" that fails to grasp heterogenous concepts.[73] Is it then really viable to think of Foucault's early style, form, and methodology in terms of montage and contradiction? It may very well be – if we only manage to peel away some of the rigid, outer layers of received and one-sided assumptions that have covered these rich concepts. First of all, rapprochements between the thought of Foucault and dialectics have already been made; Beatrice Hanssen points to "dialectical moments" in Foucault's description of biopolitical production and its negations that carry generative effects,[74] and Judith Butler sees a Foucauldian "dialectic without a subject and without teleology."[75] Most important in this regard, however, is the recognition of Foucault's own one-sided conception of dialectics. Somewhat similar to his astonishing disregard of "marxism" (as opposed to his engagement with Marx), Foucault was often categorical in his dismissal of Hegel, and by consequence of dialectics: "it was necessary to free ourselves from Hegel – from the opposition of predicates, from contradiction and negation, from all of dialectics."[76] In a short piece on this very issue, John Grant discusses how Foucault, possibly over-reliant on Alexandre Kojève's influential reading of Hegel, reduces dialectics to a binary logic of contradiction with no use for his own analysis of power relations.[77] Grant also shows how this need not be the case: with recourse to Adorno, he detaches dialectics from any necessary link with teleology and discusses how Foucault takes contradiction as "an inadequate shorthand for a constellation of concepts that include antagonism, difference and negativity;"[78] a constellation of both logical and social categories, by no means reducible to any simplistic binarism. He thus holds that Foucault, while himself not being a dialectician, "participates in dialectical thought" and that his work takes on dialectical implications.[79] Perhaps this is not as controversial as one might first think.

---

[73] Foucault, "Preface to Transgression," 38, and Michel Foucault, *The Birth of Biopolitics: Lectures at the Collège de France 1978–79*, trans. Graham Burchell (Houndmills/New York: Palgrave Macmillan, 2008), 42

[74] Beatrice Hanssen, "Between Kant and Nietzsche: Foucault's Critique" in *Critique of Violence* (London/New York: Routledge, 2000), 52.

[75] Judith Butler, *Subjects of Desire* (New York: Columbia University Press, 1987), 225.

[76] Michel Foucault, "Theatrum Philosophicum" in *Language, Counter-Memory, Practice: selected essays and interviews by Michel Foucault*, 186.

[77] John Grant, "Foucault and the Logic of Dialectics," *Contemporary Political Theory* 9, 2010, 220–238. https://doi.org/10.1057/cpt.2009.3

[78] Grant, "Foucault and the Logic of Dialectics," 226–227.

[79] Grant, "Foucault and the Logic of Dialectics," 235.

After all, Foucault said in honour to Jean Hyppolite that we may never escape Hegel,[80] and conceded as late as 1978 that regarding "the relations between dialectics, genealogy and strategy – I am working on it, and I don't know if I will ever finish."[81] In any case, this reading of a Foucault beyond Foucault, which serves Grant in his conclusion on dialectics, will here merely serve to form a hypothesis of contradiction.

A word needs to be said on the meaning of "montage" as well, given that some early definitions and denunciations of this concept seem to fit the rigid, "simplistic" logic that Foucault ascribed to dialectics. Think of Eisenstein's own, rather schematic, Marxist-Leninist application of the Hegelian schema of thesis-antithesis-synthesis (which does not keep other parts of his writing and his work from passing far beyond it),[82] or Georg Lukács's assessment of montage as a one-dimensional technique which at its best equals a good joke, but which, as representation of reality, will always result in "profound monotony."[83] Against such reductive notions of montage as a one-dimensional, binary mechanism or as a failed early modernist strategy, and in support of the analogy with Foucault's early style, we could take Georges Didi-Huberman's account of how montage operates in Bertolt Brecht's *Kriegsfibel*. Both with and against a double-sided Brecht, Didi-Huberman understands montage as an open-ended, mobile practice of "unordering," even as a form of "intoxication" in the drunken dance of Eisenstein's images, which at the same time entails the importance of "taking up a position". It is an epistemic-critical organization of cited material in which the reader's/viewer's "operative imagination" can take shape: a playing with the world that is both game and political imagination.[84] As if commenting directly on Foucault's use of epistemic breaks and archival material, Didi-Huberman takes Walter Benjamin's definition of philosophical style as "'the art of interruption, in contrast to the chain of deduction' which historians in general hold onto as a safeguard against the fundamental over-determination of becoming." This serves as the basis for his assessment that to Benjamin, "montage is thus not [...] the stylistic privilege or exclusive method of our modernity. It follows,

---

[80] Michel Foucault, "The Order of Discourse" in *Untying the Text*, ed. Robert Young (Boston, London and Henley: Routledge & Kegan Paul, 1981), 74.

[81] Michel Foucault, "Table ronde du 20 mai 1978" in *Dits et écrits II, 1976–1988*, No 278, 839–40.

[82] Eisenstein, "A Dialectic Approach to Film Form," 45.

[83] Georg Lukács, "Realism in the Balance" in *Aesthetics and Politics* (London/New York: Verso, 2007), 82.

[84] For the question of the "poetical intoxication" of montage in Brecht, Ernst Bloch and Eisenstein, and for notion of "operative imagination," see Didi-Huberman, *Quand les images prennent position*, 221–222, 118.

more generally, from every *philosophical manner of remounting history*."[85] Indeed, it is a "philosophical style" not far from how Foucault describes his own work with "historical contents" as a critical, historical-philosophical practice in "What is Critique?",[86] or how he puts it in "Nietzsche, Genealogy, History": "knowledge is not made for understanding; it is made for cutting."[87] And against Lukács' disavowal of montage in the 1930s debate on realism, Didi-Huberman recalls Brecht's reply:[88] Brecht "admits – or claims – that his work does not consist in *rendering the real*, which is to say exposing its truth, but in *rendering the real problematic*, which is to say exposing its critical points, its rifts, its aporias, its disorders."[89] Hence, it is a conception of montage beyond rigid binarism and much closer to Foucault's insistence on problematization, for example when he cautions against too easily accepting the social as the sole instance of the real, and defines his own critical work: "To undertake critique, is to render difficult the gestures that are too easy."[90]

A Hypothesis of Contradiction

We have now discussed a few aspects of style, form, and methodology in Foucault's early to mid- works, particularly his use of found material, and the way in which it is quoted, inserted and juxtaposed in his archeaologies of Western thought. These have singular effects on the reader. To put it another way, we could say that in the Foucauldian toolbox – containing what he himself used, and offered others to use – there is not only a Nietzschean hammer, but also a pair of scissors, not unlike the Eisensteinian and Benjaminian tools for cutting. But the main importance here is not to define parts of Foucault's work in terms of a certain technique or tradition, however well they fit the expanded, historical-philosophical methodological sense of montage recently given by Didi-Huberman; nor is it to prove that Foucauldian thought is compatible with some notion of dialectics. The purpose

---

[85] Didi-Huberman, *Quand les images prennent position*, 130.

[86] In this historical-philosophical practice, Foucault seeks "to desubjectify the philosophical question by way of historical contents, to liberate historical contents by examining the effects of power whose truth affects them and from which they supposedly derive[...]". See Michel Foucault, "What is Critique?" in *Politics of Truth* (Los Angeles: Semiotext(e), 1997/2007), 56–57.

[87] Michel Foucault, "Nietzsche, Genealogy, History" in *Language, Counter-Memory, Practice: Selected Essays and Interviews*, trans. Donald F. Bouchard and Sherry Simon (Ithaca, Cornell University Press, 1977), 154.

[88] Bertolt Brecht "Against Georg Lukács" in *Aesthetics and Politics* (London/New York: Verso, 2007), 82.

[89] Didi-Huberman, *Quand les images prennent position*, 109.

[90] Michel Foucault, "Est-il donc important de penser?" in *Dits et écrits II, 1976–1988*, No 296, 999.

is rather to recognize the role of contradiction and performativity: the contrasts, oppositions, and tensions in Foucault's early and mid-works are, in the reading proposed here, not merely internal differences. Rather, they are social (and other) contradictions put to play within the text, or, more precisely, in the relation between formal and textual elements organized by the author. It is true that in *The Archaeology of Knowledge*, Foucault makes some critical remarks on the notion of contradiction (archaeological analysis must steer clear from assuming both the multiple, minor and apparent contradictions to be resolved in the profound unity of discourse, and the foundational contradiction that animates every instance of discourse, as in Hegelian or Marxist dialectics).[91] Yet that does not keep other parts of his work, by means of their historical contents and quoted material, from producing contradictions within the text, just like the introductory counterpoint of Borges' "Chinese encyclopedia" and the author's laughter that sets off *The Order of Things*;[92] nor, at times, from articulating major historical contradictions, like the class interests in the penal reforms of the 18th century in *Discipline and Punish*.[93] As is evident in the complexity of Foucault's work and as has been argued on a theoretical level by many, such contradictions must not be reduced to a simplistic logical category of binary opposition: one need not go as far as Adorno; closer to Foucault, there is of course Althusser, who criticizes precisely the notion of a general "contradiction" as a simple, operative force.[94] Rather these contradictions are to be regarded as manifold relations of force: in terms of style, as we have seen, it may be the contradictions that appear in the cuts and collisions of Foucault's periodization, his highly formalized reflexivity and "geometrical structure" of writing, or, as we have looked into more closely, his way of organizing archival material in his historical-philosophical work, of mounting the forgotten voices of apparatuses that, in his hands, speak. This play of contradiction is handed over to the reader unresolved. And to some degree it is unresolvable: in analogy with the montage principle in Eisenstein which "obliges spectators themselves to *create*," it entails a particular performativity

---

[91] Foucault, *The Archaeology of Knowledge*, 149–155.

[92] Foucault, *The Order of Things*, xvi.

[93] "The illegality of property was separated from the illegality of rights. This distinction represents a class opposition because, on the one hand, the illegality that was to be most accessible to the lower classes was that of property – the violent transfer of ownership – and because, on the other, the bourgeoisie was to reserve to itself the illegality of rights: the possibility of getting round its own regulations and its own laws, of ensuring for itself an immense sector of economic circulation by a skillful manipulation of gaps in the law [...]." See Foucault, *Discipline and Punish*, 87.

[94] Louis Althusser, *Pour Marx* (Paris: François Maspero, 1965/1971), 99.

on the part of the reader, who has to "work out" the formal implications that go far beyond form. Admittedly, there is a performative aspect in all reading, and around the time Foucault was writing, this idea is articulated in various ways: Roland Barthes would emphasize the work of the reader in relation to that of the writer, suggesting that "a text's unity lies not in its origin but in its destination;"[95] Wolfgang Iser would consider the "*Appellstruktur*"[96] of the text that offers the construction of meaning to the reader; Umberto Eco imagined an unlimited semiosis of the "open work,"[97] and so on. That we use the term performativity with regards to Foucault's writing is a reflection of his own interest in the notion of performativity of speech act theory, where performative statements carry out a certain function, or produce a certain set of predefined consequences (like "The meeting is open"[98] or "I name this ship Queen Elizabeth"[99]). This is also how we described an aspect of Foucault's three found texts, *Pierre Rivière*, *Herculine Barbin*, and *Disorderly Families*, with the texts themselves being understood as acts or actions. Additionally, "performativity" can account for the theatrical or dramatic aspects of Foucault's writing, the *mise en scène* that he undoubtedly devotes himself too,[100] and for something like a performativity of the self to be possible.[101] But above all it is to describe the particular experience of reading Foucault, of how historical contents are presented to the reader in a way that they have to *do* something with it, how the form of montage obliges them to carry out a certain operation or to complete a certain juxtaposition that is not fully exhausted in the text.

In fact, the reference to montage and the 1920s and 30s Marxist debate on realism and its many adversaries is interesting in yet another way. While traditions as different as German expressionism, French surrealism, and the montage practices of Benjamin, Brecht, and Eisenstein all comprise the

---

[95] Roland Barthes, "The Death of the Author" in *Image, Music, Text*, trans. Stephen Heath (New York: Hill and Wang, 1977), 148.

[96] Wolfgang Iser, *Die Appellstruktur der Texte. Unbestimmtheit als Wirkungsbedingung literarischer Prosa.* (Konstanz: Konstanz Universitätsverlag, 1970).

[97] Umberto Eco, "The Poetics of the Open Work" in *The Role of the Reader: Explorations in the Semiotics of Texts* (Bloomington: Indiana University Press, 1979) 3, 43–66.

[98] Foucault, *The Government of Self and Others*, 61.

[99] J.L. Austin, *How to Do Things with Words*, 5.

[100] Arianna Sforzini, *Les scènes de la vérité: Michel Foucault et théâtre* (Paris: A bord de l'eau, 2017), 230.

[101] The primary example is Judith Butler's discussion of reiterative and critical forms of gender performativity. Judith Butler, *Gender Trouble: Feminism and the Subversion of Identity*, (London/New York: Routledge, 1990/1999), 33; Judith Butler, *Bodies That Matter: On the Discursive Limits of Sex* (London/New York: Routledge, 1993/2011), xxiii.

category of artistic modernism, Fredric Jameson, in his comment on what he calls "the realism/moderism controversy," also considers a French "second wave of modernism (or post-modernism) represented by the *nouveau roman* and the *nouvelle vague*, Tel Quel and 'structuralism.'"[102] And regardless of how such reappearances of modernism are possible (or whether its proper techniques can transcend it, such as in Didi-Huberman's understanding of Benjaminian montage), Jameson's identification of a second wave in 1960s France provides an interesting expansion and generalization of our identification of montage-like practices in Foucault. Following this logic, Foucault's early to mid philosophical style should perhaps be seen as guided by a modernist impulse: let us say, the modernist belief that the new forms of art will shape new forms of thought, social life, and politics. This modernist credo, resting on a notion of the transformative or revolutionary function of form, would thus underpin what Foucault is undertaking when his play of contradictions obliges the readers to a creative reading, and when the poetics of a montage-like use of archival material engages them in a certain making or *poiesis*.

Whether or not we can understand Foucault's early to mid-style – and more generally, according to Jameson, the whole formidable explosion of French philosophy in the long decade of the 1960s – as animated by modernist strategies and techniques, is obviously an open question. We can at any rate define it as an employment of formal tension and contradiction. Further, we can see that the undisputable shift in Foucault's style, which coincides with the decline of that exceptional theoretical conjuncture, consists in him leaving behind these methods. We have thus identified what constitutes the fire and intoxication in the early work, and what is "lacking" in the late work. (To some degree, this lack or absence does not only characterize the last two volumes of *The History of Sexuality*, but even Foucault's lectures at Collège de France.[103] Without foregoing the events, we can simply note that Foucault repeatedly comments on his own trampling on the spot, and on the banality and tediousness of the material at hand: the banal, flat and at once ordinary

---

[102] Fredric Jameson, "Reflections in Conclusion" in *Aesthetics and Politics* (London/New York: Verso, 2007), 197.

[103] More amply put: "[T]he lectures of 1981–2 are remarkably sedate, slow-moving, cautious even, when compared to the earlier lectures, and especially those of the mid 1970s, which are full of audacious proposals, speculations and (sometimes) abandoned hypotheses." Rosalind C. Morris, "Notes on a Double Disavowal: Conversion and the Question of Late Style," Columbia University, accessed April 11, 2024, https://blogs.law.columbia.edu/foucault1313/2016/03/09/rosalind-c-morris-notes-on-a-double-disavowal-conversion-and-the-question-of-late-style/.

sense of an anecdote of the arts of living in 1981,[104] the embarrassment in relation to Pericles' readiness to die for his word,[105] and the blandness of Plato's letters in 1983[106]). But most importantly, we have tried to demonstrate the reading of which we are guilty. Because this reading, this understanding both of a style and a form of contradiction in the early to mid- works will structure our reading of the late work, especially as it is developed in the Collège de France lectures. The hypothesis of contradiction is not only relevant to one side of the shift: it is not what separates early from late work. In a sense, it is what holds it together. The fact that Foucault so clearly stated that "I completely abandoned this style insofar as I intended to write a history of the subject"[107] does not mean that contradiction and performativity *per se* is left behind; but from having been set in play on the level of form, methodology, and philosophical style, it is now transposed to the style of life or the art of living.

In other words, the contradictions operative in Foucault's earlier writings do not disappear. Rather, they are transposed onto another register, which is that of life or the practices of the self. These ultimately play out on the social register. They do not disappear, but reappear in the relation between the technologies of the self and the technologies of domination: contradiction as antagonism between individual or collective attempts at self-government and existing government. If the earlier style initiates the reader's immediate process of a critical *poiesis* (which can be regarded as both game and political imagination), the late work rather points the reader toward another kind of *poiesis* or an *ethopoiesis*, a long and slow process – mediated in the care of the self – of forming one's habits and making one's life as a work of art.[108] It is thus a weaker kind of performativity which is not strictly bound to the act of reading, but becomes contingent upon the reader's further actions; a performativity that does not occur within a given play of contradiction, but that, if carried through, produces new contradictions in a larger game of truth. As

---

[104] Michel Foucault, *Subjectivity and Truth: Lectures at the Collège de France 1980–1981*, trans. Graham Burchell (London: Palgrave Macmillan, 2017), 26–27.

[105] Michel Foucault, *The Government of Self and Others: Lectures at the Collège de France 1982–1983*, trans. Graham Burchell (Houndmills: Palgrave Macmillan, 2010), 57.

[106] Foucault, *The Government of Self and Others*, 261.

[107] Foucault, "Le retour de la morale," 1516.

[108] In a sense also this *ethopoiesis* is a critical *poiesis*, as we shall see in the following chapter. This is also what Judith Butler's suggests: "Whereas some have dismissed [Foucault] as an aesthete or, indeed, as a nihilist, I hope to suggest that the foray he makes into the topic of self-making and, by presupposition, into *poiesis* itself is central to the politics of desubjugation that he proposes." Judith Butler, "What is Critique? An Essay on Foucault's Virtue," *Transversal*, no. 5 (2001), accessed March 2, 2021, https://transversal.at/transversal/0806/butler/en.

we shall see, this ethical and aesthetic process of *ethopoiesis* will by necessity unfold antagonistically in the social, political and economic realm. If style is a promise, as Adorno suggested, we will see how it is fulfilled in the late work.

CHAPTER 2

The Articulation of Subjectivity in the 1982 Lectures: *The Hermeneutics of the Subject*

What is a Subject? The First Steps into Antiquity: from Subjection to Subjectivation

In January 1980, Foucault opens his lecture course at Collège de France by leading the audience into the palace of the Roman emperor Septimius Severus – and thereby, into the more general domain of Antiquity, where all his following lecture courses will unfold.[1] In this palace, on the ceiling of the hall of justice in which the emperor delivered his judgments and dispensed justice, a fresco represents the exact positions of the stars on the night he was born. With this painting, the provincial background of Septimius Severus was to be understood as the starting point of a predestined trajectory that would lead up to the imperial palaces of Rome, bringing his fate into accord with the order of the world. Most importantly, the actual decision-making of one man down below was to be understood as an eternal *truth* inscribed in the star-studded sky above. The message is clear: the Roman Empire is governed in accord with truth.

With this image, Foucault departs from the previous years of lectures on the birth of the *raison d'État* of the 17th century and the theoretical works of German and American neoliberalism in *Security, Territory, Population* from 1978 and *The Birth of Biopolitics* from 1979. He leaves modernity, and from now on, will lecture about Antiquity. Yet despite the long leap backward in history, one important conceptual and methodological point serves as a bridge: the shift from the notion of power-knowledge to government-truth. In the aforementioned courses, Foucault had started developing the notion of government, which now seems to him "much more

---

[1] *The Government of the Living: Lectures at the Collège de France 1979–1980*, trans. Graham Burchell (Houndmills/New York: Palgrave Macmillan, 2014); *Subjectivity and Truth: Lectures at the Collège de France 1980–1981*, trans. Graham Burchell (Houndmills/New York: Palgrave Macmillan, 2017).

operational than the notion of power."[2] In the *Government of the Living* lectures, the introductory function of Septimius Severus' sky-painted ceiling serves to illustrate the importance of truth in relation to the workings of government, and to further "develop the notion of knowledge in the direction of the problem of truth."[3] Thus Foucault wants to "get rid of" his previously established conceptual pair of power-knowledge and replace it with that of government-truth, in order to pose the problem of the subject, which Foucault at this time defines as the general theme of all his work.[4] We can here see the fundamental structure and stakes of the remaining years of his lecture courses: government, truth, subject.

This chapter will focus on the last of this triptych, to try to answer the question: what concept of subject emerges from Foucault's late work? To this end, the 1982 lectures, *The Hermeneutics of the Subject*, are particularly important. While Foucault initiates his five lecture courses on Antiquity in 1980, the first two years of lectures largely stick to the project of *The History of Sexuality*. The *Government of the Living* from 1980 continues the work of volume 1 to trace the confessional practices and its obligatory form of truth-telling further back in history, and the 1981 lecture course *Subjectivity and Truth* is devoted to the question of sexual morality and *aphrodisia*, containing much of the material found in the second and third volumes of this work (see appendix).[5] It is true that Foucault in 1980, in his re-reading of

---

[2] *The Government of the Living: Lectures at the Collège de France 1979–1980*, trans. Graham Burchell (Houndmills/New York: Palgrave Macmillan 2014), 12.

[3] Translation modified: *Gouvernement des vivants*, 12.

[4] "I would like to say, first of all, what has been the goal of my work during the last twenty years. It has not been to analyze the phenomena of power, nor to elaborate the foundations of such an analysis. My objective, instead, has been to create a history of the different modes by which, in our culture, human beings are made subjects. [...] Thus it is not power, but the subject, which is the general theme of my research." see Michel Foucault, "Subject and Power" in *Beyond Structuralism and Hermeneutics*, eds. Hubert L. Dreyfus and Paul Rabinow (Chicago: University of Chicago Press, 1983), 208–209.

[5] In terms of its object of study and historical material, the *Subjectivity and Truth* lectures are devoted to the pre-history of sexuality: at the center of the investigation lies the Greek notion of *aphrodisia* as it appears during the first century CE, in which Foucault discovers an austere sexual morality preceding and influencing what we consider Christian sexual morality. Sources include Artemidorus' *Oneirocritica*, Plutarch's *Erotikos*, Xenophon's *Oeconomicus*, and Roman Stoics such as Musonius Rufus. It is a course that contains much of the material and many of the conclusions that in a more structured form reappear in the second and third volumes of the *History of Sexuality*, and as such, go beyond the scope of this thesis and the recapitulation offered here. The discussion of Artemidorus' *Oneirocritica* forms a substantial part of the first chapter of *The History of Sexuality Vol. 3 The care of the self*, while references to *Oeconomicus* and other works by Xenophon appear frequently in *The History of Sexuality Vol. 2 The use of pleasure*. See Michel Foucault, *The History of Sexuality Vol. 2 The use of pleasure*, trans. Robert Hurley (New York: Random House, Inc., 1990), and Michel

Oedipus Rex as a tragedy of truth-telling, identifies the element he will investigate in subsequent lecture courses: "the element of the first person, of the 'I,' of the '*autos*,' of the 'myself' in what could be called alethurgy, veridiction, or the rites and procedures of veridiction."[6] But this *autos* is subjected, on the one hand, to an *actus veritatis*, a truth act within what Foucault terms a regime of truth – "a regime defined by the obligation for individuals to have a continuous relationship to themselves"[7] – and, on the other, by the *obligation* to perform this act in confession. In 1980, Foucault is still developing the notion of productive power where even if the subject might be an agent or active part as the operator of truth or alethurgy, the individual is the very object of this alethurgy, subjected or subjugated to a predetermined confessional regime of truth: "The Christian [...] shows that putting his own truth into discourse is not just an essential obligation; it is one of the basic forms of our obedience."[8] While these lectures form a continuation of the archeology of Western governmentality[9] and the genealogy of the subject – stretching back through the centuries, as two sides of the same project – the extension of this double trajectory, which runs in parallel lines from *Security, Territory, Population* and the first volume of *The History of Sexuality*, has not yet extended its full reach. The subject is still an effect of existing power-knowledge relations, forming itself in an obligatory, predetermined, subjugating, and predominantly Christian kind of confession.

In the 1982 lectures, *The Hermeneutics of the Subject*, this changes: investigating the meaning of *epimeleia heautou*, the care of the self, among the various philosophical schools of Hellenistic philosophy, Foucault begins to consider the possibilities of a subject forming itself in an open-ended, voluntary, true discourse; one of subjectivation rather than subjugation. There is, however, one problem: Foucault does not, at any point in the lecture courses delivered during the eighties, provide a clear definition of what a subject is. He does make certain qualifications: for instance, when he indicates the proximity between the ancient Greek notion of *bios*, life, and our notion of the subject (despite the fact that "the Greeks did not know what

---

Foucault, *The History of Sexuality Vol. 3 The care of the self*, trans. Robert Hurley (New York: Random House, Inc., 1990).

[6] Foucault, *The Government of the Living*, 48.

[7] Foucault, *The Government of the Living*, 83.

[8] Foucault, *The Government of the Living*, 313.

[9] "In a sense, *raison d'État*, some genetic moments of which I tried to reconstruct two years ago, is actually a whole, let's say utilitarian and calculating reorganization of all the alethurgies peculiar to the exercise of power." see Foucault, *The Government of the Living*, 9.

subjectivity is"[10]) or when he introduces a "Cartesian moment" in the history of Western philosophy, to describe the development of an early modern notion of a knowing subject that, unlike the common ancient view, in no way is transfigured or transformed in its attaining of truth. But Foucault does not properly define "subject," which is why the following investigation will have to proceed by way of a close reading.

Another difficulty presents itself in Foucault's generally descriptive, but at times implicitly prescriptive account of this model of subjectivity. While Foucault demonstrates that the care of the self constitutes a fundamental and common principle of the philosophical attitude for the Epicureans, the Cynics, and the Stoics,[11] he also holds that this Hellenistic model retrospectively came to be "concealed historically" by the subsequent influence of Platonism and Christianity: the Platonic model characterized by knowing oneself and one's ignorance as a condition for truth, and the Christian model characterized by a circular relation between self-knowledge, self-renunciation, and the truth of the Text. So on one level, these lectures perform a historiographical, corrective task of unearthing the marginalized, concealed, or forgotten Hellenistic model of the care of the self. But on another level, which is always the case in Foucault's "histories of the present,"[12] this historical and theoretical investigation serves to illuminate the present order. Not in the critical sense of his archeological and genealogical projects, where Foucault's demonstration of the contingency of historical power-knowledge relations enables the reader to identify the contingency of power relations in their own time. On the contrary, the descriptions of the Hellenistic care of the self as a model of subjectivity takes on an implicitly prescriptive ambition in *The Hermeneutics of the Subject*. The difficulty is to distinguish between these interwined modalities, playing out in one of Foucault's richest and most voluminous lecture courses[13] – the importance and potentiality of which is

---

[10] Foucault, *Subjectivity and Truth*, 253.

[11] With regard to these philosophical schools, Foucault notes that "[t]hroughout the long summer of Hellenistic and Roman thought, the exhortation to care for oneself became so widespread that it became, I think, a truly general cultural phenomenon." See Foucault, *The Hermeneutics of the Subject*, 9. However, the Pyrrhonists (or Skeptics) are absent from Foucault's enumeration as well as from the whole lecture course, which is a curious omission for many reasons: first, because they share some positions with the Stoics and Epicureans, such as the goal of *ataraxia* (unperturbeness or peace of mind); second, as Paul Veyne has pointed out, because Foucault agreed to be called a skeptic himself. See Paul Veyne, *Foucault: Sa pensée, sa personne* (Paris: Albin Michel, 2008), 67.

[12] Foucault, *Discipline and Punish*, 31.

[13] *The Hermeneutics of the Subject* is one of the longest lecture courses Foucault gave at Collège de France; yet it does not contain all of the material on the subject that Foucault had prepared in dossiers (see the following footnote), or even what he in the first lecture announces to go through (while the

underlined by the fact that Foucault planned to use this material to write a separate book on the care of the self, outside the framework of the history of sexuality, as "a book separate from the sex series."[14]

In order to draw out the most important aspects of this subjectivity we will loosely follow Foucault's exposition in these lectures in their given order. In the following and second section, it will be shown that the Hellenistic care of the self is not merely an attentive, treating or caring work on the self, but that it also must be understood as a kind of opposition or contradiction in relation to one's surroundings, as a form of critique, which appears as both an individual and a collective endeavor. Third, Foucault affirms in this Hellenistic model an idea of subjectivity as an open-ended process of subjectivation. This is of importance both in how it relates back to his previous work on power-knowledge relations as processes of subjection – Foucault speaks of how governmentality understood as a set of "power relations in their mobility, transformability, and reversibility," cannot avoid passing through the subject defined as a self-relation – and how it leads him to define the ancient care of the self as "a self-finalization of the relationship to the self," thus introducing an important and, as we shall see, recurring figure of thought in which means and ends merge. In the fourth section, it is demonstrated that the notion of *mathēsis* and the knowledge of nature functions as a kind of veridiction – a more elaborated, systematic kind of truth-telling regarding the things of the world than subsequent forms of truth-telling that are relayed by Foucault, – and is fundamental to the subject's formation of itself. Further, this attention to the function of the knowledge of nature in the various philosophical schools implicitly answers the criticism of Hadot and others, which takes Foucault's understanding of the care of the self to be overly aesthetic, and which is analyzed toward the end of the chapter. Fifth, we will see how Foucault's brief, interjected comments on Faust – the only modern work of literature discussed in these lectures on ancient thought – serves as a reflection on the role of philosophy, which is ultimately what is at stake in these

---

Socratic-Platonic moment of *epimeleia heautou* in philosophical reflection and then the golden age of the culture of the self in the first two centuries of the common era are dealt with, the passage from pagan philosophy to Christian asceticism in the 4th and 5th century is never elaborated). See Frédéric Gros, "Course Context" in Foucault, *The Hermeneutics of the Subject*, 516–17.

[14] As Frédéric Gros points out, the book's content and themes as they are outlined by Foucault in an interview (see Michel Foucault, "On the Genealogy of Ethics: an Overview of Work in Progress" in *Ethics*, 255) correspond very well to the 1982 lectures, and to the special "thick, bound dossiers" that Foucault had prepared for them. The five dossiers were entitled "Course," "Alcibiades, Epictetus," "Government of the self and others," "Culture of the self—Rough draft," and "The Others.". See Frédéric Gros, "Course Context" in Foucault, *The Hermeneutics of the Subject*, 516.

late lectures: shall philosophy merely define theoretically the conditions of knowledge and truth, or shall it offer itself as a practice of truth? Sixth, the role of ascetic exercises and *parrēsia*, truth-telling, will be examined as such forms of practice, in Foucault's terms as a "subjectivation of truth."

This will not only provide an account of what kind of subject is gathered from *The Hermeneutics of the Subject*; it will also refute certain common and influential readings of Foucault's late work, which will be apparent in the seventh and last section of this chapter. On the one hand, there is a widespread idea that Foucault's late work on ancient philosophy indicates a turning away from politics to ethics, something which has even been taken to "legitimate neoliberal common sense," and on the other hand, it has been bemoaned as a superficial, overly aesthetic engagement with ancient thought. Pierre Hadot, for instance, took Foucault to be advancing a new form of dandyism, "a late-twentieth-century version."[15] Against these ideas it will be argued that Foucault's investigation of the care of the self – his implicit and explicit ways of linking the care of the self to a critical project and the notion of critique, i.e. his conviction that the turn to the self forms a degree zero and a point of reversibility in all relations of governmentalization – does not limit itself to a discussion of individual ethical subjects in Antiquity, but provides the ground for thinking about individual, as well as collective, political subjects in his own present, and by extension, our own present moment. Foucault acknowledges the importance of Hadot's notion of "philosophy as a way of life;"[16] in order to make clear the stakes of Foucault's project, we could call it "critique as a way of life."

The Care of the Self as a Form of Critique

In order to sort out the most important aspects of the care of the self in the 1982 lectures and, at the same time, to uncover a problematic of specific importance not only to this study, but also in relation to Foucault's work as a whole, it seems that we can align our reading around a particular and recurring set of metaphors.[17] Initially, *The Hermeneutics of the Subject* is a

---

[15] Pierre Hadot, "Reflections on the notion of 'the cultivation of the self'" in *Foucault Philosopher*, trans. Timothy Armstrong (Hernel Hempstead: Harvester Wheatsheaf, 1992), 230.

[16] Pierre Hadot, *Philosophy as a Way of Life: Spiritual Exercises from Socrates to Foucault*, trans. Michael Chase (Oxford: Blackwell Publishers Ltd, 1995), 265.

[17] The hypothesis, developed in chapter one as a transposition of a certain contradiction from the formal to the social register, is that Foucault's late work on the subject's possibility to constitute itself appears as a possible mode of contradiction operating within the power relations described in his earlier work.

course structured around gaze, vision, and visibility: from the second day of lectures when Foucault discusses Plato's well-known metaphor of the eye in *Alcibiades*, through the radical clear-sightedness of the *Therapeutae* to the mainly Stoic notion of a conversion of the gaze toward oneself, after which speech and the speaking of truth appears as the center of gravity.

The first two lectures are devoted to the Socratic insistence on the care for oneself. Foucault introduces the central notion – *epimeleia heautou* in Greek and *cura sui* in latin, "to which the historiography of philosophy has not attached much importance hitherto"[18] – and puts it next to the more famous notion *Gnōthi seauton* ("know thyself", the inscription on Apollo's temple in Delphi) in order to demonstrate how the care of oneself is actually a wider, more fundamental, and more important epigraph to ancient philosophy than the former. Even in Plato's *Apology*, where Socrates famously defines his wisdom in terms of self-knowledge and by the fact that he knows himself not to be wise, Foucault shows that he also formulates his defense repeatedly and explicitly in terms of *epimeleia heautou*: "I went to each of you privately and conferred upon him what I say is the greatest benefit, by trying to persuade him not to care for any of his belongings before caring that he himself should be as good and as wise as possible".[19] But things get a bit more complicated in *Alcibiades*. This contested dialogue displays an odd mixture of themes from both early and late Plato. And Foucault, while noting the discussion of its authenticity, decides to take its rich content at face value, as a good representation of much of Plato's work, as well as of later Platonism and Neo-Platonism.[20] This allows him to single out three elements of the Socratic-Platonic care of the self which will be investigated in their transformation in later Antiquity: government and the exercise of power, pedagogy and the focus on youth, and the principle of self-knowledge or *gnōthi seauton*.[21] The

---

[18] Michel Foucault, *The Hermeneutics of the Subject: Lectures at Collège de France 1981–1982*, trans. G. Burchell (New York: Palgrave/Macmillan, 2005), 5.

[19] Plato, *Apology* trans. G.M.A. Grube, in *Plato Complete Works*, ed. John M. Cooper (Indianapolis/Cambridge: Hackett Publishing Company 1997), 32, 36C.

[20] The debate on whether *Alcibiades* was authored by Plato was initiated by Schleiermacher in the 19th century and is still ongoing today. Foucault seems to reflect the main scholarly position in France of his day, and doubts that there is "a single expert who really, seriously questions its authenticity." He does acknowledge the possibility that it was rewritten after Plato's death, but states: "Anyway, since I have neither the competence nor the intention to discuss this, what interests me and what I find quite fascinating in this dialogue, is that basically we find here in outline an entire account of Plato's philosophy, from Socratic questioning to what appear to be elements quite close to the final Plato even to Neo-Platonism." See: Foucault, *The Hermeneutics of the Subject*, 74.

[21] Enumerating the anachronistic mix of elements from early and late Plato with regard to the care of the self, Foucault also includes "the erotics of boys," but decides not to discuss this theme and its transformation in the following centuries and Hellenistic philosophy. In this historical development

question of government or power lies in the status of Alcibiades as an aristocratic young man destined to govern others, and as such, implored to first care for himself. Because, as Socrates puts it, anyone "who is to be ruler and trustee, not only of himself and his private business, but also the city and the city's business, must first acquire virtue himself."[22] The pedagogical aspect of the Platonic care of the self is manifested in Socrates' attempt to improve the young Alcibiades' education of insufficient Athenian standards, adding to it the care of the self as a necessary link between adolescence and adulthood. The principle of self-knowledge, finally, is the most important, appearing toward the end of the dialogue "in in all its splendor and fullness," as the very answer to the question of what the care of the self is. It is also at this point that Foucault first brings up that which has "a number of echoes in Plato's other dialogues, especially the later ones: the well-known and often employed metaphor of the eye."[23] Here, in order to explain how the soul can come to know itself, Socrates takes the example of the eye. The eye sees itself in the eye of another, and more precisely – as it is reflected in the pupil – in "the best part of it, the part with which it can see".[24] In the same way, the soul can only see itself in another soul, and in the best part of it, that which is divine. This is characteristic of Platonic and neo-Platonic thought: self-knowledge as the seeing of the divine within ourselves, giving access to truth; self-knowledge as the Platonic *anamnēsis* or recollection of the divine truth or knowledge which already lies inside us; as such it is a "movement of knowledge alone, of knowledge of the self, of the divine, and of essences."[25]

All three elements of this Socratic insistence to care for oneself – as they are expressed in *Alcibiades* as the exercise of power, the education of the young, and the principle of self-knowledge – are traced by Foucault in the transformation of the *epimeleia heautou* in the Hellenistic and Roman epoch. Foucault notes that now the injunction to care for oneself applies not only to governors but to "everyone,"[26] and demonstrates how the emphasis on youth

---

the principle of self-knowledge or *gnōthi seauton*, or rather the abandonment of this principle, plays a much more important role. See: Foucault, *The Hermeneutics of the Subject*, 76.

[22] Plato, *Alcibiades* trans. D. S. Hutchinson, in *Plato Complete Works*, ed. John M. Cooper (Indianapolis/Cambridge: Hacket Publishing Company 1997), 594, 134 c.

[23] Foucault, *The Hermeneutics of the Subject*, 69.

[24] Plato, *Alcibiades* 134 c.

[25] Foucault, *The Hermeneutics of the Subject*, 78.

[26] Foucault immediately concedes that there are limitations to this generalization: "even if the Stoics and Cynics say to people, to everyone, "take care of yourself," in actual fact it could only become a practice among and for those with a certain cultural, economic, and social capability." Further, the very idea to care for oneself is often expressed in contradiction to the majority, the people, the *hoi*

and pedagogy, i.e. the pedagogical aspect of the Platonic care of the self recommended for the young Alcibiades, undergoes a radical expansion or "generalization" and comes to apply to all, to both young and old in the philosophies of the Epicureans, Cynics and Stoics. Epicurus stated in *Letter to Menoeceus* that "[n]o one should postpone the study of philosophy when he is young, nor should he be weary of it when he becomes mature,"[27] Epictetus' school accepted, alongside its young students, visitors and passers-by of all ages, while Seneca held correspondence with Lucilius, a man twelve years his junior yet still middle-aged. In this generalization of the care of the self, which comes to apply to everybody, Foucault identifies two tendencies: it gains a more accentuated "critical function," while also becoming more closely related to medicine, through notions such as cure and therapy.[28] When the care of the self functions less as a formative practice for the young and more as a corrective practice for all regardless of age, it is extended along the lines of what Foucault calls correction-liberation, as opposed to formation-knowledge. Foucault cites Seneca who employs a maxim common to the Cynics: *virtutes discere vitia dediscere est* (learning virtue is unlearning vices). This ancient notion of unlearning – a notion of critical relevance in our age too, by the way, still along the lines of "correction-liberation," but in relation to racism and privilege[29] – entails a threefold *"critique"*: a criticism of (i) the values passed down to children through nursery tales and things that form their minds from an early age (the errors we took in with the nursemaid's milk, in Cicero's words); (ii) the values reproduced in the setting of the family, and (iii) the early education given by teachers of rhetoric. To

---

polloi, as a way of distinguishing oneself, even among people with the same material conditions. See Foucault, *The Hermeneutics of the Subject*, 78.

[27] Epicurus, "Letter To Menoeceus," in *The Art of Happiness*, trans. George K. Strodach (New York: Penguin Books, 2012), §122, 155.

[28] Foucault is here distinguishing the Hellenistic care of the self mainly against the Platonic version described in *Alcibiades*, but we could naturally think of a "critical function" in Socrates too. The distinction would appear less clearly if Foucault were to take Socrates imploration of the Athenians to care for themselves in the *Apology* above, or his serving people bitter potions of what's best as opposed to what is most gratifying in *Gorgias*. On the other hand, Foucault's argument is confirmed in *Gorgias*, when Socrates concludes with a speech recommending the practice of justice and excellence not to be punished in Hades, and as a means for being able to govern the city. See Plato, *Gorgias*, trans. Donald J. Zeyl, in *Plato Complete Works*, Ed. John M. Cooper (Indianapolis/ Cambridge: Hacket Publishing Company 1997), 864–869, 522a–527e. For Foucault's "critical function," see Foucault, *The Hermeneutics of the Subject*, 93, 97.

[29] Gayatry Chakravorty Spivak, *A Critique of Postcolonial Reason: Toward a History of the Vanishing Present* (Cambridge, MA: Harvard UP, 1999), 284; Sara Danius, Stefan Jonsson, and Gayatri Chakravorty Spivak, "An Interview with Gayatri Chakravorty Spivak ," *Boundary 2*, vol 20, no. 2 (1993), 24.

Foucault, the care of the self through adult life takes on a critical function, and he even describes the unlearning of family values (with regard to Seneca's advice for Lucilius to distance himself from his parents) as a "criticism of what we in our terms would call the 'family ideology.'"[30] Without any of his usual reservations about notions of ideology and ideology critique[31] – which need not be understood as incompatible with his own work[32] – Foucault thus invokes the modern critique of family ideology (of marriage, property, and family as the basis for social domination)[33] to reveal the radically and inherently critical nature of caring for oneself. Indeed, one of the tasks of the care of the self, as he notes, is to "completely reverse the system of values conveyed and laid down by the family."[34]

In addition to this critical function, the other aspect in the generalization of the care of the self is its increased proximity to medicine. Ancient philosophy has always had a strong link to medical terminology and practice, and while this continues to be the case in Hellenistic philosophy – which is apparent in Plutarch's assertion that philosophy and medicine inhabit one *mia khōra*, one single land, as well as in the shared terminology of the Epicurean and Stoic use of the notion of *pathos* (in medical terms designating "suffering"; in Epicurean and Stoic terms ranging from illness, through passion to irrational impulses of the soul, translated as *perturbatio* and *affectus* by Cicero and Seneca) – Foucault identifies a most intense meeting

---

[30] Foucault, *The Hermeneutics of the Subject*, 96.

[31] While Foucault on many occasions criticized and defined his own project in opposition to a rather general and abstract body of "ideology critique," this mainly Althusserian school of thought is allowed to pass unpurged here. Indeed, the distance from and opposition to this favorite foe might not be as grand or diametrical as Foucault sometimes has us believe. For an interesting thesis uncovering a productive dialogue between Althusser's Ideological State Apparatuses and Foucault's "reading of the materiality of ideology," see: Warren Montag, *Althusser and His Contemporaries* (Durham and London: Duke University Press, 2013), 156.

[32] For a more general understanding of the kinship in which there "emerges a thesis common to Althusser and Foucault, namely that of a force proper to ideology, or the disciplinary, which is grasped in the [Althusserian] formula 'the individualists march by themselves:' a formula in which the thematics of subjectivation and subjection are strategically linked," see Pascale Gillot, "Michel Foucault et le Marxisme de Louis Althusser," in *Foucault(s)* ed. Jean-François Braunstein, Daniele Lorenzini, Ariane Revel, Judith Revel, and Arianna Sforzini (Paris: Éditions de la Sorbonne, 2017), 254–255.

[33] For a critique of "marriage, property, the family [...] [as] the practical basis on which the bourgeoisie has erected its domination" see Karl Marx and Friedrich Engels, *The German Ideology*, 194. For a critique of monogamous marriage as "the cellular form of civilised society, in which the nature of the oppositions and contradictions fully active in that society can be already studied," see Friedrich Engels, *The Origin of the Family, Private Property and the State*, 69. For a more general discussion of ideology, or the statement that "in all ideology men and their relations appear upside-down as in a camera obscura," see for example *The German Ideology*, 42.

[34] Foucault, *The Hermeneutics of the Subject*, 96.

point between philosophy and medicine when the *epimeleia heautou* itself is conceived as a medical operation. Foucault takes up discussions of *epimeleia heautou* in medical sources from Hippocrates and Galen,[35] but more important is the philosophers' use of the fundamental notion of *therapeuein*, a word with three different meanings: to cure or to treat, to obey one's master, and to worship. Taken in its reflexive-composite form of a therapy of the self, one can thus understand this *therapeuein heauton* of Marcus Aurelius, Epictetus, or Seneca as the threefold practice of curing oneself, being one's own servant, and devoting oneself to oneself.[36]

One of the examples that best demonstrates both this curative aspect and the critical function, is the particular community of *Therapeutae*, a religious sect in the first century BCE who retreated to communal living in the outskirts of Alexandria. In their suburban gardens the *Therapeutae* devote themselves to worship and theoretical work, they "treat the soul like doctors treat the body", and refuse to acknowledge social divisions between the poor and the affluent, dismissing even the division between slaves and free men, and welcoming women and men alike. In historical terms, this may not be an example of great significance: as a highly particular, Jewish sect from Alexandria they seem peripheral to the culture of the self in the Hellenistic world as it was practiced in the philosophical schools and centers in Athens, Greece proper, and southern Italy, not to speak of the forms it took in Rome. Furthermore, the very existence of these "therapists" has been called into question: the only original account is *De Vita Contemplativa* – a work ascribed to Philo of Alexandria, who, as Foucault points out, makes no mention of them in his other works. But if we consider that ancient genres of literary and philosophical writing differ from ours – see for instance Foucault's description of Plato's letter V as a fictional letter "intended to circulate as a manifesto" – we may understand *De Vita Contemplativa* prescriptively, rather than in any descriptive way, both with respect to the original text by Philo, as well as in Foucault's discussions of it. As mentioned, the *Therapeutae* provide an example of philosophy as cure and therapy in its proximity to medicine, and as *epimeleia* as a form of critique, breaking with some of the most important social divisions of ancient society. Further, their very *bios*

---

[35] For Hippocrates, see Foucault, *The Hermeneutics of the Subject*, 160; for Galen, see Foucault, *The Hermeneutics of the Subject*, 380–407.

[36] Foucault, *The Hermeneutics of the Subject*, 98. See also footnote 59, 105: "The striking reference here is to Marcus Aurelius who, with regard to the inner *daemon*, writes that one must "surround it with sincere service (*gnesios therapeuein*). This service (*therapeuein*) consists in keeping it pure from all passion." *Meditations*, 11.13. The expression *heauton therapeuein* is also found in Epictetus, *Discourses*, I.xix.5."

theōretikos – which in the Latinized title of the work is called *vita contemplativa* – resonates with what Foucault later in his lectures will call "spiritual knowledge" to describe a knowledge that transforms the subject[37] as well as with Pierre Hadot's notion of philosophy as a way of life, or something we could call, given the *Therapeutaes'* opposition to unjust forms of government, critique as a way of life.

Foucault describes them in great detail, and compares them to other groups: in their practice of true discourse as an art to cure, educate, and transform a subject, the *Therapeutae* and many such groups would not accept any distinction between rich and poor, between those of noble birth and those of obscure backgrounds, or between those who exercise political power and those leading lives in the shadows. Not even the opposition between free men and slaves were accepted, which is significant to Foucault: "Consequently, since there is no difference of status, we can say that all individuals are in general terms 'competent': able to practice themselves, able to carry out this practice of the self."[38] In relation to *Alcibiades* and the idea that the care of the self is above all important for those who will govern others, this general equality or ability in the care of oneself forms part of an important shift that Foucault identifies in the later philosophical traditions: while not everyone may succeed to care for themselves, everyone is *called upon* to do so. And what do the *Therapeutae* seek to achieve in this care of the self, based on religious devotion and scientific study (which to them seem inseparable), as well as on clear breaks with some of the most foundational social divisions? "Their objective is, as they say, as Philo says, to learn to see clearly."[39]

This objective of seeing clearly coincides with a collective, liberational, egalitarian, and – one might say, given that they so clearly define their own laws – autonomous way of life. Foucault takes up many aspects of this, and more evidence is found in the text itself. Philo of Alexandria states that the *Therapeutae* consist of men who "abandon their property" and give up their inheritance, "looking upon the possession of servants of slaves to be a thing absolutely and wholly contrary to nature, for nature has created all men free, but the injustice and covetousness of some men who prefer inequality, that cause of all evil, having subdued some, has given to the more powerful authority over those who are weaker."[40] Among them women are seen as

---

[37] Foucault, *The Hermeneutics of the Subject*, 229.
[38] Foucault, *The Hermeneutics of the Subject*, 118.
[39] Foucault, *The Hermeneutics of the Subject*, 117.
[40] Philo of Alexandria, *On the Contemplative Life*, § 88, trans. C. D. Yonge (London: H. G. Bohn 1854–1890/1993). http://www.earlychristianwritings.com/yonge/book34.html (17 January 2017)

"having the same feelings of admiration as the men, and having adopted the same sect with equal deliberation and decision," both "imploring tranquility and truth."[41] While Foucault does not mention either the degree of equality between the sexes or its interesting aesthetical expressions,[42] he is clear regarding the importance of its collective character, underlining that with the *Therapeutae*, you cannot understand the care of the self as something readily available to the individual, like an innate universal reason: "It can only be practiced within the group, and within the group in its distinctive character."[43] And this is what puts the Epicurean and Stoic groups similar to the *Therapeutae* in a special relation to the important and decisive idea of a constitutive dividing line in Greek, Hellenistic and Roman culture "between those of the first rank and the mass, between the best and the crowd,"[44] normally expressed in the form of political influence, riches, citizenship, revered autochtonous ancestry, or access to power. Here is a division between the few and the many, but it is not based on social status: instead it is based on the individual's relationship to himself in the way he or she has formed it collectively with others.

So with the *Therapeutae* there is a collectively *and* individually organized *bios* – or subject – which, in its study or "contemplation of nature"[45] and its refusal of what it considers "contrary to nature," develops a way of life that abandons, negates, or contradicts existing forms of government, social domination, and relations of power, welcoming people from all society into their community.[46] To Foucault, this makes the *Therapeutae*, along with the

---

[41] Philo of Alexandria, *On the Contemplative Life*, § 88.

[42] Except for the aforementioned spiritual or devotional equality between women and men, there is a curious passage describing how their festivals conclude with a gender-mixed choral singing, something which, judging from Philo's description, appears to have been unthinkable at the time. But not only is the transgression performed, its reconfiguration of the sensible leads to a new understanding: "Now the chorus of male and female worshippers being formed, as far as possible on this model, makes a most humorous concert, and a truly musical symphony, the shrill voices of the women mingling with the deep-toned voices of the men. The ideas were beautiful, the expressions beautiful, and the chorus-singers were beautiful; and the end of ideas, and expressions, and chorus singers, was piety; therefore, being intoxicated all night till the morning with this beautiful intoxication, without feeling their heads heavy or closing their eyes for sleep, but being even more awake than when they came to the feast, as to their eyes and their whole bodies, and standing there till morning, when they saw the sun rising they raised their hands to heaven, imploring tranquility and truth, and acuteness of understanding." See Philo of Alexandria, *On the Contemplative Life*, § 88–89.

[43] Foucault, *The Hermeneutics of the Subject*, 119.

[44] Foucault, *The Hermeneutics of the Subject*, 119.

[45] Philo of Alexandria, *On the Contemplative Life*, § 90.

[46] Regarding the collective, communal nature of the *Therapeutae*, Foucault makes an interesting distinction between a Hellenic and a Roman form of the philosophical care of the self. The Roman

Epicurean schools, important examples of an under acknowledged common, popular pole of the practice of the self, which at the same time they transcend through their sophisticated study of nature. The Epicurean groups "were for the most part popular communities, filled with artisans, small shopkeepers, and poor farmers, and which represented a democratic political choice, as opposed to the aristocratic choice of the Platonists or Aristotelians, and which of course, completely working class as they were, also involved an important theoretical and philosophical reflection, or anyway a doctrinal apprenticeship."[47]

We have now seen how Foucault identifies a critical and curative function in the care of the self, and how he emphasizes the importance of the collective aspect in the example of the therapeutic community in Alexandria. Foucault does not, however, declare the examples of the *Therapeutae* and the Epicureans to be of greater value than any others in his investigation, just as he does not in any way distance himself from the Stoics' austere sexual morality, Seneca's warnings against the dangers of studying history, the aristocratic values of the Pythagoreans, or the transcendental notions of the Neo-Platonists – which all run contrary to his own positions, both in theory and practice. It is therefore no easy task to disentangle the play of critical, prescriptive, or simply descriptive perspectives in Foucault's treatment of the ancient material at hand; indeed, very different interpretations can be made.[48] Yet if we look at some of his late interviews regarding *The Hermeneutics of*

---

form is practically that of the private counselor, and the Hellenic form is that of the *skhole* or school: the semi-closed schools of the Pythagoreans and Epicureans that functioned as spaces of communal living, or the open schools of the Stoics, such as the daily meetings organized by Epictetus, where people would convene during daytime. Foucault also insists on the egalitarian nature of many of these communities: against scholars who had described the Epicurean communities as strictly hierarchic, he cites Philodemus' account of how the important spiritual guidance must be characterized by friendship, reciprocity, and *parrēsia* – the act of speaking frankly, a notion that Foucault here takes up for the first time and promises to get back to later. See Foucault, *The Hermeneutics of the Subject*, 137–144.

[47] Foucault, *The Hermeneutics of the Subject*, 115.

[48] An interesting example seeking to prove a rather bold hypothesis is Patrick Gamez's recent dissertation on Foucault. Arguing against any ethical turn, ethical period, or even ethics in Foucault's work, he also – as is the case here, in this thesis – makes the case that the technologies of the self and truth-telling theorized by Foucault in his late work must be understood in relation to government, but *in continuity* with what has been described as the obligatory nature of confession most notably expressed in the first volume of the history of sexuality. Meaning that he takes Foucault's attitude toward Antiquity as thoroughly critical, regarding it as a cautionary example. While this argument is more or less the opposite of the one here, it is valuable in how it reminds us of the risks of being governed by others – in the care of the self, also. See, Patrick J. Gamez, *Foucault against Ethics: Subjectivity and Critique after Humanism*, University of Notre Dame, 2016. https://scholarsmine. mst.edu/cgi/viewcontent.cgi?article=1023&context=artlan_phil_facwork.

the Subject, we see that he emphasizes and confirms the philosophical care of the self as a "practice of freedom" (connecting it to both anti-colonial and sexual liberation struggles),[49] wanting to make both the "proximity and difference" between the ancient and contemporary moralities appear in their interplay.[50] Moreover, he regards philosophy in its critical function – i.e. a questioning of all forms of political, economic, sexual, institutional domination – as ultimately derived from the Socratic imperative to take care of oneself.[51] Hence, our focus on the critical function of the care of the self seems justifiable. And other commentators have reached similar conclusions. Laura Cremonesi, for example, holds that in Foucault, "a relation exists between the concept of critique and the interpretation of Antiquity."[52] Beyond the "chronological coincidence"[53] between these two theoretical projects in Foucault's work, Cremonesi points out that they are conceptually intertwined with their common basis in the notion of government: Foucault defines critique precisely as the "art of not being governed like that," and, as we recall, he opens his very first 1980 lecture on Antiquity with an image of , so to speak, the "true" government of Roman emperor Septimus Severus. Interestingly, Cremonesi goes on to define the Foucauldian critique as a "space of visibility," citing the 1978 lecture "La philosophie analytique de la politique."[54] Here Foucault suggests that the task of philosophy should not be to "discover that which is hidden", but to make visible what we already see;

---

[49] Michel Foucault, "L'éthique du souci de soi comme pratique de la liberté," interview with H. Becker, R. Fonet-Berancourt, A. Gomez-Müller, January 1984 in *Dits et écrits II, 1976–1988,* 1529.

[50] "From a strictly philosophical point of view, the morality of Greek Antiquity and contemporary morality have nothing in common. But if we take these moralities in what they prescribe, issue, and advice, they are extraordinarily close. The important thing is to make this proximity and difference appear, and in its interplay, to show how the same advice given by the ancient morality can play out differently in a contemporary moral style." See Michel Foucault, "Le Retour de la morale," in *Dits et écrits II, 1976–1988,* 1519–20. Foucault also stated: "What I am trying to do is provoke an interference between our reality and the knowledge of our past history." See Michel Foucault, "Truth Is the Future," interview with M. Dillon, November 1980, in *Foucault Live: Collected Interviews, 1961–1984,* Ed. Sylvère Lotringer, (New York: Semiotext(e) 1996), 301.

[51] "In its critical aspect – I take critique in a broad sense – philosophy is precisely that which calls into question all phenomena of domination on whichever level or under whichever form it appears – political, economic, sexual, institutional. This critical function of philosophy derives, up to a certain point, from the Socratic imperative: 'Take care of yourself,' which is to say: 'Found yourself in liberty, by mastering yourself.'" See Foucault, "L'éthique du souci de soi comme pratique de la liberté," *Dits et écrits II, 1976–1988,* 1548.

[52] Laura Cremonesi, "La parrēsia et l'attitude critique," in *Michel Foucault: éthique et verité, 1984,* eds. D. Lorenzini A. Revel, A. Sforzini (Paris: Vrin, 2013), 128.

[53] A coincidence not perfectly exact, given that the "What is Critique?" lecture was given in 1978 and the work on Antiquity was carried out almost entirely in the 1980s.

[54] Foucault, "La philosophie analytique de la politique," in *Dits et écrits II, 1976–1988,* no 232, 534.

what is so close that we do not perceive it. This points to another relation, another piece of conceptual common ground between this definition of Foucauldian critique and his interpretation of Antiquity that Cremonesi does not mention: between on the one hand, critique as the making visible of what we already see and on the other hand the objective of the *Therapeutae*, the very goal of their curative care of the soul, which is to learn how to see clearly, or to "see without interruption," to "perceive what is unseen by what is visible."[55] And as we shall see, any such rendering visible of the unnoticed must be preceded by, or undertaken in parallel with, a sort of necessary adjustment of vision, that is, a turning of the gaze onto oneself.

The Subject as Process and the Reversibility of Power Relations

The Greek and Roman care of the self is, as we have seen, neither a formative practice only for the young, nor a prerequisite exclusively for those in power or for those who must care for the whole city, as was the case in *Alcibiades*. As for the Platonic and Neo-Platonic emphasis on *gnōthi seauton*, finally, this insistence on the knowledge of oneself – a knowledge of the divine part of the soul (its unchanging and constant part) that will lay the foundation for all other knowledge – is completely countered by the Epicureans and Stoics, who profess a relentless labor on the self by the self, precisely in order to let truth change and transform it. In Foucault's account, the care of the self becomes a common, general formula in the art of living of Hellenistic and Roman philosophy. It is a significant shift carried out among various groups, sects, philosophical schools among the urban poor, and in the correspondence between wealthy Romans, during the course of at least five or six centuries, spanning from Epicurus in the fourth century BCE to the Roman Emperor Marcus Aurelius in the second century. And all this, Foucault says in the lecture on the 10 February, is characterized by – indeed often formulated and conceptualized as – a certain "turning" toward ourselves. It is a reflexive movement, a turn or *conversion*, frequently regarded as a conversion of the vision or gaze. Seizing upon the metaphors of visibility, Foucault cites expressions like *blepe se* (consider, or look at yourself) in Marcus Aurelius, *observa te* (observe yourself) and *respica te* (look at yourself) in Seneca, emphasizing the idea that we must look at ourselves, observe ourselves, and put ourselves under our own gaze in a continuous way: "Our attention, eyes,

---

[55] Philo of Alexandria, *On the Contemplative Life*, § 78.

mind, and finally our whole being must be turned towards the self through-out our life."[56] Foucault traces this conversion in the notion of *epistrephein pros heauton* (to turn towards the self, to convert to the self), in Epictetus, Marcus Aurelius, and Plotinus, and finds the Latin equivalent *convertere ad se* (converting to the self) in Seneca.[57] Rather than a "rigourous, 'constructed' notion" in the strict sense, Foucault defines this conversion as one of the most important technologies of the self in Western thought: a kind of nucleus, a central set of images and a practical schema extending itself through a vast and far-ranging historical field. It partly extends into Christianity, and even further into the general philosophical domain of morality, e.g. its reap-pearance in the 16th century, most notably in Montaigne.[58] Above all, however, Foucault notes its importance in political terms, with respect to what he calls the "revolutionary subjectivity:"

> It seems to me that we cannot understand revolutionary practice through-out the nineteenth century, we cannot understand the revolutionary indi-vidual and what revolutionary experience meant for him, unless we take into account the notion or fundamental schema of conversion to the revolution. So the problem is to see how this element, which arises from the most traditional technology of the self—I will say, historically the thickest and most condensed, since it goes back to Antiquity—was introduced, how conversion, this element of technology of the self, was plugged into this new domain and field of political activity, and how this element of conversion was necessarily, or at least exclusively, linked to the revolutionary choice, to revolutionary practice.[59]

In other words, this conversion to the revolution appears, according to Foucault, in the revolutionary movements of the industrial working class, most intensely around 1830–40. Foucault gives no details of this develop-ment, but the close link between the conversion to the self and the conversion to the revolution is suggested in other accounts of the same period: Eric Hobsbawm for instance, in his history of the long 19th century, underlines that the revolutionary labor movements are not merely materially deter-mined subjects, but also constituted and knitted together by developing a "common style of life" and through projects of "self-improvement."[60] Having

---

[56] Foucault, *The Hermeneutics of the Subject*, 206.

[57] Foucault, *The Hermeneutics of the Subject*, 207.

[58] Foucault, *The Hermeneutics of the Subject*, 251; Foucault, "On the Genealogy of Ethics", 278.

[59] Foucault, *The Hermeneutics of the Subject*, 208–09.

[60] In the first work in his trilogy, *The Age of Revolution*, Hobsbawm asserts that the labor movement was an organization of self-defense and revolution, but beyond the struggle it was also "a way of life" (p 214).

thus indicated that this technology of the self from Greek and Roman Antiquity reappears in the revolutionary individual as that which binds him to the collectivity of revolutionary practice, Foucault, before closing the parenthesis, notes that the history of revolutionary subjectivity "remains to be written" – an interesting deferral (or open invitation) repeated a number of times during his late lectures.[61] In fact, a similar ambition is expressed already in 1973, in the then recently launched newspaper *Libération*. In conversation with a laid off worker from the Renault factory suggests a comprehensive collective research project to run as a constant series in the

—

Further, he argues that socialism during its "formative period" between Robert Owen's New View of Society (1813–1814) and *The Communist Manifesto* (1848) parted company with the classical liberal tradition by returning "to the oldest of all human ideological traditions, the belief that man is naturally a communal being" which, as it happens, was also a general presupposition of the Hellenistic philosophies. See Eric Hobsbawm, *The Age of Revolution* (New York: Vintage Books 1996). In the second work, *The Age of Capital*, Hobsbawm describes how the political (French) revolution is swallowed by the industrial (British) revolution through the expansion of the world capitalist economy (15). Here he also notes how the turn to revolution was defined by a certain "push," where workers of very different skills, salaries, and degrees of secure employment were "pushed into a common consciousness not only by this social polarization but, in the cities at least, by a common style of life – in which the tavern ('the workman's church' as a bourgeois liberal called it) played a central role – and by a common style of thought." Hobsbawm draws the same conclusion regarding the situation in Germany in the 1860s and 1870s; not only the growing distance – in material terms – to the prosperous bourgeosie, but also the workers' associations (*Bildungsvereine*) for "self-improvement" shaped a common consciousness and accentuated revolutionary politics. Eric Hobsbawm, *The Age of Capital* (London: Abacus, 1995), 265.

[61] In the beginning of *The Government of Self and Others*, Foucault outlines this 1983 course as a study of the dramatics of true discourse within the political domain in four figures: the first concerns the shift from the public orator to the advisor in Antiquity, the second the Prince's minister in the 16th century, the third the figure of the critic in the 18th, 19[th,] and 20th centuries (the English translation wrongfully renders this as the figure of "critique"; see Foucault, *Le gouvernement de soi et des autres*, 67), and the fourth the figure of the revolutionary: "What is this person who arises within society and says: I am telling the truth, and I am telling the truth in the name of the revolution that I am going to make and that we will make together?" Of these four figures, only the first is actually discussed in the course. See Foucault, *The Government of Self and Others*, 70.

In *The Courage of the Truth*, Foucault first states that *parrēsia* can be said to appear in the modern epoch in the form of revolutionary discourse, both as a critique of the existing society and in its prophetic modality, speaking "in order to tell of a future which, up to a point, already has the form of fate." (30) Second, in his longest discussion of the issue, he states that "it would also be interesting" to analyze the revolutionary movements of the 19th and 20th century as political descendants to Cynicism, distinguishing between three different expressions: the sociality of secret associations; the organization of parties and labor unions, and the revolutionary life as true life (pp 183–186). Third, when speaking of how philosophy as a way of life disappears in the early 19th century when philosophy becomes a teaching profession, and how the legend of philosophical heroism finds its last expression in Goethe's *Faust*, before mutating and migrating into "that other, displaced and transformed form of philosophical life in the political field: the revolutionary life." (211) In his lectures at Victoria University in Toronto 1982, Foucault reiterates his wish to study "the problem of revolutionary subjectivity," but locates it to a higher degree on the level of asceticism, the personal life of individuals, and individual subjectivity. See Michel Foucault, *Speaking the Truth about Oneself*, eds. Henri-Paul Fruchaud and Daniele Lorenzini (Chicago and London: Chicago University Press, 2021), 73–74.

newspaper, precisely about the "whole tradition of workers' struggles of the 19th century, little known and poorly recounted."[62] But while it may come as no surprise that Foucault would consider investigating collective forms of self-organization and struggles in the period when he was close to the French Maoists,[63] the fact that he does so in his study of ancient philosophy and the Hellenistic form of the care of the self is perhaps more significant, indicating the political stakes inherent – but not always evident – in this project.

To return to and understand the specificity of this Hellenistic conversion to the self, Foucault relates it to the preceding Platonic notion of *epistrophē* and the later Christian notion of *metanoia*. In Plato, he says, the *epistrophē* consists first of all in turning away from appearances, then turning to care for oneself in the form of recollection, and finally in *returning* to "one's ontological homeland."[64] In the dialogues of *Alcibiades, Phaedrus, Meno*, and *Phaedo*, the conversion concerns the worldly and other-worldly, the liberation of the soul from the body, and the privileged role of knowing (*connaitre*): one turns to know oneself, to know the true, to find it within through the Platonic *anamnēsis* or recollection as the fundamental form of knowledge. The conversion in the Hellenistic and Roman culture is different, and its political implications are potentially more far-reaching. It does not lead us from this world to the world beyond, nor does it liberate the soul from the body; rather it entails a liberation within this world, within an "axis of immanence", by establishing an adequate relationship of "self to self": it is a conversion to the self which goes through lived experience, ordering this experience in exercises or *askēsis*.

The conversion in the Hellenistic and Roman culture differ also from the Christian *metanoia*, which is described by Foucault as a sudden change or a single stroke in the being of the subject, involving a transition from mortality to immortality, from darkness to light, from the devil to God, carried out in the form of self-renunciation, of a break, of a rebirth of oneself into a new life. The conversion of the Epicureans and Stoics differ also from this model: there is no sudden break within the self, but the subject's break – or what seems to be a continuously operated set of breaks – is made with its surroundings and with what keeps it enslaved, constrained and dependent. There is no

---

[67] While Foucault himself never took up any part of the project, a similar ambition might be found in Jacques Rancière's 1981 work *La nuit des prolétaires*, in which Rancière turns to the workers' archives of the 1830s and 1840s, in order to escape any prevalent essentialist and theoretically dogmatic notion of "the worker." See Foucault, "Pour une chronique de la mémoire ouvrière" (*Libération*, no 00, 22 January 1973, 6), in *Dits et écrits I, 1954–1975*, 1268.

[63] Macey, *The Lives of Foucault*, ch. 9.

[64] Foucault, *The Hermeneutics of the Subject*, 209.

internal cut or caesura, as is the case in the Christian self-renunciation, but an ongoing engagement and dis-engagement with external events, in which the self is considered an end, a point of arrival or completion. Compared to what Foucault calls the Christian trans-subjectivation, the care of the self or conversion to the self in Roman and Hellenistic culture is a "long and continuous process," an indefinite practice of auto-subjectivation.[65] This processual nature of the care of the self is important, and is related to the equally important aspect of the self as end. To Foucault, it is one of the major features of the care of the self: unlike Plato's Alcibiades one does not care for oneself in order to achieve something else, such as being able to govern, but one cares, simply, for oneself. The self is not a means to something else, but an end in itself. Following the logic all the way, Foucault notes that the same applies to the care of the self, which is a means that becomes an end, or a merging of means and ends: "There is, if you like, a sort of self-finalization of the relationship to the self."[66] Foucault returns to this further on in the lecture course: "One of the most important phenomena in the history of the practice of the self, and perhaps in the history of ancient culture, is quite probably that of seeing the self – and so the techniques of the self and all the practice of oneself that Plato designated as care of the self – gradually [during the 1st and 2nd centuries CE] emerge as a self-sufficient end."[67] Foucault calls it an "absolutization" (but immediately seems to regret the expression),[68] then a "self-finalization" of the self and a care of the self. While Foucault notes the historical importance of this event, we, in this thesis, shall note the importance of his *description* of the event, because of how it forms an important and recurring figure of thought in his own late work. Indeed, this conceptual figure in which the means and ends of the care of the self merge will reappear in Foucault's discussion of *parrēsia* (truth-telling or frank speech), as well as in his understanding of movements and associations in his own political present. It is a recurring figure of thought, a conceptual isomorphism in which means and ends coincide, and which structures Foucault's late thought: we will see this in the following chapters.

---

[65] This processual nature is evident already when Foucault traces the etymology of the word *epimeleia* in the word *meletai*, exercises, training, practice, and activity. Foucault, *The Hermeneutics of the Subject*, 84.

[66] Foucault, *The Hermeneutics of the Subject*, 83.

[67] Foucault, *The Hermeneutics of the Subject*, 176–77.

[68] Foucault does not explain the expression, nor does he specify whether it is to be understood as a self that is of absolute, ultimate importance, or if he is thinking in some kind of analogy with the Hegelian merging of subject and substance in the Absolute.

These notions of the subject as process and the self-finalization of the self form two central points: both to understand the importance and specificity of the Hellenistic philosophy to Foucault, and to understand Foucault's investigations of ancient subjectivity in relation to his previous work. The 1982 lectures produce an important shift in this regard, whereby the subject is no longer described as an effect of external power-knowledge relations, but as a reflexive process with a certain *degree* of autonomy, in which subjects can exercise and, so to speak, increase their capacity of identifying and choosing between different actions: Foucault develops this understanding of "Subject and Power" in an afterword to an American publication of his work the same year.[69] However, this shift does not break with his previous work, but rather continues and even, to some degree, completes it. To define this work as an ethical turn[70] may not be incorrect per se, but it is inadequate unless it is conceived as a turn *within* his overall project, with ramifications also for its most explicitly political aspects. Foucault's ethics is not a normative ethics – i.e. not the prescription of what actions are morally right or wrong – but rather, through descriptions of historical forms of relations to the self, his ethics is based upon an investigation into voluntary, formalized relations to the self as possible forms of subjectivation.[71] As we shall see, this investigation is developed with some apparent continuities with his previous work: we can single out three ways of understanding the links between subjectivation and subjection, between ethics and politics, between power relations and the government of self and others; in short, between Foucault's early and late work.

First, Foucault makes an important statement halfway into the course, when he recapitulates his findings about a conversion to oneself, entailing a real shift or real movement in the subject. He asks to what extent it is possible to reconstitute such an ancient ethics of the self, noting the ambitious

---

[69] "Power is exercised only over free subjects, and only insofar as they are free. By this we mean individual or collective subjects who are faced with a field of possibilities in which several ways of behaving, several reactions and diverse comportments may be realized. [...] Rather than speaking of an essential freedom , it would be better to speak of an "agonism" – of a relationship which is at the same time reciprocal incitation and struggle; less of a face-to-face confrontation which paralyzes both sides than a permanent provocation ." See Foucault, "Subject and Power," 221–222.

[70] This "ethical turn" is one of the most general characterizations of Foucault's late work, often figuring as the third leg in a (problematic and unstable) periodization of his archaelogical and genealogical phases.

[71] For a discussion of Foucault's anti-normative and normative stand, see Daniel Nica, "The Aesthetics of Existence and the Political in Late Foucault" in Viorel Vizureanu (ed.) Re-thinking the Political in Contemporary Society: Globalization, Consumerism, Economic Efficiency, (Bucarest: Pro Universitaria, 2015), 59.

attempts made during the 16th century (Montaigne), during the 19th century (e.g. Stirner, Schopenhauer, Nietzsche, dandyism, Baudelaire, and anarchist thought), as well as the banal and vacuous, "blocked and ossifed" efforts at rebuilding an ethics of the self in his own present. Despite the shortcomings of contemporary attempts, Foucault insists on the importance of a more ambitious project of this kind:

> [I]f we take the question of power, of political power, situating it in the more general question of governmentality understood as a strategic field of power relations in the broadest and not merely political sense of the term, if we understand by governmentality a strategic field of power relations in their mobility, transformability, and reversibility, then I do not think that reflection on this notion of governmentality can avoid passing through, theoretically and practically, the element of a subject defined by the relationship of self to self.[72]

In this passage, Foucault defines the political meaning of the project for the year's course – perhaps even the larger project running through all his 1980s courses – by directly linking his work on the ancient practices of the self to his previous investigations of governmentality in the important lecture courses of 1978 and 1979, *Security, Territory, Population* and *The Birth of Biopolitics*. And now, in *The Hermeneutics of the Subject*, governmentality is equalled to "power as a set of reversible relationships"[73] with the very turning point located in the subject's turn to itself and its subsequent transformation. Consequently, it is in the chain of notions of governmentality, the government of self and others, and the relationship of self to self that Foucault now can "connect together the question of politics and the question of ethics."[74]

Second, the political stakes and this ethical-political continuity transpire in the kind of examples Foucault extracts to demonstrate that there is no sudden cut or break within the subject; rather, the conversion toward oneself is conceived as a process of breaks with that which surrounds the subject and with that which keeps it "enslaved, dependent, and constrained."[75] Here, Foucault scrutinizes a set of terms and metaphors with interesting connotations, taking up the notions of flight (*pheugein*) and withdrawal (*anakhoresis*) as they appear in Dio Chrysostom and Marcus Aurelius. The notion of withdrawal or *anakhoresis*, for example, is elaborated in two meanings: the retreat of an army

---

[72] Foucault, *The Hermeneutics of the Subject*, 252.
[73] Foucault, *The Hermeneutics of the Subject*, 252.
[74] Foucault, *The Hermeneutics of the Subject*, 252.
[75] Foucault, *The Hermeneutics of the Subject*, 212.

in the face of the enemy, and "the flight of the slave who takes off into the *khora*, the countryside, thus escaping subjection and his status as slave."[76] What is at stake is liberation from slavery and dependence, an emancipation through flight, of which we may find curious analogies in the political-philosophical concepts of today.[77] These are the breaks that Foucault takes up, identifying a similar theme of liberation in Seneca, where philosophy grants one freedom like the ritual gesture of the master, who turns the slave on the spot to effectuate his liberation from subjection. This is a theme in Seneca – philosophy as liberation[78] – that Foucault stresses on many occasions. For example already in the discussion of philosophy as cure: from the pathological, morbid state of *stultitia* (commonly described among Stoics as a state of irresolution, an inability to resist and even recognize the extent to which one is governed by external forces)[79] one must exit, or actually be led out by another, because "necessary for the constitution of the subject by itself"[80] is a certain "education" or leading out by the philosopher or philosophy itself. Similarly, at another point, Foucault seizes on Seneca's definition of freedom in the *Natural Questions* as escaping slavery (*effugere servitutem*), escaping a kind of *servitutem sui*, a slavery to the self that appears when one's relations to the world has taken the form of "obligation-indebtedness."[81]

---

[76] Foucault, *The Hermeneutics of the Subject*, 212.

[77] For an investigation of "fugitive planning" and "maroon communities" of today's racialized capitalism, see Stefano Harney and Fred Moten, *The Undercommons: Fugitive Planning & Black Study* (Wivenhoe/New York/Port Watson: Minor Compositions, 2013), 26.

[78] Foucault's notion of "liberation" should not be understood as a single event liberating an original, natural, free state or subject, but as we shall see below, as a process which has no end. Illuminating in this regard is a remark made by Foucault in a 1984 interview, where he rather talks of practices of freedom: "liberation opens a field of new power relations, which one must control by practices of freedom." See Foucault, "L'éthique du souci de soi comme pratique de la liberté," *Dits et écrits II, 1976–1988*, 1530.

[79] "The *stultus* is open to the external world inasmuch as he allows these representations to get mixed up in his own mind with his passions, desires, ambition, mental habits, illusions, etcetera, so that the *stultus* is someone prey to the winds of external representations and who, once they have entered his mind, cannot make the discrimination cannot separate the content of these representations from what we will call, if you like, the subjective elements, which are combined in him." see Foucault, *The Hermeneutics of the Subject*, 131.

[80] Foucault, *The Hermeneutics of the Subject*, 134.

[81] It is interesting to see the economic-ontological entanglement both in Seneca ("stop making money for yourself" Seneca, *Natural Questions*, trans. Harry M. Hine (Chicago/London: The University of Chicago Press, 2010), 27) and Foucault's "obligation-indebtedness" in relation to the post-foucauldian attempts to understand government in terms of debt: Deleuze's remarks that man in contemporary capitalism, "is no longer man enclosed, but man in debt," in "Postscript on the Societies of Control" *October*, Vol. 59. (Winter, 1992), 3–7, and Maurizio Lazzarato's investigation of governmentality after the financial crisis in *Governing by Debt*, trans. Joshua David Jordan (South Pasadena: Semiotext(e), 2015).

Yet it is not merely what is represented in these examples and metaphors – slavery, debt, subjection – that points toward Foucauldian notions of power relations, politics, and insubordination; the way in which they relate to philosophy is significant also. As retrospective readers of these lectures, we know that Foucault in the next year's course will make a rare parenthesis in the ancient framework and devote considerable attention to Kant's "What is Enlightenment?", a text that he returns to on several occasions and that he first discusses in his 1978 lecture "What is Critique?". Without anticipating too much the discussion of this important lecture/text in chapter 4, we will simply note the resemblance between the exit from *stultitia* and the Kantian credo of enlightenment as an "exit from one's self-imposed tutelage," between Seneca's *servituem sui* and Kant's deploration of man's lack of courage to think for himself.[82] In Foucault's elaboration of these terms – breaks, flight, withdrawal, turn, education, exit – and their role in the Hellenistic and Roman practice of the care of the self, the stakes of liberation and autonomy, in some form, are clear. It thus further demonstrates the conceptual vicinity of the discussion of ancient ways of living and the Foucauldian notion of critique.

Third, and most importantly, the very form in which Foucault articulates the subjectivation of the Hellenistic care of the self in 1982, seems to respond to much of his earlier work on subjects of power-knowledge relations. Because while notions of flight, break, and exit normally signify momentary, transient, or passing events, Foucault emphasizes the extended and pro-cessual nature of these acts of conversion: "It is not a way of introducing or marking an essential caesura in the subject. Conversion is a long and con-tinuous process that I will call a self-subjectivation rather than a trans-subjectivation."[83] This Foucauldian notion of subjectivation as process is important (we will return to it at the end of this chapter, in Agamben's dismissal of Pierre Hadot's caution of over-aestheticism) because of how it relates to Foucault's earlier descriptions of subjection. In *Discipline and Punish*, for example, the disciplinary schemas appear as processes of sub-jection of the individual, by methods "which made possible the meticulous control of the operations of the body, which assured the constant subjection of its forces and imposed upon them a relation of docility-utility."[84] In *The Will to Know* the very idea that power is not a property to be acquired but a

---

[82] Immanuel Kant, "What is Enlightenment?" in *What is Enlightenment?*, ed. James Schmidt, (Berkeley: University of California Press 1996).
[83] Foucault, *The Hermeneutics of the Subject*, 214.
[84] Foucault, *Discipline and Punish*, 137.

relation, equally indicates that this is a constant, ongoing process. So in a formal sense, the notion of subjectivity as process elaborated in the 1982 lectures – a reflexive, auto-constitutive subjectivation – is what makes it a possible counterpoint to the disciplinary subjection of modern power relations, or the turning point in their transformability and reversibility. In other words, it is an elaboration of the schema expressed in *The History of Sexuality* as "[w]here there is power, there is resistance"[85]; it is the odd but irreducible term in the omnipresence of power.

On this note, having already traced Foucault's special attention to metaphors of gaze and visibility in *The Hermeneutics of the Subject*, we must consider the fact that much of his earlier work is articulated in similar terms. Already in 1963, in *The Birth of the Clinic* Foucault conceives of "the medical gaze" in the historical formation of modern medical science, uncovering, as Deleuze points out, an absolute gaze "which dominated all perceptible experiences and did not summon up sight without also summoning the other fields of perception, hearing and touch."[86] And just like the medical gaze is not a pure, liberated seeing of that which really is, but intrinsically bound to a grand transformation of knowledge and the emergence of the sciences of man, *The Order of Things* continues to enquire into how each historical formation can only see or perceive that which is given according to its conditions of visibility. The focus on the visible recedes and almost disappears in *Archaeology of Knowledge* (where the sayable and articulable is privileged in the form of statements and discursive formations), but reappears with force in *Discipline and Punish*, where the disciplines achieve their productive capacity in the individualization and formation of the subject precisely by the "diagram" of the panopticon, that is, by the implementation of an architectural and optical system that becomes a dominant political technology.[87] So Foucault's attention in his 1960s and 70s works to notions of vision and seeing in the scientific development and political technologies since the classical age seems to reappear in his 1980s reading of the ancient technologies of the self. And while Foucault does not connect the two directly, the very "reversibility" of relations of power and the fact that any reflection of governmentality must pass through the care of the self suggest how these fields of vision relate to one another: the conversion of the gaze toward oneself forms both the beginning and the end – the necessary condition and the final objective – of the critical theory and practice that

---

[85] Foucault, *The History of Sexuality, vol 1 An Introduction*, 95.
[86] Gilles Deleuze, *Foucault*, 59.
[87] Foucault, *Discipline and Punish*, 205.

opposes itself to the absolute gaze of scientific knowledge, as well as to the panoptic gaze in its generalized effects.

The Self and the Knowledge of the World: *Mathēsis* and the Study of *Physis*

To fully understand the complexity and the critical nature of the conversion to the self in Hellenistic philosophy, we must recognize a movement of opposite direction inherent in "the conversion of the gaze" toward oneself. What does it mean then, to turn the gaze on yourself? Initially, as a necessary first step or precondition, it means to turn it away from others, away from the insignificant events of the world clouding one's own vision. Citing Plutarch's treatise "On Curiosity," Foucault describes how an unhealthy curiosity about the ills and imperfections of others should be replaced with a concern for one's own flaws. This, however, does not prescribe a solely introspective, enclosed meditation on the self as something to be deciphered, attained, or analyzed. According to Plutarch, one should also be concerned with studying the "secrets of nature," reading the works of historians, and devoting oneself to various exercises. Memory exercises (a practice common throughout Antiquity, since the Pythagoreans at least: "Always remember what you have in your head, what you have learned"),[88] exercises of walking without having your attention diverted by events around you, and exercises of not giving into your curiosity; in short, exercises designed to foster concentration, to focus on the self, and to cultivate an awareness of the objective, something which is equally apparent in Marcus Aurelius, whose sheddings of curiosity strive to promote focus on one's own thoughts and actions.

But what most of all keeps this conversion of the gaze toward oneself and away from others from producing an enclosed relation of the self to the self – and here Foucault draws on the Cynics, Epicureans, and Stoics – is that it contains a gaze in the opposite direction, in the form of a systematic inquiry into nature or *physis*. This means that the Hellenistic and Roman care of the self is not only linked to the "critical function" of unlearning that we saw in Seneca, but also to a process of learning, studying and attaining knowledge in order to be able to correctly care for oneself. While in these lectures Foucault uses the term "critical" exclusively for the negative process of unlearning, we could naturally think of the positive process of learning in the

---

[88] Foucault, *The Hermeneutics of the Subject*, 221.

systematic study of nature as a form of critique, indispensable in the *Thera-peutae's* denouncement of slavery as being "against nature", or in the task that Cremonesi defines as making visible what we already see.

This double direction of the conversion toward oneself and toward the world marks an important point in the lectures, where Foucault gradually shifts his focus from gaze to speech. In the lecture of 10 February, Foucault states that he wants to consider "what is basically a much more important question" than that of conversion itself: a difficult, complex question that he has wanted to pose for some time, and which he says is at the heart of the problem of this year's lectures: "How is the relationship between truth-telling (veridiction) and the practice of the subject established, fixed, and defined?"[89] Following the movement in *The Hermeneutics of the Subject* we can see that the individual will only reach this point of truth-telling (the driving force of subjectivation) by the conversion of the gaze; the subject is only able to constitute itself in its articulation of truth once having turned to the gaze onto the self and then onto the world – a movement neatly captured in Deleuze's observation that the statement or the articulable has primacy over the visible in Foucault's work, but that the visibilities remain irreducible to the state-ment.[90] Foucault specifies this question of veridiction and subject to concern the relation between truth-telling and governing (oneself and others), the very problem Foucault says he has tried to look at with regard to madness and the prison in *The History of Madness* and *Discipline and Punish*, and which he now, leaving the question of sexuality behind, will look at in more archaic and ancient periods, in order to understand the archetypal Western subject's experience of itself. He then takes on the question slightly reformu-lated, as the relation between the knowledge of things and the return to the self, or as he finds the problem formulated already by Socrates in *Phaedrus*: "Should we choose the knowledge of trees rather than the knowledge of men?"[91] And while Socrates chose the knowledge of men, one might say that Foucault demonstrates how, in much of the Hellenistic and Roman philo-sophy, the knowledge of men had to go through the knowledge of trees, or in any case, through a certain knowledge of *physis* or study of nature. From this point, the lectures are held together more firmly by the notion of truth, as they are devoted to the study of nature and the importance of such knowledge or *mathēsis* among the Cynics, Epicureans and the Stoics. What Foucault

---

[89] Foucault, *The Hermeneutics of the Subject*, 229.
[90] Deleuze, *Foucault*, 49.
[91] "The country and the trees teach me nothing, but men in the towns teach me much." Phaedrus, 230d; Foucault, *The Hermeneutics of the Subject*, 230.

demonstrates is how this *mathēsis* is internalized and made part of the subject's actions through an *askēsis*, and finally how this *askēsis* is made up of a set of exercises concerning listening, speaking, and writing, as well as memory, truth-telling, and meditation. In order to understand Foucault's notion of philosophy, we must look briefly at his investigations of *mathēsis* among the Cynics, Epicureans and the Stoics.

Foucault notes that the Cynics' relation to knowledge is more complicated than it first may seem, and that there is no clear disqualification of the knowledge of nature among them. First of all, as Diogenes Laertius recounts, Diogenes of Sinope was a tutor for the children of the man that purchased him as slave, and Diogenes made sure they learned all the sciences. On the other hand, Foucault finds in Seneca's descriptions a very different kind of Cynic adapted to Rome's aristocratic milieu, the well-behaved Demetrius. Demetrius employs the image of the athlete, who in his training does not need to learn every existing movement or action, but only those of use in his game, which must be learned by heart and always available in the contest. Knowledge must pass a similar criterion of utility: while we cannot easily find the reasons for the ebb and flow of water, or the birth of twins, everything that can make us better and happier nature puts in plain sight for us. Demetrius thus professes a relational knowledge easily transformed into prescriptions that change who we are: fear neither men nor God, nor death, remember that it is easy to find the path of virtue, and consider yourself a social being belonging to a community. This distinction between useful and useless knowledge, says Foucault, is common to the other philosophical schools of the era, especially the Pythagoreans and Epicureans, and he uses a term from Plutarch and Denys of Halicarnassus to describe it: it is an *ēthopoēisis* or ethopoetical knowledge, one that makes the character, that builds the habits, or forms the ethos of the subject.[92]

Among the Epicureans, however, there is the important notion of *physiologia*, the study of nature, that completely changes the structure of this ethopoetical knowledge. Foucault takes up a section of the Vatican Sayings: "The study of nature (*physiologia*) does not form men who are fond of boasting and who are verbal performers, or those who make a show of the culture

---

[92] The lecture course editors specify: "In Denys of Halicarnassus, the word *ethopoiia* is found in the sense of a painting of mores: "I see then in Lysias this quality that is so distinguished that it is generally called painting of mores (*hetopoiian*)" "Lysias" in *Les Orateurs antiques*, translation G. Aujac, Paris, Les Belles Lettres, 1978, §8, p. 81. In Plutarch, however, the practical meaning is present: "Moral beauty... does not at all form the mores (*ethopoioun*) of the person who contemplates it for imitation alone." *Pericles* 153b." See Foucault, *The Hermeneutics of the Subject*, n. 15, 245.

which is envied by the masses, but men, rather, who are haughty and independent, and who take pride in what is their own and not what comes from circumstances."[93] Interestingly, *physiologia* here is opposed to *paideia*, normally a word with strong positive connotations: the culture necessary for free men (and envied by the masses). But while *paideia* here, according to Epicurus, can be used "to make a show" by "word artists," *physiologia* is not only a study of the nature of things or of what really is, nor is it a mere correction against the fear of gods (for which Epicurus is so well-known, and which made Marx call him "the true radical Enlightener of Antiquity"); above all, the Epicurean *physiologia* prepares the soul in the struggle against impulses and distractions, making man independent and bold. Foucault regards it as a criterion for setting us free, for transforming the subject, and relates it to the field of politics and law: "*Physiologia* gives the individual boldness and courage, a kind of intrepidity, which enables him to stand firm not only against the many beliefs that others wish to impose on him, but also against life's dangers and the authority of those who want to lay down the law."[94]

Foucault finds a similar distinction between *physiologia* and popular opinion in another Vatican Saying, which in a significant way ties it to the central notion of *parrēsia*: "For my part, speaking freely as one who studies nature, I would rather speak in oracles about the things useful to all men, even if no one should understand me, than gather the praise that comes in abundance from the many by giving my approval to popular opinion."[95] Here, the focus shifts from the effects to the very enunciation of *physiologia*: while it concerns "things useful to all men", emphasis is here placed on "speaking freely" (*parrēsia*) and "speak[ing] in oracles" (*khrēsmodein*). Reminding us that this free speech is the technique employed by the doctor toward the patient or the master toward the disciple, Foucault says of *parrēsia* that "it is the free hand, if you like, which ensures one's ability to select from the field of true knowledge that which is relevant for the subject's transformation, change and improvement."[96] But in this *parrēsia*, Epicurus says he would rather speak in oracles of what is useful – even if no one should understand him – than be praised by reproducing popular opinion. What is understood and praised by all changes nobody, but the

---

[93] Epicurus, "Vatican Sayings," as quoted in Foucault, *The Hermeneutics of the Subject*, 238.
[94] Foucault, *The Hermeneutics of the Subject*, 240.
[95] Foucault, *The Hermeneutics of the Subject*, 241.
[96] Foucault, *The Hermeneutics of the Subject*, 242. "La parrhesia, [...] c'est cette liberté de jeu, si vous voulez, qui fait que dans le champ des connaissances vraies on va pouvoir utiliser celle qui est pertinente pour la transformation, la modification, l'amélioration du sujet." Foucault, *L'Herméneutique du sujet*, 232.

oracular speech as prescriptive address relating to *khrēsis*, use or utility, can lead to a transformation of the subject. In the study of nature which is (potentially) useful to all, Epicurus maintains his right to speak both freely and in a way that might not be accessible to all. Whether it concerns comets, the composition of the world or the movements of atoms, it is a knowledge that will provide the foundation for a life of both "peace of mind and firm confidence," both "perfect serenity" and "renewal." Hence, it is not a Platonic knowledge of the soul as a divine essence, and it is not a Christian knowledge of God that requires a renouncement of the self: on the contrary, it is a knowledge of the world, of things, gods, and men, a knowledge whose function, as Foucault underlines, is to change the subject's being. As such, it seems more closely related toward modern, radical configurations of theoretical work. In relation to this Epicurean *physiologia* there are of course official heirs like Nietzsche, with his insistence in the *Gay Science*, on "fearlessness," the death of God, and the "almost Epicurean bent of knowledge [...] that will not easily let go of the questionable character of things."[97] But there are also larger critical projects stretching out toward the world of things and men: Freud and psychoanalysis as a new science that regards the conditions for "the subject's transformation, change and improvement," as well as Marx and the critique of political economy, a project that doubtlessly aspires to change the subject's being.

The insistence on studying the world and *physis* continues in the Stoics. For the Stoic valorization of the encyclopedic knowledge of the world, Foucault takes as an example Seneca's *Natural Questions*. It is true, Foucault concedes, that Seneca on a number of occasions criticizes the vanity of knowledge (as in *De Tranquillitate* and his characterization of the amassing of books in the library of Alexandria as a way to appease the vanity of the king),[98] that he advises Lucilius against reading too much (better to study a few books in depth)[99], and that he, as we have already seen, is critical of the instrumentalized education given to children.[100] But this does not amount to a disqualification of the knowledge of nature. *Natural Questions*, as Foucault underlines, is an immense exploration of the world, from the heavens to the earth and its rivers and seas, through air and wind to the phenomenon of meteors. Seneca attempts to *mundum circuire*, to encompass the entire world,

---

[97] Friedrich Nietzsche, *The Gay Science*, trans. Josefine Nauckhoff (Cambridge: Cambridge University Press, 2001), 246.

[98] Seneca, *On Tranquility of Mind*, IX.5, as quoted in Foucault, *The Hermeneutics of the Subject*, 260.

[99] Seneca, *On Tranquility of Mind*, IX.5, as quoted in Foucault, *The Hermeneutics of the Subject*, 355.

[100] Seneca, *Letters*, as quoted in Foucault, *The Hermeneutics of the Subject*, 261.

and seek its causes and secrets. But why does the aging Seneca concern himself with this, rather than, simply, with himself? Because, as he explains, only the study of nature can help us escape servitude to ourselves and a certain indebtedness in seeking profits and pleasures; only a detailed knowledge of the organization of the world can help us gain knowledge of ourselves and our place within it. In its first book, *Natural Questions* start and descend from the sky. Earthly phenomena are then explored in the following books, with the final and seventh book ascending once more. Only once we have encompassed the entire world, are we able to look down "from above on the circle of planets (*"terrrarum orbem super ne descipiens"*) [...] to despise the false splendors built by men."[101] Thus the all-encompassing knowledge of the world offers a view from above, in which we are to detect our place. So the turning of the gaze to oneself entails a knowledge of the world, and to Foucault this knowledge has a spiritual modality, it is a "spiritual knowledge," in that it is characterized by its transformative effects on the knowing subject. Foucault takes Marcus Aurelius' *Meditations* as another example of the Stoic form of spiritual knowledge. Instead of seeking the view from above, looking down at the world, Marcus Aurelius directs the gaze toward things as close as possible: "Look at the inside (*eso blepe*). Neither the quality (*poiotēs*) nor the value (*axia*) of anything must escape."[102] So first, in the Greek of Marcus Aurelius, *blepein*, looking closely. Then *"legein par'heautou,"* to say the things for ourselves, which does not simply amount to recalling the name of a thing, but to a kind of verbalization to fix the thing in our mind. This exercise will secure the grandeur of the soul by "testing" the thing, which is to say, determining its own isolated value for man as "citizen of the most eminent city in which other cities are like households,"[103] i.e. man as citizen of the world, but also as member of communities of a lesser order. Marcus Aurelius' exercises often tend to grasp each thing as a composite form or false unity of smaller elements (Foucault does not quote the more peculiar ones, for example when he suggests that one should separate notes of delightful songs in order not to get carried away). In considering each thing part by part and in its totality, one can acquire a sovereign indifference of tranquility and harmony with divine reason. Consequently, as Foucault notes, these exercises tend toward a sort of dissolution of individuality, setting them apart from Seneca's founding of the subject's singularity and stable being of the self.

---

[101] Seneca, *Natural Questions*, preface to book I, as quoted in Foucault, *The Hermeneutics of the Subject*, 277.

[102] Marcus Aurelius, *Meditations*, VL3, trans. mod., see Foucault, *The Hermeneutics of the Subject*, 291.

[103] Foucault, *The Hermeneutics of the Subject*, 291.

Foucault summarizes his long readings of Seneca and Marcus Aurelius in four points, clearly showing that the act of turning the gaze on oneself is not merely a way of attaining knowledge of oneself, of the individual's soul, the human being, or its internal psychic life, but constitutes a modalization of the knowledge of things in the world, defined as a spiritual knowledge. First, this involves the subject changing his position and thus his perspective, rising to the summit of the universe or penetrating into the heart of things; the subject cannot properly know by remaining in his given place. Second, this altered position lets the subject grasp the reality and the "value" of things, and Foucault specifies that "what is meant by 'value' is the place, relations, and specific dimension of things within the world, as well as their relation to, their importance for, and their real power over the human subject insofar as he is free."[104] (Here Foucault's formulation about value as the power of things over the human subject seems to fit Seneca's discussion of the enslavement inherent in "making money for yourself"[105] as much as the modern critique of the commodity.[106]) Third, this spiritual knowledge involves a kind of self-viewing (a "*héauto-scopie*"), in which the subject sees itself in the truth of its being. Fourth, the subject should now be able to achieve freedom, and in this freedom the happiness and perfection of which it is capable; in short, a transfiguration of the subject.

Foucault considers the prospects of writing a history of this spiritual knowledge, from its glory in late Antiquity through the process that comes to limit, cover up, and finally efface it, by the development of another, decidedly more rationalist understanding of the role of knowledge (*connaissance*). Already in the opening lectures, Foucault describes the historical decline of the care of the self in Western philosophy as an omission and obfuscation of its importance throughout the centuries, summed up in what he calls the "Cartesian moment"[107] in the 16th and 17th centuries,

---

[104] Foucault, *The Hermeneutics of the Subject*, 308.

[105] "A free person is one who escapes enslavement to himself, which is constant, unavoidable, oppressing by day and by night equally, without break, without respite. Enslavement to oneself is the most severe enslavement, but it is easy to shake it off if you stop expecting a lot from yourself, if you stop making money for yourself [...]." See Seneca, *Natural Questions*, 27.

[106] For a modern critique of value and how relations of things have power over people, see for example Marx's discussion of how the production of relative surplus-value revolutionizes production and the composition of society, leading to a "real subsumption" of labor to capital." Marx, *Capital vol. 1*, 645.

[107] Foucault argues that Descartes (at the summit of a process initiated already with the early theological tradition, Saint Thomas, and scholasticism) in *Meditations* significantly "requalifies" the *gnōthi seauton* ("know thyself") into the basic self-evidence and form of consciousness which is the first ontological condition and condition for knowledge. Subsequently, he "disqualifies" the *epimeleia heautou* and its inherent spirituality, that is, the subject's search and practice to achieve access to the

when the last efforts of spiritual knowledge among thinkers like Pascal and Spinoza gave way to the dawning systematizations of Descartes and Leibniz. This is a massive and to a certain degree overlooked breach between ancient and modern philosophy – however not a definitive one. If the distinction suggests that "Spinoza is one of the last ancient philosophers and Leibniz one of the first modern philosophers,"[108] the "spiritual" relation between subject and truth would reemerge after Kant. For Foucault, the 19th century philosophy – he mentions Hegel, Schelling, Schopenhauer, Nietzsche, and then also the Husserl of the *Krisis* and Heidegger – links a critique of the conditions of knowledge to a transformation in the subject's being, thus, as he puts it, rediscovering, "without saying so," the ancient care of the self. In a way, Foucault is correcting our understanding of the affinities between ancient philosophy and the modern critical philosophy to which he counts himself, while at the same time reserving some space for a transformative knowledge of the world within the latter.

The Example of Faust

While such an historical investigation of spiritual knowledge would interest Foucault, it is with even greater enthusiasm that he suggests a more limited study of this development, devoted to the literary figure of Faust. According to Foucault, such a study would serve to disentangle the relationship between intellectual and spiritual knowledges in the later period, between the 16th and 18th centuries: from Cristopher Marlowe's *Doctor Faustus*, written in 1592, to Lessing's and Goethe's later renderings of the story. According to the *Faustlegende* and its numerous expressions in literary works, Faust was a scholar who, disillusioned with the empty and instrumental character of the sciences, turned to magic and necromancy, to eventually enter a pact with the devil. Foucault takes Goethe's Faust as the hero of a spiritual knowledge that is disappearing, and quotes the protagonist's opening monologue: "Philosophy, sadly! jurisprudence, medicine, and you also, sad theology!... I have studied you in depth, with passion and

---

truth. This "Cartesian moment" may surely bring to mind another moment when Foucault invoked Descartes as the author of another constitutive cut: when, in *The History of Madness*, Foucault took Descartes' treatment of madness in *Meditations* as symptomatic of a much broader tendency of excluding madness. This first cartesian cut in Foucault's oeuvre has certainly garnered more attention, but it seems that the later one signals an equally important event: not in the constitution of the Western notion of Reason, but of the Western notion of subjectivity. See Foucault, *The Hermeneutics of the Subject*, 14.

[108] Arnold Davidson "Introduction" in Foucault, *The Hermeneutics of the Subject*, xxv.

patience; and now here I am, poor fool, no wiser than before."[109] Here, says Foucault, we see scholarly fields that precisely do not constitute a spiritual knowledge, because they do not in any way transfigure the subject. Hence nothing remains for Faust but to throw himself into the practice of magic, which takes over the tranformative function of spiritual knowledge. Despite the brevity of Foucault's remarks, a couple of things are particularly interesting. First of all, *Faust* is the only modern work of literature – or set of works – discussed by Foucault in the lectures on truth and subjectivity in Antiquity.[110] It is also a recurring reference: already in *The Lectures on the Will to Know* from 1970–1971, Foucault employs Faust and Mephisto-pheles as the figures of knowledge-power, while in these 1982 lectures he regards Faust as "the last nostalgic expression of a knowledge of spirituality which disappeared with the Enlightenment,"[111] and similarly in *The Courage of the Truth* of 1984, as the final expression of the process in which philo-sophical life disappears from the field of philosophy, which from that point develops into solely a teaching profession.[112]

Perhaps the unique status of Faust as a literary object of reflexion in Foucault's work on Antiquity may justify a minimal excursion. Because the story does not only illuminate the opposition between intellectual and spi-ritual knowledge during the previous centuries, between the dead science and the vitality of magic as the legend itself has it, but also, as we shall see, the relation between the care of the self and action, and in the end, the very question of what philosophy is and what it can be. This question was likely urgent to Foucault himself during this period: the formidable explosion of philosophical thought in France during the 1960s and 1970s (with all its connections to the broad political mobilization of the same period) had clearly started to wane, a period of ebb visible also in Foucault's own non-published books and "lengthy silence." Recall the words of Goethe that Nietzsche once borrowed – "In any case, I hate everything that merely instructs me without augmenting or directly invigorating my activity"[113] – and it is no surprise that Foucault turns to the Weimar poet's rendering of

---

[109] Goethe, *Faust*, as quoted in Foucault, *The Hermeneutics of the Subject*, 310.

[110] In *The Courage of the Truth*, Foucault mentions Diderot's *Rameau's Nephew* in relation to cynic-ism, but never discusses it in any detail. Without references to specific works, he also lists the names of Dostoevsky, Baudelaire and Flaubert, Beckett and Burroughs. See Foucault, *The Courage of the Truth*, 185–189.

[111] Foucault, *The Hermeneutics of the Subject*, 310.

[112] Foucault, *The Courage of the Truth*, 211.

[113] Friedrich Nietzsche, "On the Uses and Disadvantages of History for Life" in *Untimely Meditations*, trans. R.J. Hollingdale (Cambridge: Cambridge University Press, 1997), 59.

the story. Because who, or perhaps what, is the Goethian Faust? At the outset, he is the lonely and isolated scholar of particularized knowledges. He is a man without any other to tell him the truth or direct him, a man without community, and above all, a man without a cause. Yet he constantly professes action: "Im Anfang war die Tat!"[114] In that sense, he is what Seneca would call a *stultus*, someone without memory, constantly changing the direction of his life, letting the representations of the external world get mixed up with his own desires, passions, and habits. The *stultus* has no proper will because he does not will himself and because he does not care for himself, leaving all his actions futile and without common direction. Faust may have found in magic what he sought in spiritual knowledge in the first place, but he does not care for himself in a proper way. Curiously, in these lectures principally devoted to the care of the self, Foucault makes no mention of Faust's direct confrontation with the character "Care" toward the end of the second book of Goethe's *Faust*, in which the figure of care is directly opposed to Faustian action. In the shape of four grey women, Want, Debt, Distress, and Care appear at night outside the aging Faust's palace.[115] As the first three figures/phenomena have no place in a rich man's home, only Care can enter, and a highly ambiguous scene follows. Goethe's portentous and menacing Care knows that she is unwanted and feared – "In an ever-changed disguise / All men's lives I tyrannize" – and she is characterized by her destructive, passifying effects: "When a man is in my keeping, / All his world is dead or sleeping."[116] In part, this grimness may be explained by the rich German word *Sorge*, which denotes worry, sorrow, trouble, and anxiety, in addition to the "care" of *epimeleia/cura*. Yet nothing is easily gathered from this suggestive meeting. On the one hand, it is indeed with the arrival of Care, in her unannounced presence, that Faust, reflecting for himself, for the first time seems ready to renounce his supernatural powers; in their confrontation, he also restrains himself in order not to use sorcery against Care. On the other hand, he refuses to be stilled by care and defiantly vows to continue his "race across the world", desiring and achieving new things. He refuses to recognize the power of Care who in turn responds by blinding him. Now without eyesight, Faust

---

[114] "In the beginning was the Deed!" Faust professes action, as here, at the outset of *Faust Part One*, when Faust is writing with Mephistopheles still in the shape of a poodle in his room, but also toward the end of *Faust Part Two*, in the dialogue with Care, and by the dikes and dams before his death. See next footnote.

[115] Johan Wolfgang von Goethe, *Faust Part Two*, Trans. David Luke (Oxford/New York: Oxford UP, 1994/2008), 217.

[116] Goethe, *Faust Part Two*, 219.

still pursues his "last great project" to drain a seaside area. Keen on its completion, he rejoices at the sound of spades, unable to see that no ditches have been dug, but only the grave in which he will soon be buried, dug at the order of Mephistopheles, who returns to collect his debt. Thus, another ambivalent or double scene follows. Undoubtedly, Faust's death can be seen as a consequence of his refusal of care, and of the continued work on his "foolish dams and dikes."[117] Too little care, and too much action it seems. Yet – given the full trajectory or the aggregate logic of Faust's life, given the heroism in which his final undertaking is couched, and given what another Faust-reader identified as the typically ancient virtue of living in the present[118] – it is most likely that his deeds and his relentless action save the Goethian Faust's soul in the end, when the author lets a band of angels rescue him from the devil.

To conclude this parenthesis on Faust: not only does Goethe's *Faust* show us that philosophy itself is dried up and devoid of any transformative power; it also demonstrates that without philosophy, or at least philosophy as a form or care of the self, the protagonist is doomed to flicker without any other direction than toward a final settling of his acquired debt.[119] The fact that Goethe saves Faust's soul in recognition of his heroic deeds, and portrays care as a serious threat of pacification is interesting (perhaps we should have guessed it already by the color: grey like her sisters Want, Debt, and Distress, the Goethian Care impedes action, reminiscent of Mephistopheles' famous lines written twenty years before, in the first part of Faust: "My friend, all theory is grey, and green / The golden tree of life."[120]): it can even be taken analogically with, or as a blueprint for, the idea that Foucault's turn to ancient philosophy is a turn away from politics. An idea which, in its most tendentious form, suggests that his work on the care of the self is simply preparing the ground for the neoliberal consumer subject, deprived of real agency.[121] In any case, this Goethian conflict and contradiction between care and action confirms the shift that Foucault identifies in the philosophy of the

---

[117] Goethe, *Faust Part Two*, 222.

[118] Pierre Hadot, *N'obulie pas de vivre: Goethe et la tradition des exercices spirituels.* (Paris: Albin Michel, 2008), 15–21.

[119] A perhaps even more clear example of this Faustian lack of care of the self is found in Thomas Mann's *Doctor Faustus*, where the protagonist Adrian Leverkühn's complete disregard of caring for himself is made strikingly visible by his friend Serenus Zeitblom's constant worry and careful attention.

[120] Johan Wolfgang von Goethe, *Faust Part One*, trans. David Luke (Oxford/New York: Oxford UP, 1987/1998).

[121] Jean-Loup Amselle, "Michel Foucault and the Spiritualization of Philosophy," in *Foucault and Neoliberalism*, 164–69.

16th and 17th centuries in a striking way: such a conflict is unthinkable in the Hellenistic and Roman philosophy. For the ancients, the very opposite is the case: to be considered of any value at all, an action must be carried out in accordance with a preceding work on the self; and it is the care of the self, rather than the ensuing action, that transfigures the subject. And the Goethian care-action conflict becomes unthinkable, or at least undone, once again. If Faust serves to illustrate how the philosophical life or spiritual knowledge dies in the domain of philosophy proper, it should be kept in mind that Foucault, returning to the issue in the 1984 lectures, sees its resurgence and continuation precisely in the field of political struggle, as the stylization of life within revolutionary movements. Which is to say, when the care of the self and spiritual knowledge is articulated in individual-collective organization, the conflict between care and action, which seemed insuperable to Goethe, is resolved once more. As Foucault puts it: "Exit Faust, enter the revolutionary." But this is to forego the events; for now, it suffices to note that the ancient care of the self implies practice and as such action, which is made clear in the final words of the lecture, directing attention to what lays ahead in the course: "After *mathēsis, askēsis.*"[122]

Askēsis and the Practice of Truth in *Parrēsia*

In addition to the study of nature and the knowledge of the world in the form of *mathēsis*, the care of the self must be carried out in the activities and practices of *ascesis*. In a treatise on the matter, Roman Stoic Musonius Rufus says that the acquisition of virtue requires theoretical knowledge (*epistēmē teoretikē*) and practical knowledge (*epistēmē praktike*), and as such, the distinction between *mathēsis* and *askēsis* goes back to the earliest Pythagorean texts, and can also be found in Plato. But it is the ascetic practices from the first and second centuries that Foucault will study. Here he makes a first important distinction: ascesis is not – as we may think, following the Christian tradition with its associations to renunciation, austerity, abstention, or interdiction – the subject's subjection to a certain law: "In reality *askēsis* is a practice of truth."[123] Parallel to spiritual knowledge it is a practice of truth in which the subject constitutes itself. Rather than a renunciation of any particular element of the self, i.e. a reducing, ascesis is about equipping and providing the subject with what will protect and guide it in the future. This is called *paraskeuē* (or *instructio* in Latin), a kind of preparation of the

---

[122] Foucault, *The Hermeneutics of the Subject*, 311.
[123] Foucault, *The Hermeneutics of the Subject*, 317.

individual for the events of life. *Paraskeuē*, says Foucault, is the structure of permanent transformation of the true discourses into a morally acceptable behavior; the transformation of *logos* into *ethos*. Therefore, in contradistinction to the Christian ascesis of self-renunciation and its objectification of the self in a kind of confessional true discourse, the philosophical ascesis is defined as a "subjectivation of true discourse"[124] in exercises on oneself. Foucault underlines this fundamental difference as a central element of the whole lecture course. Unlike the Christian confession, the Hellenistic and Roman conversion to the self does not take the self as an object of knowledge, but as the subject – or ever unstable outcome – of ascetic practices of truth. This subjectivation of true discourse can be understood in terms of Seneca's notion of *facere suum* (making one's own) of a certain truth or knowledge: appropriating the discourse you recognize as true, taking this philosophical discourse that you listen to or read and write about, and making it your own. So parallel to the processes of unlearning and learning, parallel to breaking with that which enslaves you and acquiring *mathēsis*, *askēsis* is a practice of truth which entails a kind of implementation or application, or better yet, a reflected attempt at merging thought and action, truth and life. To grasp the role of truth in this, we shall look briefly at Foucault's discussion of the techniques of listening, reading, writing, and speaking (while not going into the discussion of mental exercises of abstention, presumption of evils, etc).

In Plutarch's treatise on listening (*Peri tou akouein*, translated as *De audiendo*: On Listening), Foucault finds the idea that listening is both the most passive sense – we can't stop hearing like we can stop seeing by closing our eyes – and the one best fitted to receive *logos* and learn virtue. This technique can be practiced, purified, and enhanced by various means: by silence, whose importance is neatly stressed by the example of the Pythagoreans, who required five years of silence from those who joined their communities; by the physical disposition of the listener who must express his tranquil and pure soul, resting immobile, completely still and attentive according to Philo in his *On contemplative life*; and by directing one's attention to the *pragma*, the philosophical signification and prescription, reserving a moment for recapitulation and meditation once the listening is over in order to receive it properly. This underlines the practical nature of philosophy, as a set of techniques engaging even our bodily disposition.

The issue of reading and writing is treated briefly and summarized by Foucault as: "first, read few books; read few authors; read few works; within

---

[124] Foucault, *The Hermeneutics of the Subject*, 333.

these works, read a few passages; choose passages considered to be important and sufficient."[125] This minimalist approach is best understood in relation to the important processes of memorization and application of knowledge, or rather the interiorization of the written word, of *logos* into *ethos*: what Foucault calls the subjectivation of true discourse. Rather than an exegetical approach of asking oneself what the text means, it is a matter of restating what one finds as true, engraving it in the mind and making it *prokheiron* (ready at hand) as a principle of action. This process forms a part of the important exercises of meditation, *meletē* or *meditatio*, and the related training or application in *gymnazein*. Meditation concerns an engraving in the mind, and the *gymnazein* the testing of the precepts in reality. In a similar fashion, reading cannot be taken alone: Foucault lets Seneca remind us that one must never only read or only write, but alternate between them. On the importance of writing in the practice of the self, Epictetus states that one must meditate (*meletan*), write (*graphein*) and train (*gymnazein*). But the writing exercises he devises are as little concerned with form or style as with the self as the object of the writing: they are called *hypomnēmata*, aids to memory, and relate to the texts referred to as reading notes for the use of study or meditation as care for the self, even though on occasion they may have circulated in correspondence or were used in treatises for others to read. This, says Foucault, is different from the reappearance of the genre of self writing in the 16th century, when, well after the influence of Augustine's confessions, the correspondents are concerned with autobiography and description of oneself, with stating the truth about oneself. During the first and second century, writing as an exercise of ascesis and care of the self is rather concerned with how to become a subject of veridiction, of speaking the truth of philosophical discourse. It is the spoken true discourse that, when compared to reading and writing, is by far the most important ascetic technique. It is here that for the second time, and more substantially, Foucault takes up *parrēsia* (which we have already touched upon in relation to Epicurus): a term central to the two following years of lectures, which conveys the act of truth-telling, of speaking candidly, or frank speech.[126]

In Foucault's discussion of *parrēsia* in 1982, it is practiced in a more limited and interpersonal setting, either between spiritual master and disciple or between friends, as compared to the *parrēsia* in the public and political sphere in the 1983 and 1984 courses. Foucault cites the Roman Epicurean

---

[125] Foucault, *The Hermeneutics of the Subject*, 355.
[126] Foucault, *The Hermeneutics of the Subject*, 366.

Philodemus' treatise *Peri Parrēsias,* and notes that in the Epicurean school it is necessary for every individual to have a *hegemon,* a spiritual guide or director, who would practice *parrēsia.* Observing the right moment or *kairos,* the parresiast must take great care to speak not too early and nor too late, not too harshly if it is directed to a young person in public, but rather "with pleasure and gaiety."[127] Further, Foucault finds that Philodemus encourages the disciples to practice *parrēsia* toward one another, which contradicts the later idea that the Epicurean schools were strictly hierchically organized: here is a *parrēsia* which circulates in a double – both vertical and horizontal – formation. "Along with friendship," Foucault notes about *parrēsia,* "it was one of the conditions, one of the fundamental ethical principles of guidance for the Epicureans."[128] Another example of this kind of truth-telling is found in Galen, who almost two hundred years after Philodemus, in his *On the Passions and Errors of the Soul,* states that in order to avoid self-deception, we need someone to tell us the truth, without flattery or self-interest. This person should be no "technician of the soul," but a man of moral qualities, and above all, a person capable of *parrēsia.*[129]

What is interesting in both these cases – and significant of how Foucault discusses Hellenistic *parrēsia* in relation to subjectivation in these lectures – is that the subjectivation of truth does not occur in the act of speaking, but through listening. Unlike the Christian subject formed in confession, where one speaks the truth of oneself, here it is "the master's discourse [that] must obey the principle of *parrēsia* if, at the end of his action and guidance, he wants the truth of what he says to become the subjectivized true discourse of his disciple."[130] In the Christian confession, the guided subject must produce the discourse of which he himself is the referent or object. In the examples of Hellenistic philosophy, on the other hand, subjectivation appears on the side of the silent, listening disciple while it is the guiding person who speaks, and who must be present in the true discourse. Not as referent (he does not have to speak about himself), but, as Foucault says, "as a coincidence between the subject of enunciation and the subject of his own actions. 'This truth I tell you, you see it in me.'" This is interesting because of how it differs not only from the structure of the confessing subject, but also from the following years of lectures on the philosophical *parrēsia* where subjectivation takes place on the part of the

---

[127] Foucault, *The Government of Self and Others,* 46.
[128] Foucault, *The Hermeneutics of the Subject,* 137.
[129] Foucault, *The Hermeneutics of the Subject,* 398.
[130] Foucault, *The Hermeneutics of the Subject,* 366.

speaking subject. But above all, it is important in how Foucault seizes upon this coincidence between the subject of enunciation and the subject of action: a coincidence which takes place precisely in the articulation of truth. This coincidence mirrors his introductory definition of the care of the self as something that must be an end in itself, where any action must coincide with its objective. Something similar is noted in Seneca's discussion of *licentia*, the latin equivalent of *parrēsia*: "This is the essential point: let us say what we think and think what we say; let speech harmonize with conduct."[131] *Parrēsia* is a free speech, released from set rules and rhetorical procedures, to be shaped according to a given situation. But regardless of the form it takes, it is defined by a commitment and a bond on the part of the speaking person: the truth expressed must be his own. It must harmonize with conduct, it must coincide with action. This is most central to Foucault's understanding, in which *parrēsia* is "both a technique and an ethics, an art and a morality."[132] So to conclude this brief note on Foucault's notion of *ascēsis* as a practice of truth, we can say that truth, or rather truth-telling and *parrēsia*, provides the moment or test in which the subject's long work on itself may manifest itself as a coincidence between speech and action. As such, it is another expression of the important and recurring figure of thought, the figure of merging means and ends, which, as we will continue to see, seems to connect different parts of Foucauldian ethics with a politics of subjectivation.

Historical Stakes and Validity of the Ancient Lessons

In the above, we have seen how, in his 1982 lectures, Foucault investigates the Hellenistic care of the self in the parallel movements of unlearning, learning (*mathēsis*), and exercises related to truth (*ascēsis* and *parrēsia*). We have emphasized the critical stakes or critical potential in Foucault's explicit designation of a critical function in the practice of unlearning, but also more implicitly in the learning or *mathēsis*, in the form of a critique that determines the "value" of things in relation to and power over people, as well as in the kind of examples Foucault raises, such as Philo of Alexandria's *Thereapeutae* or Seneca's metaphors of slavery, flight, and liberation. Following Foucault's supposition of a certain "reversibility" regarding the individual care of the self as a strategic turning point or point of resistance in relations of power and government, we have demonstrated, somewhat similarly, how his expli-

---

[131] Seneca, as quoted in Foucault, *The Hermeneutics of the Subject*, 406.
[132] Foucault, *The Hermeneutics of the Subject*, 368.

cation of the Hellenistic self-care as a continuous process of subjectivation sets it in dialogue with his earlier work on processes of subjection, a relation of potential antagonism, contradiction or opposition. Thus, *The Hermeneutics of the Subject*, which is arguably Foucault's furthest foray into the realm of ancient ethics, makes it clear that the late work still can't be considered as an "ethical turn," if this is understood as a turn away from politics to something like the individual's moral character. On the contrary, this work contains, as Foucault puts it, an assertion that "power relations, governmentality, the government of the self and of others, and the relationship of self to self constitute a chain" in which he attempts to "connect together the question of politics and the question of ethics."[133]

In addition to this, these lectures offer a response to some of the specific criticisms leveled against his work of this period, especially toward the second and third volumes of *The History of Sexuality*. In the following, we will look at how *The Hermeneutics of the Subject* disqualifies a large part of the criticism, while confirming the accuracy of another part. With Jean-François Pradeau, we can frame a part of the problematic between two somewhat similar objections regarding the historical accuracy of Foucault's understanding of ancient doctrines.[134] First the "for the most part Italian" criticism of Foucault's "discutable" use of ancient doctrines in *The History of Sexuality*: "Unwilling to recognize the critical and 'subversive' character of the modes of life proposed by the philosophical schools, Foucault has overestimated the extent of ancient liberty, and unduly separated, in the philosophical doctrines, the ethics of the culture of the self from its theoretical and political correlates."[135] The other objection consists in Pierre Hadot's fear that "by defining his ethical model as an aesthetics of existence, Foucault might have been advancing a cultivation of the self which was too purely aesthetic."[136] Hadot stressed that the turning to oneself always had the ultimate aim of turning to – to belong to – a cosmic whole of nature, humankind, and universal reason. As we shall see, the first part of this critique of the last two volumes of the *History of Sexuality* is in some ways undone and anticipated

---

[133] Foucault, *The Hermeneutics of the Subject*, 252.

[134] Jean-François Pradeau, «Le sujet ancien d'une éthique moderne » in *Foucault: Le courage de la vérité*, ed. Frédéric Gros (Paris : Presses Universitaires de France, 2002).

[135] Jean-François Pradeau, « Le sujet ancien d'une éthique moderne », 141. See also Mario Vegetti, "Foucault et les Anciens" in *Critique* 471–72, no. 42 (August–September 1986), 925–32.

[136] Pierre Hadot, "Reflections on the notion of 'the cultivation of the self'," trans Timothy J. Armstrong, *Foucault Philosoper* (Hemel Hempstead: Harvester Wheatsheaf, 1992), 230 Translation corrected from "ethic of existence" to "aesthetics of existence." See *Michel Foucault philosophe* (Paris: Éditions du Seuil, 1989), 268.

by Foucault himself in *The Hermeneutics of the Subject*; regarding Hadot's longstanding objection, an interesting and rather recent reply has been given by Giorgio Agamben.

To what extent is Foucault's work on ancient subjectivity susceptible to the critique Pradeau cites? In the important issue of *Critique* devoted to Foucault in 1986, Mario Vegetti notes a "tension in Foucault's genealogical style", the result of him privileging the continuity of Antiquity in contrast to the epochal ruptures he identified in Modernity; a move founded on a privileging of the "*énoncé*" at the expense of the modes of enunciation, which brings his late work closer to a traditional kind of history of philosophy or history of ideas.[137] The last two volumes of *The History of Sexuality* is thus said to be marked by a deep fascination for and even "seduction" by Antiquity.[138] Along with an exaggeration of ancient liberty and freedom and a sort of undifferentiated stylization of existence, Foucault, according to Vegetti, fails to account for any relations of power and for the links between ancient mathematics, astronomy, biology, and anthropology to social, political, and religious powers.[139] It is true that *The History of Sexuality, Vol. 3: The Care of the Self* gives a generalizing account of "the culture of the self", describing a slow but rather coherent movement beginning with Socrates, Plato, and Xenophon developing through the Epicureans and Stoics, reaching its peak with the Stoic Epictetus during the imperial period of the first and second centuries of our era. Moreover, the conclusions point unanimously in the direction of a Stoic morality of control over oneself (*dokimazein*) by practicing the ability to separate or distinguish (*diakrinein*) between events which lie within or outside one's own control. But in the lectures of 1982, as we have seen, the account is far more rich and complex; we must also bear in mind that with its important introduction of the notion of *parrēsia*, the main focus of the 1983 and 1984 courses, Foucault leaves the Stoic morality and the themes of self-control in favor of political truth-telling and confrontational true discourse.

As for the "unduly separation" between philosophical doctrines and its theoretical correlates or foundations, it is true that Foucault does not repeat the feat of Marx, who in his doctoral dissertation – after a thorough analysis of the general and specific differences between the atomistic teachings of

---

[137] Mario Vegetti, "Foucault et les anciens," 925.

[138] First "seduced" by Antiquity, then by neoliberalism; interesting how some readers put their criticism in terms of passivity, promiscuity, and lack of self-control when it comes to Foucault. See Daniel Zamora, "Introduction" in *Foucault and Neoliberalism*, 3.

[139] Mario Vegetti, "Foucault et les anciens," 930.

Democritus and Epicurus – reaches the conclusion on the ethical and political level, where Epicurean atomistics is hailed "as the natural science of self-conscioussess."[140] But as we have seen, Foucault gives a rather detailed and differentiated account of his own, regarding the important aspect of *physiologia*, the knowledge of nature (*physis*), in the process of achieving self-sufficiency (*autarkeia*), of being dependent only on oneself. Foucault takes up Epicurus' recommendation of continuous work in *physiologia* in order to achieve serenity, and Seneca's determination in *Natural Questions* to study the natural phenomena and passing through the cycle of the world as a precondition for ethics and the conversion to the self.[141] Diametrically opposed to these we find the Cynic Demetrius and his double list of things useless and useful to know: instead of fruitless speculations about natural phenomena like the origin of earthquakes, the causes of storms, or the reason for the conception of twins, one should devote oneself to rules for conduct and self-control. But Foucault also distinguishes between the first two: whereas the function of Epicurean analysis is "basically to free us from the fears, apprehensions, and myths," the Stoic need to know nature is not about dispelling these fears, but rather about "placing ourselves within a wholly rational and reassuring world, which is the world of a divine Providence; [...] a sequence of specific, necessary, and rational causes and effects that must be accepted if we really want to free ourselves from this sequence in the form, the only possible form, of acknowledgement of its necessity."[142] Here the Stoic pondering on "acceptance" and "acknowledgement of necessity" appear in all clarity, as opposed to the Epicurean attempt to free us from fears; hence, we can see that the criticism offered by Pradeau is anticipated and to a large degree abated.

More to the point is Vegetti's critical characterization of the privileging of the "*énoncé*" at the expense of the modes of enunciation, in other words a lack of attention to the material, historical conditions of enunciation rather than to its varying and different theoretical-philosophical contexts. For instance, the late lectures can hardly be said to conform with the methodology Foucault outlines in his first lectures on Antiquity, the 1970–1971 course, *Lectures on the Will to Know*: "I have tried to get rid of textuality by situating myself in the dimension of history, that is to say locating discursive

[140] Marx, *The Difference Between the Democritean and Epicurean Philosophy of Nature*, Marx-Engels Collected Works Volume 1. Progress Publishers (Online Version: Brian Basgen Internet Archive; marxists.org, 2000).
[141] Foucault, *The Hermeneutics of the Subject*, 266.
[142] Foucault, *The Hermeneutics of the Subject*, 278.

events that take place, not within the text or several texts, but through the fact of the function or role given to different discourses within a society."[143] A good example of this is Foucault's materialist reading of epic poems and tragedies. Foucault takes Hesiod's invocation and use of *dikē*, i.e. the notion of justice, in *Works and Days*, which when compared to Homer's epics takes on a different social and didactic function, offering a kind of agrarian time-keeping while incriminating "the gift-eating kings" from the perspective of small farmers.[144] The will to knowledge in this first lecture course is thus thematized in analogy with the Nietzschean will to power and in direct relation to economic and political struggles. The question regarding the 1982 lectures, then, is how we shall understand the "golden age of the culture of the self" in similar, material terms. To put if differently: if we accept Ellen Meiksins Wood's suggestion that philosophy was the discourse that replaced the epic poem as one of the central conduits of wisdom and values in the Greek world, and her assertion that its systematic analysis and dialectical form "reflected social conditions which [...] were most fully developed in the Athenian democracy,"[145] the question is: how does the importance of the care of the self in the Hellenistic period relate to the decline of democracy, to the imperial regimes, and to its corresponding social divisions? Foucault gives no clear answer in *The Hermeneutics of the Subject* or any of the other lecture courses; his position is even contradictory. In 1983, he considers the shift of *parrēsia* from the political to philosophical sphere as a result of the decline of democracy.[146] But just a year later in *The Care of the Self*, Foucault is hesitant toward the validity of such a simple explanation of a "weakening of the political and social framework" (the fall of democracy) in which those individuals "less firmly attached to the cities, more isolated from one another, and more reliant on themselves, [...] sought in philosophy rules of conduct that were more personal."[147] Similarly, while none of the 1980s courses at the Collège de France display the accentuated historical materialism of his 1970 course *Lectures on the Will to Know* – of grasping discursive events "dispersed between institutions, laws, political victories and defeats, demands, behaviors, revolts, reactions"[148] – Foucault rehearses and restates some of this work in the 1981 lectures *Wrong-Doing, Truth-Telling* in Louvain, suggesting that

---

[143] Foucault, *Lectures on the Will to Know*, 198.

[144] Foucault, *Lectures on the Will to Know*, 92.

[145] Ellen Meiksins Wood; *Peasant-Citizen and Slave: The Foundations of Athenian Democracy*, (London/New York: Verso, 1988), 170–171.

[146] Foucault, *The Government of Self and others*, 342.

[147] Foucault, *The Care of the Self*, 41.

[148] Foucault, *Lectures on the Will to Know*, 194.

he still subscribes to this form of analysis and its conclusions.[149] In any case, Vegetti's critical assessment that the late Foucault privileges philosophical statements over their historical and material conditions, their economic and political contexts, seems to a large degree correct.

The other kind of criticism leveled against Foucault's late work to be discussed here contains the objections raised by Pierre Hadot against Foucault "advancing a cultivation of the self which was too purely aesthetic – that is to say, I fear, a new form of dandyism, a late-twentieth-century version."[150] Hadot notes a lack of acknowledgment on Foucault's part of the important Stoic aspect of belonging to the whole of humanity and cosmic reason, and implies that Foucault's notion of the cultivation of the self remains superficially on the level of appearances, of the dandy's supposedly simple-minded quest for beauty and his unfettered cult of the self; on the level of sensorial and bodily pleasures rather than the morally elevated joys of virtue and reason.[151] First of all, we have already noted that Foucault, in the *Hermeneutics of the Subject*, had considered the Stoic attempt to place oneself "within a wholly rational and reassuring world, which is the world of a divine Providence."[152] Second, that the Foucauldian aesthetics of existence would purport to something like a "personal fulfillment through a stylization of life, as if halting thought" is refuted in an unusually direct manner by lecture course editor Frédéric Gros, who in the "Course Context" states: "These generalizations are facile, excessive, but above all wrong, and in a way the whole of the 1982 course is constructed in opposition to these unfounded criticisms. Foucault is neither Baudelaire nor Bataille. There is neither a dandyism of singularity nor a lyricism of transgression in these final texts. What he will

---

[149] Michel Foucault, *Wrong-Doing, Truth-Telling*, trans. Stephen W. Sawyer (Chicago: The University of Chicago Press, 2014), 49–50.

[150] Pierre Hadot, "Reflections on the notion of 'the cultivation of the self'" in *Foucault Philosopher*, trans. Timothy Armstrong (Hernel Hempstead: Hairvester Wheatsheaf, 1992), 230.

[151] Hadot invokes Seneca to remind us that the Stoics did not simply find joy in the "self" but "in the best part of the self", in the "true good". And the "'best part' of the self is ultimately a transcendental self" which means that the self has to be transcended and in some sense overcome: "Stoic exercise aims in fact at going beyond the self, at thinking and acting in union with universal Reason." (Pierre Hadot, "Reflections on the notion of 'the cultivation of the self,'" 226). Hadot acknowledges that his insistence on the transcendental self and universal reason might not be compatible with the Foucauldian project, but when claiming that Foucault "brackets" these aspects of ancient philosophy, he fails to acknowledge Foucault's explicitly stated knowledge and critique of the imperative function of universal reason in late Stoic thought; "In late Stoicism, when they start saying, 'Well, you are obliged to do that because you are a human being,' something changes. It's not a problem of choice; you have to do it because you are a rational being." *see* Foucault, "On the Genealogy of Ethics", *The Foucault Reader*, 356.

[152] Foucault, *The Hermeneutics of the Subject*, 278.

think of as the Hellenistic and Roman ethic of the care of the self is actually more difficult and also more interesting. It is an ethic of immanence, vigilance, and distance."[153]

How, then, shall we understand such an ethics? Distance is the reflexive condition required for one to contemplate one's own actions and their reciprocal effects on the self – not in order to withdraw from action, but to prepare oneself for it – and vigilance is the careful, attentive gaze reconverted back to the self.[154] Immanence, on the other hand, is what seems to constitute the blind spot of critics like Hadot.[155] For Foucault, immanence refers here to the very position of the self within and *as* this very relation: "The self with which one has the relationship is nothing other than the relationship itself… it is in short the immanence, or better, the ontological adequacy of the self to the relationship."[156] This immanence, this notion of the subject as the very relationship to oneself, is also the decisive point in Giorgio Agamben's careful discussion of Hadot's objections:

> There is only a subject that is never given in advance, and the work to be constructed is the constructing subject itself. This is the paradox of the care of the self that Hadot does not manage to understand when he writes that "it is not a matter of the construction of a self, but on the contrary, of an overcoming of the I." "Self" for Foucault is not a substance nor the object-tifiable result of an operation (the relation with itself): it is the operation itself, the relation itself. That is to say, there is not a subject before the relationship with itself and the use of the self: the subject is that relationship and not one of its terms.[157]

Agamben – who sets out to prove that Hadot's manifold criticism of Foucault's understanding of the ancient sources "each time and point by point […] is a matter of factual inexactitude" when compared to what is stated in the lectures of *The Hermeneutics of the Subject* – thus holds that the divergences between Hadot and Foucault are less a question of what constitutes an aesthetic sphere, and more about their respective conceptions of ethics and subject. What Agamben so clearly brings forth is that for Foucault, there

---

[153] Frédéric Gros, "Course Context", in Foucault, *The Hermeneutics of the Subject*, 530.

[154] Foucault, *The Hermeneutics of the Subject*, 222–223.

[155] It may be noted that, Hadot, in the text quoted above, did not have access to the material we have today; neither the lectures nor the notes. The text by Hadot quoted below, however, is published in 2002, a year after the publication of *The Hermeneutics of the Subject*.

[156] Foucault, From the dossier "Culture of the self" as quoted in Foucault, *The Hermeneutics of the Subject*, 533.

[157] Agamben, *The Use of Bodies*, trans. Adam Kotsko (Stanford: Stanford University Press, 2015), 101.

is no preexisting, foundational subject: "The practice of the self is that operation in which the subject adequates itself to its own constitutive relation and remains immanent to it."[158] Indeed, following Agamben's suggestion, not only is there no foundational subject in Foucault, there is not even a subject, but only a process of subjectivation.

Hadot's critique that there is something lacking in the Foucauldian notion of "style of existence," and that it was "expedient to parenthesize" the unfashionable notions of universal reason and universal nature, seems to imply that there is something all too simple, simplified, and easily achieved in Foucault's aesthetics of existence. An oft-quoted source in this critique is an interview in which Foucault discusses the aesthetics of existence:

> What strikes me is the fact that in our society, art has become something which is related only to objects and not to individuals, or to life. That art is something which is specialized or which is done by experts who are artists. But couldn't everyone's life become a work of art? Why should the lamp or the house be an art object, but not our life?[159]

It is perhaps not strange, if this statement has added to some readers' sense of banality, superficiality, or simplicity regarding the aesthetics of existence and the notion of life as a work of art. To begin with, one is struck by the informal, abrupt, and seemingly unspecified manner by which Foucault, in this conversation held in English with Dreyfus and Rabinow in 1983, casts out the apparent paradox or incongruity: "But couldn't everyone's life become a work of art?". Referring to the same interview and statement as above, Hadot states that while he also holds that "philosophy is an art of living, a style of life that touches on all of existence" he would "however, hesitate to speak, as Foucault does, of an 'aesthetics of existence,' both in connection with Antiquity and, in general, as the task of the philosopher. Michel Foucault understands [...] this expression in the sense that our own life is the work of art that we must make."[160] Hadot understands the work of art and the notion of aesthetics as belonging to a modern, autonomous domain of beauty independent of good and evil, whereas the Greek notion of beauty, if applied to a person, could only denote a moral value. Thus, he firmly places the work of art in the context of fine art, which, somewhat curiously, so many other interpreters have too. But some further inspection

---

[158] Agamben, *The Use of Bodies*, 104.
[159] Foucault, "On the Genealogy of Ethics", *The Foucault Reader*, 350.
[160] Pierre Hadot, «Un dialogue interrompu avec M. Foucault» in *Exercises spirituels et philosophie antique* (Paris: Albin Michel, 2002), 231–32.

is needed to see that Foucault is not at all talking about art in the modern sense of the word, of fine art; his examples are a lamp and a house. These objects are clearly not artworks in that sense of the word, and thus "art" must be understood in the more general sense as *technē* or craft: as the art of living, the art of government, or more generally, art in the sense of making, doing, of craftmanship. This means that the notion of life as work of art does not refer to the "purely aesthetic" realm of beauty, but to the subject as an ongoing, processual work or practice, which seems to confirm Agamben's remarks.

In Agamben's view, it is Hadot's presupposition of a transcendent subject that prevents him from understanding the Foucauldian problematic of immanence, which lies at the heart of his notions of the subject and the technologies of the self. Agamben writes: "Hadot does not succeed in detaching himself from a conception of the subject as transcendent with respect to its life and actions, and for this reason, he conceives the Foucauldian paradigm of life as work of art according to the common representation of a subject-author who shapes his work as an object external to him."[161] But such subject-author, Agamben adds, is precisely what Foucault had questioned already in his 1969 text "What is an author?". Here, the written work constitutes the possibility and place in which the writing subject can disappear: "In short, it is a matter of depriving the subject (or its substitute) of its role as originator, and of analyzing the subject as a variable and complex function of discourse."[162] Hence, the care of the self as an aesthetics of existence is not something easily achieved in Foucault's development of these terms. Rather it is a process of subjectivation that, through the labor of *mathēsis* and *askēsis* and by taking on the world as a "test,"[163] entails a form of "becoming other" in which the outcome can never be anticipated or taken for granted. Perhaps it is somewhat like a mirror image of the definition of discourse Foucault provides us with in *The Archaeology of Knowledge*: "not the majestically unfolding manifestation of a thinking, knowing, speaking subject, but, on the contrary, a totality, in which the dispersion of the subject and his discontinuity with himself may be determined."[164]

To conclude, in more general terms, our attempt at defining the subject in *The Hermeneutics of the Subject* – a subject as self-relation, as process, as

---

[161] Agamben, *The Use of Bodies*, 104.

[162] Foucault, "What is an Author" in *Language, Counter-Memory, Practice*, trans. Donald F. Bouchard (Ithaca, NY: Cornell University Press, 1977) , 138.

[163] Foucault, *The Hermeneutics of the Subject*, 486.

[164] Foucault, *The Archaeology of Knowledge*, 55.

subjectivation of truth, and as indefinite reflected practice – it should be acknowledged that Foucault's problematization of subjectivity forms a part of a larger tendency in French philosophy during this period. A good example of this is when Jean-Luc Nancy, a few years later, invited a large cohort of the philosophers who had emerged during the 1960s and 70s to consider the question "Who Comes after the Subject?". Taking this shared reflection on subjectivity as emanating from the teachings of Marx, Nietzsche, Freud, Husserl, Heidegger, Bataille, and Wittgenstein, and from the historical postwar conditions, Nancy describes it as a "critique or deconstruction of interiority, of self presence, of consciousness, of mastery, of the individual or collective property of an essence [...], of the firmness of a seat (*hypo-keimenon, substantia, subjectum*) and the certitude of an authority and a value (the individual, a people, the state, history, work)."[165] These common traits apply to much of Foucault's work; further, we could say that it is shaped along the lines of an empiricist critique of transcendental philosophy. While it is not systematically elaborated as such by Foucault – that is, while not devised with concepts like, let us say, Humean perceptions and principles – it can be understood as an attempt to identify or grasp a subjective agency in the double movement of an experience of the world and an experience of the self. Having invoked contrary models of subjectivity as different as those of Platonic *anamnēsis* or the Cartesian *cogito* as a subject preceding practice and knowledge, Foucault states that in the course, he wanted to demonstrate that for Hellenistic philosophy, "reality was thought of as the site of the experience of the self and as the opportunity for the test of the self," which means that subjectivation is what appears simultaneously in practice, or in the practice of self, whether this is practice in truthful discourse, in writing, in actions, or in meditation.[166] Perhaps this is why we can hear echoes of what Deleuze states in *Empiricism and Subjectivity*, where "[t]he subject is defined by the movement through which it is constituted," and where it is said that "subjectivity is essentially *practical*."[167] That Foucault himself in *The Hermeneutics of the Subject* – despite of, or perhaps in line with its very title – does not provide a strict theory of the subject, is likely because the notion of the subject is both the principal and ultimate question of his full oeuvre,

---

[165] *Who Comes After the Subject?* Eds. Eduardo Cadava, Peter Connor, Jean-Luc Nancy (New York and London: Routledge, 1991), 4.

[166] Foucault, *The Hermeneutics of the Subject*, 486. For the distinction between different practices, see 425–426.

[167] Deleuze, *Empiricism and Subjectivity*, trans. Constantin V. Boundas (New York: Columbia University Press, 1989) 85, 104.

irreducible to a single definition.[168] Or as Deleuze puts it: "The fact that there is no theoretical subjectivity, and that there cannot be one, becomes the fundamental claim of empiricism."[169] On the other hand, if we take the term in a somewhat different meaning, it can be objected that Foucault's work on subjectivation is not empirical enough: we have seen that Foucault never realizes his proposed investigations of the "revolutionary subjectivity" in its actual, historical collective movements, and we have noted the criticism of Vegetti that Foucault in his late work gives too much interpretational weight to the *enoncé* over the *énonciation*, to the philosophical statement over its social, political, material context. But here it must be noted what is at stake in Foucault's last lecture courses at the Collège de France. It is not the history of sexuality that is being rewritten, nor the history of madness, it is the history of philosophy. This is what is made clear when Foucault discusses the example of Faust, which also, at the same time, makes clear that the question of philosophy is not a strictly theoretical, historiographical endeavor, but a rewriting geared toward practice, action, spiritual knowledge, or indeed, philosophy as way of life.

A final remark regarding this history of philosophy, which is largely invoked implicitly, and of which Foucault remains taciturn in terms of names and events. A rare point of context is provided when Foucault credits Pierre Hadot with "an absolutely fundamental and important analysis" of the spiritual nature of Hellenistic philosophy, indispensable for his own attempt to "recover" the Hellenistic and Roman care of the self as a model of subjectivity historically concealed by Platonism and Christianity.[170] But no references are given when, in the first lecture, he cautions against the common understanding of the care of the self as a "sad expression" of the individual's withdrawal from collective morality; there is only an editorial footnote, providing an impressive detective work through a predominantly French historical tradition, tracing this "prejudice" back to a work by classical scholar Gilbert Murray from 1912.[171] Hiding in the open, however, there may also be

---

[168] "What I have refused is precisely to take a theory of the subject as given on beforehand – like it could be done for example in phenomenology or existentialism – and, based on that theory of the subject, to ask the question of whether we can know, for example, how this or that form of knowledge is possible. [...] I very much had to refuse any *a priori* theory of the subject to be able to make this analysis of the possible relations between the constitution of the subject or different forms of subject and the games of truth, the practices of power, etc." See Foucault, "L'éthique du souci de soi comme pratique de la liberté," 1527.

[169] Deleuze, *Empiricism and Subjectivity*, 104.

[170] Foucault, *The Hermeneutics of the Subject*, 216.

[171] Foucault, *The Hermeneutics of the Subject*, 13, 23 n 47.

the most well-known and general expression of this position: Hegel's dismissal of Hellenistic thought in his *Lectures on the History of Philosophy*. Hegel makes a common periodization of the first classical works between Thales and Aristotle, then Hellenism or "Greek philosophy in the Roman world", and finally Neoplatonism and its entanglement with Christian thought. But according to his own schema of the Spirit's dialectical movement through history, Hegel assigns the Greek philosophy in the Roman world with a purely negative, antithetical position. Compared to the corresponding movement in *Phenomenology of Spirit*,[172] it is more distinctly stated in the lectures on the history of philosophy: after the classical period's universalization of thought as science, the dogmatism of the Stoics, Epicureans and Sceptics can only offer the particular as opposed to the universal, only abstract indifference and unperturbability of Spirit as opposed to the concrete ethics and science of Plato and Aristotle, all set in a general unhappiness of the Roman world where "everything noble and beautiful in spiritual individuality" has been destroyed. For Hegel, "[t]his is the age of complete despotism, of the decline of all public or community life; there is a withdrawal into private life and private interests."[173] Thus, the turn to the self is characterized as a negatively motivated move: having lost their faith in polytheism, pantheism, and the natural elements, as well as from partaking in the state or political life, Hegel sees individuals escaping their own abstraction of thought, seeking comfort in the "abstraction of self" as an indifferent and unperturbed subject, and in "this inner freedom of the subject as such."[174]

Foucault does not relate in any explicit way to this Hegelian understanding of Hellenistic philosophy, but given its general influence and his other remarks on Hegel's role in the legacy of ancient philosophy,[175] it deserves mention. It also has the merit of already having been countered, on what we can call empiricist grounds, in ways not so unlike Foucault's: while Hegel sees the Hellenistic philosophy and its notions of a self-sufficient subjectivity as an expression of abstraction and loss of faith, as being cut off from the truth

---

[172] G. W. F. Hegel, *Phenomenology of Spirit*, trans. A. V. Miller (Oxford: Oxford University Press, 1977) 119–138.

[173] G. W. F. Hegel, *Lectures on the History of Philosophy 1825–6 Volume II: Greek Philosophy*, trans. R. F. Brown and J. M. Stewart (Oxford/New York: Oxford University Press, 2006), 317.

[174] G. W. F. Hegel, *Lectures on the History of Philosophy*, 265.

[175] For example, Foucault refers to a common (mis)understanding regarding individual freedom in ancient Greece as completely subsumed under the city state to Hegel. See Foucault, «L'éthique du souci de soi comme pratique de la liberté» 1527. And in his final lecture in 1982, Foucault defines the *Phenomenology of Spirit* as the summit of a Western philosophical tradition trying to resolve the relation between the world as object for knowledge and the site in which the knowing subject appears. See Foucault, *The Hermeneutics of the Subject*, 487.

in a kind of impotent despair and disbelief, it has also been singled out as one of the first attempts in philosophy for men to understand themselves in their "real life-process", "in their actual, empirically perceptible process of development under definite conditions,"[176] as Marx formulates it in *The German Ideology*. In Foucault's words, "the practice of the self does not function on the axis opposing this world here to the other world," but rather as the condition for the subject's liberation within this world.[177] In that sense, the historical stakes of the old Foucault in the Hellenistic and Roman philosophy are not so different from the young Marx: "Only now the time has come in which the systems of the Epicureans, Stoics and Sceptics can be understood. They are the philosophers of self-consciousness."[178]

---

[176] Karl Marx and nd Friedrich Engels, *The German Ideology*, trans. C.J. Arthur (Prometheus Books, 1998), 43.

[177] Foucault, *The Hermeneutics of the Subject*, 210.

[178] Karl Marx, *The Difference Between the Democritean and Epicurean Philosophy of Nature*, Marx-Engels Collected Works Volume 1. Progress Publishers (Online Version: Brian Basgen Internet Archive; marxists.org, 2000).

CHAPTER 3

Parrēsia: Truth-Telling in the Political Domain

What Is Truth?

To ask the question of truth in relation to Foucault's late work will not point us toward discussions of truth versus falsehood, or what conditions make a statement true. Foucault does not define truth according to any common standard: he does not take it as a propositional correspondence to facts, neither does he consider it as a fundamental ontological condition like the Heideggerian original truth of unconcealment, nor does he reengage his own previous work on how statements will only be considered true if a number of historically contingent discursive conditions are fulfilled. Truth plays an important role in Foucault's late work, not with respect to what truth is, but in what it does: its importance lies in its effects on the subject. We could say that truth here is not grasped in how it can be verified, but in how it verifies the subject. It has therefore a constitutive function. So the question of truth will not dwell on its content, but will concern the act of speaking the truth, or, as Foucault also calls it, the *dire-vrai*, the truth-telling, veridiction, and *parrēsia*, the ancient Greek notion of speaking frankly. How is the act of binding oneself to truth, and to speak the truth, the highest exercise of freedom? That – especially if this act is carried out within the political domain – can be taken as the central question of Foucault's last two lecture courses at the Collège de France, *The Government of Self and Others* from 1983 *The Courage of the Truth: The Government of Self and Others II* from 1984. In this chapter, we shall see how truth is the event in which philosophy confronts politics, and at the same time realizes itself as a kind of action.

Let us recall that Foucault started investigating the act of speaking the truth in its constitutive effects on the speaking subject in the first volume of *The History of Sexuality*, with regard to the practice of Christian confession, as a form of subjection in which the subject is obliged to state the truth about him- or herself, a truth that is largely given or codified beforehand. Through the 1980 and 1981 lectures, Foucault is still mostly concerned with the *obligation* of speaking the truth, before he shifts his perspective to consider the possibility of speaking the truth, i.e. a voluntary stating of the truth, a truth by which the subject constitutes itself with a higher degree of independence. This subjectivation of truth is developed in *The Hermeneutics of the Subject*, and, as we saw in the previous chapter, concerns the individual subject, in a kind of general context of the care of the self. In Foucault's last two lecture courses at the Collège de France, truth is not investigated as a test or decisive moment for the individual subject in the care of the self, or in the practice of philosophy as a way of life, but rather as a test for philosophy proper, embodied by the philosopher, and practiced in the political sphere of democratic or autocratic government. Here *parrēsia* signifies a kind of free-spokenness, a courageous stating of the truth, a frank speech vis-à-vis political power that Foucault traces along its course during antiquity, and that, despite its different and varying manifestations, at one point he even defines as a central task for modern philosophy.[1]

From these last two years of lectures, we shall single out three clearly discernable models, three different forms of truth-telling that appear in the political sphere: the so-called political *parrēsia* practiced at the Assembly of Athenian democracy; the philosophical *parrēsia* exemplified by Plato as political advisor to the Syracusean ruler Dionysius; the truth-telling of the Cynics, where truth takes the form of life itself, the naked life as it is manifested in the streets and on the square by the Cynic philosopher. But first, we shall look at the strange parenthesis constituted by the opening lecture on Kant's "What is Enlightenment?" and the significance of Foucault's anachronistic insertion of this text in his lectures on antiquity. While Foucault's introductory remarks on Kant seem to confirm many of the arguments about *The Hermeneutics of the Subject* made above in chapter two (e.g. the importance of the notion of governmentality in relation to the work on ancient technologies of the self, the importance of the notion of critique both in relation to the individual practices of *mathēsis-askēsis* and the function of *parrēsia*, the relatedness of the notions of unlearning and emancipation to the Kantian "sapere aude!"), the following lectures on *parrēsia*, as will be argued, articulate two new and additional propositions, the first explicit and the second implicit. First, the aforementioned assertion that *parrēsia* can be understood as a specific way of speaking the truth (despite its shifting and at times opposing meanings and values), which has reemerged as the task for

---

[1] Michel Foucault, *The Government of Self and Others: Lectures at the Collège de France 1982–1983*, trans. Graham Burchell (Houndmills: Palgrave Macmillan, 2010), 348–49.

philosophy to reinvigorate and restitute: a truth-telling concerning govern-ment, a truth-telling for philosophy to make into its own purpose.

Second, as an implication of the first, Foucault's remarks on different ancient practices of truth – the political *parrēsia* practiced at the Athenian Assembly, the philosophical *parrēsia* of the political advisor, and the Cynic form of *parrēsia* as life – must be considered as models for the philosophical practice of *parrēsia* today. To the extent that such a consideration has been undertaken, both scholarly and activist readings have singled out the Cynics and their heroic philosophical life in perpetual revolt as the philosophical and political position of greatest interest to our present, and as the one with which Foucault himself identifies.[2] There may be many reasons for this – that Foucault devotes so many lectures to the analysis of the Cynics, that a certain fascination and enthusiasm comes through his normally non-evaluative, descriptive accounts of the ancient philosophical traditions, and above all, perhaps, that the Cynics form an endpoint in Foucault's work on antiquity; both in the sense that he announced in the beginning of the course that he would go through this material "in order to return, after this several years long Greco-Latin 'trip,' to some contemporary problems", but even more so because it came to be the very last thing he lectured on before his death, thus forming his last words. As will be demonstrated in the following, however, this endpoint should not be taken as a conclusion, summit, or completion of the ancient trip, nor as the moment of finally recovering the missing piece in the thoroughly sought-through territories of ancient thought in its relation to truth, government, and the care of the self. On the contrary, it will first be argued that the position that Foucault investigates most intensely from the perspective of his own political present, the one that he might be the most invested in, is not the heroic and sovereign Cynic, but the unglamorous position of the political advisor, more specifically Plato's mission to Syracuse. Here, we will consider Marcelo Hoffman's argument about a close link between the content of these lectures and the political situation in France at the time they were given.[3] Second, regardless of the rebellious character of the Cynic life, and the enthusiasm it provoked in many of Foucault's readers – and possibly Foucault himself – it will be demonstrated that a number of implications that stem from a Cynic project enters into a contradictory or conflictual relationship with some of the most fundamental principles of Foucault's late work: both the insistence on becoming other and the

---

[2] See for example Michael Hardt, "Militant Life", *New Left Review* 64 (2010), 160.

[3] Marcelo Hoffman, *Foucault and Power* (London/New York: Bloomsbury, 2015).

insistence on the impossibility of being led toward autonomy in the Kantian "*Sapere Aude!*", which we take as an expression of the recurring conceptual figure related to subjectivation, the figure in which the means must coincide with the ends.

Does this, then, mean that the only coherent philosophical and political position that we can extract from Foucault's late work on *parrēsia* is that of the political advisor – the one who whispers in the ear of the Prince, the one who sits on the side of power and government? Does it mean that any oppositional action is lost with such a disavowal of the Cynics' rebellious life? Certainly not. Continuing to trace the implicit and explicit critical potentialities of this material along with Foucault's references to his own political present, we shall be able to identify three possible critical positions in the following chapters. But in order to do so, we must start by looking at Foucault's insertion of Kant's "What is Enlightenment?" in the first lecture of the 1983 course *The Government of Self and Others*.

Kant and "What is Enlightenment?"

Opening his 1983 course, Foucault warns that "this year's lectures will be a bit disjointed and scattered." The caution seems justified already by the fact that he traces the notion of *parrēsia* from tragedy in Euripides, through rhetorics and historiography in Isocrates, Thucydides, and Plutarch, to philosophy in Plato and Socrates.[4] But perhaps this disjointedness is most clear with regard to the opening lecture on Kant's "What is Enlightenment?" and its sudden engagement with modern thought. It is true that Foucault in the final lecture explains his inclusion of Kant's short and late text by the fact that it is emblematic of the moment when philosophy, through the critique of Enlightenment, became aware of the same problems as those that were connected to *parrēsia* in antiquity.[5] But up to that point, the text that Foucault introduced as "something of a blazon, a fetish for me" has remained in suspense, distinctly separated from the main material of the course by two millennia, and from its delivery in the auditorium of the Collège de France

---

[4] The course unfolds with a first lecture on Kant, a second on the political function of *parrēsia* and its necessary relation to courage and risk; then follows the long section (three lectures) on the *parrēsia* in Euripides' play *Ion*, and then a brief but important interlude devoted to the political *parrēsia* in Thucydides, Isocrates, and Plutarch, before another long section (also three lectures) on Plato's journey to Sicily and his role as advisor to Dionysius of Syracuse, and finally a couple of lectures both set to conclude the previous lectures and to recount the Socratic *parrēsia* in *The Apology*, *Phaedrus*, and *Gorgias*.

[5] Michel Foucault, *The Government of Self and Others: Lectures at the Collège de France 1982–1983*, trans. Graham Burchell (Houndmills: Palgrave Macmillan, 2010), 350.

by two centuries. The clean cut between the Kantian lesson and the subsequent lectures on ancient practices of *parrēsia* produces a strange effect. To some degree it remains that way, since Foucault's brief retrospective justification does not fully explicate the ripples sent through the ancient notion of the government of the self. Yet a closer look on the discussion of *Aufklärung* (Foucault consistently uses the German word, suggesting that he is principally discussing its Kantian definition) suggests a number of ways to understand its function in the greater framework. In the following we will try to unravel four aspects: the insistence on autonomy; the relation to critique; the merging of subject and subject matter in the figures of the public and the *Zeitschrift*, and finally the ontology of the present. These will determine our reading of the subsequent lectures on ancient truth-telling in the political domain. Let us start with the question itself.

What is Enlightenment? "Enlightenment," says Kant in this text from 1784, "is mankind's exit from its self-incurred tutelage.[6] Tutelage is the inability to make use of one's own understanding without the guidance of another. Self-incurred is this inability if its cause lies not in the lack of understanding but rather in the lack of the resolution and the courage to use it without the guidance of another. *Sapere aude!* [Dare to know] Have the courage to use your own understanding! is thus the motto of enlightenment."[7] Foucault, in his reading, immediately seizes upon this unspecified "exit",[8] and the fact that despite characterizing (to some extent) a historical period, Kant does not define Enlightenment in any positive way or by any kind of belonging, immanence, or accomplishment, but simply as "'*Aus-*

---

[6] Translation modified: "tutelage" substituted for "immaturity" in continuity with Foucault's terminology in the English translation. The German word is *Unmündigkeit*, and lacks a clear equivalent in English, denoting both legal minority in terms of age and legal, civil "immaturity," thus including both children and women, who as *unmündigen* must be represented by a "guardian" or "*Vormund*" in legal matters. The American translator James Schmidt notes that "Kant's use of these terms echoes that of Ernst Ferdinand Klein, who in an article on freedom of the press published a few months earlier in the *Berlinische Monatsschrift* had called on those kings and princes who had taken on the role of *Vormündern* over their *unmündigen Kinder* to follow the example of Frederick the Great and grant them freedom of expression." See Immanuel Kant, "An Answer to the Question: What is Enlightenment?" trans. James Schmidt, in *What is Enlightenment?*, ed. James Schmidt (Berkeley: University of California Press, 1996), 63, n 1.

[7] Kant, "An Answer to the Question: What is Enlightenment?", 58.

[8] While Foucault uses Piobetta's French translation, and while the English translator of Foucault translates Foucault's French translation, he consults a number of English translations to account for the nuances in *Ausgang*/exit/way out and *Unmündigkeit*/immaturity/tutelage/minority. In the following we shall use Schmidt's English translation as cited above. See Foucault, *The Government of Self and Others*, 40 n. 1. For a further discussion on English translations of Kant's "Was ist Aufklärung?" see James Schmidt's blog, "The Words We Have Lost: Translating Kant on Enlightenment," May 28, 2013, https://persistentenlightenment.com/2013/05/28/translatingkant1/.

gang,' as a way out, exit, a movement by which one extricates oneself from something, without saying anything about what one is moving towards."[9] Is this unspecified call for movement "without saying anything about what one is moving towards" an expression of the Kantian critical virtue of not trespassing beyond the boundaries of possible knowledge, of refraining from speaking of that which we cannot know? Or is it the necessary, self-assigned license of any liberatory project of not having to formulate the precise workings of the liberated state of things? Perhaps both. As we shall see, it is not the unspecified answer to the question of Enlightenment – which seems to rhyme with Foucault's own unconditional devotion to the transformation of the self toward something unknown, and the necessity of "becoming other" – that Foucault objects to. Rather, it is its specifications.

Further, asks Foucault, is this an active or passive process? And does Man's exit, "*der Ausgang des Menschen,*" refer to humanity, or only to certain societies, or yet only to certain individuals? (Recall what was mentioned in the previous chapter, when Foucault discussed the typical Greek division between the few and the many, apparent in the philosophical communities seeking salvation only for their own members). Foucault also notes Kant's double modus in the definition of Enlightenment, shifting between the descriptive and the prescriptive: from "man's exit from his self-imposed tutelage" to the imploration of "*Sapere aude!*" Having raised these general and very open questions about the exit and about man, Foucault turns to the notion of *Unmündigkeit* or tutelage. Tutelage is not a state of natural powerlessness, because men are perfectly capable of deciding upon their own actions, and neither is it a state of oppression, of violence, in which somebody else has seized power over them and appropriated their ability to act. Tutelage occurs after one has given up responsibility for one's own conduct, and to Kant, the reasons that many remain minors all their lives are laziness and cowardice, as is made clear in his examples: "If I have a book that has understanding for me, a spiritual who has a conscience for me, a doctor who judges my diet for me, and so forth, surely I do not need to trouble myself. I have no need to think, if only I can pay; others will take over the tedious business for me."[10] A book to replace the understanding or *Verstand,* a spiritual director to replace the moral conscience or *Gewissen,* a doctor to replace his own knowing and decision – to Foucault the matter is clear: "I do not think it is

---

[9] Michel Foucault, *The Government of Self and Others: Lectures at the Collège de France 1982–1983,* trans. Graham Burchell (Houndmills: Palgrave Macmillan, 2010), 27.
[10] Translation modified, Foucault's "spiritual director" substituted for "pastor." See Kant, "An Answer to the Question: What is Enlightenment?", 58.

too much of an over-interpretation of this text to say that in these three apparently extraordinarily flat and familiar examples (the book, the spiritual director, the doctor) we rediscover, of course, the three Critiques."[11]

Autonomy and the Problem of *Leitung* or Being Led

When Foucault brings up Kant's critical enterprise in relation to the process of Enlightenment, he raises the issue of autonomy. The process of exiting from tutelage is defined as the relation between the use of reason (as prescribed with the notions of critique and enlightenment) and the extent to which we are under the direction (*Leitung*) of others: "Consequently, what *Aufklärung* has to do, and is in the process of doing, is precisely to redistribute the relationships between government of self and government of others."[12] But how is this done? How is this exit from tutelage made, how is the autonomous use of reason of the critical enterprise applied after having been neglected, unknown and unpracticed, or, ultimately, how does one suddenly dare to think when one has been lazy and cowardly all one's life? This is the problem, and this is also where Foucault identifies – and perhaps magnifies – certain contradictions in the text.

According to Foucault, in what he sees as a first hypothesis, "Kant establishes that individuals are unable to get out of their condition of tutelage by themselves."[13] And why are they "unable"? For the same reason they are in a state of tutelage in the first place: out of cowardice and laziness. So, to Foucault, in what he calls Kant's second hypothesis, the question is the following: if most people are unable to exit tutelage, can the individuals who think for themselves lead the others toward Enlightenment? Here, Foucault is very clear – perhaps more so than Kant. These few people who do think for themselves would then "decide to play the role of liberators", and by virtue of their own autonomy exert authority over others, who will not be led toward enlightenment but, as a consequence of being led, will remain in tutelage. The

---

[11] If I take a book "that has understanding for me", I am doing the opposite of what is articulated in the first critique, *The Critique of Pure Reason*, where Kant urges us to make legitimate use of our understanding, i.e. within the legitimate limits of our reason: books may certainly be read, but not taken as authorities or substitutes for our own thinking. Taking a spiritual leader as the first principle for one's conduct is the negation of *The Critique of Practical Reason*, where Kant grounds the moral law in reason, in moral conscience or *Gewissen*, more precisely in the categorical imperative and the autonomy following upon its implementation. Foucault is not as clear on the relation between the relying on the doctor's judgment and the third critique, *Critique of Judgment*, but sees a kernel of what will later form the domain of this work. See Foucault, *The Government of Self and Others*, 30.
[12] Foucault, *The Government of Self and Others*, 33.
[13] Foucault, *The Government of Self and Others*, 33.

result is a kind of antinomy. But there are some differences between Kant's argument and Foucault's account: Kant's argument moves from the level of individual (who according to Kant is not "unable" as Foucault says, but for whom it is "difficult" to leave the condition of tutelage which has become a second nature to him) to the level of the public for whom, on the contrary, it is "more likely; indeed, it is nearly inevitable" to enlighten itself.[14] There is the problem of those who Foucault calls "liberators" and who, as Kant has already noted with some irony, "kindly" assume the responsibility of directing others. In this passage on the public, Kant states that if the public has been put under the yoke of these industrious few to reach enlightenment, prejudice (presumably implanted by being directed, led, and put under the authority of others) will swing back and they might force their very guardians into submission. That is why he concludes that the public can achieve enlightenment only slowly, and that revolution, while it might bring an end to tyranny, will never "reform" thought itself. Foucault's account is slightly different and more accentuated. Answering his own question of why it is not possible for a few to lead others toward enlightenment, he says:

> Why is this? Precisely because they began by placing others under their authority, so that these others, being thus accustomed to the yoke, cannot bear the freedom and emancipation they are given. They force, they constrain precisely those who want to free them because they have freed themselves to come back under the yoke, the yoke which they accepted from the other out of cowardice and laziness and under which they now wish to bring back those who want to free them. Consequently, he says, the law of all revolutions—this was written in 1784—is that those who make them necessarily fall back under the yoke of those who wanted to free them.[15]

This is not exactly what Kant says, even though his argument is somewhat convoluted:[16] according to Kant, who makes a distinction between different

---

¹⁴ Kant, "An Answer to the Question: What is Enlightenment?", 59.

¹⁵ Foucault, *The Government of Self and Others*, 34.

¹⁶ "Daß aber ein Publikum sich selbst aufkläre, ist eher möglich; ja es ist, wenn man ihm nur Freiheit läßt, beinahe unausbleiblich. Denn da werden sich immer einige Selbstdenkende, sogar unter den eingesetzten Vormündern des großen Haufens, finden, welche, nachdem sie das Joch der Unmündigkeit selbst abgeworfen haben, den Geist einer vernünftigen Schätzung des eigenen Werts und des Berufs jedes Menschen, selbst zu denken, um sich verbreiten werden. Besonders ist hiebei: daß das Publikum, welches zuvor von ihnen unter dieses Joch gebracht worden, sie hernach selbst zwingt, darunter zu bleiben, wenn es von einigen seiner Vormünder, die selbst aller Aufklärung unfähig sind, dazu aufgewiegelt worden; so schädlich ist es, Vorurteile zu pflanzen, weil sie sich zuletzt an denen selbst rächen, die, oder deren Vorgänger, ihre Urheber gewesen sind." See Immanuel Kant, *Was ist Aufklärung? Ausgewählte kleine Schriften* (Hamburg: Felix Meiner Verlag, 1999), 21–22.

kinds of guardians, the public will force the guardians who have thrown off the yoke of tutelage to come back under it "if they are incited to do so by some of their guardians who are incapable of any enlightenment," while in Foucault's reading, the public, simply by having been put under guardianship, will force the enlightened guardians back under the yoke.[17] Kant does not define any "law of all revolutions"; these words are Foucault's own. Further, Kant does not say that the public will end up with new lords or despots, though Foucault does. Rather, he argues that the public will end up with new prejudices.[18] Thus, the dangers of leading and being led, as discussed in Kant's text, are magnified by Foucault, for whom the enlightened guardians will be brought back under the yoke of tutelage even without the unenlightened guardians there to incite the masses to do so.

The point here is not to inculpate Foucault for a one-sided Kant-reading, but to ask the question what such reading may suggest. If Foucault draws a conclusion from this text – that he returned on so many occasions, a text which fascinated him in its attempt to define its own epoch and context – then he draws out a bit more than what Kant put in it. But, what is this 'more' that Foucault articulates? Presumably Foucault's own position, or his attempt to formulate the problem is the impossibility of being led toward enlightenment by another, simply because enlightenment cannot be mediated in that sense. Just as autonomy does not occur in the governing of others but in the governing of the self, any process of liberation or emancipation must take the form of a relation of the self to the self. As we can see, Foucault is not particularly interested in what Kant says about the public actually being able to

---

[17] First, Kant somewhat contradictory states that the Public might force those few self-thinking people who have already cast off the yoke of tutelage to "stay" (*bleiben*) under it. Second, the "guardians" or *Vormündern* are divided into two subcategories: those who have cast off the yoke of tutelage and those who are unable to do so, while both generally, precisely as guardians, put the masses under the yoke of tutelage. Perhaps matters are complicated by the fact that the pronouns "them" (*ihnen* and *sie*) could refer to either one of the subcategories, or just the general category. Foucault, in his reading, seems to refer exclusively to the self-thinking subcategory of guardians: the fact that they have led the public will keep the public incapable of not being led. That Kant sees this refusal of enlightenment among the public as a result of the influence of the guardians incapable of Enlightenment is confirmed by his distinction between those guardians who implant prejudices and their descendants: "So it is harmful to implant prejudices, because they ultimately revenge themselves on those who originated them or on their descendants." See Kant, "An Answer to the Question: What is Enlightenment?", 59.

[18] "So it is harmful to implant prejudices, because they ultimately revenge themselves on those who originated them or on their descendants. Therefore a public can achieve enlightenment only gradually. A revolution may perhaps bring about the fall of an autocratic despotism and of an avaricious or overbearing oppression, but it can never bring about the true reform of a way of thinking. Rather, new prejudices will serve, like the old, as the leading strings of the thoughtless masses." See Kant, "An Answer to the Question: What is Enlightenment?", 59.

achieve enlightenment so long as it goes about it slowly; he is more interested in the contradictions that exist within the text. His first objection concerns the question of *Leitung* and government, and the positive role Kant assigns to Frederick the Great: "after having stated and demonstrated at some length that there cannot be an individual agent or individual agents of this liberation, he now introduces precisely the King of Prussia."[19] To Kant, the public will reach enlightenment only if it is given freedom, and by granting it this freedom, Frederick is the guarantor of the public use of reason. Apart from questioning the logic that requires a *deus ex machina* provided by the royal sovereign,[20] Foucault – to put it mildly – does not seem convinced by the argument that both the king and the public will benefit from the public use of reason. What Kant says about Prussia as "an illuminating example to such a government that public peace and unity have little to fear from this freedom,"[21] Foucault reformulates as: "The more you allow freedom of thought, the more sure you will be that the people's mind will be shaped to obedience."[22] In Kant's account, the possibility of mutual benefits for the sovereign and his subjects rests on the distinction he makes between the "public" and "private" use of reason: the private use of reason is carried out by the individual in his or her civic post, where one as part of society's great machine must obey orders; the public use which is made by man "*as a scholar [Gelehrter] before the entire public of the reading world.*"[23] While Foucault does not dwell on the issue, it is evident that he cannot accept Kant's suggestion that Enlightenment for all will be achieved through a free exchange of ideas in the public and intellectual sphere, while obeying in the "private" professional and civic sphere. Foucault had already dismissed such a public, universal use of reason (of a more or less teleological kind) most clearly in his *Archaeology of Knowledge* and its descriptions of discourses as historically conditioned practices defined by ruptures, thresholds, and exclusions,[24] and he had criticized its subsequent Habermasian form of "communicative rationality" in a much later text;"[25] what is more, he had devoted much of his

---

[19] Foucault, *The Government of Self and Others*, 37.

[20] As another example of this role of an agent or external driving force, Foucault takes Kant's 1798 text "The Conflict of the Faculties" and the role he assigns to the "revolutionary enthusiasm" in the French Revolution. See Foucault, *The Government of Self and Others*, 39.

[21] Kant, "An Answer to the Question: What is Enlightenment?", 62.

[22] Foucault, *The Government of Self and Others*, 38.

[23] Kant, "An Answer to the Question: What is Enlightenment?", 60.

[24] Foucault, *The Archaeology of Knowledge*, 188.

[25] "Subject and Power" was written in English as an afterword to Dreyfus and Rabinow's *Michel Foucault: Beyond Structuralism and Hermeneutics* and published in 1982. Here Foucault sums up and

work to unearthing the normalizing effects of a number of practices which would fall under the "private" use of reason, investigating for example how the discipline of private obedience produced docile bodies and loyal, productive subjects.[26]

Enlightenment as a Question of Critique

Perhaps Foucault's attention to the contingent solutions, strange turns, and contradictions in Kant's text is simply an attempt to reserve for himself the possibility of reformulating its central problem: how is this exit from self-incurred tutelage possible, how is it to be carried through, and how is it to be defined? Because not only does he decline Kant's suggestion of a slow and harmonious process of public enlightenment moving through the public use of reason. It also seems that he has already started to answer Kant's question in his own right, albeit in a more preliminary manner. In the lectures he had prepared for *The Government of Self and Others*, Foucault addresses the notion of truth-telling in the face of power, and truth-telling as a practice of freedom. In the previous year's lectures on the care of the self in Hellenistic philosophy, Foucault had emphasized both the practical, critical and conflictual nature of the process of exiting from self-incurred tutelage in the form of breaks with that which enslaves you – the study of nature – and the so-called *ethopoiēsis* of giving form to one's existence. But even before that Foucault had turned Kant's question in a similar conflictual, oppositional direction, with respect to the task of critique.

In this opening lecture on Kant's "What is Enlightenment?", the notion of critique is summoned explicitly, as we have seen, by Foucault's reference to Kant's critical project – the examples of the book, the *Seelsorger*, and the doctor, which metonymically are taken as standing in for each of the three Critiques. But it is also evoked implicitly, considering that the same text by Kant forms the major point of reference in Foucault's 1978 lecture "What is Critique?". Foucault actually wrote several texts, very different in their scope and function, that engage closely with "What is Enlightenment?"[27] Each of

---

reformulates much of his previous work in terms developed during his later Collège de France courses. See Foucault, "Subject and Power" in *Beyond Structuralism and Hermeneutics*, 210, 218.

[26] "[D]iscipline produces subjected and practised bodies, 'docile' bodies. Discipline increases the forces of the body (in economic terms of utility) and diminishes these same forces (in political terms of obedience)." See Foucault, *Discipine and Punish*, 138.

[27] First, the already mentioned "What is Critique?", which was given as a lecture at the French Society of Philosophy on May 27, 1978. The second text is the introduction to the English translation of Georges Canguilhem's *On the Normal and Pathological* which was published the same year. The third, most directly linked both to Kant's text and to Foucault's own lecture of 1984 by their many

these texts overlap in certain ways. However, it is in "What is Critique?" that Foucault gets closest to providing an answer to the Kantian question of Enlightenment. This is done in a roundabout or reversed way. Attempting to answer the question "What is Critique?", Foucault gives the following preliminary definition: critique is to be understood as the attitude of not wanting to be governed like that, or as "the art of not being governed so much." Critique becomes the movement by which the subject questions truth with respect to its effects of power and questions power with respect to what it holds to be true. And this definition, he says, "is not very different from the one Kant provided: not to define critique, but precisely to define something else. It is not very far off in fact from the definition he was giving of the *Aufklärung*."[28] So if Enlightenment, as Kant defines it, equals critique, as Foucault defines it, it seems that the notion of critique has been smuggled in implicitly into the 1983 lectures on the government of self and others. Now, the following analysis of the 1983 lectures will mainly be informed by another, explicitly stated aspect of Foucault's reading of Kant , namely "the ontology of the present" which describes – and prescribes – philosophy's attempt to interrogate its own present. But as we shall see in the next chapter, Foucault's implicit invocation of critique in the midst of these courses on antiquity may help us further understand that to which we shall turn in a moment, the ancient forms of truth-telling in the political domain during antiquity. But first, two more points from the Kantian lecture, beginning with Foucault's interest in the *Zeitschrift* as a mode of publication.

The Public as Subject of Enlightenment:
The *Zeitschrift* as a Form of Public

The text on Enlightenment was written by Kant in September 1784, and published in *Berlinische Monatsschrift* in December that same year. Foucault notes that there is nothing out of the ordinary in Kant writing a text for a journal, noting a few other of Kant's contributions to the same and other journals. What is special in this case, however, is that Kant hinges the very question of the text – the definition and possibility of Enlightenment – on the notion of *Publikum* or the public, and the public at this time, as Foucault demonstrates, is made up precisely by journals; the journal or *Zeitschrift* itself being an Enlightenment invention. The public to which Kant refers, and

---

similarities, is the "What is Enlightenment?" included in Dreyfus and Rabinow's *Foucault Reader* in 1984. This is not the place to undertake a comparative study, and we will return to "What is Critique?" in the following chapter.

[28] Foucault, "What is Critique?", 47.

which should be understood as the learned, scholarly relations between writers and readers, took place not at the university (this would acquire such a function only during the 19th century through the grand reforms of higher education), neither was it primarily in the circulation of books nor finally, in anything resembling what today is called "public debate" or "public opinion" (phenomena linked to material and cultural conditions developed in the 19th and 20th centuries through mass media and the nascent sociology). The late 18th century public to which Kant attaches such importance is, says Foucault, "a reality established and delineated by the existence of institutions like learned societies, academies, and journals, and what circulates within this framework."[29] It thus seems that the subject of the text (the public on its way to Enlightenment) is manifested in and carried out by the object of its *publication.* Foucault's attention to how form and content coincide in the text's locus of publication may be understood in the light of how he begins his reading: within the first lines of Kant's text, in the very definition of Enlightenment, Foucault identifies an important aspect. Enlightenment as objective and end is not defined by Kant in any positive way, but only by the means with which one achieves it, i.e. as the "exit", or in Foucault's words as "a movement by which one extricates oneself from something, without saying anything about what one is moving towards."[30] A similar operation appears already in "What is Critique?", when Foucault notes that critique only exists in relation to something other than itself, as an instrument to achieve something yet unknown, "as a means for a future or a truth that it will not know nor happen to be", before he goes on to state that critique, at the same time, "is akin to something like virtue," something that is an end in itself.[31] This may explain why Foucault seizes upon how the text is set to circulate within the very public – the relations established and constituted by the specific form of the journal – which its argument holds as the subject of Enlightenment. That Foucault draws our attention to this ouroboros of means and end, of the public as at the same time subject, subject matter and object of publication and mediation, is never really discussed in the literature on Foucault and "What is Enlightenment?".[32] Yet he is clear of the importance

---

[29] Foucault, *The Government of Self and Others*, 8.

[30] Foucault, *The Government of Self and Others*, 27.

[31] Foucault, "What is Critique?", 42–43.

[32] Many commentators content themselves with noting Foucault's repeated interest in Kant's text, and its most obviously important aspect, Kant's turn to interrogate his own time, to ask the question of the present. See for example Elden, *The Late Foucault*, 195.

in how Kant's text "puts the notion of the public, to which the publication is addressed, at the very heart of its analysis."[33]

Perhaps the problem is that Foucault – as with most matters he brings up concerning "What is Enlightenment?" – does not specify in what sense it is important in relation to the questions of truth and subjectivity with which he is concerned during these years, nor does he situate it within any specific problematic developed elsewhere. Instead, it remains suspended in relation to the following lectures. One way to consider the issue of public/publication is in relation to Foucault's scepticism of the Kantian assertion of private obedience and a public reason in the form of the universal. The role of the *Zeitschrift* points us away from the problems of being released from *Unmündigkeit* toward the possibilities of the exit, as Foucault sees them: away from the antinomy of enlightened guardians leading others toward emancipation, away from anything like a neutral, unmediated sphere for the public use of reason, toward that which is precisely the mediated nature of such public, and toward the notion of a very particular public as means and end. Thus, the Enlightenment invention of the journal – along with the act of writing for it – offers the constitution of a new *Publikum*, a new particular form of public indispensable to the very objective of Enlightenment. That the means of the publication merges with the end of the public does not entail that the means cease to be means, in what could be regarded as a philosophy or politics of immediacy, or perhaps mediacy. On the contrary, the example of the *Zeitschrift* underlines Foucault's emphasis on the mediated nature of any emancipatory project. Understood this way, within the limits and processual temporality of the circulation of certain journals, the exit from self-incurred tutelage appears much closer to something like Seneca's exit from *stultitia*, described in the previous chapter as a gradual turning toward oneself, through an extended and formalized engagement with philosophy or with a philosopher. And if Foucault's brief notes on Kant's question of enlightenment in this sense forms a description of a liberatory project where means and ends merge, where message and medium coincide in the constitution of new publics, it enters into a play of strange echoes with some of his own theoretical and practical interventions in various struggles for autonomy. As will be suggested in chapter 5, it resonates in the descriptions of Solidarnosc, the Polish labor union that by its existence negates the interdiction of labor unions and opposes the laws against strikes with strikes. Or, as we shall see later in this chapter, it may be taken in a more or less

---

[33] Foucault, *The Government of Self and Others*, 8.

conflictual relation with the following year of lectures on the Cynics; the philosophers who mock and bark at their auditors, display a shocking behavior, and perform parodies and negative reflections in a kind of "grimace of truth" in order to change or, for that matter, lead their co-citizens into a true life.

The Ontology of the Present

A brief, but important final point to take up from the lecture on Kant concerns the so-called "ontology of the present," a crucial notion for how Foucault understands his own work, both in general and, as will be argued, in these specific lectures. Foucault says that there are two post-Kantian philosophical traditions: one following Kant's critical project, especially the first critique, of defining the limits and possibilities of true knowledge; this analytics of truth is pursued by the Anglo-Saxon tradition of analytic philosophy. Then there is another critical questioning of the kind that Kant undertakes in "What is Enlightenment?" and "The Conflict of the Faculties", a questioning directed at the heart of the present:

> This other critical tradition does not pose the question of the conditions of possibility of a true knowledge; it asks the question: What is present reality? What is the present field of our experiences? What is the present field of possible experiences? Here it is not a question of the analytic of truth but involves what could be called an ontology of the present, of present reality, an ontology of modernity, an ontology of ourselves.[34]

This is the tradition that Foucault sees unfolding in the work of Hegel, Nietzsche, the Frankfurt School, Max Weber, and it is, to no surprise, the tradition to which he counts his own work. Whether he concerned himself with the great confinement of the mad in the 17th century, the birth of the human sciences after the Classical Age, or the development of the modern prison and a number of related disciplinary apparatuses, Foucault was always a historian of the present. At one point he even replicated the Kantian attempt to directly interrogate and define his own epoch. In place of Kant's late 18th century Enlightenment, Foucault's 1979 lectures *The Birth of Biopolitics* are animated by the question "what is neoliberalism?", surveying the economic paradigm of the late 20th century.

It is not difficult to understand Foucault's partition of the Kantian heritage, nor the meaning of the ontology of the present; it should be equally

---

[34] Foucault, *The Government of Self and Others*, 20–21.

clear why Foucault sees his own work in this tradition. Rather, the question is: what does it mean to speak of an ontology of the present, to insist on this direct questioning of one's own epoch and its possible experiences, in the midst of a long series of lectures on antiquity? Given the lack of explanation of how it relates to the subsequent material of the course – given the mute presence of this imperative next to the following lectures on *parrēsia* and the political advisor – it seems to function as a reminder. As a way of saying: I may speak of antiquity, but make no mistake as to what is really at stake, what epoch I really invite you to think about in terms of truth-telling in the political sphere and the government of self and others. Understood this way, Foucault's discussion of "Was ist Aufklärung?" as an ontology of the present unhinges all his following lectures: no longer can they be taken as a commentary on a remote past, at a safe distance of two millennia. They concern the here and now.

"Political *Parrēsia*" and the Public Speaker

In *The Government of Self and Others*, as we have noted, the main concept is *parrēsia* and the main theme is truth-telling. But the *parrēsia* that Foucault discusses in these lectures is not exactly the same as the one he had introduced a year before, in *The Hermeneutics of the Subject*, when it was culled from the golden age of the culture of the self, as the truth spoken by the master or spiritual guide to the apprentice, by the honest person to his friend, or between the members of a spiritual community or philosophical school. In 1983, already on the first occasion that Foucault mentions the term *parrēsia*, he qualifies it as "true discourse in the political realm."[35] It will mainly concern the public orator and political advisor. Reminding his audience of the general project, Foucault describes his work in three displacements: from the analysis of forms of knowledge to the rules of veridiction; from the analysis of power and historical forms of domination toward the technologies of governmentality; from a theory of the subject[36] to the historical analysis of forms of subjectivation in the technologies of the self. Now, *parrēsia*, says Foucault, is located at the inter-

---

[35] Foucault, *The Government of Self and Others*, 6.

[36] While the first two displacements can be located within Foucault's work, the third displacement from "a theory of the subject" seems to describe a departure point located outside his own work, a problem that was never his own and that also his earlier work sought to move beyond. Instead, one can think of the third displacement as moving from, let us say, an analysis of forms of subjection "to the historical analysis of forms of subjectivation in the technologies of the self." See Foucault, *The Government of Self and Others*, 5.

section of the obligation to speak the truth, techniques of governmentality, and the constitution of the relationship to oneself. Thus, *parrēsia* is a central concept. Further, it is of strategic importance to Foucault, interconnecting the different levels of the government of the self and the government of others, in a way that continues the previous year's project of linking together the fields of ethics and politics. Despite the stated ambition to connect the investigation of true discourse in the political domain to the "still open dossiers" on governmentality he worked on in 1978 and 1979, this is one of several points the lectures never reach; but it is made clear that they form a part of the same conceptual framework. In this section we shall look at Foucault's first, general remarks on *parrēsia*, and consider the figure of the public orator or public speaker, precisely to be able – in the following chapters – to relate it to the field of governmentality and thus be able to locate it within Foucault's larger body of work.

First Remarks on *Parrēsia* in The Government of Self and Others

After the first lecture on Kant, after a brief reminder of the previous year's definitions of *parrēsia* and a bibliographical note on the strikingly scarce research previously devoted to the term (which was at the time generally unknown), Foucault devotes the first more precise textual analysis to a testimony of the political-conflictual properties of *parrēsia*: Plutarch's text on Dion in *Parallel Lives*. Here, the Syracusan youngster Dion meets Plato, who has appeared on the shores of Sicily; he becomes the Athenian philosopher's pupil and prospers under him, deciding to bring to him his brother-in-law, Dionysius the Elder, tyrant of Syracuse. When Plato is lecturing on the subject of the virtue and happiness of tyrants, Dionysius asks why he came to Sicily in the first place: "To find a good man," says Plato, with the implication that the search is still open. Insulted and outraged, Dionysius plots to have Plato sold into slavery during his passage back to Athens, leaving Dion as the sole practitioner of *parrēsia* at the court.

Having summarized the text, Foucault asks what actually characterizes this *parrēsia*. Considering that Plato could have stated the same thing about tyrants and virtue at another occasion and to another audience without the same, dramatic consequences, Foucault gives a preliminary definition: *parrēsia* is a truth not defined by its content, but by how it is spoken, as "a way of telling the truth."[37] A few distinctions are made: *parrēsia* is not an art of demonstration or teaching, and does not belong to the field of pedagogy;

---

[37] Foucault, *The Government of Self and Others*, 55.

nor is it an art of persuasion or discussion, and does not belong to rhetoric or eristic. Unlike these, the truth-telling of *parrēsia* cannot be defined by analyzing the internal forms or structures of discourse, nor by the effects it wants to achieve. In fact, Foucault again formulates the problem in terms of means and ends: "Since we cannot situate *parrēsia* in an end envisaged by the discourse, where can we situate it?"[38] Looking at the risk involved for the speaker, whether it is Dion or Plato, he concludes: "*Parrēsia* is to be situated in what binds the speaker to the fact that what he says is the truth."[39] It is situated in the speaker's act of binding him or herself to the truth and to the action of speaking it. And since it cannot be situated "in an end envisaged by the discourse" we infer that this means of binding oneself to the truth is an end in itself, and that *parrēsia* is the *sine qua non* of a certain event, with unknown effects on the speaker and the interlocutor. To be clear, these are not just any effects, as is evident in the example of Plato and Dion before Dionysius: "Parrhesiasts are those who, if necessary, accept death for having told the truth."[40] This means that risk – the readiness to state the truth at whatever cost – is an important element in Foucault's description of *parrēsia*, implying a situation of unequally distributed power or force. We can thus continue to identify certain continuities between different parts of Foucault's late work; patterns that appear as its very core or essence. To begin with, the binding of oneself to the truth as an end in itself resembles both, on the one hand, the subjectivation of truth and the act of making truth one's own, and on the other, that which we previously defined as a recurring conceptual figure: the figure of merging means and ends in the "self-finalization" of the care of the self as it is formulated in *The Hermeneutics of the Subject*. Further, the aspect of the unknown effects, the unforeseen consequences of *parrēsia* recalls Foucault's emphasis on the Kantian definition of Enlightenment as exit from one's self-assumed tutelage into something yet unknown, as well as his understanding of subjectivity as process and his general insistence on the importance of becoming other. Finally, as opposed to the obligation to speak the truth in the Christian confession, the example of Plato's *parrēsia* before the tyrant is an active, free, voluntary and reflected act of speaking the truth – conflictual and inscribed in an unequal relation of force – somewhat like the "reflected intractability" of critique in relation to government.[41]

---

[38] Foucault, *The Government of Self and Others*, 56.
[39] Foucault, *The Government of Self and Others*, 56.
[40] Foucault, *The Government of Self and Others*, 56.
[41] Foucault, "What is Critique?", 47.

In addition to these continuities or common elements in the different parts of his late work, Foucault makes two remarks that tie this notion of political *parrēsia* to his work in more general ways: he defines it in terms of Nietzschean truthfulness and of a certain "dramatics" of discourse. While he had rendered the *parrēsia* of the spiritual guide in the previous year's lectures as free-spokenness (*franc-parler*), Foucault now suggests that the term needs to be understood differently:

> I think we can propose to translate it as "veridicity" (*véridicité*). The parrēsiast, the person who uses *parrēsia*, is the truthful man (*l'homme véridique*), that is to say, the person who has the courage to risk telling the truth, and who risks this truth-telling in a pact with himself, inasmuch as he is, precisely, the enunciator of the truth. He is the truth-teller (*le véridique*). And (maybe we will be able to come back to this, I don't know if I will have the time) it seems to me that Nietzschean veridicity is a way of putting to work this notion whose distant origin is found in the notion of *parrēsia* (truth-telling) as a risk for the person who states it, a risk accepted by the person who states it.[42]

Foucault does not return to the issue (which illustrates the preliminary, tentative nature of these lectures), but this Nietzschean veridicity or truthfulness, this invocation of a concept of one of the philosophers he claimed he had studied the most,[43] suggests how he relates *parrēsia* to a modern philosophy of action and contestation. Given the emphasis on courage in this context of *parrēsia*, Foucault is perhaps referring to the truthfulness in the fifth book of *The Gay Science*, "We Fearless Ones" which Nietzsche himself returns to in *On the Genealogy of Morality*.[44] In this passage, Nietzsche regards the will to truth as a potential will to death because there is a risk and a "dangerousness of 'the will to truth' or 'truth at any price'".[45] But for Nietzsche, truth and truthfulness is a double-edged sword, both emancipatory and dangerous, both morally necessary and yet ungrounded and unstable. In addition to the perils involved, truthfulness and this will to truth carries a kind of promise; those who are truthful "affirm another world,"[46] which means that rather than being the expression of any simple correspondence, and regardless of any possible metaphysical implications, truth

---

[42] Foucault, *The Government of Self and Others*, 66.

[43] Foucault, "Interview de Foucault," in *Dits et écrits II, 1976–1988*, 1522.

[44] Friedrich Nietzsche, *On the Genealogy of Morality*, trans. Carol Diethe (Cambridge: Cambridge University Press, 2006), 112.

[45] Friedrich Nietzsche, *The Gay Science*, trans. Josefine Nauckhoff (Cambridge: Cambridge University Press, 2001), 201.

[46] Friedrich Nietzsche, *The Gay Science*, 201.

is the precondition for transformation. Let us recall Foucault's 1967 text "Nietzsche, Freud, Marx": "For Nietzsche, the interpreter is the truthful man (*le veridique*); he is truthful (*veritable*), not because he seizes a sleeping truth in order to proclaim it, but because he pronounces the interpretation that every truth has for its function to conceal."[47] Read this way, the reference to Nietzsche seems to invoke both the relentless hermeneutics Foucault drew from the Nietzschean, Freudian, and Marxian heritage, and the way in which Nietzsche himself regarded this will to truth both as an affirmation of another world, and as an unbending courage. As such it comes close to Foucault's notions of critique: it is a truthfulness that challenges the given order, and that does so through a "politics of truth"[48] by showing "that things are not as evident as one thinks."[49]

This truth-telling is an affirmation of alterity, which is why Foucault can say that *parrēsia* does not belong to the "pragmatics" of discourse where positions, statements, and consequences are regulated and to some extent given in advance – he takes the example of performative statements, such as when someone declares a meeting to be open – but to what he calls a "dramatics" of true discourse. This "dramatics" is doubly interesting. To begin with, because it is within the potential history, forms, and structures of such dramatics of true discourse that Foucault identifies four different and significant "figures" or historical agents to study. First, the double figure that comprises both the public orator and the Prince's counselor in antiquity: "How did we pass from a *parrēsia* which, as you will see in a moment or next week, characterizes the public orator, to a conception of *parrēsia* which characterizes the dramatics of the Prince's counselor, speaking and telling him what he must do?"[50] Second, the figure of the minister of the 16th century, when the art of government begins to acquire its eminence and autonomy, and when the minister addresses his true discourse to the monarch in the name of the *raison d'état*, establishing a new kind of knowledge of the state. Third, the figure of the critic (not "critique" as the English translation has it),[51] and the development of critical discourse during the 18th, 19th, and 20th centuries; fourth, appearing alongside the critic during the last three centuries, the figure of the revolutionary, rising to speak the truth in the name of the revolution that shall be made. Of these Foucault only manages to

---

[47] Michel Foucault, "Nietzsche, Freud, Marx," in *Dits et écrits I, 1954–1975*, 600.
[48] Foucault, "What is Critique?", 47.
[49] Foucault, "Est-il donc important de penser?", 999.
[50] Foucault, *The Government of Self and Others*, 69.
[51] Foucault, *The Government of Self and Others*, 70.

discuss the double figure of the public orator and the Prince's counselor in antiquity; in fact he says from the outset that he might not have time to go through them all. Yet it is as if, not to lose track of the overarching discussion that he is hoping to reach, Foucault repeatedly raises the same points of reference to mark out its field: governmentality, critique, revolution.

What is more, the "dramatics" of true discourse connects Foucault's lectures on truth-telling in antiquity to a fascinating strand that can be traced through the full body of his work. In *Les scènes de la vérité*, Arianna Sforzini shows to what extent Foucault's multifaceted work can be understood through his consistent use of terms, themes, and metaphors relating to the theatre: masks, scenes, stages, tragedies, and indeed, dramatics, from the early radio lectures in 1963 when the language of madness is discussed in terms of tragedy and theatre, to the dramatization and theatrical staging of Cynic life in 1984. Thus Sforzini understands Foucault's particular definition of *parrēsia* in *The Government of Self and Others* as a dramatic discourse of truth along the lines of a Butlerian "aesthetics of the performative," which is not founded on the idea of a predetermined, individual subject, but which constructs new forms of subjectivity through its very performance.[52] This also encompasses the gestures and exercises of the Cynics, Stoics, and Epicureans, which Foucault investigated in the previous year of lectures, and which, already in 1970 in his significantly entitled text *"Theatrum Philosophicum"*, with the help of Deleuze, he raised against the Platonic transcendental truth, otherworldly idea or essence. For this reason, we can add that political *parrēsia* is another immanent, transformative practice of truth, a conflictual dramatics of true discourse in the political domain.[53] Sforzini also affirms the richness of the performative aspect of Foucault's work. In addition to describing the dramatics of truth in terms of a performative subjectivity close to Judith Butler's work in this regard, Sforzini is clear to underline – and similar to what has been emphasized above – Foucault's critical challenge to philosophy: "it indicates a practice of truth that does not strive to make people understand or learn, but to make them act and react, in a sliding movement of inventing new rules in the 'games' of true and false, in the divisions between reality and fiction, in the impositions and battles of bodies."[54] This shall suffice to demonstrate the stakes in Foucault's introduction of the notion of truth-telling in the political sphere.

---

[52] Arianna Sforzini, *Les scènes de la vérité: Michel Foucault et théâtre* (Paris: A bord de l'eau, 2017), 230.

[53] Michel Foucault, *"Theatrum Philosophicum"* in, *Language, Counter-Memory, Practice: Selected Essays and Interviews*, 168–69.

[54] Arianna Sforzini, *Les scènes de la vérité: Michel Foucault et théâtre*, 230–231.

The *Parrēsia* of the Public Speaker

Foucault demonstrates that the term *parrēsia* had a quite different meaning during the 4th century BCE, before it acquired the meaning of courage or personal virtue that Plutarch describes in Dion and Plato. In the 4th century, *parrēsia* was regarded both as a general, shared political structure and as a social and political status of a limited number of citizens. Foucault takes up Polybius retrospective definition of the Achaean regime by three major characteristics: *dēmokratia*, *isēgoria* (equality before the law), and *parrēsia*, the right of every citizen to speak at the *ekklēsia*, the general assembly.[55] But along with this assertion of an "equally" distributed right to speak the truth – equal among those freemen counted as citizens – Foucault raises a contrary example from Euripides' play *Ion*. In *Ion*, the title character wishes he was born by an Athenian mother, since only this form of autochtony would grant him *parrēsia*, the right to speak freely in Athens, a right unavailable to foreigners and practiced most frequently by those foremost citizens exercising a certain ascendancy over others. In this case, *parrēsia* is a social status, ensuring that its proprietor/practitioner can form part of the front rank of the city, and that, in the words of Euripides, his mouth will not remain "slave" (Gr. *to ge stoma doulon*), which it would without Athenian maternal ancestry. Foucault's careful analysis of the tragedy makes up a fair share of the lecture course; but since it is not of great significance for our argument it will not be further discussed here.[56] More important as a model for the public speaker is what Foucault somewhat curiously calls "Periclean *parrēsia*" which he finds in the writings of Thucydides, despite the fact that the latter does not denote it as *parrēsia*.[57] This courageous truth-telling of Pericles provides, as Foucault sketches it, a kind of chronological starting point of the historical trajectory of *parrēsia*. And not only chronological, but also qualitative, since Foucault takes it as an example of the initially good relationship between democracy and *parrēsia*; a relationship which would increasingly come apart.

—

[55] Polybius was writing in the 2nd century BCE; see Foucault, *The Government of Self and Others*, 71.

[56] Foucault introduces *Ion* at the end of the second lecture, devoting the entirety of the third and fourth lectures to it. He concludes the theme in the fifth lecture, thus making its treatment about a quarter of the full lecture course. The extended nature of the analysis might be explained by the year's improvised and somewhat "trampling" around *parrēsia* as a key concept of truth in relation to government; perhaps the analysis went on for longer than necessary (with respect to the scope of the overarching investigation) because Foucault took pleasure in the material; or perhaps its richness and complexity calls for a more careful and delimited analysis regarding the dramatics of truth. For some notes about this, and about the feminist implications of Foucault's analysis of a woman's *parrēsia* in Creusa's accusal of Apollo, see Arianna Sforzini, *Les Scenes de la vérité: Michel Foucault et théâtre* (Paris: A bord de l'eau, 2017), 167–170, 207–208.

[57] Foucault, *The Government of Self and Others*, 174.

To Foucault, there are four basic conditions for political *parrēsia*, or the *parrēsia* of the public speaker: first, there must be democracy, equality, and free speech; second, a certain power or authority exercised by some over others; third, speech must be truthful and rational; and finally, courage must be shown (since this truth will be stated in a joust or confrontation). The paradigm example, for Foucault, is Pericles: the public orator who came from a wealthy, influential and aristocratic family, and who was a political leader and general in Athens in the late 5th century.[58] Thucydides wrote down, recorded from memory and testimonies, three speeches of Pericles in his *History of the Peloponnesian War* which form a good representation of *parrēsia* and its merits for democracy at the end of the 5th century BCE. Before rendering Pericles' speech of war, Thucydides describes the many opinions voiced at the assembly for and against war against the Spartan-led Peloponnesians (who had posed a sort of ultimatum to Athens), thus highlighting the democratic notion of *isēgoria*. And then "Pericles, the son of Xanthippus, stood up to speak. At that time, he was the most influential man of Athens, the most skillful in speech and in action."[59] Here we see influence and power. Then follows the speech itself wherein Foucault finds the condition of truth according to which the truth of Pericles' discourse is bound to himself.[60] The element of risk and courage is certainly present. However, it is more visible in Pericles' third discourse, known as the discourse on the plague: military losses are piling up in plague-stricken Athens whose citizens now turn against Pericles, negotiate with the enemy behind his back, and blame him for the failure. But instead of flattering the angry Athenians, instead of shifting the blame onto someone or something else, he summons the citizens to the Assembly and reproaches them for losing courage in the face of adversity, shifting their views, and accusing him wrongly. To Foucault, this is the image of good *parrēsia*, an example that "theorizes the proper adjustment between demo-

---

[58] While Thucydides called him the first citizen of Athens, and while he is credited for having initiated the most important constructions of Acropolis, including the Parthenon, some have considered him responsible, through his structural strengthening of democracy and his favoring of the lower classes, for having set Athens in an irreversible motion into degeneration and turmoil; Plato, for example, has Socrates say that he "made the Athenians idle and cowardly, chatterers and moneygrubbers, since he was the first to institute wages for them." See Plato, *Gorgias*, trans. Donald J. Zeyl, in *Complete Works* (Indianapolis/Cambridge: Hackett Publishing Company, 1997), 859.

[59] As quoted in Foucault, *The Government of Self and Others*, 175.

[60] Foucault, *The Government of Self and Others*, 176.

cracy and the exercise of *parrēsia* and truth-telling, an exercise which, once again, necessarily entails the ascendancy of some over others."[61]

Paradoxes of Political *Parrēsia*: Descent and Historical Development

This "good *parrēsia*" forms a departure point in Foucault's account: after its descent into a "bad *parrēsia*" within a faltering democracy, and after the subsequent disappearance of democratic structures, *parrēsia* is gradually shifted into the domain of philosophy – from political *parrēsia* to philosophical *parrēsia*. Its denotation shifts to a true discourse that is directed toward the soul of the individual (which even in its most political form is directed toward the soul of the Prince). This long trajectory is traced in Foucault's course *The Government of Self and Others*, and yet, as is stated in the summary to the final lecture, it is only a part of an even larger project, an even longer historical continuum, extending back in time from the *History of Sexuality*, as a most distant genealogy of confession.[62] The transformation of the meaning and function of *parrēsia* in antiquity is produced by two paradoxes identified by Foucault in terms of the relation between *parrēsia* and democracy; two sets of problems that Foucault explicitly relates also to modern, representative democracy. The first paradox appears in *Ion* and in Thucydides' account of Pericles' speeches before the Assembly: while *parrēsia* as true political discourse can only be guaranteed by democracy, it is at the same time at odds with democracy's egalitarian structure – that is, when it takes the form of influence and power or authority over others, when it is something practiced by a select few – that is, by the front rank – or by the most distinguished citizen, as in the case with Pericles. There is here an unresolved contradictory relation between *politeia* and *dynasteia*: between, on the one hand, the democratic, egalitarian constitution, and, on the other, *dynasteia* both in its original sense of exercise of power, and in the sense of oligarchy or dynasty. With this exercise of authority over others, with this socially stratified or class-determined access to speaking the truth in public, the city is governed in a way that exhibits a tension between *parrēsia* and democracy: "True discourse and the emergence of true discourse underpins the process of governmentality. If democracy can be governed, it is because there is a true discourse."[63]

---

[61] Foucault, *The Government of Self and Others*, 180.
[62] Foucault, *The Government of Self and Others*, 359.
[63] Foucault, *The Government of Self and Others*, 184.

The second paradox appears in *Orestes*, a tragedy written by Euripides ten years after *Ion*. The paradox concerns the *parrēsia* that is called *amathēs*, uneducated, i.e., the bad *parrēsia* indexed neither to truth nor reason, but rather to something like persuasion, flattery, and rhetoric. This kind of false *parrēsia* plays an important role in the political-judicial events of the tragedy: the Argivian Assembly are persuaded to condemn Orestes to death (Orestes has killed his mother Clytemnestra to avenge his father Agamemnon; the sentence however, after many events and the divine intervention of Apollo, is never carried out). So, while the first paradox concerns *parrēsia* as social status and what we may call the anti-democratic influence of aristocratic, plutocratic, technocratic, or meritocratic tendencies within democracy, the second paradox concerns the evil twin of *parrēsia*: the bad *parrēsia* that drives out the good *parrēsia*. This second paradox holds that while there can be no democracy without true discourse, this true discourse or good *parrēsia* must survive the joust with bad *parrēsia* in the free debate of democracy; if it doesn't, then both true discourse and democracy might come to an end. The proliferation of this bad *parrēsia* in democratic Athens is acknowledged by several writers at the time: Isocrates, Demosthenes and others. Isocrates is certain of its reasons in his treatise *On the Peace*, when he reproaches the citizens at the Assembly for not paying equal attention to the speakers, for favoring those who flatter them and for throwing out speakers who do not agree with their desires. This kind of dangerous and false truth-telling appears, according to Isocrates, when "just anybody can speak:" anybody, rather than the ones belonging to the front rank or, at the very least, to the city itself and its soil by their bloodline.[64]

Bad *Parrēsia* and its Equivalents Today

The bad *parrēsia* of our time often gets labelled as populism. While populism is an ambiguous and contested term, it at least has the merit of pointing to what still seems to be the undisputed source of the problem: the people, the lower classes, the *hoi polloi*, and the possibility of popular influence.[65] What may be disputed is the desirability or necessity of such popular influence,

---

[64] As quoted in Foucault, *The Government of Self and Others*, 182.

[65] The ambiguous and contested nature of populism, and the fact thhat populism has come to be used as a way to label movements or parties of a dangerous, irresponsible, and potentially authoritarian kind is of a rather recent invention. During the 19th and early 20th century the term was used assertively in the more literal sense of belonging to the people; the pejorative sense of a threat or danger is essentially a post-war phenomenon, not without its own political agenda. See: Marco D'Eramo, "Populism and the new Oligarchy," *New Left Review*, 82 July/Aug 2013.

along with the desirability or necessity of the social divisions that structure this whole problematic. Then there are the obvious imperfections in drawing a parallel between bad *parrēsia* in antiquity and today's false truth-telling in political discourse: while Isocrates (in his aristocratic assumption that truth will only be spoken by the privileged) lamented that "just anybody can speak" and that there had appeared poor and uneducated people among the political speakers, today's biggest false truth-tellers generally belong to the political and/or economic elite, assigning the poor and uneducated to the side of the listeners, limiting their role to voting, or not voting.

Regardless of how one understands the causal relations between class divisions and how 'false' true discourse is spread, there is still the problem of how to tell apart the good from the bad *parrēsia* as it is practiced by the public orator – a problem Foucault does not pursue very far, though it remains a subterranean line of inquiry in his analyses. While the true, good *parrēsia* is characterized by courage, by speaking one's mind freely and honestly, and by unselfishly stating that which goes against prevailing opinion no matter the risk, all these things are the first claims or pretentions of *parrēsia amathēs* as well, and form the basis of how any demagogue or corrupt promoter of self-interest will present their discourses. A courageous speaking of the truth seems to be the first characteristic of the leaders of today's authoritarian political movements, when they lie, deceive, and flatter general opinion in their own bid to power and profit. Understood this way, Foucault's definition of political *parrēsia* in the image of the perfect public orator, Pericles, also provides the description of how the shrewdest and most deceitful demagogues and flatterers will appear. As for how to distinguish between them, Foucault offers no suggestion. And as easily detected as they may seem to some, the imposters of the recent anti-democratic, proto-totalitarian and nationalist, alt-right, political movements and leaders that "courageously" denounce "elites" and "fake news" have been gladly accepted and embraced by political majorities built on hundreds of millions of people in some of the world's largest representative democracies during the last decade – like the US under Trump and Brazil under Bolsonaro. This is not the place to go into any discussion of ideology, hegemony, or the complex phenomenon of working class and middle-class support for policies and candidates that cater to the economic interests of those above them, even when proving unbeneficial to the general welfare of the broader population. What is interesting here is that these policies and candidates appear in the heroic form of the truth-teller. And while Foucault does not discuss the problem of telling the true *parrēsia* and its evil twin apart – there exists in Foucault's work no qualitative definition like the Rancièrian notion of politics, which is always founded upon claiming the principle of equality – his concluding words in the lecture on February 2 1983 suggest that he noted the gravity of the problem:

> [I]n a time like ours, when we are so fond of posing the problems of democracy in terms of the distribution of power, of the autonomy of each in the exercise of power, in terms of transparency and opacity, and of the relation between civil society and the State, I think it may be a good idea to recall this old question, which was contemporary with the functioning of Athenian democracy and its crises, namely the question of true discourse and the necessary, indispensable, and fragile caesura that true discourse cannot fail to introduce into a democracy which both makes this discourse possible and constantly threatens it.[66]

These words apply both to the recent years of "post-truth," bad *parrēsia*, and the proliferation of absurdly non-factual statements from some of the world's most powerful leaders, on the one hand, and to a longer historical development, on the other, in which the truth of government has been increasingly provided by a technical or even technocratic, analytic and scientific groundwork of economic theory, policy, and interest. Indeed, this may be another way to think what Foucault calls a caesura in democracy and its form of political discourse. In any case, we can see how Foucault's attention to the public orator – and this early form of *parrēsia* as true discourse at the Assembly – forms a principal area of discussion with respect to the relation between truth and democracy, a kind of new starting point in his historical-philosophical investigation of the concept of *parrēsia*, and an invitation to reflect on the possibilities of speaking the truth, today, in the political realm of the public field.

"Philosophical *Parrēsia*" and the Political Advisor

About halfway through his 1983 lectures, *The Government of Self and Others*, following the discussion of the public orator as truth-teller at the *ekklēsia* of democracy, Foucault turns to look closer at another figure he finds in Plato's letters: the advisor of the prince, the philosopher's advice as a kind of truth-telling to the autocratic ruler of the city state. Plato's letters are texts attributed to Plato, some of which were written at a much later point in antiquity, when real or more often fictional letters had become an

---

[66] Foucault, *The Government of Self and Others*, 184.

important genre: shorter pieces meant to circulate as manifestoes, treatises, or public letters. Thus Foucault understands them as good testimonies of, if not the actual role of the philosophers of the Platonic school in Greek political life, then at least of the kind of intervention they had in mind.[67] He studies letter V, letter VIII, and most substantially letter VII, which was possibly written by Plato himself, or somebody reasonably close to him, not long after his death. The events described in the letter form a continuation of the events in Sicily described by Plutarch that Foucault brought up in his first lectures, about Plato's journey to Syracuse, and his meeting with Dion and the tyrant Dionysius I. In his account of the subsequent events, Plato gives a kind of "political autobiography" as a reply to the friends of the now deceased Dion, whom Plato had gotten to know as a young man. Foucault recounts Plato's decision to return to Syracuse as a political advisor, and shows how it is based on three things: *philia, kairos, ergon*: friendship (to Dion, the advisor to the tyrant Dionysius, who might be endangered without Plato's assistance); the opportunity or right moment (with the death of Dionysius I and the successsion of Dionysius II, a young monarch had come to power, ready to listen to the philosopher's advice); the task or real action (*ergon* as opposed to *logos*). Above all, Foucault devotes himself to explicate Plato's focus on *ergon*, the moment when philosophy ceases to be merely theory and proves itself as practice:

> [I]f the *logos* is in fact related to the construction of the ideal city, then the *ergon*, which must complete the philosopher's task with regard to politics, is actually the task of the political counselor and of the elaboration, through the Prince's soul, of the rationality of the real conduct of the city. It is by taking part directly, through *parrēsia*, in the formation, maintenance, and exercise of an art of governing that the philosopher will be not merely *logos* in the political realm, but really *logos* and *ergon*, in accordance with the ideal of Greek rationality.[68]

This responds to what we may call Foucault's insistence on the performative aspect of philosophy. It is what we identified in the form and style of the early works and their montage-like way that "obliges the reader to create" during his reading; it is what we saw in the publication of his so-called found books and his attention to their performative aspect, for example in legal battles; and it is what is at stake in Foucault's discussion of Goethe's *Faust* and the

---

[67] Foucault, *The Government of Self and Others*, 209.
[68] Foucault, *The Government of Self and Others*, 219.

deeds of which Faust thought philosophy incapable. Here, in the 1983 lectures at Collège de France, it is again a matter of how philosophy (echoing the previous year's lectures on Stoicism and Epicureanism), cannot merely be *mathēsis*, but must also be *askēsis*.[69] If philosophy is not merely an acquisition of knowledge but a way of life, a manner of being, and a work on the self, then the philosopher cannot merely occupy himself with it as a theoretical problem, but must also consider the problem of the city because it shapes the life of the many; he cannot be content with being merely the word, reason, or *logos*, but must also put his hand to work, to the task, to *ergon*. "And what is it to put one's hand to *ergon*? It is to be the real counselor of a real politician in the field of the political decisions he really has to take."[70] To put things in perspective, Foucault juxtaposes letter VII with *Alcibiades*, comparing Plato's motif to Socrates' gesture of assistance to the young Alcibiades: while Socrates enters into dialogue with the beautiful and soon to be powerful youngster, it is merely out of *eros*; Plato, on the other hand, approaches political power in order to put his hand to *ergon*. And this *ergon* means to ask the question of "philosophy's reality," the question of philosophy's essential field of intervention. While it is often held that philosophy must tell the truth about science, the conditions of secure knowledge, or the truth about truth, Foucault emphasizes the importance of this short passage in Plato's letter because it defines the reality of philosophy in a wholly different way: philosophical veridiction (whether its claims are actually true or false) consists in "speaking the truth [...] to power," something which has since become one of its permanent principles.[71]

What does it mean to speak the truth to power, and how does it function in Plato's account? Following the Greek text closely in his reading, Foucault identifies and discusses three conditions. First, philosophy can only address itself to someone who listens. Thus Plato only accepts to go to Sicily because he is assured he will be properly heard: listening forms the first proof or test of reality. The second condition is similar and connected to the first, in that it concerns the seriousness of the listener; but as we shall see, it has further implications. Plato writes: "When I arrived, I thought my first task was to prove whether Dionysius was really on fire with philosophy, or whether the many reports that came to Athens were without foundation."[72] To this end,

---

[69] Foucault makes no mention of his discussion of the *mathēsis-askēsis* problem in the various schools of Hellenistic philosophy during the previous year's course.

[70] Foucault, *The Government of Self and Others*, 219.

[71] Foucault, *The Government of Self and Others*, 230.

[72] Plato, "Letter VII" in *Complete Works*, 340b.

Plato had devised a test particularly suited to tyrants, "especially to those whose heads are full of half-understood doctrines:" one must simply, says Plato in Foucault's translation, "show such people, these tyrants, what *to pragma* is [...]; through what activities, what practices (*di'hosōn pragmatōn*) [it is practiced]; and what effort it involves and presupposes (*kai hoson ponon ekhei*)."[73] The true lover of wisdom will then throw himself at this strenuous labor, ready for all efforts. Those, however, who are not really philosophers "but have only a coating of opinions, like men whose bodies are tanned by the sun," will either give up, or claim that they have heard it all before, and pretend to master it perfectly; which is what Dionysius did. So, in addition to the courageous confrontation, on one level, speaking truth to power means to speak or transmit the essence of philosophy itself. On another level, this essence or this *pragma*, this thing that philosophy is, gets a specific definition in the *pragmata*: the practices, exercises, and activities in which one engages on a continuous basis, in everyday life. This is not insignificant: "The text says no more or less than this, which is fundamental nevertheless, that the reality of philosophy, the reality of philosophizing, that to which the word philosophy refers, is a set of *pragmata* (practices)."[74] The proof of the pudding is in the eating, it seems. Foucault again compares the letter to *Alcibiades*, and notes a series of contrasts: in *Alcibiades* there is the conversion of the gaze inward, to the eternal realities and the divine element of the soul; here it is a conversion to the self as a set of practices, much more similar to that of the Hellenistic philosophy discussed by Foucault during the previous year. The second condition is thus something like the care of the self: "The reality of philosophy is this work of self on self."[75] The third condition concerns knowledge: while Dionysius, in Plato's eyes, fails philosophy both as a form of listening and as a practice of the self, he subsequently also misunderstands it by writing a treatise on the fundamental questions of philosophy, by putting it in the form of *mathēmata*, as formulae of knowledge. This is a failure and a misunderstanding, because philosophy is not passed on through the *mathēmata* of a theoretical treatise, but through "*sunousia peri to pragma*," through cohabitation or by living together with the thing itself. It is also an argument that lies close to what Plato has Socrates say in *Phaedrus*, distinguishing real, spoken philosophy from any written account, merely built on "long hours twisting it around, pasting parts together and taking

---

[73] Foucault, *The Government of Self and Others*, 238.
[74] Foucault, *The Government of Self and Others*, 239.
[75] Foucault, *The Government of Self and Others*, 242.

them apart".[76] At this point of the letter, Plato presents a whole theory of knowledge as a complex process of what he calls the *tribē*, the rubbing or friction between five different forms of knowledge (name/ *onoma*, definition/*logos*, image/*eidōlon*, science/*epistēmē*, reason and understanding/*nous*). To Plato, this process is not compatible with any simplistic production of *mathēmata*: "For this reason anyone who is seriously studying high matters will be the last to write about them," whether they concern "the laws of a legislator or a composition on any other subject."[77] This rejection has consequences for his own written work, not least the *Laws* and the *Republic*, very much concerned with nomothetic projects. In response to this paradox, Foucault advances the hypothesis that the law-giving and constitutional propositions of these works should be taken with caution, similar to what Plato says regarding myth and how it should not be taken literally.[78] In any case, according to Letter VII, the serious activity of philosophy does not appear in the written form, but in the action or the *ergon* of Plato's agreement to meet with the one who exercises political power, and in his insistence that ultimately this *ergon* or this reality of philosophy is found in the relationship of self to self.

Philosophical Advice to Political Power as a Test of Reality

After having analyzed letter VII in its philosophical content, and in Plato's explanation for his decisions of accepting Dion's invitation, Foucault turns to the content of the advice (which also figures in Letter VIII), warning that it "risks being rather disappointing when we look at it," "more moral than really political" and "nothing which appears to be very interesting."[79] Compared to Richelieu or Machiavelli or even other political writings during antiquity, they appear as "bland platitudes,"[80] with no intention of telling

---

[76] Plato, *Phaedrus*, in *Complete Works*, 274b–279c.

[77] Plato, "Letter VII" in *Complete Works*, 344c.

[78] Here Foucault's hypothesis seems to converge with some elements of the theory of Plato's "unwritten doctrines" (Plato's metaphysical theories said to have been taught at the Academy, but never included in his dialogues) mentioned by Aristotle in *Metaphysics* and *Physics*, and professed by the Tübingen School in their attempt to reconstruct the doctrines. In a detailed engagement with the question of the oral versus the written in Plato's Letter VII in particular, Thomas A. Szlezak makes an argument somewhat similar to Foucault's, even noting that according to Plato in Letter VII, "[p]hilosophical knowledge is not a means to an end but an end in itself, and should therefore be passed on properly, with necessary circumspection, not promulgated mechanically." See Aristotle, *Physics*, 209b13–15, and Thomas A. Szlezak, *Reading Plato*, trans. Graham Zanker (London: Routledge, 1999/2005), 86.

[79] Foucault, *The Government of Self and Others*, 260.

[80] Foucault, *The Government of Self and Others*, 261.

politics what it has to do, but what the governor or prince has to be. At one point, Foucault even excuses the fact that "this Platonic advice has a rather banal appearance which makes its analysis somewhat tedious."[81] What, then, keeps him reading and analyzing these texts? Presumably two things. The first is that he finds in Plato's letter what he had found among the Stoics and Epicureans during the previous year's lectures, and something in conflict with what Plato expresses in *Alcibiades*, where the best part of oneself is found through *anamnesis* in the divine element of the soul: now, the equivalent to the best part of oneself is found in a relation to oneself that is tested, exercised, and manifested in the everyday practices of this world. As was mentioned above, in *The Hermeneutics of the Subject* Foucault describes this as a certain self-finalization of the care of the self: this "self-finalization" is Foucault's expression for the Hellenistic injunction to care for oneself not in order to be able to successfully govern others, to achieve a certain goal, or to be ready for adulthood; but to care for oneself continuously, because the self – and by consequence the care of the self – is an end in itself. In the previous chapter, we identified this kind of merging of means and ends as a recurring conceptual figure in Foucault's late work. Now it seems to buttress the reading Foucault provides of Plato's letters on several levels. One example is when he seizes upon Plato's test of Dionysius, when Plato shows the tyrant "through what activities, what practices" philosophy comes about. Because in a sense, the very test is passed only if one realizes that these means of philosophy are its end, and not something one may already know or master perfectly. Another example is Plato's rejection or critique of writing: one may write a book, but one cannot consider it as something as serious as the process of knowledge itself. In what may appear as a paradox, the means of thinking cannot be instrumentalized, because it forms an end in itself. Something similar applies to the act of speaking truth to political power: as the *ergon* and task, as the very proof or test of the reality of philosophy, it functions much like how Foucault in *The Hermeneutics of the Subject* describes *askēsis* as a practice of truth. In ascesis, there is a subjectivation of truth, an act of incorporating and making truth one's own. Important in this regard are both the concept *paraskeue*, the preparation or exercise that produces the "transformation of *logos* into *ethos*,"[82] and *gumnazein*, Epictetus' idea of the individual exercising or putting into practice a certain truth, "that is to say, training in real life, trying to endure the trial, the test of reality."[83] So, similar

---

[81] Foucault, *The Government of Self and Others*, 280.

[82] Foucault, *The Hermeneutics of the Subject*, 327.

[83] Foucault, *The Government of Self and Others*, 359.

to how the individual engaged in philosophical ascesis transforms *logos* into *ethos* in a test of reality, philosophy itself transforms *logos* into *ergon* in its own test of reality, i.e. the confrontation with political power in which it must above all reiterate itself.

This figure of merging means and ends is important as a driving force in Foucault's reading of Plato's seventh letter. And its isomorphic reappearance in different parts of Foucault's late thought suggests a more general importance: Foucault seems on his way to formulate an ethics and a politics, if not of immediacy, then perhaps a kind of "mediacy" – something one could confirm by how he framed certain public interventions.[84] But this recurring conceptual figure is only one of two things that may have motivated Foucault's relentless analysis of Plato's letters, despite the "feeble, banal, and general character of Plato's advice to his correspondents."[85] The other has to do with the figure of the political advisor, and the importance in how the philosopher does not want to remain just *logos*, but also to intervene in and affect reality. This is important not only in a general, historical sense – in how it seems "to mark one of the fundamental features of what is and will be philosophical practice in the West" and in how philosophy's practice of veridiction in relation to power has become "one of the permanent principles of its reality for at least two and a half millennia"[86] – but also for other, much more immediate reasons. At the time when Foucault is giving these lectures, the question of the political advisor had been dramatically actualized, in France as well as for Foucault himself. As Marcelo Hoffman has shown, it may very well be Foucault's own "parrhesiastic engagement with the French government [that] provoked him to plunge headlong into a sustained set of reflections on *parrēsia* for the remaining years of his life."[87]

The New Socialist Government and the Intellectuals

In 1981 the Socialist Party won a historic victory in France, and François Mitterrand became the first socialist president of the Fifth Republic, after having secured a common program and a coalition agreement with the Communist Party. This was a major political shift of government that would

---

[84] In multiple public comments and interviews Foucault took a position that refused "strategic terms" and demanded a politics coherent with the moral and ethical position otherwise held. See Foucault, "L'expérience morale et sociale de Polonais ne peut plue être effacée" in *Dits et écrits II, 1976–1988*, no 321, 1166–67, and "Sur l'attitude du gouvernement francais à propos de la Pologne" in *Signés Foucault et Cie*, ed. Philippe Artières (Paris: Editions de la Sorbonne, 2020), 121–122.
[85] Foucault, *The Government of Self and Others*, 286.
[86] Foucault, *The Government of Self and Others*, 230.
[87] Marcelo Hoffman, *Foucault and Power* (London/New York: Bloomsbury, 2015), 134.

affect the political and intellectual map in highly unexpected ways. In a short span of time, the relations deteriorated between the Mitterand government and the intellectuals on the left; an abysmal schism opened between those in power who seemed to expect unconditional support and those who may have expected more influence and greater adherence to the principles of the relatively progressive electoral platforms, *110 Propositions pour la France* and the *Programme commun*.[88] Contested issues included everything from the reform of voting rights for immigrants to the penal system, but most central was the Government's non-condemnation of the military coup in Poland led by General Jaruzelski in December 1981 and its repression of the *Solidarność* movement: a position Foucault refused to accept, and condemned in the strongest possible terms (Foucault was also a part of the French chapter of *Solidarność*; more on this below, in chapter 5). In a long and bitter war of words, government representatives wrote debate articles against the intellectuals who responded with public appeals of protest and estrangement. In an article in *Le Matin*, the minister of Culture, Jack Lang, notably accused the intellectuals of being guilty of "typical structuralist inconsequence".[89] Foucault in his turn, refused to have anything to do with the government and its representatives – or at least claimed so.[90]

This is the domestic political situation – a heated and infected public debate on how the Left should govern, and what role should be played by the intellectuals in relation to this power. It is against this backdrop that Foucault decides to lecture on the role of the privileged speakers in the assemblies of classical Greece, on the philosopher as advisor to the prince, on the true discourse in relation to government. To parts of the audience, the parallel must have been quite striking. To us, it may help explain why Foucault's reading gravitates around Plato's letters numbered VII and VIII, commenting on them in such detail. First, there is the opportunity, "a *kairos* in which, a young monarch having come to power and being ready to listen to philosophy" that is mirrored in and through a socialist and communist-backed government that, on the basis of shared ideological and political positions, for the first time since the postwar years seemed ready to listen to intellectuals on the left. Then, there is the task or action as the very reality of philosophy: "It is that Plato did not want to appear to be merely *logos*, to be

---

[88] "110 propositions pour la France: Programme de gouvernement préparé par le Parti socialiste (PS) pour l'élection présidentielle d'avril-mai 1981," September 2012, https://www.monde-diplomatique.fr/mav/124/A/51865.

[89] Jack Lang, *Le Matin*, quoted in Eribon, *Foucault*, 318.

[90] Eribon, *Foucault*, 301–2.

only discourse. [...] He wants to show that he is also capable of taking part and putting his hand to *ergon* (to action)."[91] To act at the right moment, in order to set into play a philosophical truth-telling within the political order; to be the advisor of a power that one does not necessarily support in all respects – it is not too distant from what was at stake in Foucault's immediate surroundings during the first years of the 1980s. The third point or reason for Plato to accept Dion's invitation to Sicily, namely, *philia*, was certainly a bit more complicated in Foucault's case, but not entirely lacking.

Despite his refusal to have any interaction with members of the government, Foucault actually made one significant exception: Robert Badinter, minister of justice. Badinter, a former professor of law, was someone Foucault held in high esteem, finding "their joint discussions about legal and penal problems fascinating."[92] Among the many abandoned projects of this period was a conversation between Foucault and Badinter "on the social function of punishment" to be published in the Gallimard review *Le Débat*, together with the unrealized plans of a co-organized seminar on justice and the penal system, which was to be a kind of practical discussion about some of the issues raised in Foucault's study of prisons, disciplinary society, and punishment.[93] When asked, before the events in Poland unfurled, if he would possibly consider working with the new government, he answered in the affirmative: "Working with a government implies neither subjection nor complete acceptance. One can both do the work and remain restive. I even think that the two things go hand in hand."[94] In other words, it does not seem unlikely that both the prospect and problems of working with the new French government may have piqued Foucault's interest in Plato's journey to Syracuse, and his general theoretical and historical investigation of the philosopher as truth-teller and political advisor. In any case, the fact is that the author of *Discipline and Punish* met regularly with the minister of justice of France, at a time when comprehensive reforms of the judicial system were undertaken, among them the abolition of the death penalty.

In addition to this, in 1983, Foucault also met with Michel Rocard, minister of planning, on a number of occasions. Rocard wanted to commission an official report to be written by Simon Nora, Pierre Bourdieu and Foucault on the governmental policies of culture, education and research (though this never happened). Foucault and Bourdieu had already discussed

---

[91] Foucault, *The Government of Self and Others*, 218.
[92] Macey, *The Lives of Foucault*, 461.
[93] Macey, *The Lives of Foucault*, 461.
[94] Foucault, "Est-il donc important de penser?", 998–99.

the possibility of writing a *livre blanc* on these topics to "explore a 'logic of the left,' emphasizing all the things the Socialists did nothing about, or did too little, or did so badly".[95] The aim was to have the book revised by a group of experts, and, according to Didier Eribon, it was to describe difficulties as well as solutions and concrete actions. Apparently, Foucault considered putting his hand to *ergon* as well; something that was not new to him given his engagement in GIP, the Prisoners' Information Group, even if he had never before given direct advice to government. At the same time, he was wary to "avoid the trap into which those who govern want the intellectuals to fall, and into which they often fall: 'put yourself in our place and tell us what you would do.'"[96] Discussing the current events in a 1984 interview for *Le Monde*, Foucault thus echoes his analysis of Plato and Dionysius in *The Government of Self and Others*, emphasizing the importance for philosophy to remain in a kind of exteriority toward political government, not to fall into the trap of telling those who govern what to do. The echoes, which reverberate between his study of truth-telling in antiquity and his formulations regarding strategies in the political present, are quite clear.

It is, to conclude this section, beyond doubt that Foucault in his 1983 lectures presents problems highly relevant to his own situation, the general political situation in France, as well as the intellectual and public debate at the time. It seems reasonable to assume that his reading of the political advisor of antiquity is stimulated by the acute theoretical-political questions of his own time, and by his own conflicting sense of hesitation and obligation toward a theoretical interaction with the newly elected government. Further, as we have seen, some of the positions on the role of philosophy vis-à-vis power expressed in his work on ancient forms of truth-telling (e.g. do not tell the prince what he must do, but what he must be), reappears in his own comments about events in the political present (e.g. do not fall into the trap of telling those who govern what they must do, or what you would do in their place). And as we saw in the beginning of this chapter, regarding the disparate inclusion of the discussion of Kant's "*Was ist Aufklärung?*", Foucault more or less tells us to read these lectures from 1983 and onward as an investigation of the present. Similar to how, in the first chapter of *Discipline and Punish*, Foucault sets out to write a "history of the present",[97] now, in the opening lecture of 1983, he defines and adheres to the critical tradition of an "ontology

---

[95] Eribon, *Foucault*, 307.
[96] Michel Foucault "Une esthétique de l'existence" in *Dits et écrits II, 1976–1988*, No 357, 1553.
[97] Foucault, *Discipline and Punish*, 31.

of the present".[98] But perhaps some prudence is required. While Marcelo Hoffman also shows that "some of the key theoretical developments in Foucault's analysis of *parrēsia* seemed to grow out of his experience of *parrēsia* with the French government," he does so by superimposing Foucault's interventions within the public debate in France during the early 1980s upon his definitions of *parrēsia* he gathers from antiquity, thereby producing one single figure of coinciding contours.[99] To render it so consistently however, risks overlooking the unresolved issues, the contradictions and the ambivalences in Foucault's different interventions on truth-telling within the political field. Rather than Foucault reaching his conclusion on *parrēsia* in antiquity after a certain exchange with the various representatives of the *palais de l'Élysée* in the early 1980s, like a strict theoretical application of his own previous praxis, these lectures should probably be understood as an attempt to formulate the problem, still open and complex. Surely, for instance, Foucault was ready to confront governments in the name of truths far more immersed in practicalities, particular positions, concrete courses of action, and questions of what to do, than in the name of seemingly universal philosophical statements limited to stating what those who govern "must be" – which was one of his conclusions regarding Plato's letters. Perhaps a distant parallel can shed some light on the issue. While there are many differences between Gramsci's interpretation of Machiavelli's *The Prince* as the Italian Communist party and Foucault's possible understanding of Plato's prince as the French Socialist party – not least because the former is explicit in making the connection, while the latter is not – Foucault would surely agree with Gramsci in his assertion that truth in the political field can only emanate from a partisan position rather than an "impartial" or "objective" point of view.[100] And the embrace of such partisan position may complicate the distinctions Foucault makes with regard to philosophical truth-telling, such as when he says that "Philosophy has to play a certain role in relation to politics; it does not have to play any role in politics."[101]

Finally, too much emphasis on the continuity between Foucault's own theory and praxis will overlook the other important aspect of the function of truth-telling that was raised above. The whole notion of *ergon*, the action or task, as a test of reality for philosophy – as the moment when it appears both

---

[98] Foucault, *The Government of Self and Others*, 21.

[99] Marcelo Hoffman, *Foucault and Power* London/New York: Bloomsbury, 2015, 135.

[100] Antonio Gramsci, *Selections from the Prison Notebooks*, ed. and trans. Quentin Hoare and Geoffrey Nowell Smith (New York: International Publishers, 1971), 171–172.

[101] Foucault, *The Government of Self and Others*, 318.

as the means to give advice to the highest political power and at the same proves itself as an end in itself – is important in how it shapes the definitions of both truth-telling and the technologies of the self, and in how it reappears in different parts of Foucault's late work, among the somewhat disparate elements of lectures, interviews, and political organization, acquiring a unifying function, tying them together. Or, as we shall see in the next section, potentially pushing other themes away.

The Cynics and Life itself as *Parrēsia*

In an anecdote recounted by Diogenes Laertius, Plato finds the Cynic Diogenes washing salad, and says: Had you been more polite to Dionysius, you would not have to wash your own salad. To which Diogenes replies: Had you acquired the habit of washing your own salad, you would not have been the slave of Dionysius.[102] In this scene, Foucault sees the opposition between two main modes of philosophical truth-telling in relation to political power since the 4th century BCE: to speak the truth to the Prince to form his soul, or to speak the truth in the public arena "as challenge, confrontation, derision, and criticism with regard to the Prince's action and to political action."[103] In the following section, however, we will try to illuminate another form of opposition between these modes of truth-telling: one that puts Foucault's account of Cynicism and Cynic *parrēsia* at odds or in a kind of tension not only with Plato's attempt to form the Prince's soul, or with the Socratic *parrēsia* as something that stands back from politics to direct itself toward ways of being, but with some of the most important and general points of his reading of the care of the self and *parrēsia* during the last three years of lectures at Collège de France.[104]

It is toward the end of *The Government of Self and Others*, after having traced *parrēsia* from Plato's letters through Socrates' *Apology* and other dialogues (which we will not take up here), that Foucault turns to the Cynics and their "doglike" way of barking at the citizens, of opposing themselves to habits and ridiculing traditional values, of letting naked life manifest itself as *parrēsia* on the *agora*. The same topics form the core of the last lecture course,

---

[102] This highly fictional account is set in Syracuse, perhaps because of the rumors that Plato accepted handouts from Dionysius II. For Foucault's retelling of the anecdote, see Foucault, *The Government of Self and Others*, 292. See Diogenes Laertius, *The Lives of Eminent Philosophers*, trans. Pamela Mensch (Oxford/New York: Oxford University Press, 2018), Book 6:58.

[103] Foucault, *The Government of Self and Others*, 292.

[104] For a longer version of the arguments in this section, see Karl Lydén, "Kritik av kynismen": in *Foucault och antiken*, ed. Sven-Olov Wallenstein & Johan Sehlberg (Stockholm: Tankekraft förlag, 2017).

The Courage of the Truth. Here we shall try to trace a certain tension or friction between what, in the 1984 lectures, Foucault calls "Cynicism as moral category" – i.e. Cynicism understood as a set of moral teachings to have been practiced even after historical Cynicism died out during late antiquity – and on the other hand Foucault's insistence of subjectivity as a process of becoming other, along with what we have defined as the figure of self-finalization, when the care of the self or truth-telling is a means that becomes an end in itself. Can we even identify a contradiction between the relations implied by the Cynic as an emancipatory force and the notion of the subject capable of constituting itself? If this critical attention to the Cynics specifically seems exaggerated – why not the Stoics, for example? – the following investigation should be of interest for at least two reasons, beyond the argument itself. First, Foucault demonstrates a clear enthusiasm for the Cynics' ability to express truth in the form of life as such, and points out that "with Cynicism we have a quite remarkable point which deserves some attention if we want to study the history of truth and the history of the relations of truth and the subject."[105] In Piergiorgio Donatelli's words, there is an important and marked "insistence of the late Foucault on the Cynical tradition as opposed to the Stoic tradition."[106] Second, it seems like his account of the Cynics and their alleged ability to lead us to another life and another world engages today's readers of Foucault, to a higher degree than his account of the Stoics, the Epicureans, and Plato for that matter.[107] In a review of the 1983 and 1984 lectures in *New Left Review* Michael Hardt writes: "We can only imagine how explosive would have been this notion of [the Cynics'] biopolitical militancy if Foucault had been able to deploy it not only at the safe distance of ancient Greece but also in his world."[108] Let us therefore look into the specific and paradoxical status of Foucault's Cynic: as the constant other and wretched poor; as the philosopher with a scandalous lack of doctrine; as king of

---

[105] Foucault, *The Courage of the Truth*, 174.

[106] Piergiorgio Donatelli, "Foucault, éthique et subjectivité" in *Michel Foucault: éthique et vérité 1980–1984*, ed. Daniele Lorenzini, Ariane Revel, Arianna Sforzini (Paris: Vrin 2015), 191.

[107] See the anthology *Michel Foucault: éthique et vérité 1980–1984* (cited above), especially Orazio Irrera's "Satyagraha: un alèthurgie décoloniale," Daniele Lorenzini's "Éthique et politique de nous mêmes," Laura Cremonesi's "Askêsis, êthos, parrêsia," and Marie-Odile Goulet-Cazé's "Foucault et sa vision du cynisme dans *Le Courage de la vérité*." See also Maurizio Lazzarato "Enunciation and Politics: A Parallel Reading of Democracy" in *Foucault, Biopolitics, and Governmentality*, eds. Jakob Nilsson and Sven-Olov Wallenstein (Stockholm: Södertörn Philosophical Studies 2013), 155; Edward F. McGushin, *Foucault's Askēsis: An Introduction to the Philosophical Life* (Evanston: Northwestern University Press, 2007), 163–164; Louisa Shea, *The Cynic Enlightenment: Diogenes in the Salon*. (Baltimore: The Johns Hopkins University Press, 2010), 190.

[108] Michael Hardt, "Militant Life", *New Left Review* 64 (2010), 160.

derision and king of all; as a prefiguration of the avantgarde, or, finally, as someone or something who escapes all of the above, in what must be understood in aesthetic terms, along the lines of what Bakhtin called the highly novelized nature of the Cynics.

The Constant Alterity of the Cynic

When Foucault gave these lectures, very little was published on the Cynics compared with today, and Giannantoni's *Socraticorum Reliquae*, which collected Cynical fragments and testimonies in their original language, was during this time still under publication.[109] As Marie-Odile Goulet-Cazé points out, Foucault was largely dependent on other sources: the predominantly critical perspective of the Stoics in Seneca and Epictetus, for example. It must therefore be stated that this section is not primarily a discussion of Cynicism, but of Foucault's understanding of Cynicism, and its place in his work. In addition to this, the following discussion of Foucault's lectures on Cynicism has no ambition of going through them from start to finish. In fact, let us begin with the very end, with the last, unspoken words of the manuscript from the last lecture Foucault gave at Collège de France, 28 March 1984, a few months before his death – words which, in a footnote, mark the end of the published lectures:

> But what I would like to stress in conclusion is this: there is no establishment of the truth without an essential position of otherness; the truth is never the same; there can be truth only in the form of the other world and the other life (*l'autre monde et de la vie autre*).[110]

Readers of Foucault immediately recognize the insistence on transformation, otherness, and becoming so important to his philosophical practice. This is expressed as early as the preface to *The Archeology of Knowledge* from 1969: "What, do you imagine that I would take so much trouble and so much pleasure in writing, do you think that I would keep so persistently to my task, if I were not preparing – with a rather shaky hand – a labyrinth into which I can venture, in which I can move my discourse, opening up underground passages, forcing it to go far from itself..."[111] And in an interview from 1982 in the US, Foucault refuses to respond to the question whether he is a structuralist, a Marxist, philosopher or historian: "I don't feel that it is necessary

---

[109] Gabriele Giannantoni, *Socraticorum Reliquae* (Rome: Bibliopolis 1983–1985).

[110] Foucault, *The Courage of the Truth*, 340.

[111] Foucault, *The Archeology of Knowledge*, 17.

to know exactly what I am. The main interest in life and work is to become someone else that you were not in the beginning."[112] In one form or another, we recognize the same striving toward transformation through Foucault's whole work, which in its very heterogeneity and mutability confirms his outspoken ambition to do something different with every new book. The question is how well this transformative element, this fundamental ambition to become other, is matched by the incessant insolence and, so to speak, *constant* scandal of the Cynic. Must we not regard the Cynic as someone who lives in an immutable otherness? Someone who can never strive beyond this continuous alterity? Think of Diogenes who, in his self-imposed poverty, leads his life before the eyes of all, sleeps and eats wherever he finds someplace suitable and even satisfies himself sexually on the square. As upsetting as it may be, it is at the same time a stable, constant and, in a sense, predictable negation of all traditional values. The Cynic separates himself radically from society, and vows to continue to live in this way, thereby committing himself to perpetual exteriority and to remaining the same. His voluntary exclusion puts him safely in his place, and the Cynic remains in his tub.

Perhaps this immutable otherness can be further understood by having a look at the life and *parrēsia* of the Cynic in terms of what risks they confer, in light of the previous year's lectures, *The Government of Self and Others*. In these lectures, Foucault cites the risks of truth-telling as the very condition for *parrēsia*. He takes up numerous examples: the letters of Plato and the description of Plato's and Dion's fearless truth-telling before the tyrant of Syracuse (which led to the former's expulsion); the daring speech of Pericles before the Assembly in democratic Athens, and the tragedy *Ion* by Euripides, in which Creusa eventually throws the truth at Apollo, the god who has raped her but refuses to admit paternity for the child whose existence threatens to destroy her status and marriage. In *parrēsia*, one must dare to risk everything in telling the truth before the sovereign, the people, or in an act of accusation toward power that can take many forms: "The discourse, through which someone weak, and despite this weakness, takes the risk of reproaching someone powerful for his injustice, is called, precisely, *parrēsia*."[113] But with regard to the Cynic, it is hardly the same kind of risk: the Cynic, after all, is the one who has left everything behind, who has nothing left to lose, who even strives for infamy and flogging. Consider the "foundational" anecdotes of Cynicism, when the young Diogenes approaches Antisthenes – who is

---

[112] Foucault, "Truth, Power, Self" in *Technologies of the Self*, eds. Luther H. Martin, Huck Gutman and Patrick H. Hutton (Amherst: University of Massachusets Press 1988), 9.
[113] Foucault, *The Government of Self and Others*, 133–134.

regarded as the very first Cynic, or a proto-Cynic, and who was known for not accepting pupils – and follows him around everywhere, as a kind of adherent. When Antisthenes raises his staff to strike, Diogenes offers his head and says: "Strike, for you'll not find wood hard enough to keep me away from you, as long as I think you have something to say."[114] And thus he succeeds in avoiding being struck and in becoming Antisthenes' disciple. Or think of Diogenes' complete discourteousness and insistence to have nothing, which somehow keeps him safe even as he insults the sovereign: according to the story, Diogenes is lying in the sun at the *Craneum*, the hill in Corinth, and Alexander the Great comes up to him and says, "Ask whatever you desire," to which Diogenes simply replies, "Stand out of my light."[115] While Foucault considers this Cynic defiance and the Cynic's scandalous life in general as another form of the courage of the truth, as another way of risking one's life by "displaying" it and "exposing" it,[116] this way of exposing one's life and welcoming infamy seems just as well to function as a way to eliminate any risk. In other words, the Cynic risks nothing, since he has nothing to lose (he wishes to own nothing but his staff and cloak); further, he risks nothing because of the harmlessness of his immutability, of his determination to remain in the "naked life" of humiliation and shamelessness, poverty and alterity.[117]

The truth-telling of the Cynic is evidently not about transforming his own situation: he does not want to change or alter it. He lives in a permanent state of alterity. The question appears, then, to what extent the Cynic life can lead to change or becoming-other for anybody else, or to what extent the position of the Cynic presupposes or even maintains the position of constant normality as something to attack without ever affecting. This continuous, inconclusive, and safely contained counter-conduct can perhaps be illustrated by the scene when Diogenes is entering a theater as everyone else is leaving it; when asked why, he replied, "This has been my practice all my life."[118]

---

[114] Diogenes Laertius, *The Lives of Eminent Philosophers*, Book 6:21.

[115] Ibid., Book 6:38.

[116] Foucault, *The Courage of the Truth*, 233–34.

[117] A decade prior to Agamben's influential discussion of "bare life," Foucault uses the expression to emphasize the Cynic's embrace of bad reputation (*adoxia*) and shamelessness (*anaideia*). While both conceptions of bare life may share a very general sense of lawlessness and exteriority, Foucault's bare life cannot be understood in relation to sovereignty, judicial law, and the distinction between *bios/zoē*, i.e. social life/biological life. See Foucault, *The Courage of the Truth*, 260, 297, and Giorgio Agamben, *Homo Sacer: Sovereign Power and Bare Life*, trans. Daniel Heller-Roazen (Stanford: Stanford University Press, 1998), 6–7.

[118] Diogenes Laertius, *The Lives of Eminent Philosophers*, Book 6:64.

The Scandal and Paradox of Cynicism

Foucault is clear about the reasons for his interest in the Cynics:

> The aim of this practice of the truth characterizing the Cynic life is not just to say and show what the world is in its truth. Its aim, its final aim, is to show that the world will be able to get back to its truth, will be able to transfigure itself and become other in order to get back to what it is in its truth, only at the price of a change, a complete alteration, the complete change and alteration in the relation one has to self. And the source of the transition to that other world promised by Cynicism is found in this return of self to self, in this care of self.[119]

The problem here, it seems, lies in an elision, or perhaps an elision of an elision: the Cynics, as Foucault demonstrates at other points in the lectures but does not mention here, elide or leave out how this complete transition and transformation of the relation to oneself will come about, i.e. how this care of the self should be constituted and carried out practically. This is clear in comparison to the practical instructions and concrete advice given to the Epicurean groups by their masters and the well prescribed Stoic way of life that Foucault describes in the 1982 lectures, when he initiates his work on *epimeleia heautou*, the care of the self, and *parrēsia*. In his *On the Passions and Errors of the Soul*, Galen inculcates the importance of self-devotion throughout one's whole life, and to form a relationship to someone endowed with *parrēsia* who can reveal the truth about that person; the Epictetus, for his part, gives precise directions: you must meditate, you must write, you must practice and exercise.

The Cynic, opposed to all these, offers no general rules for life, and even less does he forge them in collaboration with others within a school or community in order to develop a care of themselves: the practice of the Cynic is negative and manifested in insolence, impudence and conflict in the *bios diakritikos*, the distinct, particular and opposite life. Yet all these actions seem to be based on common, widely accepted precepts or philosophic principles of what is the right way to lead one's life. This is what Foucault calls the paradox of Cynicism: that it essentially contains the dominant traits of the other philosophies or schools of philosophy to which it was more or less contemporary, and yet it succeeds at becoming an offensive practice, a scan-

---

[119] Foucault, *The Courage of the Truth*, 315.

dal, a grimace of a philosophy.[120] Of the many traits that Cynicism has in common with the Socratic, Hellenistic, and Roman philosophical tradition, Foucault lists the view on philosophy as a preparation for life; the insistence on the care of the self; the exhortation to only study what is of use in one's existence, and, finally, the philosophical insight that life should be made to conform with the precepts that one formulates.

But apart from these resonances, a further principle, exclusive to Cynicism, is identified: the task of *paracharattein to nomisma*, the task of changing the value of the currency. Diogenes Laërtius gives different versions of the background to this in his *Lives of Eminent Philosophers*, and the section devoted to Diogenes of Sinope.[121] Among these, it could be that Diogenes' father had "restamped the coinage" or counterfeited money, that it was Diogenes himself who had counterfeited money, and/or that he had received the advice from the Oracle in Delphi to change the value of the "currency of the city" or "civic currency," which has an even clearer metaphorical sense of social customs.[122] It is an act which, by definition, appears to belong to a symbolic level, like all of Diogenes' acts described by Diogenes Laertius: like, for example, when Diogenes is walking the streets of Athens with a lantern in broad daylight shouting the words "I'm looking for a man", intended as a demonstration of the difficulty of finding someone worthy of that description. This divine task to change the value of the currency (in the metaphorical sense of habits, customs, etc), practiced with irony, derision, sarcasm, in a kind perpetual performance, in combination with the pursuit of *adoxia*, with the intended aim of tarnishing one's reputation (something completely unique and unheard of during antiquity) can of course explain the paradox in which Cynicism shares most of its features with its contemporary philosophical traditions, even while it still manages to cause a scandal.

---

[120] In Goulet-Cazé's highly appreciative commentary of Foucault's view of the Cynics, one of her more critical objections concerns Foucault's idea of this so-called syncretism and banality of Cynicism, suggesting that he is over-reliant on the "all but impartial" emperor Julian. See Marie-Odile Goulet-Cazé, "Foucault et sa vision du cynisme dans *Le Courage de la vérité*" in *Michel Foucault: éthique et vérité 1980–1984*, 116.

[121] Diogenes Laertius, *The Lives of Eminent Philosophers*, Book 6:20.

[122] The editor of Diogenes Laertius' *The Lives of Eminent Philosophers*, James Miller, explains in a couple of footnotes: "The phrase restamp the currency (*paracharattein to nomisma*) bears a double meaning, explored by Diogenes in what follows. *Nomisma* can refer not just to coinage, but to social customs, and to 'restamp' these can mean to violate custom or innovate in the social sphere. [...] In the original, what is said to be Apollo's phrase *politikon nomisma* contains a further ambiguity, since *politikon* can mean 'of a (single) city' or 'of civic life (generally).'" See Diogenes Laertius, *The Lives of Eminent Philosophers*, 269, n. 29, n. 33.

But that is probably not the whole explanation. Perhaps the most "scandalous" aspect is the absence of a written and coherent theoretical basis, it's doctrinal thinness, as well as the absence of a practice that involves other people in more permanent, lasting and transformative ways. Foucault describes the way Cynicism resembles all other philosophies yet lacks any theoretical or practical substance as its "scandalous banality".[123] And in comparison with its contemporary movements of philosophical thought – let us say, the Epicurean ambition to study *physis*, to speak the truth about nature and to deduce an ethical and political mode of life from this materialist worldview, and on the other hand the Stoic emphasis on ascesis, preparation and exercises that structure the way of being – this lack of "doctrinal mediation" and of any means of guidance, advice or positive directions seems to be a serious obstacle to arriving at a generalized Cynic care of the self.[124] The paradox and scandal of Cynicism can thus be understood as its refusal or unwillingness to define any steps toward reaching the life it calls for, its reluctance to propose even a preliminary action or practice: a theoretical-practical vacuity in the proposed transformation of the self.

The Cynic as King and Observer from Above

While the *bios kynikos*, the dog-like life of the Cynic, is famous, and while we have come to know him as naked except for his rough cloak, barefoot and almost completely without possessions, the idea of the Cynic's subordinated position does not seem to be entirely correct. There is obviously something appealing in the perspective from below, the humor and constant rebellion of the Cynic – it might even seem tempting to join ranks with the likes of Peter Sloterdijk when he hails an ideal which he likens to "pick[ing] one's nose while Socrates exorcises his demon and speaks of the divine soul", "lets a fart fly against the Platonic theory of ideas" and "answers Plato's subtle theory of eros by masturbating in public."[125] And yet, the man who lives such a dog's life, described as an urban "plebeian

---

[123] Foucault, *The Courage of the Truth*, 232.

[124] This aspect of Cynicism can be recognized also in what Foucault calls "the great exteriorization of the problem of the philosophical life in relation to philosophy." Noting its importance, Foucault does not develop or fully explain so much in his late lectures, the paradoxical or contradictory relation between this exteriorization and his insistence on philosophical life *within* philosophy, along with Hadot's notion of "philosophy as way of life." See Foucault, *The Courage of the Truth*, 237.

[125] Peter Sloterdijk, *Critique of Cynical Reason*, trans. Michael Eldred, (Minneapolis/London: University of Minnesota Press 1987), 101.

figure"[126] and representative of a "popular philosophy"[127] , has given himself the title king. With Epictetus, Foucault describes the Cynic not only as king of poverty or the king of himself (in the context of Diogenes' response to Alexander the Great's claim that "if I had not been Alexander, I would have liked to be Diogenes"), but also as the one who possesses the actual function of exerting *politeia*: not in terms of taxes, wars, the public affairs of the city, but in terms of happiness and misfortune, freedom and slavery. In this perspective, the Cynic is the restored king, who takes part in the government of Zeus and who rules over the universe, over everything and everyone. This aspect of the Cynic is often forgotten or omitted from the account of his political virtue. Diogenes Laërtius recounts the episode – which Foucault also takes up – when Diogenes is to be sold as slave. To the question of what he can do, Diogenes replies: Govern men.[128]

Foucault takes another example, from Seneca, in which the Cynic Demetrius flatly refuses a large sum of money from Caligula, stating: "If he wanted to tempt me, he should have offered me the whole Empire."[129] Foucault apparently interprets it as a difference in degree, as if the money was too little and it simply would have taken more of something. But it seems more adequate to regard it as a difference in kind. The fact that the full power over the empire is at stake coincides with the highest task that the Cynic assigns to himself, namely to govern each and every one.

The account that Foucault here gives of the Cynics' care for others, the Cynics' elevated watch over the people, contrasts to the common view of the Cynic as operating from a subordinate position. It is a perspective from above: the Cynic governs the universe, he is "restored, beyond his hidden monarchy, in true sovereignty, which is that of the gods over the whole of humankind. This is the reversal of the theme of sovereignty in the Cynics."[130] Indeed, the specialist in the field of the history of antiquity, Pierre Hadot, shows that while this birds-eye perspective is common to all ancient philosophy, it is by far most frequently employed by the Cynics:

---

[126] Sloterdijk, *Critique of Cynical Reason*, 4.

[127] Foucault, *The Courage of the Truth*, 202.

[128] Diogenes Laertius, *Lives of Eminent Philosophers Volume 2*, trans. R.D. Hicks, Book VI: 20, (Cambridge: Harvard University Press, Loeb Classical Library 1925), 31.

[129] Foucault, *The Courage of the Truth*, 193–194.

[130] Foucault, *The Courage of the Truth*, 303.

When the view from above takes on this specific form of observing human beings on earth, it seems more than ever to belong to the Cynic tradition. We find it being used with particular effectiveness by Lucian, a contemporary of Marcus Aurelius who was strongly influenced by Cynic doctrines. In Lucian's dialogue entitled *Icaromenippus*, or the *Sky-man*, the Cynic Menippus confides to a friend that he was so disillusioned by the contradictory teachings of the philosophers concerning the ultimate principles and the universe that he resolved to fly up heaven to see for himself how things were. He fitted himself out with a pair of wings – on the left side a vulture's wing and on the right side that of an eagle – and soared upwards towards the moon. [...] After Menippus has recited a long list of the crimes and adulteries he had seen committed inside people's homes, he sums up his overall impression: what he saw was a cacophonous, ridiculous hodge-podge of a play. [...] Once he leaves the moon, Menippus travels among the stars until he arrives at the dwelling-place of Zeus. There, he has a good laugh over the ridiculously contradictory nature of the prayers mankind address to Zeus.[131]

This laugh from above – along with the elements of commanding and governing in Cynicism – would not be so significant were it not combined with what we mentioned before: nothing at all. That is to say, the lack of doctrine, teachings, *mathēsis*, in sum the lack of any practice that would include or engages others in a continuous and systematic fashion. How does this king of derision then engage with his subjects? With what right and by what principle does he govern others, and with what consequences?

Cynicism and the Avantgarde

We have described the facets of Cynicism that make the Cynic an ironic, distanced and elevated figure, who professes an "other" life but remains the same, immutable in his constant alterity. The Cynic offers no theoretical and practical mediation for his listeners to engage with, but considers himself superior, with the right to command over them. Now, every aspect of Cynicism may not be embraced by Foucault, just as not all of the forms of truth-telling and ancient practices of truth in his account are taken as exemplary. Tracing the notion of *parrēsia* in Plato, for instance, Foucault recounts without further remarks how in the *Laws*, *parrēsia* is professed as a way to make the citizens uphold religious festivals, choral singing, military exercise, and good order in sexual life – not precisely the emancipatory, free, and courageous stating of truth in the face of power that he seizes upon elsewhere. Yet Cynicism as a philosophy "in which mode of life and truth-

---

[131] Hadot, *Philosophy as a Way of Life*, 245–246.

telling are directly and immediately linked to each other" has an important status for Foucault. Therefore, we must look into the sides of Cynicism that seems opposed or contradictory to the general project Foucault advances, particularly as it is framed by his reading of Kant's "*Was ist Aufklärung?*".

To Kant, as we recall, "Enlightenment is mankind's exit from its self-incurred tutelage."[132] "Immaturity" or "tutelage" is the inability to make use of one's reason or understanding without the guidance of another: to replace one's understanding with a book, one's conscience with a *Seelsorger*, and to have a doctor decide one's diet. Yet even when trying to exit this state of immaturity, one may fall back into it, if one opts to follow those who Kant defines as guardians, and who, according to Foucault, "decide to play the role of liberators:"

> Now, he [Kant] says, in reality these individuals, who are like spiritual or political leaders, cannot get humanity out of its tutelage. Why is this? Precisely because they began by placing others under their authority, so that these others, being thus accustomed to the yoke, cannot bear the freedom and emancipation they are given.[133]

Here we see one of the central points of these lectures: it is impossible to lead others to freedom. For Foucault, Kant's text on the Enlightenment links ancient philosophy with today's philosophy, it serves as a way to reflect on today's philosophy and how it relates to the present, and it lastly broaches his own work within the tradition of critical philosophy. It is opposed to the Cynic tradition of showing and governing others onto the right path. We may also recall Foucault's emphasis on the philosophical care of the self as something that was always developed within, and specific to a particular group, sect, school, or community, as opposed to the general, common population. This is another difference in the Cynic strategy:

> The Cynic battle is an explicit, intentional, and constant aggression directed at humanity in general, at humanity in its real life, and whose horizon or objective is to change its moral attitude (its ethos) but, at the same time and thereby, its customs, conventions, and ways of living.[134]

---

[132] Immanuel Kant, "What is Enlightenment?" in *What is Enlightenment?*, ed. James Schmidt, (Berkeley: University of California Press 1996), 56.
[133] Foucault, *The Government of Self and Others*, 33–34.
[134] Foucault, *The Courage of the Truth*, 280.

To change the moral attitude and ways of living of others, of those who are slaves to customs and conventions, is evidently not far from deciding to play "the role of liberators."[135] The contradiction sharpens if we turn to what Foucault calls "Cynicism as a moral category". Cynicism as a trans-historical category, as something that reappears in its religious, political, and aesthetic descendents; forms of later Cynicism as opposed to the historical, ancient Cynicism.

The first great descendent appears in Christianity, both in the doctrinal recognition such as by Saint Augustine and Saint Jerome, and in the Christian asceticism and in the mendicant orders.[136] After this religious successor, which is of less importance to the argument here, Foucault traces a political descendant in the figure of the revolutionary, and an aesthetic descendant in the modern art. The Cynicism of the revolutionary appears in the mode of existence, where life becomes an example to follow, and where life itself is a manifestation of truth: in the "scandalous forms of life"[137] of leftism, in the revolutionary life of militant movements and parties: "And it must manifest directly, by its visible form, its constant practice, and its immediate existence, the concrete possibility and the evident value of an *other* life, which is the true life."[138] Foucault sees possible examples of this Cynic scandalous true life (after the Socratic *alethes bios*) in Dostoyevsky, Russian nihilism, European and American anarchism, before its inversion in the Communist Party's "implementation of accepted values, customary behavior, and traditional schemas of conduct, as opposed to bourgeois decadence or leftist madness."[139] The third great descendant is formed by a kind of Cynicism in culture. From the literary obscenities of the medieval fabliau tradition and the carnivalesque studied by Bakthin, to Modernism and the notion of the singularity of the artistic life, the modern idea that the artist's life "should constitute some kind of testimony of what art is in its truth."[140] And this modern art – defined by Foucault as anti-Platonic, anti-Aristotelian, from Manet, Flaubert, and Baudelaire to Becket, Bacon, and Burroughs – is a practice that aims at a certain "laying bare, exposure, stripping, excavation, and violent reduction of existence to its basics. [...] The consensus of culture has to be opposed by the

---

[135] Foucault, *The Government of Self and Others*, 33–34.
[136] Foucault describes the poor, wandering Franciscans as "the Cynics of medieval Christianity," and notes that the Dominicans called themselves *Domini canes*, the Lord's dogs. Ibid, 182.
[137] Foucault, *The Courage of the Truth*, 185.
[138] Foucault, *The Courage of the Truth*, 185.
[139] Foucault, *The Courage of the Truth*, 186.
[140] Foucault, *The Courage of the Truth*, 187.

courage of art in its barbaric truth. Modern art is Cynicism in culture; the Cynicism of culture turned against itself."[141]

While we cannot go very far into the implications of all this with regards to Cynicism, we can note that a rather modern notion lurks in the background. It is a notion that Foucault never spells out, but which he seems to be doing everything to conjure, especially given how, just before his revolutionary-artistic digression, he takes up Epictetus' description of the Cynic by the military term *kataskopos*, a kind of scout which is sent out ahead of the army to observe the enemy, or, in case of the Cynic, someone who is running ahead of humanity. The implicit notion with equally military origins is, of course, the *avantgarde*. The revolutionary or artistic vanguard which has marched through so much of the 20th century and its political, critical, and aesthetic theory. To put it as briefly as possible: if the avantgarde is Cynicism in culture – for instance, in the form of modern art as Foucault claims – then Cynicism as a moral category could reasonably be discussed in terms of the critique of the avantgarde. Particularly since this critique seems full of echoes from the points of conflict we have already located between Cynicism and Foucault's general genealogy of the relations between truth and subjectivity during antiquity. In Peter Bürger's *Theory of the Avant-garde*, for example, we learn that art as an institution, and part of a larger political-economical system, neutralizes the critical and political potential of individual artworks.[142] Can we not we apply this to the wild and theatrical outbursts of the Cynic, which despite their scandalous intensity seems to have formed a constant and, in the end, non-threatening otherness in the customs of everyday life? It does not seem an unfitting analogy with regard to Diogenes himself, given that the Athenians, according to Diogenes Laërtius, held their bilious *kataskopos* in high regard and affection; they had the cask in which he slept replaced after it was broken, and buried him, when he died at the age of ninety, beneath a statue carrying a marble dog – a destiny quite different to that of Socrates, with respect to how he was treated by the same Athenians.[143]

The critique of the political, revolutionary avantgarde can help us identify another problematic. Epitomized in one principle, it may be exemplified by

---

[141] Foucault, *The Courage of the Truth*, 189.

[142] Peter Bürger, *Theory of the Avant-garde*, trans. M. Shaw (Minneapolis: University of Minnesota Press 1984), 90.

[143] Diogenes Laertius, *Lives of Eminent Philosophers*, 78.

Rosa Luxemburg's[144] critique of Lenin. Luxemburg sharply rejects the notion of the centralized vanguard party more than a decade before the October Revolution, and she does so precisely because the movement will never be able to abandon the organizational structure of a centrally ruled government once it is put in place; on the contrary, it will maintain itself at whatever cost. Luxemburg does not mince her words: "Nothing will more surely enslave a young labor movement to an intellectual elite hungry for power than this bureaucratic straightjacket, *which will immobilize the movement and turn it into an automaton manipulated by a Central Committee.*"[145] This critique articulates the risks involved when those who consider themselves as the real sovereigns, worthy to command and to govern others, decide to liberate them, to lead them out of immaturity and subordination. Or as Foucault rephrases Kant's verdict on all revolutions: "those who make them necessarily fall back under the yoke of those who wanted to free them."[146]

A Deeply Novelized Figure

If the above amounts to a critique of Cynicism, or more precisely a critique of Foucault's Cynicism from the general perspective of his last three lecture courses on the care of the self and truth-telling, and if it manages to identify a divergence or a set of contradictions, it seems that the question arises: was Foucault somehow mistaken in his fascination with Cynicism? Yet that question seems a bit absurd. The issue must probably be understood on another level, where some of the contradictions we have identified may even be resolved. Important here is Foucault's assessment that "Cynicism is always both inside and outside philosophy."[147] While Foucault refers to the philosophical life as being exteriorized by Cynicism in relation to philosophy, we shall also – in a limited, brief attempt – consider the Cynic truth-telling as an externality to philosophy in terms of its distribution, its mode of expression and reception, its circulation, as well as the kind of listening, understanding,

---

[144] This does not concern Foucault's odd reference to Rosa Luxemburg in *The Government of the Living*, regarding the exercise of power and truth. There, Foucault ascribes to Luxemburg the maxim that "if everyone were to know, the capitalist regime would not last twenty four hours". However, while the editors of Foucault's lectures find no such quote in Luxemburg's complete works (nor is it in any clear way representative of her position on class struggle and class consciousness), they note note that Cornelis Castoriadis quotes her saying so. See. Foucault, *On the Government of the Living: Lectures at Collège de France 1979–1980*, trans. G. Burchell, (New York: Palgrave/Macmillan 2014), 15 and n. 26, 20.

[145] Rosa Luxemburg, "Organizational Questions of the Russian Social Democracy (Leninism or Marxism?)", https://www.marxists.org/archive/luxemburg/1904/questions-rsd/ (January 9, 2017).

[146] Foucault, *The Government of Self and Others*, 34.

[147] Foucault, *The Courage of the Truth*, 237.

and sensibility that at once it produces and presupposes. In one word, we shall consider it on the level of aesthetics. Hegel found that there was "nothing particular to say of the Cynics, for they possess but little Philosophy, and they did not bring what they had into a scientific system."[148] But to think of Cynicism in strictly philosophical and scientific terms overlooks its particular properties; as Bracht Branham claimed almost three decades ago, it is as rhetorical or literary practice that one best understands "Cynicism's 'peculiar authority and resilience.'"[149] For the understanding we are trying to develop here, Branham's argument is interesting: it begins by emphasizing the literary side and formal inventiveness of Cynicism, and ends by tying this to the notion of *parrēsia* (this focus on *parrēsia* is interesting in itself, given that Branham's text was published in 1996, and given also that not many scholars have focused on this concept independently of Foucault, before the publication of the Collège de France lectures).[150]

In contrast to the many negative definitions and descriptions of Cynicism, like the "doctrinal thinness" that Foucault discusses, Branham underlines Cynicism's advanced literary character. While he holds that most philosophical writing at this time remained within a limited set of forms such as dialogues, epistles, memoirs, and treatises, the Cynics produced new forms or genres: they reconfigured the use of myth in burlesque and parodies, and renovated traditional forms such as the proverb. Thus, "we find Cynics like Crates and Menippus turning low or extraliterary genres such as the will or the diary into full-scale literary productions with satiric motives, or using an established form like the epistle in novel ways, for example by addressing it to a god."[151] But perhaps more significant than the development of new and existing genres in these written works, is the oral circulation of Cynicism, its

---

[148] G. W. F. Hegel, *Lectures on the History of Philosophy*, trans. E.S. Haldane and F.H. Simson (Lincoln/London: University of Nebraska Press, 1995), vol. I, 479.

[149] R. Bracht Branham, "Diogenes' Rhetoric" in *The Cynics: The Cynic Movement in Antiquity and Its Legacy*, ed. R. Bracht Branham and Marie-Odile Goulet-Cazé (Berkeley/Los Angeles, London: University of California Press, 1996), 89.

[150] Regarding the importance of the literary aspect of Cynicism, Branham cites Dudley's influential study of the Cynics, and the definition of ancient Cynicism's three primary features: "1 . the vagrant Cynic life; 2. the assault on all established values; 3. a body of literary genres." See Donald R. Dudley, *A History of Cynicism from Diogenes to the Sixth Century A.D.* (London: Methuen & Co, 1937) xi–xii. Regarding *parrēsia*, Branham writes: "Cynicism is the only philosophical movement in antiquity to make freedom a central value, and freedom of speech in particular. This fact is directly linked to the Cynic invention of satiric and parodic forms of literature without classical precedent. It is [...] a mistake, however, to think of a body of Cynic doctrines first formulated and then embodied in literary works. Cynicism originates in no small part in rhetorical and literary activity, as the exercise of *parrēsia*." See Branham, "Diogenes' Rhetoric," 82, 104.

[151] Branham, "Diogenes' Rhetoric," 85.

telling and retelling of anecdotes. Indeed, this is something that Foucault takes up, and that he calls Cynicism's particular "traditionality," its form of expression as opposed to the doctrinal traditions of Platonism and Aristotelianism:

> Cynic teaching, in the way in which it passed itself on through examples and anecdotes, found and gave rise to an interesting and important mode of traditionality. The traditionality of Cynic teaching, which was conveyed through models of behavior, frameworks of attitudes, took the form of brief anecdotes called *khreiai*, which reported in a few words a gesture, a retort, or an attitude of a Cynic in a given situation; or of longer stories, *apomnēmoneumata* (memories), in which a whole episode of the Cynic life was recounted; and also jokes and anecdotes, which were called *paigna*, and which provoked laughter (*paizei*) and were sorts of comical, ironical *khreiai*.[152]

Foucault does not draw any direct conclusions from this description. But let us consider Cynicism in its "traditionality," in its representation and circulation in various literary forms, and above all in the *khreiai*, the oral and anecdotal form that made it such a popular tradition, among common people and among the illiterate, the urban poor, and slaves. We must then leave aside the moral and political evaluation based on the attempt to grasp the actual words and actions of the Cynics (like the overly literal, historiographical scrutiny of the *khreiai* in terms of historical truth),[153] and resist the attempt of trying to separate out the good, ideal Cynic from its bad examples (which several commentators advice against).[154] Let us instead consider Cynicism as form, in its literary aspect, and understand it as a philosophy that – to a much higher degree than other Classic and Hellenistic philosophies, which manifested itself in its doctrinal content, or its practice of daily exercises – takes place in the play of its representation; as Bakhtin suggests in his essay on the epic and novel, Diogenes is a "deeply novelized" figure.[155] By this, as Branham points out,

---

[152] Foucault, *The Courage of the Truth*, 208.

[153] Heinrich Niehues-Pröbsting shows that the modern transmission of Cynicism on the basis of anecdote and apophthegm was seriously shaken when Pierre Bayle and his successors "subjected the copiously transmitted anecdotal biographical material to the standard of historical credibility [...and] reduced it to a steadily decreasing stock of anecdotes that were believed to be true." See Heinrich Niehues-Pröbsting, "The Modern Reception of Cynicism" in *The Cynics: The Cynic Movement in Antiquity and Its Legacy*, 330.

[154] Margarethe Billerbeck, "The Ideal Cynic from Epictetus to Julian" and Niehues-Pröbsting, "The Modern Reception of Cynicism" in *The Cynics: The Cynic Movement in Antiquity and Its Legacy*, 205, 364–365.

[155] Mikhael Bakhtin, "Epic and Novel" in *Dialogic Imagination*, trans. Caryl Emerson and Michael Holquist (Austin: University of Texas Press, 1981), 38.

Bakhtin does not simply mean that the Cynic appears as the character in a novel with his tub, his cloak, and his lentils: "Rather Bakhtin means something much more fundamental, namely that Diogenes is, in his terms, a 'dialogical' figure – 'a hero of improvisation not of tradition,'" and an operator of transformation.[156] What follows more generally from this novelistic understanding, is that Diogenes, or the common figure of the Cynic, initiates a game of infinite participation between the author and reader/listener. A game in which, if we continue to lean on Bakhtin, "the subjectivity of the individual becomes an object of experimentation and representation."[157] This means that the Cynics do not show or lead the way for their listeners out of servitude or tutelage by any simply derived principles or precepts of their actions, performances, or demonstrations. Rather, if there is any liberating effect, it lies in the performance itself as form, as expression, as literary practice: as something that engages the listener/spectator in a production and reproduction of sense that does not really work by concepts, but that appears as a process of making, creating, or, in other words, a *poiesis* on the part of the listener/reader/spectator. Perhaps such circulation of *khreiai* and *paigna* (anecdotes and jokes), such improvisation and popular participation in literary forms, is not so far from what Oscar Wilde meant when he said that the Greeks were a nation of art critics, practicing the *bios theōrētikos*, and uniting the two supreme and highest arts: life and literature.[158]

This is not the place to unravel the workings of such a poetical-critical sensibility as a political technology of the self,[159] but to acknowledge it as an important aspect of Cynicism. It certainly has some consequences to our objections to Foucault's reading: as opposed to the idea that Cynicism is characterized by a scandalous lack of a theoretical or practical program, by the lack of any "doctrinal mediation" as Foucault calls it, we can now see that the truth-telling of the Cynics, in the action of improvisation and even more so in the circulation of its written or oral representation, offers precisely that: a kind of mediation. It is something for the listeners/readers to engage with, due to its open-ended, and sometimes comic and humoristic form; it is a way to understand Cynicism as "the link between the concern for the truth and the aesthetics of existence."[160]

---

[156] Branham, "Diogenes' Rhetoric," 86.

[157] Bakhtin, "Epic and Novel," 37.

[158] Oscar Wilde, "The Critic as Artist" in *The Collected Works* (Hertfordshire: Wordsworth Editions, 1997), 971–72.

[159] For such an attempt, see Karl Katz Lydén, *Poems and Parables on the Political Utility of Art* (Berlin: BOM DIA BOA TARDE BOA NOITE, 2021).

[160] Foucault, *The Courage of the Truth*, 190.

This does not resolve all the points of contradiction we have identified above, namely between Foucault's account of Cynicism and his more general positions on truth-telling and the care of the self; for example, the Cynic is still in some kind of tension with the otherwise recurring figure of merging means and ends: the Cynic remains in his radically other position, and his means of demonstration, his strange and scandalous performances, can hardly be considered as ends in themselves. On the other hand, it does, to some extent, resolve the issues of the Cynic as the figure of the king/superior/governor (by inscribing this figure into a fictional, literary, meta-phorical framework), and as the embodiment or prefiguration of the problem of the avantgarde or those guardians who attempt to lead others into autonomy (by understanding the Cynic's interventions not as attempts to lead, but as performances or narratives to engage with). Thus, the critical-poetical work of reception and interpretation of Cynicism as a rhetorical, literary, and performative practice provides the reader/listener with the possibility of engaging in a reflective work on themselves. Understood this way, however, Cynicism cannot be taken alongside other traditions of Classic and Hellenistic philosophy as forms of truth-telling and of the care of the self; it can hardly, or at least not fully, be taken as philosophy. Given what Foucault calls its "traditionality," given that it is not transmitted in the form of concepts or systematic practices and exercises, Cynicism as literary prac-tice and as a kind of precursor to a much later concept of art (art not as *tékhnē*, but as fine art developed since the 18th century and through modern-ism) appears to no small extent to fall "outside" of philosophy. That does not make it less interesting – on the contrary, perhaps. But compared to the other two models of ancient truth-telling in the political field discussed by Foucault – the *parrēsia* of the public orator, and the *parrēsia* of the philosopher as advisor to the prince; both conceivable as practices in relation to modern government – it is less evident what form of veridiction, critique, or militancy a descendent of Cynicism could take today, and what function it would have in the political present. And as we gathered in the beginning of this chapter, from Foucault's sudden insertion of the Kantian question of *Aufklärung* in his lectures on antiquity, it is this political present that is at utlimately at stake.

CHAPTER 4

Foucault's Three Critiques:
Kant, Government and the Critical Attitude

What Is Critique?

In the previous chapters, it has been demonstrated that Foucault invokes the notion of critique on several occasions in his readings of ancient philosophy. For example, the care of the self acquires in Hellenistic philosophy a "critical function".[1] "Critique"[2] is used as the means by which one is to liberate oneself from one's familiar surroundings, and, furthermore, *parrēsia* must "tell the truth in the name of a critical analysis."[3] In 1983 Foucault says he will study the notion of *parrēsia* in relation to the figure of the critic in the domain of political discourse from the 18th through to the 20th century, and as Arnold Davidson and Daniele Lorenzini note, Foucault considers *parrēsia* to be of importance not only for philosophy – the task is not only "for philosophy, through the critique of the *Aufklärung*, to become aware of problems which were traditionally problems of *parrēsia* in antiquity"[4] – but also he relates it specifically to "the critical attitude" as its very genealogy. This is the position he sets out in the lectures he delivered at Berkeley, in 1983.[5]

Further, Foucault's discussion of Kant's essay "What is Enlightenment?" in his first lecture from 1983, ultimately serves to connect ancient philosophy's way of functioning with a modern critical philosophy, and toward the end of the course Foucault states: "I think that philosophy as ascesis, as critique, and as restive exteriority to politics is the mode of being of modern

---

[1] Foucault, *The Hermeneutics of the Subject*, 97.

[2] Foucault, *The Hermeneutics of the Subject*, 96.

[3] Foucault, *The Government of Self and Others*, 288.

[4] Foucault, *The Government of Self and Others*, 350.

[5] Arnold I. Davidson and Daniele Lorenzini, "Introduction" in Michel Foucault, *Qu'est-ce que la critique? suivi de La culture de soi* (Paris: Vrin, 2015), 25. This French critical edition of "What is Critique?" confirms, by its inclusion of the lecture "The Culture of the Self," our view that there is a strong link between critique and the ancient practices of the self in Foucault's work.

philosophy."[6] It is therefore time to look closer at Foucault's own definition of critique.

Apart from shorter, fragmentary, and dispersed reflections on the concept,[7] the most thorough discussion of the issue is found in "What is Critique?".[8] The text was originally presented as a lecture at The French Society of Philosophy on May 27, 1978. This is the first time Foucault works on Kant's "What is Enlightenment?", which then occurs in several, partly overlapping texts. After "What is Critique?", it appears as a fragment in the introduction to the 1978 English translation of Canguilhem's *On the Normal and the Pathological*, then in the aforementioned opening lecture of *The Government of Self and Others*, and finally it appears in *"Qu'est-ce que les Lumières?"* published as "What is Enlightenment" in Rabinow's *The Foucault Reader* from 1984. As we shall see, the very question of "What is Enlightenment?" is given at least three different replies or meanings, two of which we have already learned from the 1983 lecture. The first is Foucault's reiteration of Kant's literal reply: "Enlightenment is to exit from one's self-assumed tutelage." The second reply is Foucault's description of the act of philosophy to question its own present, in what he calls an ontology of the present. The third reply or meaning given to Kant's question, developed most clearly in "What is Critique?," is to pose it anew and in retrospect, in order to investigate what role Enlightenment has played since Kant in the development of late modern governmental reason: the development of new scientific procedures of governmentality.

In the 1978 lecture, the question "What is Critique?" is given two replies or definitions by Foucault: first, in line with the Kantian exit from tutelage, we have the very general and rather evasive characterization of what Foucault calls the critical attitude, in which critique is rendered as "the art of not being governed like that."[9] This definition, producing an eclipse in the very last lines of the text, is indeed equaled with or reformulated as the very question of "What is Enlightenment?". Apparently, there is a sort of circular movement between critique, government, enlightenment – and as we shall see below, truth-telling. Much of this relationship could be gathered already from our reading of the first lecture of *The Government of*

---

[6] Foucault, *The Government of Self and Others*, 354.

[7] A beautiful remark is made in an interview from 1981, when Foucault says that the critique necessary for social transformation means "making more difficult the most simple gestures." See Michel Foucault, "Est-il donc important de penser?", 997.

[8] Michel Foucault, "What is Critique?" in *The Politics of Truth*, trans. Lysa Hochroth and Catherine Porter (Los Angeles: Semiotexte, 2007).

[9] Foucault, "What is Critique?", 45.

Self and Others. But here, in his investigation of critique, Foucault also provides a second definition: critique may also consist in the theoretical work of a "historical-critical practice" which can also be taken as a description of his own work, as it is outlined in three coexisting dimensions: archeology, genealogy, and strategy. As it happens, both of these definitions divide into two, in equally simple and important ways: the first as both an individual and a collective movement of desubjugation; the second both as a general recapitulation of his previous work but also as a foreshadowing of a work to come, a work, as we shall see, which precisely engages with the role of Enlightenment in subsequent governmentalities of the state. To begin with, we shall go through what is at stake in these two definitions of critique. After that, we will suggest interfoliating a third – which we will extract from what we have discussed from Foucault's Collège de France lectures – so that we have three Foucauldian critiques.

The Art of Not Being Governed Like That

Being a concept that incorporates so many different polemics and various kinds of critical projects, critique, says Foucault, seems by its very function to be defined by dispersion and pure heteronomy. Yet there is, in modernity, a common critical attitude to be investigated, one that appeared in relation to another historical event. In the 15th and 16th centuries, we find a "veritable explosion of the art of governing men," a process of secularization and expansion of civil society, along with the discussion of how to govern children, the family, the poor and the army, how to govern, cities, states and also how to govern oneself: "How to govern was, I believe, one of the fundamental questions about what was happening in the 15th or 16th centuries."[10] And this question on the part of those who are governing were met by that of the governed: "how *not* to be governed?" Foucault stresses that the stakes of the latter question is not about not being governed at all, but rather, "'how not to be governed like that, by that, in the name of those principles, with such and such an objective in mind and by means of such procedures, not like that, not for that, not by them.'"[11] This is what constitutes the critical attitude, a kind of defiance and challenge, and it is what Foucault gives as a very first definition of critique: "the art of not being governed quite so much."[12]

---

[10] Foucault, "What is Critique?", 44.
[11] Foucault, "What is Critique?", 44.
[12] Foucault, "What is Critique?", 45.

For this general and somewhat evasive definition, Foucault provides three historical anchoring points: first, critique as a practice directed toward ecclesiastical rule, returning to the scriptures in order rediscover or refute their truth: "critique is biblical, historically." Second, critique as something that developed in relation to, and found its expression within, natural law, as a way of denouncing excessive or unwanted government that may infringe on the universal rights of man. Third, and somewhat more vague, critique as the refusal of government in terms of truth, on the basis of not accepting authority per se, and demanding certainty over its decrees. Foucault does not elaborate on these historical reference points, but we can note that he, for instance by mentioning Wycliffe and Pierre Bayle in relation to the critique of the scriptures, predates critical practices to points well before the 15th century, just as he states that even Kant's critiques "presumably have origins which go back way before the 15th and 16th centuries" (and thus way before this period's art of government, which he offered as a first landmark in the history of the critical attitude).[13] Perhaps Foucault here, in this 1978 lecture, is reserving a place in his historical analysis for the relation between critique and the ancient care of the self, an investigation he would later continue to hint at, but never carry through. As well as the links we have already mentioned between the practices of the self and the will not to be governed like that, there are further indications in his reading notes from this period: at one point Foucault studies the different philosophical schools in their attitude to the Roman imperial dictatorship,[14] and in another dossier of handwritten notes entitled "Critique" Foucault collects some of the material that appears in *The Hermeneutics of the Subject* on the critique of "family ideology," stating that "the practice of the self must play a critical role."[15]

In addition to these appearances of the term "critique" in his accounts of the ancient practices of the self, Foucault also defines the critical attitude along the lines of an *ēthos*, in a way that displays similarities with how the care of the self is defined as an ethics and *parrēsia* as a morality in *The Hermeneutics of the Subject*.[16] In "What is Critique," Foucault states that critique on the one hand only exists in relation to something else, as an instrument or a means to achieve a truth or a future yet unknown; as such it

---

[13] Foucault, "What is Critique?", 42.

[14] Michel Foucault, Fonds Foucault à la BNF (NAF 27830). Boite_023-17-chem, accessed March 19, 2024. https://eman-archives.org/Foucault-fiches/collections/show/662.

[15] Michel Foucault, Fonds Foucault à la BNF (NAF 27830). Boite 72, Critique. (Not available online).

[16] "[I]t seems to me that the analysis of governmentality—that is to say, of power as a set of reversible relationships—must refer to an ethics of the subject defined by the relationship of self to self." See Foucault, *The Hermeneutics of the Subject*, 368.

is subordinated to philosophy, politics, literature, law, etc. On the other hand, it is "supported by a more general imperative," suggesting somewhat paradoxically that while it always exists as a means for something else, it seems at the same time to be an end in itself: "There is something in critique which is akin to virtue."[17] On the one hand, we may recall how Foucault in *The Hermeneutics of the Subject* describes *parrēsia* as indexed both to the truth and to the very act of truth-telling, defining it in a similar paradoxical or double way as "both a technique and an ethics, an art and a morality."[18] On the other hand, we of course recognize the recurring figure of the merging of means and ends we had first encountered in the description of the Hellenistic relation to the self, in this thesis' second chapter.[19]

So even though critique only exists in relation to something else, it has a value in and for itself; it falls within a "more general imperative," within the confines of "virtue," and hence, we may conclude, it belongs to a certain *ēthos*. In a sense, we may even say that years before Foucault investigates the care of the self, according to Pierre Hadot's notion of "philosophy as way of life" – whether as the *bios theōrētikos* among the *therapeutae* in Philo of Alexandria, the shedding of fine words and revered speech in favor of an undaunted truth-telling (*parrēsia*), the search for knowledge in Epicurus, the *forma vitae* of Seneca,[20] or the life as a manifestation of truth among the cynics – Foucault advances something we can call "critique as way of life." After Foucault has established this ethical imperative of critique, he gives a further, slightly more elaborated definition, which provides us with some important distinctions:

> And if governmentalization is indeed this movement through which individuals are subjugated in the reality of a social practice through mechanisms of power that adhere to a truth, well, then! I will say that critique is the movement by which the subject gives itself the right to question truth on its effects of power and question power on its discourses of truth. Well, then!:

---

[17] Foucault, *The Hermeneutics of the Subject*, 43.

[18] Foucault, *The Hermeneutics of the Subject*, 368.

[19] Regarding the notion of critique as virtue, and a reading of Foucault that develops along similar lines, we should recall Judith Butler's essay: "Foucault also refers to such arts of existence as producing subjects who 'seek to transform themselves in their singular being, and to make their life into an oeuvre.' We might think that this gives support to the charge that Foucault has fully aestheticized existence at the expense of ethics, but I would suggest only that he has shown us that there can be no ethics, and no politics, without recourse to this singular sense of poiesis." see Judith Butler, "What is Critique? An Essay on Foucault's Virtue," *Transversal*, no. 5 (2001), accessed March 2, 2021, https://transversal.at/transversal/0806/butler/en.

[20] Foucault, *The Hermeneutics of the Subject*, 429–30

> critique will be the art of voluntary insubordination, that of reflected intractability. Critique would essentially ensure the desubjugation of the subject in the context of what we could call, in a word, the politics of truth.[21]

To be noted here is that while *individuals* "are subjugated in the reality of a social practice," it is the *subject* that appears in the movement of critique. Whether this subject is individual or collective – or both – remains unspecified. This treatment of "individuals" can be explained by the fact that in *Discipline and Punish*, Foucault analyzed the workings of power in its individualizing properties,[22] while he investigated the totalizing effects of biopower directed to the whole population in *Society Must Be Defended*.[23] This dual nature of power is confirmed a year later in the lecture entitled "Omnes et singulatim," when Foucault notes that the inevitable effects of state power are both individualization and totalization: "Opposing the individual and his interests to it is just as hazardous as opposing it with the community and its requirements. [...] Liberation can only come from attacking, not just one of these two effects, but political rationality's very roots."[24]

   This splitting into two of Foucault's notion of critique, as both individual and collective, is confirmed in other parts of "What is Critique?" At the very end of the lecture, Foucault concludes that if it is necessary to investigate knowledge in its relationship to domination, "it would be, first and foremost, from a certain decision-making will not to be governed, the decision making will, *both an individual and collective* attitude which meant, as Kant said, to get out of one's minority." (Italicization added). Finally, the issue is elucidated by a reply given by Foucault in the discussion following the lecture, where he emphasizes the collective aspect, the issue of revolt, the importance of the spiritual tradition in class struggle, and the fact that critique goes beyond the theoretical work of philosophy:

> I am wondering... if one wants to explore this dimension of critique [the dimension of the will not to be governed thusly, which might imply some "fundamental anarchism" or "originary freedom"] that seems to me to be so important because it is both part of, and not a part of, philosophy. If we were to explore this dimension of critique, would we not then find that it is supported by something akin to the historical practice of revolt, the non-

---

[21] Foucault, "What is Critique?", 47. Translation slightly modified.

[22] Foucault, *Discipline and Punish*, 193.

[23] Foucault, "*Society Must Be Defended*," 247.

[24] Michel Foucault, "Omnes et Singulatim: Towards a Criticism of Political Reason." In *The Tanner Lectures on Human Values vol II*, ed. S. McMurrin (Salt Lake City: Univ. Of Utah Press, 1981), 225–254.

acceptance of a real government, on the one hand, or, on the other, the individual experience of the refusal of governmentality? [...] When one sees that these experiences, these spiritual movements [of Mysticism] have very often been used as attire, vocabulary, but even more so as ways of being, and ways of supporting the hopes expressed by the struggle that we can define as economic, popular, and in Marxist terms as the struggle between the classes, I think we have here something that is quite fundamental. In following the itinerary of this critical attitude whose history seems to begin at this point in time, should we not now investigate what the will not to be governed thusly, like that, etc., might be both as an individual and a collective experience?

It is beyond doubt that Foucault's definition of critique, as the will not to be governed thusly, must be understood both as an individual and collective practice. To us, as retrospective readers, after the publication of his lectures on *The Hermeneutics of the Subject* four years later, it is not difficult to imagine such an individual practice. After all, Foucault develops his understanding of the care of the self both explicitly and implicitly in terms of critique: the "critique" of family values and received wisdom; the exit from *stultitia*; the conversion or turn to oneself; the study of the world or of nature and the Epicurean disqualification of divine and worldly powers, the breaking with that which enslaves you, the aim of *askēsis* as making one's actions coincide with the truths one professes; the exercises to prepare oneself to face the world without fears, etc. Despite the fact that no small part of this care of the self presupposes an exchange with others and may be developed within communities, groups, schools and other forms of collectivities, it designates an individual subjectivation. As for collective subjectivity, the collective practice of critique understood as popular struggle or as revolt considered in "What is Critique?", is never properly theorized in Foucault's subsequent (or previous) work – yet at times, as we shall see, he does make some remarks to suggest its form. But first, we shall look at the other definition of critique provided by Foucault in 1978: critique as historical-philosophical practice.

The Historical-Philosophical Practice

While Foucault sees the critical attitude neatly expressed in the Kantian notion of Enlightenment and *Sapere aude!*, he acknowledges that to Kant himself, this was not really a question of challenging government: "It would also be easy to show that, for Kant, autonomy is not at all opposed to obeying the sovereign."[25] These remarks on Kant's adherence to political authority are

---

[25] Foucault, "What is Critique?", 49–50.

developed further by Foucault in 1983 and *The Government of Self and Others* lectures, when, as we saw in the previous chapter, he discusses Kant's essay with regard to the role of Frederick the Great and the relation between the private and public use of reason.[26] In "What is Critique?", he merely notes that with Kant, while one does not let someone else say "obey," the obedience is founded on autonomy. So if there is a gap already in Kant between the courage of Enlightenment and the application of the three critiques (by which you attain autonomy and still obey the sovereign), Foucault notes that of these 18th century phenomena it is the latter that gets the upper hand during the course of the 19th century: it is apparent in the development of positivist science, the development of a State system that refines its instruments for rationalizing the economy and society, and their combination in a science of the state. But while these processes of rationalization, systematization, objectivation, and technicalization were expected to strengthen individuals in their quest for autonomy, they resulted in an ever tighter grip of governmentalization. At the extremes of this development, Foucault sees two forms of power that extends their logic so far that they come to resemble each other: Fascism and Stalinism. Thus, the question is: "how is it that rationalization leads to the furor of power?"[27] Foucault cites a German tradition of questioning the effects of the *Aufklärung*, from Hegel through Nietzsche, Husserl, and Weber to the Frankfurt School, and situates his own task along these lines: one must study the continuous workings of the Enlightenment in order to grasp Modernity.

To study the afterlife of the Enlightenment means that one has to engage in a historical and philosophical practice which is neither a history of philosophy nor a philosophy of history, but, as Foucault calls it, a "historical-philosophical practice."[28] Under this rubric, Foucault draws a theoretical, rather abstract sketch of his own work up to that point; a sketch which is also a methodological reflection. To begin with, this work forms its very own relation to the historical processes which it considers. Rather than taking the results provided by historians as received and ready-made facts, the historical-philosophical practice sets out to write history in its own manner, to "fabricate history, as if through fiction."[29] Fabrication, fiction – these terms reflect what we discussed in chapter one as Foucault's creative, montage-like use of archival material. At the same time, the careful

---

[26] Foucault, *The Government of Self and Others*, 37–39.
[27] Foucault, "What is Critique?", 54.
[28] Foucault, "What is Critique?", 55.
[29] Foucault, "What is Critique?", 56.

work to organize historical material in relation to each other, in oppositions or contradictions that generate meaning, testifies to the immanent perspective and the ambition "to desubjectify the philosophical question by way of historical contents."[30]

But what are these historical contents? How are they selected? Foucault actually gives a general, formal reply to these questions. The empirical mode of incorporating and mounting historical contents is an attempt to represent mechanisms of coercion and elements of knowledge, and above all, to identify the relations between them. Think of the section on the timetable in *Discipline and Punish*, and the use of cross-quotations from various treatises on army discipline, school regulations and rules for employees at workshops, forming a rather coherent whole that becomes visible in each of its parts: "'At the last stroke of the hour, a pupil will ring the bell, and at the first sound of the bell all the pupils will kneel, with their arms crossed and their eyes lowered. When the prayer has been said, the teacher will strike the signal once to indicate that the pupils should get up, a second time as a sign that they should salute Christ, and a third that they should sit down'".[31] The purpose is not to reveal the occurrence of error, illusion, or illegitimacy in these mechanisms, but rather to show how they form a continuity, and how this nexus of knowledge-power constitutes the acceptability of a system, "be it the mental health system, the penal system, delinquency, sexuality, etc."[32] This analysis of the interplay between knowledge-power and the acceptability of a system is what Foucault calls the archeological level.

To then follow the breaking points of a system, to trace its emergence as a singularity with multiple determining elements beneath it, moves the analysis onto the next level. Here, one must shed any notion of a preconceived original causality or an overarching historical explanatory model. Rather than envisaging a singular, original genesis, it is about tracing a certain formation of knowledge-power in its many and combined causal or determining relations, thus uncovering the process of its emergence: this is what Foucault calls the genealogical level. Finally he describes a strategic level of analysis that pays attention to the individuals and groups that operate within and are operated by these systems: how they appear in a certain slippage or perpetual mobility, and how this slippage also leaves room for a certain agency. These three levels – archaeology, genealogy, and strategy – do not operate separately or successively. They are coexisting dimensions of the same historical-philo-

---

[30] Foucault, "What is Critique?", 56.
[31] Foucault, *Discipline and Punish*, 150.
[32] Foucault, "What is Critique?", 61.

sophical practice. (While Foucault's important concepts of archaeology and genealogy have often been used to define different periods of his work, he describes them both here and elsewhere as simultaneous processes of the same undertaking.)[33] So in the work of fabricating history, of grasping and mounting "historical contents" to produce something almost like a fiction, Foucault proposes new ways to grasp the historical contingency of various power-knowledge formations. His historical-philosophical practice demonstrates the acceptability of a certain system, the way it was articulated, and – pointing to its temporary and perhaps even fragile nature – the way it can be taken apart, or at least dislocated or reversed within the very strategic field that induced it. And it does so guided by a certain impulse: the will or decision of not being governed like that.

The Three Critiques

In our reading of "What is Critique?", critique has been taken to mean two things: critique as the theoretical, epistemological-philosophical work defined as historical-political practice, and critique as the individual and collective formation against specific forms of governmentalization. And both, according to Foucault, amount to Kant's question: what is enlightenment? As we have seen, for Kant, "enlightenment is man's release from his self-incurred tutelage". One must dare to think for oneself, instead of relying on external authorities: "If I have a book that has understanding for me, a pastor who has a conscience for me, a doctor who judges my diet for me, and so forth, surely I do not need to trouble myself. I have no need to think, if

---

[33] That archaeology and genealogy have been used to periodize Foucault's work is not without sense, given that Foucault regarded all of his 1960s works archaeologies: *The History of Madness* is initially described as an archaeology of the silence of madness in relation to the monologue of psychiatry (Foucault later removed this description and his whole first preface, considering archaeologies as only possible to undertake with respect to what has been said; on the other hand, the term "archaeology" is also used within the same book in relation to alienation, cultures, and knowledge); *The Birth of the Clinic* is an "archaeology of the medical gaze," while *The Order of Things* is an "archaeology of the human sciences." The very concept itself is discussed in *The Archaeology of Knowledge*. As opposed to these, and after Foucault's methodological reflection "Nietzsche, Genealogy, History" from 1971, *Discipline and Punish* and the first volume of *The History of Sexuality* are often considered genealogies, with the former, for example, discussing the "genealogy of modern society". Yet Foucault himself seems to have regarded them as inseparable, or at least as coexistent or simultaneous forms of analysis: "Archaeology is the method specific to the analysis of local discursivities, and genealogy is the tactic which, once it has described these local discursivities, brings into play the desubjugated knowledges that have been released from them." see Foucault, *"Society Must Be Defended,"* Foucault, *"Society Must Be Defended,"* 10–11.

only I can pay; others will take over the tedious business for me."[34] Let us return to Foucault's understanding of these famous words:

> Now I do not think it is too much of an over-interpretation of this text to say that in these three apparently extraordinarily flat and familiar examples (the book, the spiritual director, the doctor) we rediscover, of course, the three *Critiques*. The first, in fact, addresses the question of *Verstand*; the second, that of the *Seelsorger*, that is, the problem of moral conscience; and with the problem of the doctor you can see at least one of the kernels which will later form the domain of the *Critique of Judgment*. These three concrete examples of the book, the spiritual director, and the doctor are not usually accorded much philosophical, juridical, or political status, but they are the three *Critiques*.

There is nothing exaggerated about this interpretation, in which Kant is affirming his previous work, positing the aggregate critical project as a precondition for the exit from the state of immaturity or tutelage. It adds up rather well: *The Critique of Pure Reason* teaches us how to use our *Verstand* legitimately, within the constraints of our reason and what we can know, not submitting to doxa or substituting books for our understanding; *The Critique of Practical Reason* teaches us how not to let desire but the categorical imperative guide our maxims; and *The Critique of Judgment* – on which Foucault is less clear – can perhaps be taken in its application of the reflecting judgment as opposed to following the doctor's orders. It is true that Foucault, in "What is Critique?", also registers a certain gap or distance between the courage of enlightenment and Kant's idea of obedience to the sovereign power as well as how the Kantian critical heritage functioned within the rationalization or technicalization of society during the 19th and 20th centuries. But if we simply take Foucault's insistence on the presence of the three critiques in Kant's familiar examples, we have an interesting series of equivalences. If Foucault's notion of critique to some extent equals the Kantian notion of enlightenment, which equals the exit from one's self-incurred minority, which equals the application of the Kantian critiques – then we seem to have arrived at the strange equivalence between Foucault's and Kant's critical projects, or at least certain aspects of them. But how does one consider any kind of parity between theses of such different "conditions of enunciation,"[35] between such mutually exclusive premises, extrinsic oppositions, and generally incompatible concepts? It seems better not to.

---

[34] Kant, "An Answer to the Question: What Is Enlightenment?", 56.
[35] Foucault, *The Archaeology of Knowledge*, 153.

Instead, we shall limit this unexpected relation to a formal analogy. Can we apply the general architecture of Kant's three critiques to Foucault's work and his general philosophical and political practice? As we shall see, there may be good reasons to, and in fact, similar suggestions have been made by Deleuze and others.[36] But while Deleuze understands Foucault's "unique neo-Kantianism" most substantially in relation to the *Critique of Pure Reason*, in a discussion of Foucault's "statements," "visibilities," and what Deleuze describes as a kind of epistemological "light" in relation to Kant's time, space, and understanding, the following will be more interested in the third critique – above all what we will define as Foucault's third critique. It must be stressed that the following rudimentary, formal and thematic application of the three critiques to Foucault's work is not a philosophical argument: it is not to claim any essential, theoretical common ground between the Kantian critiques and Foucauldian project, and it is not to fit Foucault's nonsystemic, heterogenous and historicist oeuvre into the Procrustean bed of a philosophical system such as transcendental idealism. The idea is simply to use this tripartite schema as an analogous interpretive model, to sketch the overarching stakes in the Foucauldian notions of truth-telling, government, and critique. This will allow us to enlarge the perspective, to enrich Foucault's discussion of critique with material he subsequently developed, and to form a triple definition of philosophical practice congruent with propositions he made himself.

So, if we are to somehow replicate the Kantian model, then between Foucault's two given definitions of critique – the historical-philosophical practice and the will not to be governed like that – we will add another "critique:" Foucault's notion of truth-telling in the political field, a practice he thematized in the form of *parrēsia* in his 1983 lectures *The Government of Self and Others*. Here, we must proceed with caution, as Foucault at no point defines this practice as critique. Yet he develops this notion of truth-telling precisely as an intervention with regard to government. What Foucault discusses as political and philosophical *parrēsia* – the political *parrēsia* of the public speaker, exemplified by Pericles before the assembly in Athens, and the philosophical *parrēsia* of the philosopher as political advisor, such as Plato before the tyrant of Syracuse – is determined by both a kind of learned, philosophical practice and, above all, a manifest will of not being governed like that. So on the one hand, we can clearly see the relation to Foucault's

---

[36] See Deleuze, *Foucault*. See also: Amy Allen, *The politics of our selves: power, autonomy, and gender in contemporary critical theory* (New York: Columbia University Press, 2008).

definition of critique as insubordination; on the other hand, this situated and delimited truth-telling directed toward political power appears as distinctly different from the "individual and collective attitude [...] to get out of one's minority," not to speak of its aspect of revolt, individual refusal of power, or popular struggle: it merits to be considered on its own terms.

One more word on the application or replication of this schema before we attempt to draw it: while Kant's three critiques are formed by three particular works, *The Critique of Pure Reason*, *The Critique of Practical Reason*, and *The Critique of Judgment*, what we propose with regard to Foucault does not refer to specific books or other forms of actualized, achieved work; nor does it refer to an overarching, continuous systematic theoretical project, such as demonstrating or proving the human subject's autonomy. Instead, these critiques refer to three possible fields of action. In this regard, our attempt may be similar to how Deleuze identifies the three dimensions of knowledge, power, and self in some of Foucault's works, and then underlines that these are not closed cases, but ways for Foucault to continuously ask: "What are the new types of struggle, which are transversal and immediate rather than centralized and mediatized? What are the 'intellectual's' new functions, which are specific or 'particular' rather than universal? What are the new modes of subjectivation, which tend to have no identity? This is the present triple root of the questions: What can I do, What do I know, What am I?"[37] Unlike Deleuze's rephrasing of the Kantian questions, however, the following Kantian-Foucauldian triad is based on the two definitions of critique that Foucault gives himself, with the notion of *parrēsia* in the political domain interceding them. Thus, we have the following three Foucauldian critiques:

1. The first critique: to "know knowledge," to define the (historical) conditions of our understanding and the limits of reason.[38] Here we have Foucault's own theoretical work, his historical-philosophical practice as it is formulated in "What is Critique?" as an archeological, genealogical, and strategic project, stretching from the *History of Madness* to the *History of Sexuality*. To Foucault himself, this category of critique could in its broader sense include the work of other thinkers, and consequently works yet unwritten.

2. The second critique: the problem of moral conscience, of making decisions in practical matters where the alternative actions are defined by a given situation. Here we have the political and philosophical *parrēsia*, that of Pericles

---

[37] Deleuze, *Foucault*, 114–115.
[38] Foucault, "What is Critique?", 50.

and that of Plato; that of speaking the truth in the public sphere, and that of speaking the truth directly to political power. This critique is based on Foucault's 1983 Collège de France course on truth-telling in the political domain during antiquity. But above all it consists in its present-day equivalents, in the potential actions these forms of *parrēsia* propose to us, and the way in which they were practiced and considered by Foucault. This means, on the one hand, the public intellectual's work: in Foucault's case writing and signing petitions, organizing and participating in demonstrations, writing shorter pieces in newspapers, and engaging in a public debate. On the other hand, it means the role of the political advisor that Foucault discussed so thoroughly in the example of Plato, and that – in relation to the French Socialist government of his own time – he considered with such ambivalence, yet seemed ready to take up.

3. The third critique: the will of not being governed like that. Here we have what Foucault calls the art of voluntary insubordination, the movement in which an individual or collective subject takes shape in a politics of truth. It is a general and evasive definition of critique, which, according to Foucault, lies both inside and outside philosophy. However, at least a part of it, the part that lies the closest to philosophy, gets a further articulation: in Foucault's subsequent investigation of the technologies of the self, primarily in the 1982 lectures, individual subjectivation appears as both a care of the self – which he also calls the art of living, the aesthetics of existence, the style of life – and a form of critique. The other part, the reflected intractability of a collective subject, does not receive the same attention, since Foucault never undertakes any systematic study of the technologies of collective struggle. We shall, however, return to this important broader negation of government in the following chapter. Finally, a parenthetic addition: despite the fact that Foucault locates these acts of insubordination in a "politics of truth" that remains largely unspecified – stretching from practices of the self to outright social revolt – we should perhaps, in this third critique, accord space also for fiction, and the more general phenomenon that Foucault, at least at some point, considers capable of subversion. In keeping with Kant's *Critique of Judgment* and its considerations of the reflective judgment of beauty, we can include the transformative potential of art, which Foucault in his earlier work above all recognizes in the possible transgression and "outside" of modern literature.

In general terms, there are of course certain risks in producing a schema such as the one presented above. For example, reasonable objections can be raised against the totalizing effects of casting one philosopher in the mold of another: Amy Allen's similar (but different with respect to her own divisions and objectives) use of Kant's questions to summarize Foucault's work[39] has been criticized for creating a false coherence and "continuous whole" in which Foucault's productive contradictions and internal differences disappear.[40] The three Foucauldian critiques proposed here, however, are not so much an attempt to summarize his multifaceted body of work, as they are an attempt to identify what Foucault, for himself and for others, considered as fields of possible action; in that sense it may be the closest one could get to what Judith Revel discusses as the impossible Foucauldian "testament."[41] In any case, there are risks inherent in all schematization. And as regards the accuracy of the Kantian analogy, we can note that Foucault himself, on a number of occasions, seems to use this tripartite model to sort out the stakes of his work, to define what he describes as his "historical ontology," his genealogy, or even the very task of philosophy. True to his habit of quoting works and thinkers without naming them or providing any reference, the statements appear somewhat hermetic, but on closer inspection, they point rather directly to the Kantian heritage. In one of the last lectures of *The Government of Self and Others*, when Foucault sums up the course and defines its philosophical and political stakes, he says: "I think that philosophy as ascesis, as critique, and as restive exteriority to politics is the mode of being of modern philosophy. It was, at any rate, the mode of being of ancient philosophy."[42] Given the context and the discussion that leads up to the statement, the references are clear: "ascesis" refers to the practice of the self and thus to what above falls under the third critique; "critique" refers to the theoretical work of the first critique and its attempt to know knowledge; "restive exteriority to politics" refers to Foucault's whole discussion of Plato as political advisor, and to philosophy's attempt to speak truth to political

---

[39] Allen uses Kant's *four* questions (not only "What can I know?" and "What ought I do?" and "What may I hope?") to structure Foucault's work as the archaeologies of discourse, the genealogies of discipline and normalization, and the techniques of the self, respectively: "And, as with Kant, it is the fourth and final question – 'what is man?' which we might recast in Foucauldian terms as 'what has human subjectivity been and what might it become?' – that sums up the first three and provides the guiding thread that runs throughout Foucault's work as a whole." See Allen, *The Politics of our Selves: Power, Autonomy, and Gender in Contemporary Critical Theory*, 40.
[40] Guilel Treiber "What ought I do?" *materiali foucaultiani*, volume IX numero 17–18, January–December 2020, 51,52.
[41] Revel prefers to discuss Foucault's "heritage" and "tool box," and considers the significance of Foucault's reference to René Char on the issue: "Our heritage is not preceded by any testament." See Judith Revel, "Un héritage de Foucault. Entre fidelité et libres usages," *Theory Now* Vol 2, Nº 1 (January–June 2019): http://dx.doi.org/10.30827/TNJ.v2i1.8599.
[42] Foucault, *The Government of Self and Others*, 354.

power, i.e. the second critique in the model above. Further, there is a remark in "The Culture of the Self" that may be a bit more clear, and that reflects the Kantian order and the critical model above: "I think the ontological history of ourselves must analyze three groups of relations: our relations to truth, our relations to obligation, our relations to ourselves and to others."[43] It thus seems fair to say that Foucault himself was thinking of his work precisely in these terms.

On a more specific note, still with respect to this proposition surrounding the three Foucauldian critiques, a few more things can be said. First, while briefly sketched in the model above, these three critiques are investigated in more detail in the three preceding chapters of this thesis, if only in a slightly reversed order. What is here defined as Foucault's first critique, the "historical-philosophical practice," corresponds to the material discussed in chapter 1 above, devoted to the style, form, and methodology of Foucault's early to mid work. What is defined as the second critique, that of the role of the public intellectual and the political advisor, corresponds to or rather emanates from the political and philosophical *parrēsia* discussed in chapter 3, regarding truth-telling in the political domain during antiquity. What is defined as the third critique, or at least the part of it concerning individual subjectivation, is discussed in chapter two, devoted to the care of the self as a critical practice.

Second, these three forms of critique are not mutually exclusive categories; we have already argued in chapter 1 that Foucault's particular montage-like use of archival material or "historical contents" produces a performative, creative reading, or in his words, something like a fiction. Evidently, there is a dimension of this theoretical work that must be grasped aesthetically, akin to the function of the third critique.

Third, as has been suggested, the relation to the Kantian critiques is to be taken analogically, on a formal and thematic level: it is not a philosophical argument to reconcile their extrinsic oppositions, and it is neither to claim that anything like the Kantian systematicity upholds and unites the Foucauldian critiques. Regarding this systematicity, let us recall that Kant, in his critique of pure theoretical reason had set out from understanding to establish *a priori* categories to demonstrate the causal laws of nature and the bounds of our knowledge. In his critique of practical reason, he sets out to claim that while the law of freedom is unprovable, as an idea of reason, it is

---

[43] Michel Foucault, *Qu'est-ce que la critique? suivi de La culture de soi*, 84 and n. 10, 102–103, n." med "and 102–103, n. 10.

nonetheless constitutive for morality. The third critique, on aesthetic judgment, functions in Kant as the point of mediation between these two strictly separate fields; it opens up the possibility of a free play between the faculties, and makes space for a *sensus communis*.[44] This is hardly the case in Foucault: there is no strict contradiction or incompatibility to be resolved between what we have defined as his first and second critique, and there is very little explicit discussion on the interrelation between these three "groups of relations," as he calls them, in "The Culture of the Self." Yet to some extent, the analogy applies in this regard as well: the third modality of critique found in Foucault, i.e. the "will not to be governed like that," unites the first two by accounting for their very impulse or motivation. In its individual manifestation – the individual subjectivation, consisting in both theory and praxis, in both study and in the laborious application of truth – the third Foucauldian critique can be taken to mediate between theoretical work and political action. In its collective manifestation, the matter is less clear.

Fourth and finally, a word on the somewhat sudden inclusion of the phenomenon of art in the third critique (Foucault's most substantial efforts in this regard are found in his early work on literature, but his interest in visual art is manifest in the texts on Manet and Magritte). Is the "politics of truth," in which the subject of critique appears, wide and open-ended enough to accommodate something as large as the notion of art? Despite Foucault not raising any aesthetic questions in "What is Critique?" there may be reason reserve some space, or, at the very least, to keep open the possibility thereof. Many have pointed to the correspondences between Foucault's early work on literature and his late work on truth-telling and the technologies of the self, suggesting, for example, that there is an "underground link" between literature and *parrēsia*.[45] In a sense, we argued similarly in chapter 1 of this thesis, by describing Foucault's "found texts" as a manifestation of the common stakes in the force of writing and the radically other life as a manifestation of truth. But to point to the coexistence of certain elements is not to assume that the conceptual structures to which they belong, these early and late parts of Foucault's work, are easily reconciled or compatible on a theoretical level. While interesting claims have been made that Foucault's attention to literature as a site of "resistance" prefigures themes in his notion of critique – and that the considera-

[44] Immanuel Kant, *The Critique of the Power of Judgment*, trans. Paul Guyer and Eric Matthews (Cambridge: Cambridge University Press, 2000), 8, 120, 122, 139, 173–176.
[45] Azucena G. Blanco, "Foucault on Raymond Roussel: The Extralinguistic Outside of Literature," *Theory, Culture and Society*, 40 (1–2), 161–178. https://doi.org/10.1177/0263276420950458.

tion of "this performative intervention of literature [...] is an early development of some aspects of the critical discourse of *parrēsia* that Foucault elaborated in the 1980s" – such linkage must accommodate Foucault's early notions of transgression and of the "extralingustic," i.e. literature as an outside to language, with his late notion of an immanent subjectivity in the practices of the self and the notion of critique.[46] This, however, is beyond the scope of our present investigation. Instead, suffice it to note, as others have shown, that when Foucault's interest in literature wanes at the end of the 1960s, it cedes its place – and arguably its function within his thought – to an attention to forms of power and resistance, to collective struggles in the real, and finally to technologies of the self and the forming of an *other* life.[47] This common locus in the Fouauldian oeuvre, this shared function of pointing toward a certain agency of the subject, is not so surprising after all – the aesthetic writing cedes its place to an exploration of the technologies of the self, or the aesthetics of the self, the aesthetics of existence, the aesthetic character of the art of living.[48] And even if Foucault does not conceive of the aesthetics of the self or of "the life as a work of art" – and surely not of the art of not being governed like that – in modern terms of fine art, but in terms of *techne*, the two notions of art and the two notions of aesthetics are by no means unrelated. While their historical, practical, and conceptual links are not investigated here, both may be included in this third critique.

To conclude: having studied Foucault's "What is Critique?" we have taken his double definition of critique, added a third based on his subsequent work, and proposed the model of three Foucauldian critiques: namely, a sense of critique that applies to theoretical work, as proposed by his own historical-philosophical practice; critique as truth-telling in the political field, directed toward the public or the government, and third, a notion of critique formed by an individual and collective will not to be governed like that. Each of these critiques could be further examined and problematized, but at least the first two categories should be clear in what they are referring to. The third modality of critique, however, the collective art of insubordination, remains

---

[46] Azucena G. Blanco, "Foucault on Raymond Roussel: The Extralinguistic Outside of Literature," 178.

[47] Philippe Artières, Jean-François Bert, Mathieu Potte-Bonneville and Judith Revel, "Présentation" in Michel Foucault, *La grande étrangère: à propos de litterature*, 15–19.

[48] Recall, for example, Foucault's well-known remarks on Baudelaire's "modernity" and "modern man" (who makes his very existence into a work of art) as extensions of the Kantian critical attitude. Michel Foucault, "What is Enligthtenment?" in *The Politics of Truth*, trans. Lysa Hochroth & Catherine Porter (Los Angeles: Semiotexte, 2007), 109.

undetermined with regard to its position in Foucault's work and practice. We shall thus turn to this matter in the next chapter.

191

CHAPTER 5

Toward a Third Critique

Ontologies of the Present

In the previous chapter, a schema of three critiques was drawn up to sum-marize three great strands in Foucault's work and life, and, arguably, serving as his philosophical testament. From the 1978 lecture "What is Critique?" we took Foucault's own double definition of the concept to form the first and third modes of critique, modeled loosely on Kant's three critiques. We had inserted between these, a further mode, based on our reading of Foucault's 1983 lectures concerning *parrēsia* in the political domain during antiquity. Thus, what we call the first Foucauldian critique is the "historical-philosophical practice" of theoretical work. This is also how Foucault retrospectively understands the methodology of his early to mid works; the second critique is the truth-telling of the public intellectual and the political advisor, tasks with which Foucault engages to various degrees during his career;[1] and the third critique refers both to the individual and collective movement of desubjugation, resulting from the "will of not being governed like that." As we can see, the definitions of the first and second modes of critique are reasonably clear in that they refer to *faits accomplis* in Foucault's own life and work, or to future but similar – and therefore easily imagined – practices by others. The content of the third critique, at least in its collective form, is far more abstract. To begin with, it is not further discussed in Foucault's work: while the individual mani-festation of the art of not being governed like that can be taken as an object of investigation in Foucault's later lectures at the Collège de France on the care of the self (as has been demonstrated in chapters 2 and 4), these lectures are never devoted to the movement of collective desubjugation. As Foucault remarks in the discussion following his lecture on critique at the French Society for Philosophy, "this dimension of critique that seems to me to be so important because it is both part of, and not a part of, philosophy"

---

[1] For a recent compilation of petitions and open letters signed by Foucault, see *Signés Foucault & Cie*, ed. Philippe Artières (Paris: Éditions de la Sorbonne, 2020).

would have to be defined primarily as practice, or in his own words, as "revolt:" as the collective "non-acceptance of a real government," or "the individual experience of the refusal of governmentality."[2] With the tools and traces Foucault left, how might we go developing a more elaborate understanding of the collective art of not being governed like that, or what we call the Foucauldian third critique?

Perhaps we can define the matter in terms of truth – more precisely, truth and subjectivity. If the first critique is concerned with "regimes of truth" and with defining the conditions of truth, and if the second critique is concerned with speaking the truth to political power or in relation to government, the third critique can be understood as a practice of truth. It does not primarily relate to truth conceptually or discursively, as is the case with the first two critiques, but rather in terms of action. Now, critique has a subject. If the multiple subjects of the first critique are the writer and the readers that constitute themselves as such, and if the subject of the second critique is philosophy or rather the philosopher who tests reality by not remaining mere *logos* and by confronting political power, the subject of the third critique is being formed in a practice or politics of truth, as a subject of action in a kind of non-acceptance of government. In order to shed some light on what such a practice of truth and such a subject could be, we shall look at a few significant engagements with present events that Foucault undertook during this late period of his work and life: above all his lecture course on neoliberalism, but also his engagement with the Polish *Solidarność* movement, and his reflections on the role of labor unions.

The first "engagement" is of a theoretical nature and concerns the lectures of 1979, *The Birth of Biopolitics*. Despite the title, these lectures are more or less completely devoted to the origins and contemporary emergence of neoliberalism, the theoretical framework and governmental practice that was gaining strength as an ideological movement and political project at that particular moment, to dominate global political economy for the decades to come. The lecture course is important for several reasons: first of all, this is the point where Foucault most literally replicates the Kantian attempt to define the conjuncture and historical epoch to which he belongs, an attempt which, in his 1983 lectures, he would define as an ontology of the present: "an ontology of the present, of present reality, an ontology of modernity, an ontology of ourselves."[3] While Kant asked "What is Enlightenment?", Fou-

---

[2] Foucault, "What is Critique?" 75.
[3] Foucault, *The Government of Self and Others*, 21.

cault asks: "What is neoliberalism?" Further, this is the point where Foucault most clearly undertakes what he just months earlier had formulated as the task of critique in "What is Critique?": to ask the question of what role Enlightenment has continued to played between its historical epoch and today, through a process in which knowledge as positivist science "is going to play an increasingly determinant part in the development of productive forces and, such that, in addition, state-type powers are going to be increasingly exercised through refined techniques."[4] With this question – what is neoliberalism, animated by the investigation of the continuous effects of the Enlightenment as processes of governmentalization[5] – Foucault begins to characterize the workings of present-day government (arguably a precondition for any attempt not to be governed like that), grasping it in an inseparable relation with economy. Finally, *The Birth of Biopolitics* constitutes an interesting threshold as the last time Foucault works on modernity – all subsequent lecture courses and published works are devoted to antiquity – while the methodology and terminology, for instance his discussion of the *truth* of liberal *government*, puts it in a direct relation to his subsequent work. In Chapter 1 we identified Foucault's use of "found texts" as an *Archimedean point* in relation to his writing, in order to grasp the breaks and continuities in style, form, and methodology between Foucault's early/mid and late works. In the following we will argue that *The Birth of Biopolitics* could be regarded as a *critical point*, in the general sense of its importance for understanding Foucault's notions of critique and the ontology of the present, and in the more precise sense of allowing for the coexistence of otherwise separate forms, i.e. the methodologies of the first critique, and methodologies of what we call the second and third critiques.[6] *The Birth of Biopolitics* constitutes the

---

[4] Foucault, "What is Critique?", 50–51.

[5] In "What is Critique?", it is shown that Kant's 1784 question leads to more questioning, of a predominantly German kind: "for what excesses of power, for what governmentalization, all the more impossible to evade as it is reasonably justified, is reason not itself historically responsible?" Foucault both distances himself from and attaches himself to this kind of questioning: he traces his own heritage in the French epistemological tradition of Cavaillès, Bachelard and Canguilhem, but cites a "fellowship" with the Frankfurt School. See Foucault, "What is Critique?", 51. In *The Birth of Biopolitics,* on the other hand, Foucault distances his own work from this critique of Enlightenment heritage, perhaps when considering the Weberian ideas of disenchantment and economic rationality, or Adorno and Horkheimer's instrumental reason: "Undertaking the history of regimes of veridiction—and not the history of truth, the history of error, or the history of ideology, etcetera— obviously means abandoning once again that well-known critique of European rationality and its excesses, which has been constantly taken up in various forms since the beginning of the nineteenth century." See Foucault, *The Birth of Biopolitics*, 35.

[6] The critical point in thermodynamics defines the temperature and pressure at which a liquid and its vapor can coexist.

point at which modernity is still the epoch under investigation. But by means of the methodology and terminology – truth-telling and government – it is developed more substantially and effectively in his lectures on antiquity. This point of overlapping methodologies should make it even more clear that Foucault, in his diagnosis of the dominant governmentality of the present, defines the conditions and the very "arena" in which processes of subjectivation, truth-telling, the care of the self, and critique as a way of life will have to unfold today.

The second engagement concerns Foucault's far-ranging solidarity work with the Polish *Solidarność* movement. In its scope and duration it can only be compared with Foucault's work with GIP (*Groupe d'informa-tion sur les prisons;* the Prison Information Group) in the early 1970s: a thorough practical and activist engagement that preceded and in part led up to *Discipline and Punish.* On the issue of Foucault's practical solidarity with Poland, the secondary literature covering it and its relation to his theoretical work is, as Marcelo Hoffman has pointed out, "shockingly sparse.".[7] It is not likely that this sparsity will be much allayed below, given that Foucault provide so little material himself. Nevertheless, we can con-sider some significant continuities between Foucault's theoretical work and how he understood was drawn to the form of *Solidarność* at this moment. On Foucault's part, it is indeed a practical engagement. Yet, despite the fact he never wrote anything substantial on the events, some of the public inter-ventions he made – e.g. petitions and newspaper interviews – offer glimpses of his thought on subjectivity and critique, as it is laid out elsewhere. These glimpses and continuities point toward certain qualifications of the form of collective insubordination.

The third engagement consists in Foucault's exchange with the labor union *La Confédération française démocratique du travail* (CFDT), most notably the long conversation with its general secretary Edmond Maire, published in *Le Debat.*[8] Here Foucault makes an interesting, unprecedented remark, when he characterizes the trade union as a *"veridique,"* a truth-teller in the public sphere. He thereby transfers a concept, developed in relation to antiquity, to his own political present, thus activating or setting into play the terminology developed in his lectures on ancient modes of truth-telling, in which the speaking of the truth is always linked to a certain subjectivation of

---

[7] Marcelo Hoffman, *Foucault and Power* (London/New York: Bloomsbury, 2015), 126.

[8] This chapter will not return to Foucault's polemics with the Socialist government; while it is certainly a turn to his own present, it would, in terms which have already been established, qualify as part of a second critique; it has been discussed in chapter 3, and to some extent in chapter 4.

the truth, i.e., a reflexive, transformative process of becoming other. Not only does the application of this important concept in a new field confirm what has been suggested through the previous chapters, i.e. that the processes of subjectivation as Foucault studies them through ancient material are not only relevant to individual, ethical subjects during antiquity, but also to political, collective subjects in the present. As we shall see, the very same notion of veridiction also places these subjects and struggles in an interesting position in relation to the "truth" of liberal and neoliberal government. In the following, we shall look at these three engagements with the present, and try to identify their interconnections – despite their large differences – in light of what has been investigated in the previous chapters. Thus, hopefully, we shall be able to suggest one possible form of the third critique.

"What is Neoliberalism?"

It may seem strange that *The Birth of Biopolitics*, despite its title, discusses the notion of biopolitics only on a few occasions. In fact, this particular lecture course is devoted to discussing liberalism – more specifically neoliberalism. This is not so strange, however, once we acknowledge that to Foucault, the governmental reason of biopolitics is framed within the more general regime of liberalism: "only when we know what this governmental regime called liberalism was, will we be able to grasp what biopolitics is."[9] And so the prolegomenon becomes the study itself, as a major attempt to know what liberalism was evolving into during the 20th century, which defines much of it still today. Foucault studies the theoretical origins of neoliberalism and its German–Austrian–US emergence, devoting much of the course to the influence of Walter Eucken and the so-called Ordoliberals of the 1930s in Freiburg. He traces the dissemination of these ideas by Ludwig von Mises and Friedrich von Hayek during the 1950s–1960s when they are brought to the Chicago School, the bastion from which this German model achieves further diffusion in the US among economists like Gary Becker, and in France among economists and strategists close to Giscard d'Estaing during the 1970s. The lectures are neutrally descriptive, with Foucault largely maintaining a distance between himself and the material under scrutiny. But even within this seemingly nonpartisan account of liberal doctrines, we can find notes on the economy of truth-telling and government which, as we shall argue, have large but under discussed ramifications for his later use of these concepts in other contexts. In any case, Foucault is unearthing the very theoretical funda-

—

[9] Foucault, *The Birth of Biopolitics*, 22.

ment of the political-economic paradigm that had started to be implemented during the postwar period, and that was taking shape at an ever faster pace around him at the time of the lecture course.

It is doubtless a rare and important event when in the lectures of 1979 Foucault, in a manner unprecedented during his 14 years at the Collège de France, turns to scrutinize his most immediate present. And it is striking that he does so only months after having delivered "What is Critique?", in which for the first time he engages with Kant's attempt to define his own epoch in "What is Enlightenment?" But what may be even more important is the fact that Foucault here develops a definition of government in strictly economic terms: government is inseparable from economy. On the one hand, this represents something new in Foucault's thought, a "radicalization"[10] in political-economic terms, which provides a sort of horizon against which all his subsequent Collège de France lectures on the government of self and others arguably must be – but rarely is – understood.[11] On the other hand, this political-economic radicalization can be considered as a culmination of an ever-present tendency in Foucault's work. It marks in a more extensive way a kind of affirmation (an affirmation that is also a kind of reversal, as we shall see), of those flashes, present throughout his earlier works, where Foucault seeks to account for the determining relations between great economic processes and power effects in society. Let us recall that in *The History of Madness* Foucault considers "the Great Confinement" to be incited by mercantilist policies against falling wages,[12] and in *Discipline and Punish* he regards petty crime as a direct function of the bourgeoisie's rise to power, and its necessary allocation of certain economic practices to a separate, socially contained sphere: "Delinquency, solidified by a penal system centered upon the prison, thus represents a diversion of illegality for the illicit

---

[10] Radicalization may be understood not only as a stronger emphasis or accentuation, but in its etymological sense of relating to the *radix*: the genealogy of government and the "radically economic state" traces its economic roots. See below.

[11] In the two last courses at Collège de France, "government" refers to both the self-control or *enkrateia* on the part of the individual and the "good government" of the city-state; the fact that Foucault retains the term "government" indicates not only that he assumes an essential relationship between these two kinds of government, but also their relationship between them and the modern economic government he had examined in *The Birth of Biopolitics*. See *The Government of Self and Others*, 269–270 and *The Courage of the Truth*, 274.

[12] "Confinement had the same meaning throughout Europe, in these early days at least. It was one of the first responses that the seventeenth century offered to the economic crisis that was affecting the whole of the Western world: wages were falling, unemployment was widespread and the money supply was dwindling, probably as a repercussion of the crisis in the Spanish economy." See Foucault, *The History of Madness*, 64.

circuits of profit and power of the dominant class."[13] A perhaps lesser-known example is found in the inaugural Collège de France course *Lectures on the Will to Know*, when Foucault highlights the economic or proto-economic aspects of ancient Greece during the archaic period, for instance in his discussion of how the introduction of money served to maintain the landowners' position as a ruling class.[14] We can thus see that, from the very outset of his archaeological and genealogical projects, Foucault takes into account labor, circulation, and the role of money as determining factors of social transformation. Indeed, even the notion of government as economy was introduced by Foucault already a year prior to the investigation of neoliberalism, in his previous lecture course *Security, Territory, Population*, in order to account for the development of the reason of the state and the expanding notion of government from the 16th century to the 18th century. These two courses form a kind of diptych, the former tracing a line between a "pastoral power" (the model of the shepherd guiding his flock toward salvation) to the government of population within a set territory, passing through the very moment when "the essence of this government, that is to say, of the art of exercising power in the form of economy, will have what we now call the economy as its principal object."[15] But this notion of government as economy will be further developed in *The Birth of Biopolitics*.

The Beautiful, All-new and Rational State in Germany

Just as a certain "impossibility" of literary and cinematic representation may have been born in the ruins of nuclear annihilation in Marguerite Duras and Alain Resnais' *Hiroshima mon amour* ("You saw nothing in Hiroshima. Nothing."),[16] a new impossibility of political sovereignty – and concomitantly "the radically economic state"[17] – is born from the ruins of the Third Reich, after the same war but in another kind of void, when the new West German Republic is invented. In Germany, year zero, "a state – which history, defeat,

---

[13] Foucault, *Discipline and Punish*, Trans. Alan Sheridan (Vintage Books: New York, 1995), 280.

[14] Foucault, *Leçons sur la volonté de savoir*, 143.

[15] In these lectures Foucault accounts for the reappearance and flourishing of the notion of government in the 16th century (the government of children, of oneself, of the state, etc). Here, the general meaning of government still coincides with that of economy, in the original, ancient sense of *oikos*, of managing a household. Foucault traces the notion of government through the mercantilists and physiocrats to a point in the 18th century when, with Quesnay, economic government means "economic" in its modern sense. Foucault, *Security, Territory, Population*, 95.

[16] *Hiroshima mon amour*, directed by Alain Resnais (Argos Films, 1959), 00:03:30. See also Marguerite Duras, *Hiroshima mon amour*, trans. Richard Seaver (New York: Grove Press, 1961), 15.

[17] Foucault, *The Birth of Biopolitics*, 86.

or the decision of the victors had just outlawed – [...] rediscovers its law, its juridical law, and its real foundation in the existence and practice of economic freedom. History had said no to the German state, but now the economy will allow it to assert itself."[18] It is a "radically" economic state because its very roots are economic. Foucault argues that it constitutes something new in the way governmentality has been organized and rationalized since the 18th century. For the physiocrats, for Turgot and other 18th century economists, the problem was to limit the government of a legitimate and functioning state in order to allow economic liberty; "the problems the Germans had to resolve was the exact opposite: given a state that does not exist, how can we get it to exist on the basis of this non-state space of economic freedom?"[19] This post-war construction of modern, liberal governmentality introduces a recurring definition in these lectures: neoliberalism as the reversal of an order in which a solid state granted restricted space and freedom for economic exchange, to a kind of government determined by and founded upon economy as the unbound market.[20] It also provides some context to a brief and obscure passage in "What is Critique?", referring to "the recent development of the beautiful, all-new and rational State in Germany."[21] Does Foucault have his mind set on the emergence of neoliberalism across the Rhine, already in his discussion of critique ? It seems that way. It is in any case beyond doubt that the stakes of "What is Critique?" – for instance the Statist-scientific development of "procedures to rationalize the economy and society"[22] – animates *The Birth of Biopolitics*.

The early neoliberal development in the Anglo-American zone of Germany – which occurred during the parallel processes of reconstructing a peace economy, ensuring coordinated planning, and providing social measures deemed necessary to prevent further outbreaks of fascism and Nazism – is described as having implemented some of the ideas that Eucken and the so-called Ordoliberals had developed theoretically before the war. Among these, there is the central insistence on a market free from large monetary and fiscal interventions of a Keynesian kind, but not a market considered as self-regulating and natural, as in earlier liberal and neoclassical thought. It is instead a market that, in order to acquire its supreme price-setting function, must be optimized by public force, as Wilhelm

---

[18] Foucault, *The Birth of Biopolitics*, 85–86.
[19] Foucault, *The Birth of Biopolitics*, 86–87.
[20] Foucault, *The Birth of Biopolitics*, 131.
[21] Foucault, "What is Critique?", 51.
[22] Foucault, "What is Critique?", 50.

Röpke, one of the economists associated with Eucken's journal *Ordo*, points out: "The free market requires an active and extremely vigilant policy."[23] Foucault unravels a chain of events starting on 18 April 1948, when a scientific report delivered at a moment of otherwise "fully-fledged keynesian policy" (the report was delivered by a committee consisting of Eucken and fellow economists from the Freiburg School, as well as Christian Democratic and Socialist representatives) stated, among other things, that "the direction of the economic process should be assured as widely as possible by the price mechanism."[24] The results of the report were summed up efficiently ten days later in a speech by future chancellor Ludwig Erhard: "We must free the economy from state controls."[25] Foucault quotes Erhard's determination to steer clear from both anarchy and an interventionist "termite state" that would eat up society, and his political-economic conviction that "only a state that establishes both the freedom and responsibility of the citizens can legitimately speak in the name of the people."[26] In Foucault's understanding, it is the very legitimacy of the state that is at stake: against the political project of the National Socialist State, it is only the purity of an unfettered economy and economic growth that will produce a breach in history and memory, establishing a "permission to forget"[27] in the form of a radically economic state. These economic policies, Foucault notes, were not greeted enthusiastically by all: as prices rose in the months following deregulation, the German Socialists demanded Erhard's resignation, and by November 1948 there was a general strike calling for a return to a state-controlled economy. The strike was defeated, and the prices stabilized toward the end of the year. Apart from such direct con-testation, the British occupying power with its Labour Party ties and strong inclination toward Keynesian policies had to be appeased, while at the same time the important support from the Christian Democrats had to be secured by maneuvering internal ideological reluctance, such as when the vice president of the Christian Miners' union projected the social economy

---

[23] Wilhelm Röpke, *The Social Crisis of Our Time*, Part II, ch. 3, p. 228:, as cited in Foucault, *The Birth of Biopolitics*, 133.

[24] Foucault, *The Birth of Biopolitics*, 80.

[25] Ludwig Erhard as quoted in Foucault, *The Birth of Biopolitics*, 80–81.

[26] Ludwig Erhard as quoted in Foucault, *The Birth of Biopolitics*, 81.

[27] Foucault situates this permission to forget and its breach in time, along with economic growth, at the heart of the German political-economic system. He even sketches an analogy with Max Weber's description of wealth as regarded as a sign of God's salvation in the 16th century Germany: "In twentieth century Germany, an individual's enrichment will not be the arbitrary sign of his election by God, but general enrichment will be the sign of something else: not, of course, of God's election, [but] the daily sign of the adherence of individuals to the state." Foucault, *The Birth of Biopolitics*, 85.

of neoliberalism as a middle way between capitalism and socialism: a rhetorics Foucault describes as "completely hypocritical [...], simply intended to get the Christian inspired trade unions of the time to swallow the pill."[28] Eventually even the *Sozialdemokratische Partei Deutschlands* (SPD), "somewhat late, but fairly easily," came over to the neoliberal program. Foucault gives a brief sketch of the ten-year transition from the 1949 *Bad Dürkheim* congress, when class struggle as a political strategy and socialization of the means of production as a political goal, were still part of the party program, through the significant 1955 book *Socialism and Competition* by economist, SPD member, and future minister of economy and finance Karl Schiller (a book that, with its view on socialism *and* competition, preceded the Social Democrats' embrace of the free market), to the 1959 *Bad Godesberg* congress where the demand for the socialization of the means of production was renounced and instead private ownership was declared as legitimate and beneficial.

Socialist Governmentality

At this point of his investigation, Foucault makes an interesting digression: why, he asks, did the Social Democrats adopt neoliberal policies? First, for "a necessary and indispensable reason of political tactics:" a party that had strived within the legal framework of the old sovereign state to transform its political structure and abolish the capitalist mode of production, simply had no place within the new economic-political regime founded upon the principles of profitable enterprise, unregulated market, and growth.[29] They needed to adapt, and they did it so well that they were able to form a government in 1969, with Willy Brandt as chancellor. Second, Foucault adds, because socialism does not have a governmental rationality of its own. One might argue that socialism has a historical rationality, an economical rationality, an administrative rationality, but: "I do not think that there is an autonomous socialist governmentality."[30] According to Foucault, this great lacuna has far-reaching consequences: to begin with, it produces the question that is never addressed to liberalism, but always is in relation to socialism, namely: is it true or false? For this reason, it produces a peculiar form of validation: the question of how well it conforms to a text or set of texts considered to harbor the truth of socialism. Finally, the absence of a proper

---

[28] Foucault, *The Birth of Biopolitics*, 88.
[29] Foucault, *The Birth of Biopolitics*, 90.
[30] Foucault, *The Birth of Biopolitics*, 92.

governmental rationality means that to bring any kind of socialism into existence, it must be alloyed with established forms of governmentality, whether it is the "hyper-administrative" police-state of the German Democratic Republic in the East or the "unhappy symbiosis" with neoliberalism in the Social Democratic Federal Republic of Germany in the West.[31] The question is, in Foucault's words:

> What would really be the governmentality appropriate to socialism? Is there a governmentality appropriate to socialism? What governmentality is possible as a strictly, intrinsically, and autonomously socialist governmentality? In any case, we know only that if there is a really socialist governmentality, then it is not hidden within socialism and its texts. It cannot be deduced from them. It must be invented.[32]

Foucault contents himself with these brief remarks about the fundamental lack that characterizes socialism; the issue is a mere parenthesis in his wider explanation for the social democratic shift to neoliberal policies in Germany. Nonetheless, a couple of remarks can be made. First, considering the changing political landscape and global proliferation of neoliberalism in the decades following Foucault's lectures on the subject, it is impossible not to be struck by the general, almost predictive accuracy of Foucault's characterization of how social democratic parties face a tactical necessity to adopt a neoliberal agenda, by which they undermine their very *raison d'être*. The transition of the German Social Democrats is replicated throughout the world: from clearing all Marxist remnants in the Party programs and policies (most notably the socialization of the means of production),[33] to dismantling the Keynesian policies of sustaining aggregate demand by large-scale public investments;[34] from operating the more or less global wave of deregulation

---

[31] "In actual fact, and history has shown this, socialism can only be implemented connected up to diverse types of governmentality." Foucault, *The Birth of Biopolitics*, 92.

[32] Foucault, *The Birth of Biopolitics*, 94.

[33] In Sweden during the 1970s the Social Democratic Party had been commissioned by their unionized members to adopt the so-called "Employee funds" (*Löntagarfonderna*) or Rehn-Meidner Plan, a project of public taxation to be reinvested in shares of private companies, in order to gradually socialize them. Commissioned by the social democratic trade union confederation *Landsorganisationen*, and drafted primarily by economist Rudolf Meidner, the original document aimed at discontinuing capitalist ownership and made explicit reference to Marx. During the late 1970s and throughout the 1980s the party leadership did what they could to stall, defer, postpone, and gradually impede the implementation of the highly controversial funds. See David Harvey, *A Brief History of Neoliberalism* (New York: Oxford UP, 2005), 112–115.

[34] *The End of Parliamentary Socialism: From New Left to New Labour*, eds. Colin Leys and Leo Panitch (London/New York: Verso, 1997), 237, 240.

and privatization of the public sector, to limiting the legal right to strike.[35] Second, it must be acknowledged that the hypothesis itself, the notion of a non-existent socialist governmentality, is general, categorical and unspecified in a way that creates difficulties. Here, the word "socialism" refers to both the state capitalism of East Germany under the Communist Party's totalitarian rule and the capitalism of West German Social Democracy. Whether this reflects Foucault's "nominalism" or a rhetorical procedure of the moment, its general and indistinctive sense complicates analysis.[36] Ambiguity also belies the notion of "socialist governmentality" which could be taken either as a contradiction in terms, or as a sort of tautology; either socialism is irreconcilable with anything of the centralized and hierarchal kind that Foucault had previously discussed with respect to governmentality,[37] or, assuming that governmentality could appear between equals in their management of the common, socialist governmentality would be indistinguishable from socialism itself (and if socialism remains to be realized, so does its governmentality). Such apparent antinomies are not likely to have been part of Foucault's own conceptualization of the matter. While he does not discuss any further the idea of a distinct form of socialist governmentality in his lectures, the issue clearly stays with him: in 1983, it is the very subject of a book of interviews or conversations he plans to write with Didier Eribon.[38] The book never materialized, and it is difficult to imagine the

---

[35] "Reduced Right to Strike in Sweden," *Sveriges arbetares centralorganisation* (SAC), accessed March 10, 2024, https://arkiv.sac.se/en/Reduced-right-to-strike-in-Sweden.

[36] Regarding Foucault's "nominalist method," see Foucault, *The Birth of Biopolitics*, 94, and Michel Foucault, "Preface to The History of Sexuality, Volume Two," trans. William Smock, in *The Essential Works: Ethics*, ed. Paul Rabinow (London/New York: Penguin Books, 2000), 200.

[37] This would certainly be the case regarding the first definition Foucault gives *Security, Territory, Population*: "First, by "governmentality" I understand the ensemble formed by institutions, procedures, analyses and reflections, calculations, and tactics that allow the exercise of this very specific, albeit very complex, power that has the population as its target, political economy as its major form of knowledge, and apparatuses of security as its essential technical instrument." This definition, also consisting of the increased governmentalization and administrization at the expense of discipline, sovereign power and the state of justice, seems to be gradually generalized in the same course, and further stretched towards something like "that which relates to government" in *The Birth of Biopolitics*. Even if one were to take the different governmentalities of the police state, the 18th century economists, and the neoliberal state form in the original sense provided by Foucault (it might not be wrong to do so), it always seems to refer to a set of overlaying hierarchic, vertical or pyramid-shaped power relations, impossible to reconcile with anything called socialism. See, Foucault, *Security, Territory, Population*, 108.

[38] Foucault starts reading material on Léon Blum and the Popular Front government, seemingly intent to explain the failures and missed opportunities of the relatively radical government of the years 1936–38 precisely in terms of the absence of socialist governmentality (something that would also apply to Mitterand's Socialist government in the 1980s). Foucault begins interviews with Eribon, and the publishing house provides him with a researcher, but he abandons the project because his

outcome of such an investigation that would form a study or critique of "the parties and the party function" and in some positive sense seek to define a socialist governmentality, a left governmentality, or a certain "governing in a different way."[39] It is perhaps even more difficult to imagine the place such an investigation would have in the Foucauldian oeuvre, next to his critical archaeological and genealogical work.

The Market as Site of Veridiction

To return to the main question of the lectures – what is neoliberalism? – we must look closer at Foucault's notion of the "radically economic state." This particular state form is a radicalization of what Foucault considers in classical liberalism, in the first three lectures of the course, leading up to his introduction of the topic of neoliberalism. Here Foucault takes up the notions of "interests," "regime of truth" – defined as a discourse that renders certain practices intelligible and interrelated, and at the same time legislating between what is true and false among them – and the market as a "site of veridiction" for governmental practice. In the first lecture, Foucault recapitulates the previous year's course on the transition from the 16th and the 17th centuries, when the government of the economic field of taxes, tolls, price regulations and market codifications, and so on, was simply conceived as the exercise of sovereign rights, to the mid-18th century, when government had to be externally and systematically defined and validated, or, in other words, when political economy emerged as the regime of truth for economic government. This regime of truth as the principle of self-limitation of government is to be found, more specifically, in the changing role of the market. As opposed to the way in which the market had functioned during the middle ages, as a site of justice – of the just price and regulation, essentially of jurisdiction in Foucault's terms – the market appeared in the middle of the 18th century as something natural, producing what some economists called the natural price, thereby providing a form of veridiction. This natural field, the economists realized, reveals something like a truth; not only the true price, but a truth that distinguishes between correct and incorrect governmental practice. If left on its own, the market provides the blueprint or "speaks" the truth for correct government: "inasmuch as it enables production, need, supply, demand, value, and price, etcetera, to be linked together

---

work with volumes two and three of *The History of Sexuality* is again running smoother, and, according to Eribon, because the question proved too big for such a small project. See Eribon, *Foucault*, 306–07.

[39] Eribon, *Foucault*, 306.

through exchange, the market constitutes a site of veridiction, I mean a site of verification-falsification for governmental practice."[40] The market had obviously been of great concern to earlier governmental practices such as mercantilism, but it is, according to Foucault, only in the 18th century that it acquires the function of veridiction. No single cause lies behind the development of this fundamental phenomenon of Western governmentality; it would have to be explained by a more substantial investigation of multiple and articulated factors. Here, Foucault points to: the monetary situation of stable currencies and the influx of gold; economic and demographic growth; the new role of technicians in government, and the development of economic concepts. But it is perhaps not the "intelligibility of the process" that is of interest, as much as how Foucault formulates it in terms of truth-telling.[41]

The "irruption" of the market as a site of veridiction is a prismatic moment in the lecture course and in Foucault's late work in general. To begin with, and in addition to being an early instance of Foucault's shift from the conceptual pair power-knowledge to government-truth, the very term veridiction, i.e. the speaking of the truth, points both backwards and forwards in Foucault's work: forwards, because it will be employed frequently in the lectures devoted to antiquity when Foucault discusses the Greek and Roman practices of truth-telling in *parrēsia* and *licentia*; backwards, because introduced in *The Birth of Biopolitics*, veridiction is employed precisely to articulate the stakes of his earlier works. Thus, the histories of madness, punishment and surveillance, and sexuality are now formulated as investigations of the shift from jurisdiction to veridiction, forming a greater critical project of "the genealogy of regimes of veridiction."[42] The "veridiction of the market" is also a strikingly atypical use of the term. It is unlike the other forms of veridiction to which Foucault refers: the courageous truth-telling of the parrhesiast; the shifts from physical treatments and punishments to imploring the madman and criminal to state the truth about himself; the individual confession as production of desire and sexuality. In contrast to these examples, the veridiction of the market is a non-personal, non-human "speaking" of the truth, a technical or automated kind of truth-telling, a non-discursive speech. Unlike the practice *parrēsia* or speaking the truth to power,

---

[40] Foucault, *The Birth of Biopolitics*, 32.

[41] The irruption of the market as a site of veridiction cannot be ascribed to a single cause. It needs to be understood by establishing its "intelligibility." This is how Foucault defines genealogy in his historical-philosophical work in "What is critique?". See Foucault, "What is critique?", 64, and Foucault, *The Birth of Biopolitics*, 33.

[42] Foucault, *The Birth of Biopolitics*, 33–36.

the veridiction of the market is not a critique, not a negation or protest. It does not respond to anything. It has neither referent nor interlocutor, but is the object of constant attention of those who govern. At the same time, there are continuities beyond these atypical features. Just like the two models in antiquity that Foucault discusses (i.e. the Periclean model of speaking the truth at the Assembly for the democratic city-state to function and the Platonic model of acting as a political advisor and of speaking the truth to form the Prince's soul in the autocratic Syracuse), liberal, modern governmentality needs its own form of truth to function. But while the two ancient models of truth-telling and government clearly are of a spoken, discursive kind, where concepts are used and *logos* formed in relation to an interlocutor – and where the response equally operates on a conceptual, discursive level – the veridiction of the market is not really speech, it is not even *monologos*, but unspoken and non-discursive in its nature. It is impossible to respond to. It cannot be argued with, so to speak. Could such non-discursive truth-telling then be opposed with other forms of non-discursive truth-telling? Perhaps, as we shall see below. Similar to Daniele Lorenzini, who alongside his exegetical tracing of the development of the concept "regime of truth" through different texts by Foucault tries to grasp its most central but also most evasive function, we can perhaps approach veridiction in a similar way: not as a "merely analytical or methodological tool: it carries in itself a critical force, and this is why it can still be useful for us, today."[43] So, this notion of veridiction of the market is an important point in the lecture course, in that it allows one to make connections with other parts of Foucault's work, as well as allowing one to recognize how it functions within the lectures' scope of understanding liberalism. Foucault defines the constitution of the market as a site of veridiction as an "absolutely fundamental phenomenon in the history of Western governmentality."[44] As such, it continues to play a central role in his account of neoliberalism.

In relation to early neoliberalism's recognition of the social sphere, the commitment to the market among US American neoliberals is "much more radical, much more complete and exhaustive."[45] When Ordoliberal Alexander Rüstow coined the term "neoliberalism" at the Walter Lippman colloquium in Paris in 1938, he was outlining a *Gesellschaftspolitik* which was an "enterprise society" not only in economic terms, but also a *Vitalpolitik*

---

[43] Daniele Lorenzini, "What is a Regime of Truth?" *Le Foucauldien*, 2 February, 2015. DOI: 10.16995/lefou.2.
[44] Foucault, *The Birth of Biopolitics*, 33.
[45] Foucault, *The Birth of Biopolitics*, 243.

which included "warm" measures against the "cold" effects of competition.[46] As opposed to this, US neoliberalism further emphasized the economic interests of individuals, projecting an "unlimited generalization of the form of the market" with regard to the social sphere.[47] Foucault takes up a number of striking examples here: child rearing as an investment in human capital; marriage as a form of contractual commitment of input and output; crime as a supply-demand relation that the rational individual subject considers in light of the risk of punishment. These cases of generalization of economic analysis are considered by Foucault in strictly theoretical terms, within the neoliberal perspective. To the present-day reader of these lectures, after four decades of neoliberal economic subsumption of social relations, Foucault's commentary may seem overly distanced. To some extent, he acknowledges neoliberalism's ontological aspect: "Liberalism in America is a whole way of being and thinking."[48] But he does not cite any critical reflections of the struggles in opposition against this early development of neoliberalism, despite the fact that such critical work was already underway at the time;[49] in relation to the idea of marriage as a contractual affair of input and output, for example, there is an important feminist critique of unpaid domestic work as reproductive labor necessary to capital.[50] To assess the critical value of these lectures on neoliberalism, we need to pay attention to certain examples and how they relate to other parts of Foucault's work; we need also to recognize the limits of Foucault's perspective, and to acknowledge the fact that

---

[46] Alexander Rüstow, *Colloque Walter Lippmann*, 83, as cited in Foucault, *The Birth of Biopolitics*, 242.

[47] Foucault, *The Birth of Biopolitics*, 243.

[48] Foucault, *The Birth of Biopolitics*, 218.

[49] In relation to the neoliberal notion of human capital there is a critical mirror image in Mario Tronti's description of "the capitalist's struggle to dismantle and recompose in his own image the antagonistic figure of the collective worker." Tronti's *Workers and Capital* was published already in 1966, and it set off a movement of *operaismo*, *post-operaismo*, and *autonomia* that would develop alongside neoliberalism and critically diagnose it. Some of its articulations are not so far removed from Foucault. A year prior to *The Birth of Politics*, at the invitation of Althusser, Antonio Negri gave a series of lectures at l'École normale in Paris, furthering Tronti's analyses of social capital and the subject of labor. Between Foucault and the tradition(s) of Tronti and Negri there is a general but important common feature: just as, for Foucault, resistance is always possible – indeed, it is even implied in every relation of power – Tronti insisted on the working class as a decisive subject in the historical development of capitalism, with its struggles as a driving force behind capital's adjustments and developments. See Mario Tronti, *Workers and Capital*, trans. David Broder (London/New York: Verso, 2019), 29, and Antonio Negri, *Marx Beyond Marx*, trans. Harry Cleace, Michael Ryan and Maurizio Viano (London: Autonomedia/Pluto, 1991).

[50] This critical claim was advanced by the Wages for Housework movement. See Mariarosa Della Costa and Selma James, *The Power of Women and the Subversion of the Community* (Bristol: Falling Wall Press, 1972).

Foucault is investigating neoliberalism before the fact, so to speak; before it became a globally dominant economic and political program.

A Critique of Neoliberalism

When Foucault describes the neoliberal use of the veridiction of the market as a corrective to political government, he argues that it forms a reversal of the *laissez-faire* policy of classical liberalism: rather than the government letting the market be, the market is attended to and optimized, it is used to gauge the validity, to object to the actions, or to criticize the excesses or futility of governmental actions; it is even turned into a "permanent economic tribunal confronting government."[51] In this optimization and generalization of the market, he identifies potential effects both in the form of objective changes in the labor market, and in the form of a subjective transfiguration, i.e. a transformation of the subject's ways of being under neoliberalism. One example appears in his discussion of the possible French introduction of a "negative tax," a *de facto* payment or benefit to individuals to assure income at a certain level, a potential measure "clearly visible in the economic policy of Giscard and Barre."[52] First, Foucault notes that the lack of any redistributive purpose "reintroduces that category of the poor and of poverty that all social policies, certainly since Liberation, but in reality all the policies of welfare, all the more or less socializing or socialized policies since the end of the nineteenth century, tried to get rid of."[53] Then he echoes Marx's description of industrial capitalism's "creation of that monstrosity, an industrial reserve army, kept in misery in order to be always at the disposal of capitalist exploitation."[54] Foucault observes that with nothing but such a minimum security guaranteed by a negative tax, there will be "a kind of infra- and supra-liminal floating population, a liminal population which, for an economy that has abandoned the objective of full employment, will be a constant reserve of manpower which can be drawn on if need be, but which

---

[51] Foucault, *The Birth of Biopolitics*, 247.

[52] This financial measure ties together the different geographic points of neoliberal development in the lectures: the consideration of a negative tax appears in and around the French government in the late 1970s (president Giscard d'Estaing had appointed economy professor Raymond Barre as both prime minister and minister of economy and finance), but Foucault credits its invention to US neoliberal thought, and underlines its roots in the German Ordoliberalism and its dictum that no "player" shall ever risk or be allowed to fall out of the "economic game." As he points out, it is obviously also a kind of optimization of the market, securing supply of labor. See Foucault, *The Birth of Biopolitics*, 207.

[53] Foucault, *The Birth of Biopolitics*, 206.

[54] Translation modified; Marx, *Capital* vol 1, trans. Ben Fowkes (Middlesex: Penguin Classics, 1976), 618.

can also be returned to its assisted status if necessary.[55] Another example is found in his reflection on the transformation of the liberal notion of *homo economicus*: from the earlier 19th century subject of interests and exchange, to the neoliberal version of *homo economicus* as entrepreneur. By radicalizing and individualizing the Ordoliberal notion of *Gesellschaft* or enterprise, by developing the theory of human capital – in which the selling of one's labor is not considered as work but as profiting from one's own human capital, turning every worker into a capitalist – the individual subject can be understood as an entrepreneur of himself. While Foucault may have been interested in many forms of critique of the state,[56] he has no illusions of the radically economic state, or the further radicalized economy of neoliberalism (in which the entrepreneurial subject would produce his own happiness), as one of pure freedom:

> In other words, considering the subject as *homo oeconomicus* [...] means that the individual becomes governmentalizable, that power gets a hold on him to the extent, and only to the extent, that he is a *homo oeconomicus*. [...] Homo *oeconomicus* is the interface of government and the individual.[57]

The model of *homo economicus* as entrepreneur is thus one of the most recent models for governing and "individualizing" individuals. The freedom available to this figure is freedom in the modern sense it acquires during the 18th century, namely the freedom and security of exchange: "the possibility of movement, change of place, and processes of circulation of both people and things."[58] The liberal subject as *homo economicus* and entrepreneur must be understood as an individualizing effect of power of the kind that Foucault discusses in "Omnes et Singulatim," as a figure inscribed in his overall project of making visible the arbitrary, historically contingent – and thus confrontable – nature of power and forms of government.[59] Consequently – despite the fact that Foucault does not generally pass any judgments in his descriptions of neoliberalism[60] – it might be wrong to call the historical account of neoliberalism in *The Birth of Biopolitics* non-partisan, disinterested, or distanced; or, like Stuart Elden, to say that it is "historical rather than political,"

---

[55] Foucault, *The Birth of Biopolitics*, 206.

[56] In relation to neoliberalism, Daniel Defert stated: "For Foucault, the critique of the state appealed to him, but more as anarchist than as liberal." see Stuart Elden, *Foucault's Last Decade*, 103.

[57] Foucault, *The Birth of Biopolitics*, 252.

[58] Foucault, *Security, Territory, Population*, 48–49.

[59] Foucault, "Omnes et singulatim: Towards a Criticism of Political Reason," 254.

[60] Although, he does at one point acknowledge its "coefficient of threat." See Foucault, *The Birth of Biopolitics*, 233.

or "an attempt to grasp the historical conditions of possibility of political order, rather than an endorsement of or opposition to a specific political programme."[61] Because the "attempt to grasp the historical conditions of possibility of political order" could very well be understood as the political modus operandi for the Foucauldian genealogical method.[62]

At the same time, there are important limits to Foucault's analysis. Foucault sets out to study the current crisis in governmentality, saying that if the modern world is characterized by the recurring crises of capitalism, one could also identify a set of crises within liberalism. And while capitalism and liberalism may appear conjoined, the "crises of liberalism are not just the pure and simple or direct projection of these crises of capitalism in the political sphere."[63] This underlying assumption – never developed or further discussed – determines the entire investigation of governmentality. Yet the position stands in some contrast to the one articulated in earlier works by Foucault, where economic processes are taken to determine social and political transformations to a larger degree.[64] So, while *The Birth of Biopolitics* forms Foucault's most systematic account of the relation between government and economy, presenting government as essentially economic and indexed to the truth of the market, it retains a kind of autonomy on the part of politics and governmentality *vis-a-vis* the economy and the crises of capitalism. It thus reverses the causal order deployed in the analysis of, for example, *The Lectures on the Will to Know* where the new political structures in the archaic period of classical antiquity appear as a function of specific interests in the accumulation of wealth.[65] That governmentality in Foucault's account is irreducible to economic relations is not a

---

[61] Elden, *Foucault's Last Decade*, 103.

[62] As has been argued in the previous chapter, to make visible the historical conditions of possibility of a political order is also to start to make visible how it is made impossible, undone, or dismounted: "Let us say, roughly, that as opposed to a genesis oriented towards the unity of some principal cause burdened with multiple descendants, what is proposed instead is a *genealogy*, that is, something that attempts to restore the conditions for the appearance of a singularity born out of multiple determining elements of which it is not the product, but rather the effect. A process of making it intelligible but with the clear understanding that this does not function according to any principle of closure." See Foucault, "What is Critique?", 64.

[63] Foucault, *The Birth of Biopolitics*, 70.

[64] Recall the examples in the beginning of this chapter: in *The History of Madness*, the "Great Confinement" is seen as propelled by a mercantilist understanding of economic relations and falling wages, in *Discipline and Punish*, legal reforms regarding petty crime is described as a direct function of class domination and the bourgeoisie's rise to power, and so on.

[65] See for instance Foucault's analysis of the legal constitution of the city state under Solon, and how its *nomos* functions as a diversion from class struggle, "hid[ing] the fact that the political distribution of power maintains and renews the mode of appropriation of wealth." Foucault, *Lectures on the Will to Know*, 161.

problem per se – quite the contrary, as has been argued.[66] But the emphasis on the theoretical development of liberalism – a focus on doctrinal content more continuous with his subsequent studies of ancient philosophical schools than his previous work and its use of archival material[67] – prevents Foucault from recognizing important aspects of the process: while Foucault states that what is at stake in neoliberalism is ultimately the survival of capitalism, he does not take into account the technical transformations and social contradictions of the latter.[68] To do so, he would perhaps have had to investigate government not only in relation to his own concept of "regimes of truth," but something like "regimes of accumulation," a concept forged precisely to analyze more closely the relation between the crises of government and the crises of capitalism.[69]

The notion of regimes of accumulation was systematized three years prior to Foucault's investigation of neoliberalism, by Michel Aglietta in his *Régulation et crises du capitalisme* from 1976. Aglietta's "regulationist" approach holds that the recurring crises of capitalism are actually due to the tension between what he calls the regime of accumulation, which defines the historically shifting forms of capitalist accumulation or creation of surplus value, and the forms of its regulation, which includes the state and economic policies. Like most other periodizations of capitalism,[70] Aglietta locates a break in the early 1970s: in his terms it is a crisis of Fordism that leads to the emergence of Neo-Fordism, but while he sees this as an expansion or the totalization of the logic of accumulation, insinuating itself into all parts of the lives of the wage-earners, he does not conceive it in terms of neoliberalism, and is careful not to draw any conclusions at such a preliminary stage of its development.[71] Yet it is in this vein, and with the benefit of hindsight, that

---

[66] Jacques Bidet argues for a complimentary relation between the Marxian analysis of the market and the Foucauldian analysis of the organization or governmentality. See Jacques Bidet, *Foucault avec Marx*, 67.

[67] Can we already here see what Vegetti called the "tension in Foucault's genealogical style," resulting from a privileging of the "*énoncé*" at the expense of the modes of enunciation, in other words the doctrine itself rather than the discursive formation making that doctrine possible? See Vegetti, "Foucault et les anciens," 925.

[68] Foucault, *The Birth of Biopolitics*, 164.

[69] The differentiated understanding of capitalism provided by the notion of regimes of accumulation is precisely what Foucault is lacking when he states: "if we accept that in a Marxist type of analysis, in the broadest sense of the term, it is the economic logic of capital and its accumulation that is determinant in the history of capitalism, then you can see that in fact there can only be one capitalism since there is only one logic of capital." See Foucault, *The Birth of Biopolitics*, 164.

[70] See for example Giovanni Arrighi, *The Long Twentieth Century* (London/New York: Verso, 2010), 221.

[71] "A new regime of intensive accumulation, Neo-Fordism, would arise from the crisis, articulating the progress of capitalist accumulation to the transformation of the totality of conditions of existence

someone like David Harvey could later grasp neoliberalism as a reinvention of certain forms (or regimes) of accumulation – and above all, something that Foucault does not consider but of central importance, as a project emanating from specific class interests.[72] Harvey argues that neoliberalism essentially is a project of restoration of class power (citing an increased share of national income by the richest percent of the population, an increased concentration of wealth, as well as a decrease in real wages and the minimum wage, and a deterioration in both common property rights and the legal framework of workers' rights), showing that it is not so much through the creation of surplus value that the capitalist accumulates but through the redistribution of existing wealth that neoliberalism further enriches the richest part of society. For Harvey, then, neoliberalism marks a kind of return to what Marx called primitive accumulation,[73] though in its neoliberal form, Harvey refers to it as "accumulation by dispossession".[74]

Finally, we must recall that while Foucault traces neoliberalism's theoretical roots decades back in time, he is still studying the phenomenon before its most substantial implementation. In *A Brief History of Neoliberalism*, Harvey regards the years 1978–80 as the revolutionary starting point of this tumultuous era, and of the four events he singles out, only China's beginning of liberalization of its economy occurred before Foucault held his 1979 course *The Birth of Biopolitics* (the changing of direction at the US Federal Reserve, the election of Thatcher and the election of Reagan all played out sub-

---

of the wage-earning class – whereas Fordism was geared simply to the transformation of the private consumption norm, the social costs of mass consumption continuing to be met on the margins of the capitalist mode of production. See Michel Aglietta, *A Theory of Capitalist Regulation: The US Experience*, 168.

[72] David Harvey, *A Brief History of Neoliberalism* (Oxford/New York: Oxford University Press, 2005), 159–65.

[73] Primitive accumulation (acquiring value with force, more or less) is Marx's term for the accumulation preceding capitalistic accumulation, which provides its necessary conditions: both surplus value to be turned into capital, and available, "free" labor power. Marx describes it as "the historical process of divorcing the producer from the means of production," and scoffs at the idyllic standard version of political economy: "In actual history it is notorious that conquest, enslavement, robbery, murder, briefly force, play the great part." Karl Marx, *Capital* vol 1, ch. 26, 873–76.

[74] First developed in *Spaces of Hope*, the notion of "accumulation by dispossession" is further discussed by Harvey in *A Brief History of Neoliberalism*. Like Giovanni Arrighi, who builds on the work of Fernand Braudel and the Annales school, and shows that each historical "cycle of accumulation" enters an increased level of financialization when it draws to an end, Harvey notes the central role of financialization in neoliberalism. Along with this financialization of a particularly "speculative and predatory style," Harvey lists three more features of the neoliberal accumulation by dispossession: privatization and commodification, the management of crises, and state redistributions, all of them transferring wealth from the public sphere and common property, from wage earners and low income households, to the top earning segment of society.

sequently). Hence, the actual development of neoliberalism, and its new forms of accumulation and governmental practices, takes place after Foucault's inquiry into the matter.[75] The events of this development shed light upon what Foucault could not know, but to some extent also what, given the limits of his perspective, he could not account for.

What *The Birth of Biopolitics* shows us is some of the most important features of neoliberalism as governmental practice. While modern government is essentially economic with liberal government having to adhere to the veridiction of the market, neoliberal government is a radicalization of this relationship, expanding its logic to cover ever more social relations. This means among other things that the veridiction of the market does not only speak the truth of how a state must be governed. With the notion of homo economicus as an interface of government and the individual conceived as an entrepreneur of him- or herself, we can see how this veridiction of the market "speaks" directly to individuals, providing the truth of how the individual subjects must govern themselves. The neoliberal constant optimization and generalization of the market thus ensures that society, from the individual to the state, is governed in accordance with truth. So if *The Birth of Biopolitics* and some of the other works mentioned above offer a critique of neoliberalism, they, as theoretical works, obviously belong to what, in previous parts of this thesis, we called the first modality of critique. To imagine something akin to the third modality of critique of neoliberalism, i.e. critique in the sense of opposing or refusing government – of not being governed like that – one may be served not only by theoretical works, but by certain features of two labor unions (engaged in very different struggles) that Foucault interacted with around this time.

Foucault and *Solidarność*
– Where Means Become Ends Again

During the early 1980s, Foucault's largest non-theoretical engagement was with the "Polish question," specifically the organized support for the labor union, *Solidarność*, against the increasingly repressive, militarized Polish state. This engagement surpasses others of the kind in terms of intensity,

---

[75] For Harvey, too, it took some time to reach this conclusion. Before his history of neoliberalism, Harvey describes the historical transition from the rigidities of Fordism-Keynesianism to a new regime of accumulation which he tentatively calls "flexible accumulation." See David Harvey, *The Condition of Post-Modernity: An Enquiry into the Origins of Cultural Change* (Oxford: Basil Blackwell, 1989), 173.

duration, and public scale,[76] and it differs in several respects from Foucault's oft discussed relation to the Iranian struggle against the Shah and its transformation into the Islamic Republic. While Foucault had traveled to Iran as a journalistic chronicler of sorts for *Corriere della Sera*,[77] he goes to Poland as an activist. And while Foucault in Iran tried to grasp the events with concepts that he was yet to develop more substantially elsewhere, and that he used speculatively in relation to a movement that would take a very different direction than he had predicted – Foucault's enthusiasm for the "political spirituality" in a struggle that led to the regime of the ayatollahs have produced a long debate[78] – his brief characterizations of *Solidarność* articulate important features of his own thought that are of interest for our investigation here. We shall now look into the nature of this engagement.

Little has been written on Foucault's solidarity with the struggle in Poland, in light of his theoretical work. To some degree, Marcelo Hoffman's *Foucault and Power* is the exception, with Hoffman himself noting a lack of literature on the issue. But while Hoffman considers Foucault's position on Poland in relation to the French government – suggesting that his condemnation of the French non-interventionist policy propelled him into his studies of *parrēsia* – we shall look a bit closer at how Foucault related to the Polish movement of opposition and struggle. The following may not provide the "sustained

---

[76] During this period, Foucault's support for Soviet dissidents is consistent and important, but carried out on a case to case basis. His engagement with gay rights, gay culture, and sexuality is always carried out within the movement and the community, limited to contributions and interviews in publications like *Gai Pied*. See Michel Foucault, "De l'amitié comme mode de vie" in *Dits et écrits II, 1976–1988*, no 293, 982.

[77] Foucault's Italian publisher Rizzoli had started cooperating with *Corriere della Sera*, and asked him for regular contributions. Foucault made two visits to Iran, and wrote eight articles on the events leading up to the Islamic revolution. He was enthusiastic about the possibility "to grasp what is happening right now, because these days nothing is finished, and the dice are still being rolled," embracing the new format and its possibilities: "There are more ideas in the world than the intellectuals often imagine. [...] We have to be there and assist at their birth and their exploding force." Michel Foucault, *Dits et écrits II, 1976–1988*, no 293, 982.

[78] Regarding what Foucault wrote in 1978 about "Islamic government" and how he was impressed by "its attempt to open up a spiritutal dimension in politics" in the brewing state before the revolution, he was opposed directly at the time in *Nouvel Observateur*. See, for example, Atoussa H., "An Iranian Woman Writes" in *Foucault and the Iranian Revolution*, eds. Janet Afary and Kevin B. Anderson (Chicago and London: The University of Chicago Press, 2005), 209–10. The same book contains English translations of Foucault's writings on Iran, and a strong criticism of Foucault by its editors. For an interesting attempt to contextualize Foucault's writings on Iran, for a demonstration of the contituity between his notion of a "political spirituality" in Iran and his notion of spiritual knowledge in *The Hermeneutics of the Subject*, and for a critique of how Afary and Anderson "misconstrue" Foucault's work, see Behrooz Ghamari-Tabrizi, *Foucault in Iran* (Minneapolis/London: University of Minnesota Press, 2016).

analysis"[79] of Foucault's relation to Poland and *Solidarność* that has been called for – a difficult task considering that Foucault neither wrote any substantial theoretical commentary about this union *cum* social movement, nor, quite expectedly, did he offer any systematic reflections about his own engagement in the cause. But looking closer at the public statements he made, we shall try to demonstrate what it is that makes Foucault consider *Solidarność* such a remarkable vehicle for ethical, political, and critical mobilization.

When *Solidarność* was formed in September 1980, it had been preceded by strikes and protests that had won the right to form unions. But with the rapid growth of the movement and demands for self-government, repression intensified again.[80] In December 1981, the newly instated First Secretary General Wojciech Jaruzelski declared martial law and set off a wave of arrests, severe repression, and deadly force.[81] Foucault, who had lived in Poland two decades earlier, serving as lecturer and cultural attaché in Warsaw in 1958–59,[82] had been following the events with special interest.[83] When French Foreign Minister Claude Cheysson, speaking on radio *Europe 1* about Jaruzelski's deployment of military troops in the streets, declared that it was a purely internal affair with no possibility for outside intervention, Foucault was among the many who reacted forcefully. From his immediate response

---

[79] Marcelo Hoffman, *Foucault and Power* (London/New York: Bloomsbury, 2015), 126.

[80] Poland in 1980 was facing an economic crisis, and strikes had appeared at factories in protest to rising prices and falling real wages. When the crane operator and activist Anna Walentynowicz was dismissed from the Gdansk shipyard, a strike broke out demanding her reinstatement. The strike spread across the country to factories and mines, and the demands soon included the right to strike, the right to form labor unions, free speech, and the restoration of the rights of political prisoners and expelled students. The strikers won the right to strike and to form unions, and a month later, in September 1980, the nationwide labor union *Solidarność* (Solidarity) was formed by Lech Walesa and others. Growing rapidly, striving for a "self-governed republic" and organizing nationwide strikes as large as one of 14 million workers, *Solidarność* had by its legal status as a legitimate representative of workers, autonomist ambitions, and its great popular support become a serious threat against the ruling Communist Party. See Shana Penn, *Solidarity's Secret* (Ann Arbor: The University of Michigan Press, 2005), 58.

[81] Under pressure from the Soviet Union, the Party Central Committee replaced its first secretary Stanislaw Kania with General Wojciech Jaruzelski, already acting as Prime Minister and Minister of Defence, Commander in Chief, and General of the Army. See Shana Penn, *Solidarity's Secret*, 87.

[82] Foucault was the director of the newly opened *Centre Français*, lecturing on Apollinaire among other things, and writing on *Madness and Civilization*. He had to leave the country (advised so by his superiors) after having had a relationship with a man who had acted as police informer. *See* David Macey, *The Lives of Foucault*, 85–86.

[83] In 1977, Foucault had signed petitions in support of imprisoned members of KOR (Committee for Defense of Workers), and in 1980 he supported the "Free Learning in Poland" initiative. See David Macey, *The Lives of Foucault*, 445.

penned together with Pierre Bourdieu and published in *La Libération*,[84] there were to be a string of texts, petitions, and interviews by Foucault in support of the Polish people, parallel with his voluntary work in *Comité Solidarność en France*, the French *Solidarność* committee founded by exiles. The extent of this engagement, where he "spent hours on repetitive bureaucratic tasks" in its financial section,[85] is perhaps only comparable to his work in the *Groupe d'Information sur les Prisons* (GIP) in the early 1970s, characterized by a similar "working alongside" rather than "speaking for"[86] its implicated subjects, whether prison inmates or Polish workers.[87]

To understand Foucault's "exceptional devotion" we must consider the importance of the very form of *Solidarność*. Hoffman takes up an interesting analogy made by Foucault on French radio in response to the Foreign Minister's proclamation of non-intervention: "Who is the socialist, but I would say who is the European who would accept to say today that the Commune of Paris in 1871 was nothing but an internal French affair? I believe that for one century now we know that a worker put in prison for a strike, that a prohibited union, that an army that occupies a city are never an internal affair of a country."[88] It is a strange analogy; if one thing has become certain since the Paris Commune, it is that European governments, including socialist ones, as Foucault had pointed out the day before,[89] have made it standard procedure to regard imprisoned workers, prohibited unions and

---

[84] This short text was published in *Libération* on the 15 and 17 December, reproduced in part in *Le Monde* on the 18 December, and read out by Yves Montand on *Europe 1* on 15 December. Toward the end, we may recognize a slight echo of Foucault's critique of the lacking Socialist governmentality: "In 1936, a socialist government was faced with a military putsch in Spain; in 1956, a socialist government was faced with repression in Hungary. In 1981, the socialist government is faced with the Warsaw coup. We do not want its attitude today to be that of its predecessors." See David Macey, *The Lives of Foucault*, 440.

[85] David Macey, *The Lives of Foucault*, 444. Seweryn Blumsztajn, the head of the French chapter, describes Foucault's work as a treasurer and recalls his "long accounts, complete with all the figures. I couldn't help thinking he had better things to do." Didier Eribon, *Foucault*, trans. Betsy Wing (Cambridge, Massachusetts: Harvard UP, 1991), 303.

[86] Michel Foucault and Gilles Deleuze, "Intellectuals and Power" in, *Language, Counter-Memory, Practice: Selected Essays and Interviews*, 209. For a description of the diverse members and shared tasks in the running of GIP, see Macey *Lives of Michel Foucault*, 264–69.

[87] Both engagements were defined by a similar refusal of any division of labor or of delegating the less glamorous, time-consuming or manual work to others. Foucault and his partner Daniel Defert had founded GIP, and for the two years the group was active, Foucault was running things also on a very basic level: "addressing envelopes, drafting press releases and handing out leaflets were all part of his daily life." Macey, *Lives of Michel Foucault*, 257.

[88] Michel Foucault, "Émission radiophonique sur la situation en Pologne," 16 December 1981, C 154, Audio Cassette, Fonds Foucault, Institut Mémoires de l'Édition Contemporaine, Paris, France. As quoted in Marcelo Hoffman, *Foucault and Power* (London/New York: Bloomsbury, 2015), 130–31.

[89] See footnote 84 above, on the text by Foucault and Bourdieu in *Libération*.

occupied cities as internal affairs. In any case, Foucault makes it clear that he regards *Solidarność* as a legitimate workers movement, aligned with historical workers' struggle.[90] But perhaps the analogy rather concerns the Paris Commune, as it points to a feature of *Solidarność* that Foucault returns to on several occasions. Let us recall that the Paris Commune – so brief, with such a bloody end, with few concrete victories – is often celebrated for its very form, its consistent attempt to constitute itself according to the ideas it was fighting for, and that its greatest accomplishment was its own "working existence."[91] This is precisely what Foucault seizes upon with regard to *Solidarność*, emphasizing the fact that this workers' initiative was giving itself its own form in accordance with its very objectives, even leading up to the demands of self-government.

After a visit to Warsaw in September 1982, Foucault gives several interviews that confirm this point.[92] In *Libération*, he cites a general sense that the West has not only abandoned the Poles, but it has abandoned itself in its neglect of the right to basic self-determination: "An academic told me:

---

[90] Regarding this case of a workers movement in a "workers' state," Moishe Postone has argued convincingly – if in a particular Marxist tradition rather distant from Foucault and the perspectives discussed here – that the "actually existing socialism" of the communist regimes cannot be regarded as an imperfect negation of capitalism, but should rather be seen as a "(failed) form of capital accumulation." See Moishe Postone, *Time, Labor, and Social Domination* (Cambridge: Cambridge University Press, 1993/2003), 7.

[91] Marx's well-known assessment of this "government of the people by the people," is that its greatest achievement was its own "working existence;" see Karl Marx, *The Civil War in France* in *Marx: Later Political Writing*, ed. & trans. Terrell Carver (Cambridge: Cambridge University Press, 1996), 192. (Foucault, even as he is trying to rid himself of Marxism, singles out Marx's writings on the Commune as important, see Michel Foucault, "Méthodologie pour la connaissance du monde: comment se débarrasser du marxisme" in *Dits et écrits II, 1976–1988*, no 235, 612.) Kristin Ross defines the "communal luxury" as an equality in abundance and an aesthetic condition in which divisions of labor and of work and play are overcome in a general "*process* of making;" see Kristin ross, *Communal Luxury: The Political Imaginary of the Paris Commune* (London/New York: Verso, 2015), 64. And even films focus on this open-ended making and evolving political form in which means and ends merge, in which emancipation is being "worked out," with Peter Watkins' *La Commune* making this aspect into its very theme and mode of cinematic production. *La Commune (Paris, 1871)*, directed by Peter Watkins (13 Production, 2000). For Marx's definition of the Commune as "the political form at last discovered under which to work out the economical emancipation of labour," see Marx, *The Civil War in France*, 187.

[92] Foucault travels to Warsaw with the last of sixteen convoys organized by *Médécins du Monde* and *Varsovivre*, partly funded by the French government. The reason he gives for his journey is that the Poles need to be visited, to be heard and to be talked to, and that these things then must be passed on to the French. See Foucault, "En abandonnant les Polonais, nous renonçons à une part de nous mêmes" (Interview with P. Blanchet, B. Kouchner, and S. Signoret), *Le Nouvel Observateur*, no 935, 9–15 October 1982, in *Dits et écrits II, 1976–1988*, no 320, 1160.

'The first thing that I ask of you, is that you care a bit for yourselves.'"[93] Whether or not Foucault was told these exact words – whether or not he was treated to the very dictum of *epimeleia heautou*, which he himself had taken up from relative historical oblivion in his Collège de France lectures a few months earlier – he makes sure to formulate the support for *Solidarność* and the Polish people not only, and perhaps not even primarily, as a means for their struggle, but as an end in itself, as part of the objective of caring for "ourselves." Solidarity here is not only a means, but an end at the same time: this is not just congenial with the propositions in *Hermeneutics of the Subject*, but, in fact, also with how Foucault describes *Solidarność* and the larger Polish movement.

First, he emphasizes that the recent Polish experience of not remaining passive and not accepting government forms an individual and collective "morale"[94] and a certain "moralization;"[95] it confirms the importance of a preparatory work in relation to action – the role of *paraskeue* and in the forming of an *ethos* in Stoic and Epicurean philosophy – and it appears as a concrete example of his idea of a reversibility in the "chain" of power relations, governmentality, and the relationship of self to self, in which politics and ethics are connected.[96] Despite the fact that the rights and liberties obtained in 1981 had been annulled by Jaruzelski in 1982, Foucault underlines that the experience among the Poles of disavowing the regime cannot be undone: "Now, after Solidarity [...] people will be much stronger in resisting all the small mechanisms by which they are made to if not agree, at least accept the worst."[97] The individual and collective "morale" thus aligns with the "virtue" of the critical attitude defined in "What is Critique?": in the ability to resist "the small mechanisms" that elicits obedience we can see the will of not being governed like that taking form. Instead of the *spiritualization* of political life that impressed Foucault in Iran right before the revolution (and that came to mean something entirely else and brutally repressive after

---

[93] Michel Foucault, "Il n'y a pas de neutralité possible," (Interview with D. Eribon and A. Lévy-Willard), *Libération*, no 434, 9–10 October 1982, in *Dits et écrits II, 1976–1988*, no 319, 1159.
[94] Foucault, "Il n'y a pas de neutralité possible," 1158.
[95] Michel Foucault, "L'expérience morale et sociale des Polonais ne peut plus être effacée," Interview w. G. Anquetil, Les Nouvelles littéraires, n 2857, 1982, pp 8–9. in *Dits et écrits II, 1976–1988*, no 321, 1164–65.
[96] Foucault, *Hermeneutics of the Subject*, 237, 484–87, 333, 252.
[97] Foucault, "L'expérience morale et sociale des Polonais ne peut plus être effacé," 1165.

the Islamic Republic was established) the *moralization* of life is carried out as a first kind of application or realization of the movement itself.[98]

Second, and most importantly, Foucault describes *Solidarność* as an instance of merging means and ends not only on the level of individual morality, but on the level of collective, organizational form:

> What is remarkable in the whole history of the Solidarity movement is that one has not only struggled for liberty, democracy, the usage of fundamental rights, but through [by means of] the usage of rights, through liberty and democracy. The form of the movement is its coinciding end. Look at what is happening today: against the anti-strike law, the docks of Gdansk reply by striking.[99]

We detected this recurring figure of "absolutization" or self-finalization in *Hermeneutics of the Subject,* recalled having seen it in "What is Critique?", and encountered it again in the discussion of Kant's "Was ist Aufklärung?" and of the philosopher's truth-telling in the political field in *The Government of Self and Others.* But here, with regard to *Solidarność,* it is expressed most clearly: "The form of the movement is its coinciding end." We can thus note a common conceptual ground for Foucault's understanding of critique, of ethical models of individual subjectivity in antiquity, and forms of political movements and collective subjectivity in his own present. Perhaps the terminology of coinciding means and ends with regard to a workers' movement brings to mind other philosophical discussions of the subject, such as the notions of a proletarian general strike that functions as a "pure" means,[100] or a revolutionary "pure immediate violence" that dissolves any distinction between means and ends.[101] But unlike the idea of a mythical force that "defies description" and that marks the passage from capitalism to socialism,[102] or the revolutionary "divine violence" that transcends the law and founds new

---

[98] Michel Foucault, "What Are the Iranians Dreaming About?" trans. Karen de Bruin and Kevin B. Anderson, in *Foucault and the Iranian Revolution,* eds. Janet Afary and Kevin B. Anderson (Chicago and London: The University of Chicago Press, 2005), 207.

[99] Foucault, "L'expérience morale et sociale des Polonais ne peut plus être effacée," 1163.

[100] Georges Sorel, *Reflections on Violence,* trans. T. E. Hulme revised by Jeremy Jennings (Cambridge: Cambridge University Press, 2004), 147–50.

[101] For Walter Benjamin's discussion of the general strike as violence, his problematization of violence as a means to a just or unjust end, and his conclusion that the only acceptable form of violence is a revolutionary "divine" violence, see Walter Benjamin, "Critique of Violence" in *Reflections: Essays, Aphorisms, Autobiographical Writings,* ed. Peter Demetz, trans. Edmund Jephcott (New York: Schocken Books, 1986), 300.

[102] Georges Sorel, *Reflections on Violence,* 140.

epochs,[103] Foucault's notion of coinciding means and ends remains on a level of immanence. It is a conceptual figure that may shift between description and prescription, but there is no prophecy, and no sudden act of transcendence. Whether it is used to grasp the individual's finalization of every action in the relation of self to self, or a popular movement's struggle for democratic self-determination, it denotes the actual technologies, practices, and actions by which an individual or collective subject constitutes itself according to what it holds as true. Perhaps the emphasis on and enthusiasm for the merging means and ends in *Solidarność* also comes as a lesson learned after the events in Iran, when the spiritualization of politics hailed by Foucault was instrumentalized by the Islamic Republic for very different ends than those he had imagined. In his final text on the issue, a kind of justification of his own revolutionary enthusiasm written after the brutal government of the new state had become evident and after the criticism he drew, he defends the right to revolt, and defines himself as the opposite to the strategist who calculates the utility of "this death, this cry, this uprising" in relation to a certain objective: he is an "anti-strategist," i.e. one for whom means and ends must coincide.[104]

The Truth-telling of the Labor Union

In 1983, in a conversation with the general secretary of the French labor union CFDT, Foucault defines the union as a *veridique*, a truth-teller, thus applying the concept already used to describe "the veridiction of the market," and further developed around the notion of *parrēsia* in his work on the ancient technologies of the self. This significant but little discussed event, when Foucault considers a collective subject in his political present as an agent of veridiction, shall be investigated in the following.

Foucault approached the labor union *Confédération française democratique du travail* (CFDT) in 1981 – which at the time was the second largest labor union in France[105] – together with Pierre Bourdieu, a mere day after

---

[103] Walter Benjamin, "Critique of Violence," 300.

[104] "It is all the same to me if this strategist is a politician, a historian, a revolutionary, or a partisan of the shah or of the ayatollah, for my theoretical ethics are on the opposite side. My ethics are 'antistrategic.' One must be respectful when a singularity arises and intransigent as soon as the state violates universals." See Michel Foucault, "Is it Useless to Revolt?" trans. Karen de Bruin and Kevin B. Anderson, in *Foucault and the Iranian Revolution*, 266–67.

[105] The CFDT has its roots in the catholic workers movement and was in its early history a Christian union. After a postwar period of deconfessionalization and more radical alignment with the *autogestion* or self-management during the 1960s and 1970s, it took centrist turn in 1977, moving away from its demands of socialized enterprises and distancing itself from political parties; its support of

their co-authored "Les rendez-vous manquées" ("The Missed Encounters," denouncing Foreign Minister Cheysson announcement of the French policy of non-intervention towards Poland). The idea was to establish, also in France, "worker-intellectual links" of the kind that had played a significant role in the development of *Solidarność*. Foucault's and Bourdieu's steps towards the CFDT thus started in the relation to Solidarność and the Polish struggle, but the idea was also to work on other common points of interest.[106] The objective is clearly stated in an internal CFDT document: "They wish, within the limits of their own competence, to find joint forms of work to promote thinking about the period our country has been experiencing since 10 May 1981."[107] This is the date of the election which brought Mitterand and the Socialist Party to the Élysée Palace:[108] Foucault has obviously not let go of the problem of socialist governmentality he raised in 1979, and his public fallout with the government of the left is one of the reasons for approaching the CFDT.[109]

Concretely, the cooperation with CFDT resulted in two publications, both in 1983: Foucault's participation in a book on social security edited by CFDT, in the form of an interview with its National Secretary Robert Bono, and a lengthy conversation with its General Secretary Edmond Maire, published in the review *Le Débat*. In the former, Foucault somewhat reserved on the subject, noting a general lack of theoretical-analytical force. While the existing theories of social security developed by thinkers like Keynes and Beveridge in the first half of the 20th century have become obsolete, the present moment has not contributed with any of its own. Referring to the period inaugurated in 1973 with the international financial crisis, the oil embargo, and the collapse of the Bretton Woods system, he states that "the crisis that we are going through, which soon will have lasted for ten years, has

---

Mitterand's Socialists in the 1981 election was the last instance of this kind. The reason for why Foucault and Bourdieu approached the CFDT was probably not only what it was, but what it was not: it was not the CGT, *Confédération générale du travail*, which was the largest labor union in France as well as more militant, but which also had strong links to the communist party, and by extension, to the Soviet Union and the newly instated Polish military rule. CFDT on the other hand, had started scaling down cooperation with the CGT in 1977, and had already made connections with *Solidarność* after Walesa's visit to France in October 1981.

[106] Macey 444–45.

[107] Macey, 445.

[108] The Socialists won the election as the major part of the Union of the left, in which the Socialist Party, the Communist Party and the more centrist Radical Movement of the Left (*Mouvement radical de gauche*, MRG) had agreed upon The Common Program.

[109] Eribon, *Foucault*, 305.

led to nothing interesting nor new in these fields."[110] In one sense, Foucault's observation of the severe lack of intellectual instruments confirms both the impetus of *The Birth of Biopolitics* – i.e. the necessity at that point of time, to interrogate the present and ask the question: what is neoliberalism? – and the difficulty of engaging with problems of political economy without considering the technical transformations within capitalist accumulation. As a response to the question whether unions can help solving this problem, and function as the site from which new forms of analyses can emerge, Foucault states that if the current predicament stems from the changing role of the state, the response must come from what constitutes its counter-balance or counter-power: "What proceeds from union actions may thus, in effect, open a space of intervention."[111] So to the question of unions and theory, Foucault replies with an affirmation of action. And as we shall see, this possible role of unions in the political-economic field of action is further developed in the conversation with Edmond Maire.

In the long exchange with Maire, Foucault raises questions of the union's relation to the non-salaried part of the population, the complicated role of unions in a period of slow or zero economic growth (Foucault refers again to the unprecedented post-1973 stagflation, and to the idea that demanding higher wages would produce more inflation, and in the long run more unemployment). Further, he discusses the possibilities of unions in periods of crisis and de-unionization, and the strange case of a Left government that has, contrary to the historical tradition in France, come to power unaccompanied by any social movement.[112] But the most important part – for our attempt to demonstrate a reciprocal relation between Foucault's readings of ancient philosophy and his political present – comes after the opening discussion and definitions of union action and class struggle.[113] If Maire is somewhat at pains to clarify how CFDT's notion of class and class struggle differ

---

[110] Foucault, "Un système fini face à une demand infinie" (Interview with Robert Bono), in *Securité sociale: l'enjeu*, Paris, Syros, 1983, *Dits et écrits II, 1976–1988*, no 325, 1192.

[111] Foucault, "Un système fini face à une demand infinie" in *Dits et écrits II, 1976–1988*, no 325, 1193.

[112] In preparation for the talk with General Secretary Maire, Foucault had read several documents produced by or about CFDT, analyzing the crisis of unions in the face of increasing unemployment rates, and he had met with Pierre Rosanvallon, historian and sociologist working closely with CFDT, and Simon Nora, old collaborator with Pierre Mendès France, former Prime Minister and leader of the Radical Party on the moderate left. See Foucault, "La Pologne, et après?," Interview with Edmond Maire, *Le débat*, no 25, May 1983, in Foucault, *Dits et écrits II, 1976–1988*, no 334, 1315.

[113] In this initial exchange, Maire affirms that for the CFDT, class is not only defined in economic terms with respect to its position in the mode of production, but also in relation to a possible organization of self-managed production, and that their common project remains building a self-managed society. See Foucault, "La Pologne, et après?, 1318.

from the Marxist definition they reject, he is met by Foucault's suggestion, based on what he has extracted from the Union's own documents, that it is not the frontal opposition between two fixed classes that is the fundamental idea of struggle to the CFDT. Instead, the union would engage in various, different conflicts ultimately forming a struggle against an undefined heterogenous adversary, which – in a way characteristic of Foucault's own position – puts the struggle itself at the center. As he put it elsewhere: "when they [Marxists] talk about class struggle as the motor of history, they above all strive to know what the class is, where it is situated, whom it includes; but never what, concretely, the struggle is."[114]

Maire agrees that there are multiple forces of domination, and that the adversary is not one single class. Therefore, explains Maire, the class action of the CFDT cannot be limited to representing only their members in labor conflicts, but also the other salaried part of the population: those working in small businesses, those employed on a minimum wage, i.e. the part which has no contractual force: "The political tension we provoke is not merely a theoretical tension on the role of the union. It appears because we pose delicate problems."[115] Maire connects these problems of "social categories [...] without guarantees" to the present conjuncture, and the union's readiness to address broader political and economic questions. Foucault responds:

> It is obviously not about substituting the union function for the political function. But about covering the failures or silences of the political by the union. What has happened is simply that the government and the parties in power have omitted speaking the truth, posing the problem, naming the difficulties that await us. Had they done so, you would have contented yourselves to say: "We, from our point of view as unionists, we wish this or that thing." Your discourse would have remained, in a way, a unionist's discourse.
>
> You find yourselves invested with the function of the truth-teller, very important in public life![116]

These are significant words. First: when Foucault states that the government has "omitted speaking the truth, posing the problem, naming the difficulties that await us" he refers to Maire's vindication of the parts of the population that falls outside safety and guarantees. Foucault had already touched upon

---

[114] Foucault, "Non au sex roi," interview with B.H. Lévy, *Le Nouvel Observateur*, no. 644, 12–21 March 1977, 92–130 in Foucault, *Dits et écrits II*, no. 200, 268.
[115] Foucault, "La Pologne, et après?," 1323.
[116] Foucault, "La Pologne, et après?," 1323.

the emergence of such a liminal population in *The Birth of Biopolitics*, floating along the poverty line as a constant reserve of manpower, as an optimization of the labor market, and as one of the objectives of the neoliberal policies in France.[117] In the conversation with Maire, he regards this precarization as a theoretical and political lacuna that still needs to be addressed. In fact, a large part of the discussion between Maire and Foucault circles around this new, unstable and unpredictable economic conjuncture and how to handle it from the point of view of the working class, when – as neither Maire nor Foucault fail to register – the composition of this class is undergoing an objective transformation in France, as in most of the Western World. Considering their subsequent decline and further shift to the center, the CFDT may not have offered much of a bulwark or viable set of strategies against this decomposition of the working class. Nonetheless, judging from the concerns expressed by their General Secretary in 1983, it seems that they actively attempted some form of resistance, by seeking to identify and counter some of the central problems and effects of neoliberalism. There is thus a shared critical perspective of the present situation.

Second: when Foucault is saying that the union finds itself invested with the function of the truth-teller, he is using the expression *l'homme veridique*, a term he most recently had employed in relation to the ancient practices of truth-telling and *parrēsia*.[118] This "veridicity" or truthfulness of *l'homme veridique* reflects the ethical nature of truth-telling: it is by binding oneself to the truth, by being, in a way, the truth that one speaks, by posing the truth as both a technique and a virtue, that it is operative and meaningful. That this acutely political truth-telling – with regard to the political and economic sphere – relates to a domain of collective and individual technologies of the self is further confirmed when Foucault defines the union member in ethical terms: "The union member distinguishes himself greatly from the politician. The passion for power of the latter is opposed to a rule of personal, ethical behavior of the other – essential, I would even say constitutive, of the union militant."[119] How shall we then understand this truth act or "veridiction" of the labor union? If it is a concept that, to some extent, is transferred from the discussion of ancient practices of truth, in what way does it relate to these?

---

[117] Foucault, *The Birth of Biopolitics*, 206.

[118] The expression appears for example when Foucault explains the notion of *parrēsia* with a parallel to Nietzschean *Wahrhaftigkeit*, in English "veracity" or "truthfulness": "The parrhesiast, the person who uses *parrēsia* is the truthful man (*l'homme véridique*), that is to say, the person who has the courage to risk telling the truth, and who risks this truth-telling in a pact with himself, inasmuch as he is, precisely, the enunciator of the truth." See Foucault, *The Government of Self and Others*, 66

[119] Foucault, "La Pologne, et après?," 1324.

As we have seen in *The Government of Self and Others*, the lectures he gave in the early months of 1983, just prior to the conversation with Maire, two major forms or moments of veridiction are investigated: the philosophical veridiction or *parrēsia* of Plato in front of the tyrant Dionysius, and the Periclean moment or the political *parrēsia* in the Assembly of the democratic city-state. These are the two forms of truth-telling in the political field we have defined as the second Foucauldian critique. Compared to these models of truth-telling, it is clear that the CFDT does not practice any version of philosophical veridiction; it does not appear in the form of an advisor to political government, and it is not defined by the erudite, abstract practice of philosophical discourse testing its "reality" against the field of politics.[120] Nor can the veridiction of the CFDT be understood, at least not primarily, on the level of political *parrēsia*, the courageous speaking of the truth in the public realm of the Assembly. Here one must consider by what function the labor union speaks the truth, in what kind of public sphere, with what relation to actual government, and by what means it exercises its influence over the citizens or decision makers. Foucault observes that "when Edmond Maire speaks, in his capacity as a unionist of course, what he says has a political dimension and becomes a political event."[121] But the reason that this becomes a political event is not only, as Foucault says, that union representatives are considered incapable of speaking about economic policies. Further, the reason that it becomes an event with a potential influence is not because Maire and the CFDT, like Thucydides says of Pericles, are "the most skillful in speech and action."[122] Nor is it because they belong to society's privileged few, for which Euripides' Ion strived , the *proton zugon* or "front rank" of Athens endowed with *parrēsia*, revered and listened to by tradition and because of their social standing.[123] In relation to this "political *parrēsia*" which Foucault identifies in the 5th century BCE and defines as true discourse, the intervention of CFDT, arguably, operates on a wholly different level. The force of the union's truth-telling does not reside in its argument, and it does not operate on the level of discourse. Its force ultimately consists in potential union action: the withdrawal from or refusal to work, to strike, or other forms of mobilisation of workers employed across various sectors of production. In other words, it ultimately rests on the union's organic connection to the

---

[120] Foucault, *The Government of Self and Others*, 353.
[121] Foucault, "La Pologne, et après?," 1322.
[122] Thucydides, *History of the Peloponnesian War* (London: Penguin Books, 1972) Book One, 139, p. 118, as quoted in Foucault, *The Government of Self and Others*, 175.
[123] Foucault, *The Government of Self and Others*, 99.

productive force of labor, and thus its capacity to intervene directly in the sphere of production. This underlying, inescapable force of the unionist truth-telling is not discussed explicitly by Foucault when, perhaps to the surprise of its general secretary,[124] he defines the union as invested with the function of a *veridique*. But it would not be far from his earlier, Clausewitzian analyses of politics and its *rapports de force*,[125] and Foucault touches on the issue when inquiring about the union as an "ultra-democratic project" intervening with all its "force" in a public debate.[126]

Hence, we can consider this kind of truth-telling not only as a self-reflexive practice – in which a subject, in this case a collective one, binds itself to the truth – but at the same time as a veridiction, which may intervene in a kind of public discourse, though the force of which is not primarily discursive. The force of the veridiction of the labor union rests upon action: organized, collective action within production. This is arguably why Foucault insists on the "tension with the whole political apparatus [...] provoked by the exercise of this unionist function of 'speaking the truth.'"[127] It is a non-discursive speaking of the truth, or perhaps rather a doubly discursive and non-discursive speaking of the truth: the "tension" is not produced by the argument, but by a whole other function of the "speaking" subject, which belongs to another domain, the domain of action. This veridiction of the union forms a striking counterpart to a phenomenon Foucault described in *The Birth of Biopolitics*: the market as a site of veridiction for liberal and neoliberal government. While the veridiction of the market is driven by capital (as a part of its process of circulation) and provides a kind of "verification" for liberal government, the veridiction of the union, on the other hand, obviously represents labor, yet forms an unasked-for correction of the "socialist" government of the French socialist party. And while the veridiction of the market constitutes a kind of non-speech, a non-discursive speaking of the truth, the veridiction of the labor union is situated somewhere between speaking the truth of a problem that the government has "omitted" posing, and imposing the force of potential action. Could we think of other forms of veridiction that opposes, in a non-dis-

---

[124] It is a bit difficult to assess the general secretary Edmond Maire's view on the issue: his statements on the union's function and strategy oscillates between still claiming the the CFDT's heritage of direct action revolutionary unionism, and imagining a social mobilization, against the "exceptional actions" of strike and the street protest, to be reinvented as proposals and experimentation, in what seems to be a field without forces and conflicts. See Foucault, "La Pologne, et après?," 1339, 1331.

[125] Foucault, "*Society Must Be Defended*," 15.

[126] Foucault, "La Pologne, et après?," 1322.

[127] Foucault, "La Pologne, et après?," 1323.

227

cursive way, the veridiction of the market? We shall try to draw the outlines of such a practice in the following.

Coinciding Means and Ends: Critique, Veridiction and Left Governmentality

In this chapter we set out to draw the contours of what we have called Foucault's third critique or third modality of critique – i.e. the collective "non-acceptance of a real government" that Foucault points to in "What is Critique?" in 1978. Looking at three of Foucault's major political engagements with present events during this period – posing the question "what is neoliberalism" in his 1979 Collège de France lectures, engaging in the Polish *Solidarność* movement, discussing strategic possibilities with the labor union CFDT – we wanted to consider this third form of critique in terms of truth and practice. As opposed to the theoretical work on regimes of truth in the first critique, and in contrast to the act of speaking the truth in relation to political power in the second critique, the third critique refers to practice; a non-discursive practice of truth. Briefly, we can say that under a government that is essentially economic, resting on the veridiction of the market, the third critique is a collective manifestation of a truth which, as both means and the end of the movement, opposes and falsifies the truth of government. Let us develop this more concretely.

In *Security, Territory, Population* from 1978 – one possible threshold to Foucault's late work – Foucault defines the essence of modern government as "the art of exercising power in the form of economy."[128] A year later, in his 1979 lectures, *The Birth of Biopolitics*, Foucault characterizes the market as that which makes possible the falsification and verification of governmental practice: "In this sense, inasmuch as it enables production, need, supply, demand, value, and price, etcetera, to be linked together through exchange, the market constitutes a site of veridiction, I mean a site of verification-falsification for governmental practice."[129] As has been argued, this represents something new in Foucault's thought: a "radicalization" in political-economic terms, forming a sort of horizon against which his work on the tech-

---

[128] In these lectures Foucault accounts for the reappearance and flourishing of the notion of government in the 16th century (the government of children, of oneself, of the state, etc), and from this point when the general meaning of government coincides with that of economy (in the original meaning of managing a household), through the mercantilists and physiocrats, to a point during the 18th century when economy acquires its modern meaning. Foucault, *Security, Territory, Population*, 95.

[129] Foucault, *The Birth of Biopolitics*, 32.

nologies of the self – to the extent that we follow Foucault and regard them in relation to the political present – must be, but rarely is, understood. We have already seen that the care of the self, as Foucault develops it in *The Hermeneutics of the Subject*, can amount to processes of critique and liberation – keeping in mind that liberation to Foucault is not an attainable, free and happy state, but a practice without end.[130] While these practices of breaking with what enslaves engages with issues often remote from the field of economy, such as the study of nature, family ideology, religion, curiosity, indebtment to yourself, and dependence on external events – and while we today can think of processes of critique and liberation that may not be reducible to economic relations, such as struggles for equality in terms of race, sexuality, gender – it seems that we, with regard to the present, have to ask one fundamental question. What does it mean to care for oneself, to free oneself from that by which one is enslaved, and thus to govern oneself, when one is already governed as an economic entity, in accordance with economic rationality, in what Foucault calls the "radically economic state"?

It is likely that this existing essentially economic government, these existing forms of subjection or subjugation, will determine what form the critical and emancipatory individual care of the self must take. It is also likely that this government will mark an absolute limit of what the individual care of the self or the government of oneself can achieve in terms of liberation and autonomy. To cross that limit, the individual care of the self must become collective. The collective struggle of not being governed like that does not have this problem, since it will not let itself be limited in the same way – certainly not, for example, when it is carried out as outright "revolt." The problem is, of course, to know how and under what form this collective insubordination will appear. And the specific problem here is to state something about that form, despite the general and evasive nature of Foucault's own definition – critique as the art of not being governed like that. Foucault was never willing to prescribe strategies, or point out ways of action. First because of how he considered the role of the philosopher, the theorist, or the intellectual. In "Intellectuals and Power," for example, he states that the task of the intellectual is not to awaken consciousness, and it is not to give the masses knowledge: "they *know* perfectly well."[131] Second because of how he considered philosophy and theoretical work as a potential struggle, and therefore, like all struggles, always local and regional. How could he then

---

[130] Foucault, "L'éthique du souci de soi comme pratique de la liberté" in *Dits et écrits II, 1976–1988*, no 356, 1530, and "Une ésthetique de l'existence" in *Dits et écrits II, 1976–1988*, no 357, 1152.
[131] Foucault and Deleuze, "Intellectuals and Power," 207.

provide anything programmatic to be applied to singular struggles or processes of insubordination? This unwillingness to provide positive definitions of notions like critique and struggle, or anything that could be understood as models for action, is also manifest in Foucault's consistent habit of abandoning projected works whenever they ventured too far away from the critical and descriptive, toward the constructive and prescriptive. We have already mentioned the book on socialist governmentality earlier in this chapter; we can also recall the white paper to be written together with Pierre Bourdieu for the Socialist government,[132] or the study of the workers' movement during the 19th century that he considered in *Liberation*.[133] As we know, none of these proposed projects were realized.

For these reasons, it would be misguided to formulate Foucault's third mode of critique – the movement in which a collective subject challenges government in a politics of truth – in a definite way. For such a critical practice will always be singular and defined by its specific conditions; events like revolt and social struggles are largely unpredictable and overdetermined, intangible and acutely historically contingent in their appearance. What we will do here is simply to continue to generalize certain features of Foucault's three turns to the present, and provide a simple sketch. While Foucault's most substantial attempt at an ontology of the present, *The Birth of Biopolitics*, sets out to ask what neoliberalism is, this is a specification of the larger question of what, today, government is. To Foucault, it seems that this latter question was problematized in a sudden and unexpected way in 1980 by the Polish labor union and popular movement *Solidarność*, in their demand for self-government, and above all, in their *way* of struggling for liberty, democracy, and fundamental rights "*through* the usage of rights, *through* liberty and democracy."[134] In this description of Solidarność, we recognize the figure of thought that Foucault had already used to define critique and the care of the self: the figure of "self-finalization," according to which means and ends merge. This important, recurring figure of thought, or perhaps even an ethical-political principle of Foucault, now comes to characterize a broad popular movement. Somewhat similarly, he employs one of his central concepts to describe the workings of the French labor union *La Confédération française démocratique du travail* (CFDT): Foucault identifies the union's function of "truth-telling" and its conflictual status in

---

[132] Eribon, *Foucault*, 307.

[133] Foucault, "Pour une chronique de la mémoire ouvrière" (*Libération*, no 00, 22 January 1973, 6), *Dits et écrits I, 1954–1975*, 1268.

[134] Foucault, "L'expérience morale et sociale des Polonais ne peut plu être effacé," 1163. Emphasis added.

relation to the political apparatus.[135] Foucault thus takes a conceptual figure and a key concept from his studies of ancient forms of subjectivation and uses it to define a phenomenon in his own political present. This opens up for a whole set of possible analogies, parallels, juxtapositions, and connections. Or to put it more correctly, it confirms these connections, whose more or less open, more or less subterranean network of communication we have tried to map through notions such as government, governmentality, and critique. In any case, these are the central points we have identified in the later Foucault's three turns to the present. This gives us the following:

- The third mode of critique opposes, in a given situation or on a principal level, government as a particular effect, measure, policy or set of policies indexed to the truth of the market.
- This act of opposition in a "politics of truth" is concomitant with the formation of a collective subject, a process of collective and individual subjectivation, in a movement whose form is its coinciding end.
- This critical practice takes the function of truth-telling, which does not primarily appear as a kind of public discourse, but as an intervention based on collective force or action (such as the union's use of strike), as a non-discursive veridiction opposing the equally non-discursive veridiction of the market.

To clarify what is at stake, we can compare this form of critical practice to what we defined as the second mode of critique, and the examples of truth-telling in the political field from Foucault's 1983 lectures *The Government of Self and Others* upon which we based this definition. To speak the truth to political power in the democratic city-state of ancient Athens – for citizens that is, and not women, slaves, or foreigners – was a matter of taking the word in the assembly, and to try and secure a majority. Truth was needed for democracy to function, and it was spoken in an open public debate by those courageous (and aristocratic and influential) enough, as was noted in the description of Pericles and his speeches on the Peloponnesian war. To speak the truth to political power in the autocratic city-state, it was a matter of seizing the right moment and to speak directly to the prince. To the extent that truth was needed, it resided in the prince or tyrant himself, and to the extent that it was spoken, its purpose was to form the prince's soul and thus change the direction of government. These forms of truth-telling are of a discursive kind. (Possible equivalents of these two models of ancient truth-

---

[135] Foucault, "La Pologne, et après?", 1324.

telling in the political field in the present would be the intellectual intervening in public debate, and, the intellectual, theorist, or specialist acting as political advisor to government – both still discursive kinds of truth-telling.) But opposed to these models, as Foucault demonstrates in *The Birth of Biopolitics*, the truth that forms the basis for modern, liberal and neoliberal government is provided by the veridiction of the market. It is a non-discursive, non-personal truth-telling, in that it is impossible to oppose with arguments. That is why Foucault's definition of the union as invested with the function of truth-telling is so important: the force of the union's truth-telling does not lie in its arguments and is not of a discursive kind; it is a force that rests on potential action in the labor market. And the fact that the union's truth-telling is not primarily or at least not only of a discursive kind, allows us to think of other non-discursive forms of truth-telling, opposing itself to the non-discursive truth-telling or veridiction of the market.

This third critique is admittedly a sketch. It is an attempt to see if it is possible to somewhat specify Foucault's elusive definition of collective insubordination. Perhaps a few remarks can shed some more light on its meaning. First, the reason for our emphasis on the third critique as a practice of truth is that truth works on each of the three levels listed above. It is what connects them to one another. In a general sense, it opposes itself to government by speaking its own truth, which may denounce or disregard, on a discursive level, anything like the veridiction of the market. Further, it is a practice of truth in the ethical sense of subjectivation, found in the "moralization" of *Solidarność* or the "ethical" formation of the CFDT member: to Foucault, the subject constitutes itself in a subjectivation of true discourse, making the truth one's own, "becoming the subject of enunciation of true discourse".[136] Finally, this critical function of truth-telling rests on the collective force of potential action; it is a non-discursive veridiction opposing the equally non-discursive veridiction of the market. So, the third mode of critique is bound together by a truth-telling that moves between the discursive and non-discursive, between speech and action. When Deleuze distinguishes between the discursive and the non-discursive in Foucault, between the sayable and the visible (where the visible is characterized by actions, diagrams, the panopticon, etc), he quotes a part of Foucault's portrait of Raymond Roussel: "to speak and to show in a simultaneous motion... [a] prodigious... interweaving."[137] Perhaps the third critique's truth-telling, moving between the

---

[136] Foucault, *The Hermeneutics of the Subject*, 333.
[137] Deleuze, *Foucault*, 67.

discursive and the non-discursive, can be understood as such a prodigious interweaving.

Second, despite Foucault's apparent appreciation of the CFDT's notion of multiple adversaries in the class struggle, it seems that, in this sketch of a critique of government as a generalized market, we have ended up with two diametrically opposed adversaries facing each other: capital and labor. On the one hand, we have the veridiction of the market; and while the market may be a site of veridiction for liberal government, it is above all a site for exchange, realization of value, and circulation of capital. On the other hand, we have the veridiction of the labor union, whose force ultimately rests on its organizational relation to the productive force of labor power. It seems it has to be this way, given the way in which Foucault defines the workings of neoliberalism. Whether it is the labor union or some other actor that assumes the function of truth-telling against market veridiction, it seems it must – by necessity – be done with non-discursive force, for to remain on a discursive level in a political game with economic government is, according to Foucault, a futile battle.[138]

Third, while Foucault assigns the function of truth-telling to a labor union, this does not mean that this third critique, these struggles in the economic and political sphere, must be limited to the labor union. The receding influence of unions is evident to both Foucault and his unionist interlocutor already in 1983, and the process have since then continued in most parts of the world. While organized labor is weakened, and while strike action may appear less frequently and with less force, it does not follow that struggles in the labor market, within production, or in relation to capital accumulation will disappear; other, and new forms of collective action could emerge.[139] In relation to this point, Foucault's analysis of neoliberalism must perhaps be updated on a specific point: during the decades of its implementation, it has become clear that neoliberal governmental practices tend to be combined with non-liberal policies in the non-economic sphere. And

---

[138] "[T]to enter into the political game of the new Germany, the SPD really had to convert to these neo-liberal theses, if not to the economic, scientific, or theoretical theses, at least to the general practice of this neo-liberalism as governmental practice." Foucault, *The Birth of Biopolitics*, 90.

[139] On the contrary, according to some. Following in the aforementioned tradition of periodizing capitalism by its "regimes of accumulation" (Aglietta, Arrighi, Harvey; see above) there have also been attempts to periodize different forms of struggle against capital. Joshua Clover argues for instance that unionization and strikes belong to a period of overlapping regimes of industrial capitalism: it was preceded by riots in the port and the marketplace, and it is being succeeded by overdetermined riots (linked also to race and racialization) in the sphere of circulation. See Joshua Clover, *Riot, Strike, Riot* (London/New York: Verso, 2019).

to the extent that neoliberal government then relies also on other forms of veridiction than the strictly economic – to the extent that it even relies on *parrēsia amathēs*, the bad, coarse and persuasive *parrēsia* of racist and sexist incitement of violence toward indigenous populations, people of color, LGBT communities and women – the effects of which are inseparable from "the art of exercising power in the form of economy," one could think of many different forms of this third critique, more or less articulated with the negation of the veridiction of the market. In recent decades there have been blockades, occupations, social strikes, refusals, slowdowns, closed highways, and organized standstills; climate activism is likely to increase, and other forms remain to be invented and put into practice. To conclude this discussion of the diverse possibilities and possible forms of the third mode of critique, we can perhaps compare its possible effect or way of functioning to the theoretical work of the first critique. While the first critique on a theoretical level, by its strategic and genealogical investigations, identifies new positions to occupy in power relations, the same can be done, on a practical, experimental, and social level, by the third mode of critique.

Finally, and incidentally, it seems that this third critique can provide an answer to another Foucauldian question. Let us recall that we have defined the third mode of critique as a practice of truth and a non-discursive truth-telling that contradicts the veridiction of the market, grounded in a certain "rule of personal, ethical behavior,"[140] and that, on a larger collective level, refers to democratic self-government: as Foucault notes about *Solidarność*, "[t]he form of the movement is its coinciding end."[141] Can this be the answer to the question that one cannot pass? The question that Foucault never relinquished, and that we have returned to on a number of occasions, namely that of the non-existence of a socialist governmentality. It may seem inappropriate to use the same answer twice. But perhaps Foucault's questions – that of critique and the aporia in calling for a predefined governmentality of something yet to exist – are not that different, given their common basis in a politics of truth, or even, as we have shown, an economy of truth. Of course, objections can be made to this way of posing a somewhat elaborated definition of the Foucauldian critique as a preliminary answer to an even larger problem: it is too evasive, perhaps even too Foucauldian a definition. Or: how could one possibly define socialist governmentality in relation to a practice of truth, but without any principle of equality? Even Nietzsche's truthful man

---

[140] Foucault, "La Pologne, et après?," 1324.
[141] Foucault, "L'expérience morale et sociale des Polonais ne peut plu être effacé," 1163.

must strive for justice to be truly great![142] Admittedly, it provides little firm ground. There are only two regulative principles: the practice of freedom or self-government, and the coincidence between means and ends (from which, however, some would say, equality follows by necessity). If Marx was "at his most *anarchisant* or communalistic when writing about the Commune,"[143] perhaps *Solidarność* brought out something similar in Foucault. And in fact, this "working existence" and movement that embodies its own objective is not so far from what Foucault seizes upon when Epicurus says: "You must practice philosophy for yourself and not for Greece:"[144] a practice which forms its own end.

----

[142] Friedrich Nietzsche, "On the Uses and Disadvantages of History for Life" in *Untimely Meditations*, trans. R.J. Hollingdale (Cambridge: Cambridge University Press, 1997), 88–89.

[143] Ross, *Communal Luxury*, 108.

[144] Epicurus, "Vatican Sayings," 76, as quoted in Foucault, *The Hermeneutics of the Subject*, 239.

Conclusion

This thesis has set out to demonstrate that the ancient technologies of the self and forms of truth-telling that Foucault investigates in his last three lecture courses at Collège de France is articulated – both formally and conceptually – with the question of political government and "the art of not being governed like that," i.e. Foucault's own definition of critique. It has been shown that these readings of antiquity relate intensely, and in several ways, to the present moment. We have seen Foucault lecture on the Periclean *parrēsia* at the assembly, and on Plato as a reluctant advisor to the tyrant of Syracuse, when, in his own time, there was intense debate on the French intellectuals' relation to the newly elected Socialist government in the early 1980s. We have contended that Foucault's notion subjectivation as an open-ended, emancipatory practice – developed in his readings of ancient philosophy – complements and responds to his earlier notion of modern power relations according to which subjection is both ongoing and constant. Finally, we have seen Foucault apply the figure of "self-finalization" to the form of the movement *Solidarność,* and ascribe the function of truth-telling to a French labor union, suggesting the possibility of a non-discursive practice of truth, operative in the political-economic sphere. Hence, both the care of the self and *parrēsia* – whether as ancient practices or present configurations – can be said to take on the function of critique. The question of the subject posed by Foucault in his work on antiquity is not merely an ethical subject, as many have gathered: it is also a political subject, and it holds the seeds for how to understand political forms collective of subjectivation in the present.

This reading of Foucault's late work has covered a vast terrain, and it has engaged with different kinds of material: from the lectures on antiquity and ancient philosophy, through the discussion of Kant and the question of the Enlightenment, to the 1979 lectures *The Birth of Biopolitics* devoted to neo-liberalism, and finally to his engagement with *Solidarność* and his interaction with the French labor union CFDT. The eclecticism of the material under investigation is on the one hand motivated by the unfinished nature of Foucault's late work; the absence of any major concluding publication – with the later Foucault, we reach no endpoint or summit, such as with *Discipline and Punish*, for example, which was the culmination of years of research on penal and punitive practices, and his practical engagement with GIP. On the other hand, it is motivated – in methodological terms – by what we have described as a transversal hermeneutics: the attempt to identify significant formal and conceptual continuities that operate on different levels in Foucault's work. Most important in this regard has been the identification of the recurring figure of thought that posits the merging of means and ends as an essential characteristic of some of the most central points of Foucault's late work and political practice. These include: the definition of critique as both a means and a virtue; the description of the care of the self, as characterized by a "self-finalization"; the discussion of Plato before Dionysios and philosophy's "test of reality" in the encounter with political government; the analysis of Kant's way of calling for enlightenment of the public in an Enlightenment publication, and the attention to the very form of *Solidarność* embodied its objectives. In order to grasp the most important points, let us make a brief summary.

In the first chapter, we discussed the stylistic shift that occurs with Foucault's late work. It was argued that while the play of contradictions – which we defined as a montage practice and something present in the earlier writings – disappears stylistically the late work, it nonetheless reappears *in potentia* in the form of the style of life and the care of the self as critical projects.

In the second chapter, engaging with *The Hermeneutics of the Subject* from 1982, the question of the subject in Foucault's late work was raised. Noting its implicit and explicit, formal and conceptual links with the notion of critique, we endeavored to show that this subject, which is able to constitute itself in a careful and truthful practice in relation to itself, neither falsifies nor falls outside any meaningful relation with Foucault's earlier work on subjection, according to which the subject emerges only as an effect of power-knowledge relations. On the contrary, Foucault's insistence on subjectivity as an indefinite process places the notion of an auto-constitutive subject in a necessary relation with the earlier notion of subjection, or, so to speak, puts it *in* the existing power relation as the instance of resistance. This is confirmed by Foucault's explicit assertion that any notion of opposition, resistance, and "reversibility" of power relations and forms of governmentality must pass through the question of the practice of the self. The discussion of the subject in this second chapter formed the basis for the later chapters on collective, political subjects in the present.

The third chapter posed the question of truth, and of truth-telling in the political field, which Foucault discussses in *The Government of Self and*

Others from 1983 and *The Courage of the Truth* from 1984. Foucault takes up the *parrēsia* of the public speaker within the political assembly, and – through a reading of Plato's letters about Dionysios, the tyrant of Syracuse – the *parrēsia* of the philosopher who speaks the truth to political power, assuming the function of political advisor. This chapter also noted the contradictory role that the Cynics' understanding of *parrēsia* plays in Foucault, and in relation to many of the other themes that he addresses in the late lectures.

In order to sort out the stakes of this vast and varied material, it was proposed in the fourth chapter to consider a tripartite division of the meaning of Foucault's work and practice: a schema of three Foucauldian critiques. While loosely modeled on the Kantian critiques, the Foucauldian critiques do not consist in individual works, but rather constitute possible fields and forms of intervention: thus the first critique consists in Foucault's definition of (largely his own) theoretical work as historical-philosophical practice; the second critique consists in philosophy's necessity of testing its own reality against government, and the third critique consists in the collective, non-philosophical expression of the will of not being governed like that.

In the fifth chapter, we attempted to articulate a possible form of such a third mode of critical practice in Foucault. This was tied to, on the one hand, Foucault's notion of how modern, liberal and neoliberal government is indexed to the veridiction of the market, and on the other, Foucault's remarks on a particular kind of truth-telling posed by the collective, political-economic subject of a labor union. The third mode of critique could then be proposed in the form of a practical, non-discursive truth-telling against the equally non-discursive logic of the market, as a movement or formation whose form – following Foucault's characterization of the "remarkable" feature of *Solidarność* – is its coinciding end.

To conclude, we can recall Foucault's way of asking the two questions "What is Critique?" and "What is Enlightenment?", equating the one with the other. Here it is tempting to extend the chain of identity once more, in order to raise a question to which it has long been thought he never gave a direct response: "What is philosophy?". With the recent publication of *Le discours philosophique*, we now have an explicit answer: philosophy is that which must say what there is; it must undertake a diagnostic of the present.[1] Foucault remained true to this definition, with his notion of an "ontology of the present," developed precisely in his reading of "What is Enlightenment?". But that is only one definition, parallel to which Foucault was developing

---

[1] Michel Foucault, *Le discours philosophique* (Paris: Seuil/Gallimard, 2023), 17.

another. In the beginning of the 1980s, not long after (yet very distant from) the period when the ground was crumbling beneath his and everybody's feet, in an "immense and proliferating criticizability of things, institutions, practices, and discourses,"[2] it seems that Foucault's study of the ancient technologies of the self is an attempt to find the meaning and task of philosophy anew. To the question "what is philosophy?", the answer is no longer only the diagnostic of the present, but also a notion of practice, of caring for oneself in a practice or truth. In Pierre Hadot's words, it is philosophy as a way of life. But given our chain of identity, we can perhaps say that for Foucault, the answer would have been *critique* as a way of life.

Krinein, the greek verb and distant origin in the etymology of critique, means among other things to "separate." To separate, to cleave, to cut: it is the kind of work undertaken in Foucault's early and mid work with its periodizations, collisions, and the cutting inherent in the practice of montage. It is also the work undertaken by the subject trying to liberate or cut itself off from that which "enslaves" or binds it, according to Seneca. Today it is not (only) the knowledge of nature that will let us engage in a practice of liberation, but rather, I conclude, the critique, the cleaving, the truth-telling that contradicts the veridiction of the market and the truth of economic government in its paroxysmal consumption of living beings and nature.

This is my reading of *The Birth of Biopolitics* and Foucault's study of the ancient notion of the care of the self, whose close ties to the notion to critique have been foregrounded. Whether or not this is a political-philosophical standpoint and practice of the self that Foucault could have reached or ever approved of, I cannot know. But, to close the circle back to where it started: I do this reading because the promise of style and form in his early and mid work allows me – even urges me to.

---

[2] Foucault, *"Society Must Be Defended?"*, 6.

Bibliography

Public Archives

Bibliothèque nationale de France (BNF)

Fonds Foucault (NAF 27830). Boite 72, Critique. (Not available online.)

Fonds Foucault (NAF 27830). Boite 023-17-chem. https://eman-archives.org/Foucault-fiches/collections/show/662. Accessed March 19, 2024.

Printed Sources

Foucault, Michel. Articles:

Foucault, Michel. "Theatrum Philosophicum." In *Language, CounteLanguage, Counter-Memory, Practice: Selected Essays and Interviews. ed. Donald F. Bouchard. Ithaca: Cornell University Press, 1977.*

Foucault, Michel. "What is an Author" in *Language, Counter-Memory, Practice.* Translated by Donald F. Bouchard. Ithaca, NY: Cornell University Press, 1977.

Foucault, Michel. "Omnes et Singulatim: Towards a Criticism of Political Reason." In *The Tanner Lectures on Human Values*, vol II, edited by S. McMurrin. Salt Lake City: Univ. Of Utah Press, 1981.

Foucault, Michel. "Subject and Power." In *Beyond Structuralism and Hermeneutics*, edited by Hubert L. Dreyfus and Paul Rabinow, 208–209. Chicago: University of Chicago Press, 1983.

Foucault, Michel. "On the Genealogy of Ethics". *The Foucault Reader.* New York: Pantheon Books, 1984.

Foucault, Michel. "Truth, Power, Self" in *Technologies of the Self*, edited by Luther H. Martin, Huck Gutman and Patrick H. Hutton. Amherst: University of Massachusets Press, 1988.

Foucault, Michel. "Truth Is the Future," interview with M. Dillon, November 1980. In *Foucault Live: Collected Interviews, 1961–1984*, edited by Sylvère Lotringer. New York: Semiotext(e), 1996.

Foucault, Michel. "On the Genealogy of Ethics: an Overview of Work in Progress." In *Ethics.* London: Penguin Books, 2000.

Foucault, Michel. "What Are the Iranians Dreaming About?" Translated by Karen de Bruin and Kevin B. Anderson. In *Foucault and the Iranian Revolution*, edited by Janet Afary and Kevin B. Anderson, 207–209. Chicago and London: The University of Chicago Press, 2005.

Foucault, Michel. "An Interview with Michel Foucault." In *Death and the Labyrinth: The World of Raymond Roussel*, translated by Charles Ruas, 171–177. London/New York: Continuum, 2006.

Foucault, Michel. "What is Critique?" In *Politics of Truth*, edited by Sylvère Lotringer, translated by Lysa Hochroth & Catherine Porter, 55–81. Los Angeles: Semiotext(e), 2007.

Foucault, Michel. "What is Enligthtenment?" In *Politics of Truth*, edited by Sylvère Lotringer, translated by Lysa Hochroth & Catherine Porter, 55–81. Los Angeles: Semiotext(e), 2007.

Foucault, Michel. "La parrēsia et l'attitude critique." In *Michel Foucault: éthique et verité, 1984*, edited by D. Lorenzini A. Revel, A. Sforzini. Paris: Vrin, 2013.

Foucault, Michel. "Sur l'attitude du gouvernement francais à propos de la Pologne" in *Signés Foucault et Cie*, edited by Philippe Artières. Paris: Editions de la Sorbonne, 2020.

Foucault, Michel. Articles in *Dits et écrits I, 1954–1975*:

Foucault, Michel. "Entretien sur la prison: le livre et sa méthode." In *Dits et écrits I, 1954–1975*, edited by Daniel Defert and François Ewald, Collab. Jacques Lagrange. Paris: Gallimard, 2001.

Foucault, Michel. "Nietzsche, Freud, Marx." In *Dits et écrits I, 1954–1975*, edited by Daniel Defert and François Ewald, Collab. Jacques Lagrange. Paris: Gallimard, 2001.

Foucault, Michel. "Pour une chronique de la mémoire ouvrière" (Libération, no 00, 22 January 1973, 6). In *Dits et écrits I, 1954–1975*, edited by Daniel Defert and François Ewald, Collab. Jacques Lagrange. Paris: Gallimard, 2001.

Foucault, Michel. Articles in *Dits et écrits II 1976–1988*:

Foucault, Michel. "Est-il donc important de penser?" *Liberation*, May 30–31, 1981. In *Dits et écrits II 1976–1988*, edited by Daniel Defert and François Ewald, Collab. Jacques Lagrange. Paris: Gallimard, 2001.

Foucault, Michel. "Interview de Foucault." In *Dits et écrits II 1976–1988*, edited by Daniel Defert and François Ewald, Collab. Jacques Lagrange. Paris: Gallimard, 2001.

Foucault, Michel. "L'éthique du souci de soi comme pratique de la liberté," interview with H. Becker, R. Fonet-Berancourt, A. Gomez-Müller, January 1984. In *Dits et écrits II 1976–1988*, edited by Daniel Defert and François Ewald, Collab. Jacques Lagrange. Paris: Gallimard, 2001.

Foucault, Michel. "L'expérience morale et sociale de Polonais ne peut plue être effacée" in *Dits et écrits II 1976–1988*, edited by Daniel Defert and François Ewald, Collab. Jacques Lagrange. Paris: Gallimard, 2001.

Foucault, Michel. "La philosophie analytique de la politique." In *Dits et écrits II 1976–1988*, edited by Daniel Defert and François Ewald, Collab. Jacques Lagrange. Paris: Gallimard, 2001.

Foucault. "La Pologne, et après?" Interview with Edmond Maire, *Le débat*, no 25, May 1983. In *Dits et écrits II 1976–1988*, edited by Daniel Defert and François Ewald, Collab. Jacques Lagrange. Paris: Gallimard, 2001.

Foucault, Michel. "Non a sexe roi". In *Dits et écrits II 1976–1988*, edited by Daniel Defert and François Ewald, Collab. Jacques Lagrange. Paris: Gallimard, 2001.

Foucault, Michel. "Pouvoirs et stratégies". In *Dits et écrits II 1976–1988*, edited by Daniel Defert and François Ewald, Collab. Jacques Lagrange. Paris: Gallimard, 2001.

Foucault. "Un système fini face à une demand infinie." In *Dits et écrits II 1976–1988*, edited by Daniel Defert and François Ewald, Collab. Jacques Lagrange. Paris: Gallimard, 2001.

Foucault, Michel. "Une esthétique de l'existence." In *Dits et écrits II 1976–1988*, edited by Daniel Defert and François Ewald, Collab. Jacques Lagrange. Paris: Gallimard, 2001.

Foucault, Michel. Books:

Foucault, Michel. *The Archaeology of Knowledge*. Translated by A.M. Sheridan Smith. New York: Pantheon Books, 1972.

Foucault, Michel. *The Birth of the Clinic: An Archaeology of Medical Perception*. Translated by A.M. Sheridan. London: Tavistock Publications Limited, 1973.

Foucault, Michel. *I, Pierre Rivière, having slaughtered my mother, my sister, and my brother*. Translated by Frank Jellinek. Lincoln/London: University of Nebraska Press, 1975.

Foucault, Michel, *Language, Counter-Memory, Practice: Selected Essays and Interviews*. Ed. Donald F. Bouchard. Ithaca: Cornell University Press, 1977.

Foucault, Michel. *Herculine Barbin dite Alexina B*. Paris: Gallimard, 1978.

Foucault, Michel. *The History of Sexuality Volume 1: An Introduction*. Translated by R. Hurley. New York: Pantheon Books, 1978.

Foucault, Michel. *The Order of Discourse*. In *Untying the Text*, edited by Robert Young, 65–77. Boston, London and Henley: Routledge & Kegan Paul, 1981.

Foucault, Michel. *The History of Sexuality Vol. 2 The use of pleasure*, Translated by Robert Hurley. New York: Random House, Inc., 1990.

Foucault, Michel. *The History of Sexuality Vol. 3 The care of the self*. Translated by Robert Hurley. New York: Random House, Inc., 1990.

Foucault, Michel. *Discipline and Punish: The Birth of the Prison*. Translated by A. Sheridan. New York: Vintage Books, 1995.

Foucault, Michel. *Abnormal: Lectures at the Collège de France 1974–75*. Translated by Graham Burchell. London: Verso, 2003.

Foucault, Michel. *"Society Must Be Defended": Lectures at Collège de France 1975–1976*. Translated by D. Macey. New York: Picador, 2003.

Foucault, Michel. *The Hermeneutics of the Subject: Lectures at Collège de France 1981–1982*. Translated by Graham Burchell. New York: Palgrave/Macmillan, 2005.

Foucault, Michel. *The Order of Things*. Translated by Alan Sheridan. London/New York: Routledge, 2005.

Foucault, Michel. *History of Madness*. Translated by Jonathan Murphy and Jean Khalfa. London/New York: Routledge, 2006.

Foucault, Michel. *Security, Population, Territory: Lectures at Collège de France 1977–1978*. Hampshire/New York: Palgrave/Macmillan, 2007.

Foucault, Michel. *The Birth of Biopolitics*. Translated by Graham Burchell. New York: Palgrave Macmillan, 2008.

Foucault, Michel. *The Government of Self and Others: Lectures at the Collège de France 1982–1983*, translated by Graham Burchell. Houndmills: Palgrave Macmillan, 2010.

Foucault, Michel. *The Courage of the Truth (The Government of Self and Others II): Lectures at the Collège de France 1982–1983*, translated by Graham Burchell. Houndmills: Palgrave Macmillan, 2011.

Foucault, Michel. *Mal faire, dire vrai: Fonction de l'aveu en justice – cours de Louvain, 1981*. Louvain/ Chicago: Presses universitaires de Louvain/University of Chicago Press, 2012.

Foucault, Michel. *La grande étrangère: à propos de litterature*. Edited by Philippe Artières, Jean-François Bert, Mathieu Potte-Bonneville, and Judith Revel. Paris: Éditions de l'EHESS, 2013.

Foucault, Michel. *Lectures on the Will to Know: Lectures at the Collège de France 1970–1971*. Translated by Graham Burchell. New York: Palgrave Macmillan, 2013.

Foucault, Michel. *The Government of the Living: Lectures at the Collège de France 1979–1980*. Translated by Graham Burchell. Houndmills/New York: Palgrave Macmillan, 2014.

Foucault, Michel. *Language, Madness and Desire: On Literature*. Minneapolis: University of Minnesota Press, 2015.

Foucault, Michel. *Qu'est-ce que la critique?, suivi de La culture de soi*. Eds. Henri-Paul Fruchaud and Daniele Lorenzini. Paris: Vrin, 2015.

Foucault, Michel. *Subjectivity and Truth: Lectures at the Collège de France 1980–1981*. Translated by Graham Burchell. Houndmills/New York: Palgrave Macmillan, 2017.

Foucault, Michel. *Speaking the Truth about Oneself: Lectures at Victoria University, Toronto, 1982*. Chicago: The University of Chicago Press, 2021.

Foucault, Michel. *Le Discours Philosophique*. Paris: Seuil/Gallimard, 2023

Other Printed Sources

"110 propositions pour la France: Programme de gouvernement préparé par le Parti socialiste (PS) pour l'élection présidentielle d'avril-mai 1981." In *Manière de voir*, no. 124, August–September 2012. https://www.monde-diplomatique.fr/mav/124/A/51865. Accessed April 14, 2024."Reduced Right to Strike in Sweden." *Sveriges arbetares centralorganisation (SAC)*. https://arkiv.sac.se/en/Reduced-right-to-strike-in-Sweden. Accessed March 10, 2024.

Adorno, Theodor W. "Late Style in Beethoven." In *Essays on Music*, translated by Susan H. Gillespie. Berkeley: University of California Press, 2002.

Afary, Janet and Anderson, Kevin B. *Foucault and the Iranian Revolution: Gender and the Seductions of Islamism*. Chicago and London: The University of Chicago Press, 2005.

Agamben, Giorgio. *Homo Sacer: Sovereign Power and Bare Life*. Translated by Daniel Heller-Roazen. Stanford: Stanford University Press, 1998.

Agamben, Giorgio. *The Use of Bodies*. Translated by Adam Kotsko. Stanford: Stanford University Press, 2015.

Allen, Amy. *The Politics of Our Selves: Power, Autonomy, and Gender in Contemporary Critical Theory*. New York: Columbia University Press, 2008.

Alpert, Avram. *Global Origins of the Modern Self*. Albany: SUNY Press, 2019.

Althusser, Louis. *Pour Marx*. Paris: François Maspero, 1971.

Armstrong, Timothy J., ed. *Michel Foucault, Philosopher*. New York: Harvester Wheatsheaf, 1992.

Aristotle, *Physics*, translated by C. D. C. Reeve. Indianapois: Hackett Publishing Company, Inc., 2018. Indianapolis/Cambridge

Arrighi, Giovanni. *The Long Twentieth Century.* London: Verso, 2010.

Artières, Philippe and Potte-Bonneville, Mathieu, eds. *D'après Foucault: Gestes, luttes, programmes.* Paris: Editions Points, 2012.

Atoussa H. "An Iranian Woman Writes." In *Foucault and the Iranian Revolution*, edited by Janet Afary and Kevin B. Anderson, Chicago and London: The University of Chicago Press, 2005.

Austin, J.L. *How to Do Things with Words.* Oxford: Clarendon Press, 1975.

Bakhtin, Mikhael. *The Dialogic Imagination.* Translated by Caryl Emerson and Michael Holquist. Austin: University of Texas Press, 1981.

Barthes, Roland. "The Death of the Author." In *Image, Music, Text.* Translated by Stephen Heath. New York: Hill and Wang, 1977.

Benjamin, Walter. *Reflections: Essays, Aphorisms, Autobiographical Writings.* Ed. Peter Demetz, Translated by Edmund Jephcott. New York: Schocken Books, 1986.

Bergeron, Louis. *Les Capitalistes en France.* Paris: Gallimard/Juillard, 1978.

Bidet, Jacques. *Foucault avec Marx.* Paris: La Découverte, 2015.

Blanchot, Maurice. "Michel Foucault as I imagine him." In *Foucault/Blanchot.* New York: Zone Books, 1987.

Blanco, Azucena G. "Foucault on Raymond Roussel: The Extralinguistic Outside of Literature." *Theory, Culture and Society*, 40 (1–2). https://doi.org/10.1177/026327 6420950458.

Branham, Robert Bracht & Goulet-Cazé, Marie-Odile, eds. *The Cynics: The Cynic Movement in Antiquity and Its Legacy.* Berkeley: University of California Press, 1996.

Brecht, Bertolt. "Against Georg Lukács." In *Aesthetics and Politics.* London/New York: Verso, 2007.

Butler, Judith. *Gender Trouble: Feminism and the Subversion of Identity.* London: Routledge, 1999.

Butler, Judith. "What is Critique? An Essay on Foucault's Virtue." *Transversal*, no. 5 (2001). https://transversal.at/transversal/0806/butler/en. Accessed April 14, 2024.

Butler, Judith. *Bodies That Matter: On the Discursive Limits of Sex.* London: Routledge, 2011.

Bürger, Peter. *Theory of the Avant-garde.* Translated by M. Shaw. Minneapolis: University of Minnesota Press, 1984.

Cadava, Eduardo, Connor, Peter and Nancy, Jean-Luc, eds. *Who Comes After the Subject?* New York: Routledge, 1991.

Clover, Joshua. *Riot, Strike, Riot.* London/New York: Verso, 2019.

Cremonesi, Laura. "Askêsis, êthos, parrêsia." In *Michel Foucault: éthique et vérité 1980–1984*, edited by Daniele Lorenzini, Ariane Revel, and Arianna Sforzini, Paris: Vrin, 2015.

D'Eramo, Marco. "Populism and the new Oligarchy." *New Left Review*, 82, July/Aug 2013.

Deleuze, Gilles. "À propos des nouveaux philosophes et d'un problème plus général." *Minuit*, no. 24, May 1977.

Deleuze, Gilles. *Empiricism and Subjectivity.* Translated by Constantin V. Boundas. New

York: Columbia University Press, 1989.

Deleuze, Gilles. "Postscript on the Societies of Control." *October*, Vol. 59 (Winter, 1992).

Della Costa, Mariarosa, and James, Selma. *The Power of Women and the Subversion of the Community.* Bristol: Falling Wall Press, 1972.

Didi-Huberman, Georges. *Quand les images prennent position: L'Oeil de l'histoire, 1.* Paris: Les Éditions de Minuit, 2009.

Diogenes Laertius. *Lives of Eminent Philosophers,* Translated by R.D. Hicks. Cambridge: Harvard University Press, Loeb Classical Library, 1925.

Diogenes Laertius. *The Lives of Eminent Philosophers.* Translated by Pamela Mensch. Oxford/New York: Oxford University Press, 2018.

Dos Passos, John. *U.S.A.* London/New York: Penguin Books, 2001.

Duras, Marguerite. *Hiroshima mon amour.* Translated by Richard Seaver. New York: Grove Press, 1961.

Döblin, Alfred. *Berlin Alexanderplatz.* Translated by Michael Hofmann. London/New York: Penguin Books, 2019.

Eco, Umberto. "The Poetics of the Open Work." In *The Role of the Reader: Explorations in the Semiotics of Texts.* Bloomington: Indiana University Press, 1979.

Eisenstein, Sergei. *Film Sense.* Edited and translated Jay Leyda. New York: Harcourt, Brace & World, 1947.

Eisenstein, Sergei. *Film Form: Essays in Film Theory.* Edited and translated by Jay Leyda. New York: Harcourt, Brace & World, 1977.

Elden, Stuart. *Foucault's Last Decade.* Cambridge: Polity Press, 2016.

Engels, Friedrich. *The Origin of the Family, Private Property and the State.* Translated by Alick West. London: Verso, 2021.

Epicurus. *The Art of Happiness.* Translated by George K. Strodach. New York: Penguin Books, 2012.

Eribon, Didier. *Foucault.* Translated by Betsy Wing. Cambridge, Massachusetts: Harvard University Press, 1991.

Farge, Arlette, and Foucault, Michel. *Disorderly Families: Infamous Letters from the Bastille Archives.* Translated by Thomas Scott-Railton. Minnesota: University of Minnesota Press, 2016.

Faustino, Marta, and Ferraro, Gianfranco, eds. *The Late Foucault.* London: Bloomsbury, 2020.

Gamez, Patrick J. *Foucault against Ethics: Subjectivity and Critique after Humanism.* University of Notre Dame, 2016. https://scholarsmine.mst.edu/cgi/viewcontent.cgi?article=1023&context=artlan_phil_facwork.

Genette, Gérard. *Paratexts: Thresholds of Interpretation.* Translated by Jane E. Lewin. Cambridge: Cambridge University Press, 1997.

Giannantoni, Gabriele. *Socraticorum Reliquae.* Rome: Bibliopolis, 1983–1985.

Gillot, Pascale. "Michel Foucault et le Marxisme de Louis Althusser." In *Foucault(s)*, edited by Jean-François Braunstein, Daniele Lorenzini, Ariane Revel, Judith Revel, and Arianna Sforzini, Paris: Éditions de la Sorbonne, 2017.

Gordon, Colin. *The Foucault Effect which introduced Foucault's concept of governmentality to a larger audience*. Chicago: The University of Chicago Press, 1991.

Gordon, Colin. Foucault News. "Foucault, neoliberalism etc." January 2015 https://foucault news.files.wordpress.com/2015/01/colin-gordon-2015.pdf.

Goulet-Cazé, Marie-Odile. "Foucault et sa vision du cynisme dans Le Courage de la vérité" in *Michel Foucault: éthique et vérité 1980–1984*.

Gramsci, Antonio. *Selections from the Prison Notebooks*, edited and translated by Quentin Hoare and Geoffrey Nowell Smith. New York: International Publishers, 1971.

Grant, John. "Foucault and the Logic of Dialectics." *Contemporary Political Theory* 9 (2010): 220–238. https://doi.org/10.1057/cpt.2009.3.

Gros, Frédéric. "Avertissement." In Michel Foucault, *Les aveux de la chair*. Paris: Gallimard, 2018.

Gros, Frédéric. "Course Context." In Foucault, Michel. *The Hermeneutics of the Subject: Lectures at Collège de France 1981–1982*. Translated by Graham Burchell. New York: Palgrave/Macmillan, 2005.

Gutting, Gary. "Introduction." In *The Cambridge Companion to Foucault*, edited by Gary Gutting, New York: Cambridge University Press, 2005.

Hadot, Pierre. "Reflections on the notion of 'the cultivation of the self'." In *Foucault Philosopher*, translated by Timothy Armstrong. Hemel Hempstead: Harvester Wheatsheaf, 1992.

Hadot, Pierre. "Un dialogue interrompu avec M. Foucault." In *Exercises spirituels et philosophie antique*. Paris: Albin Michel, 2002.

Hadot, Pierre. *N'obulie pas de vivre: Goethe et la tradition des exercices spirituels*. Paris: Albin Michel, 2008.

Hanssen, Beatrice. "Between Kant and Nietzsche: Foucault's Critique." In *Critique of Violence*. London/New York: Routledge, 2000.

Hardt, Michael. "Militant Life". *New Left Review* 64 (2010).

Harvey, David. *The Condition of Post-Modernity: An Enquiry into the Origins of Cultural Change*. Oxford: Basil Blackwell, 1989.

Harvey, David. *A Brief History of Neoliberalism*. Oxford/New York: Oxford University Press, 2005.

Harney, Stefano, and Fred Moten. *The Undercommons: Fugitive Planning & Black Study*. Wivenhoe/New York/Port Watson: Minor Compositions, 2013.

Hegel, G. W. F. *Lectures on the History of Philosophy*, Translated by E.S. Haldane and F.H. Simson. Lincoln/London: University of Nebraska Press, 1995.

Hegel, G. W. F. *Phenomenology of Spirit*. Translated by A. V. Miller. Oxford: Oxford University Press, 1977.

Hegel, G. W. F. *Lectures on the History of Philosophy 1825–6 Volume II: Greek Philosophy*. Translated by R. F. Brown and J. M. Stewart. Oxford/New York: Oxford University Press, 2006.

Hobsbawm, Eric. *The Age of Capital*. London: Abacus, 1995.

Hobsbawm, Eric. *The Age of Revolution*. New York: Vintage Books 1996.

Hoffman, Marcelo. *Foucault and Power*. London/New York: Bloomsbury, 2015.

Irrera, Orazio. "Satyagraha: une alèthurgie décoloniale." In *Michel Foucault: éthique et vérité 1980-1984*, edited by Daniele Lorenzini, Ariane Revel, and Arianna Sforzini, Paris: Vrin, 2015.

Iser, Wolfgang. *Die Appellstruktur der Texte. Unbestimmtheit als Wirkungsbedingung literarischer Prosa*. Konstanz: Konstanz Universitätsverlag, 1970.

Jameson, Fredric. "Reflections in Conclusion." In *Aesthetics and Politics*. London/New York: Verso, 2007.

Kant, Immanuel. *Was ist Aufklärung?* In *Ausgewählte kleine Schriften*. Hamburg: Felix Meiner Verlag, 1999.

Kant, Immanuel. "An Answer to the Question: What is Enlightenment?" In *What is Enlightenment?*, edited by James Schmidt. Berkeley: University of California Press, 1996.

Kant, Immanuel. *The Critique of the Power of Judgment*, translated by Paul Guyer and Eric Matthews. Cambridge: Cambridge University Press, 2000.

Katz Lydén, Karl. *Poems and Parables on the Political Utility of Art*. Berlin: BOM DIA BOA TARDE BOA NOITE, 2021.

Lazzarato, Maurizio. "Enunciation and Politics: A Parallel Reading of Democracy." In *Foucault, Biopolitics, and Governmentality*, edited by Jakob Nilsson and Sven-Olov Wallenstein, Stockholm: Södertörn Philosophical Studies, 2013.

Lazzarato, Maurizio. *Governing by Debt*. Translated by Joshua David Jordan. South Pasadena: Semiotext(e), 2015.

Lemm, Vanessa. "The Embodiment of Truth and the Politics of Community." In *The Government of Life: Foucault, Biopolitics, and Neoliberalism*, edited by Vanessa Lemm and Miguel Vatter. New York: Fordham University Press, 2014.

Leys, Colin, and Leo Panitch, eds. *The End of Parliamentary Socialism: From New Left to New Labour*. London/New York: Verso, 1997.

Lorenzini, Daniele, Revel, Ariane and Sforzini, Arianna, eds. *Michel Foucault: éthique et verité, 1980–1984*. Paris: Vrin, 2013.

Lorenzini, Daniele, Ariane Revel, and Arianna Sforzini, eds. *Michel Foucault: éthique et vérité 1980–1984*. Paris: Vrin, 2015.

Lorenzini, Daniele. "Éthique et politique de nous mêmes." In *Michel Foucault: éthique et vérité 1980-1984*, edited by Daniele Lorenzini, Ariane Revel, and Arianna Sforzini, Paris: Vrin, 2015.

Lorenzini, Daniele, and Arnold I. Davidson. "Introduction." In *Qu'est-ce que la critique? suivi de La culture de soi*, edited by Henri-Paul Fruchaud and Daniele Lorenzini. Paris: Vrin, 2015.

Lorenzini, Daniele. "What is a Regime of Truth?" *Le Foucauldien,* February 2, 2015. DOI: 10.16995/lefou.2.

Lukács, Georg. "Realism in the Balance." In *Aesthetics and Politics*. London/New York: Verso, 2007.

Luxemburg, Rosa. "Organizational Questions of the Russian Social Democracy (Leninism or Marxism?)", https://www.marxists.org/archive/luxemburg/1904/questions-rsd/ (Accessed January 9, 2017).

Lydén, Karl. "Kritik av kynismen" in *Foucault och antiken*, edited by Sven-Olov Wallenstein & Johan Sehlberg.

Macey, David. *The Lives of Michel Foucault*. London: Vintage, 1994.

Marx, Karl. *Capital: Volume 1*. Translated by Ben Fowkes. Middlesex: Penguin Classics, 1976.

Marx, Karl. *The Civil War in France*. Edited and translated by Terrell Carver. Cambridge: Cambridge University Press, 1996.

Marx, Karl, and Friedrich Engels. *The German Ideology*. Translated by C.J. Arthur. Prometheus Books, 1998.

Marx, Karl. *The Difference Between the Democritean and Epicurean Philosophy of Nature*. Marx-Engels Collected Works Volume 1. Progress Publishers (Online Version: Brian Basgen Internet Archive; marxists.org, 2000).

McGushin, Edward. *Foucault's Askēsis: An Introduction to the Philosophical Life* (Evanston: Northwestern University Press, 2007.

Meiksins Wood, Ellen. *Peasant-Citizen and Slave: The Foundations of Athenian Democracy*. London/New York: Verso, 1988.

Montag, Warren. *Althusser and His Contemporaries*. Durham and London: Duke University Press, 2013.

Negri, Antonio. *Marx Beyond Marx*. Translated by Harry Cleace, Michael Ryan, and Maurizio Viano. London: Autonomedia/Pluto, 1991.

Nica, Daniel. "The Aesthetics of Existence and the Political in Late Foucault." In *Re-thinking the Political in Contemporary Society: Globalization, Consumerism, Economic Efficiency*, edited by Viorel Vizureanu, 59. Bucarest: Pro Universitaria, 2015.

Niehues-Pröbsting, Heinrich. "The Modern Reception of Cynicism" in *The Cynics: The Cynic Movement in Antiquity and Its Legacy*.

Nietzsche, Friedrich. "On the Uses and Disadvantages of History for Life" in *Untimely Meditations*. Translated by R. J. Hollingdale. Cambridge: Cambridge University Press, 1997.

Nietzsche, Friedrich. *The Gay Science*, translated by Josefine Nauckhoff. Cambridge: Cambridge University Press, 2001.

Nietzsche, Friedrich. *On the Genealogy of Morality*, translated by Carol Diethe. Cambridge: Cambridge University Press, 2006.

Pavón-Cuéllar, David. "Foucault's Marxism." *Continental Thought & Theory*, 327–345 (2022).

Penn, Shana. *Solidarity's Secret*. Ann Arbor: The University of Michigan Press, 2005.

Philo of Alexandria. *On the Contemplative Life*. Translated by C. D. Yonge. London: H. G. Bohn, 1854–1890/1993. http://www.earlychristianwritings.com/yonge/book34.html (Accessed January 17, 2017).

Plato. "Letter VII." In Plato: *Complete Works*, edited by John M. Cooper, Associate Editor D. S. Hutchinson. Indianapolis: Hackett Publishing, 1997.

Plato. "Letter VIII." In Plato: *Complete Works*, edited by John M. Cooper, Associate Editor D. S. Hutchinson. Indianapolis: Hackett Publishing, 1997.

Plato. *Alcibiades*. Translated by D. S. Hutchinson. In *Plato Complete Works*, edited by John M. Cooper. Indianapolis/Cambridge: Hackett Publishing Company, 1997.

Plato. *Apology.* Translated by G.M.A. Grube. In *Plato Complete Works*, edited by John M. Cooper. Indianapolis/Cambridge: Hackett Publishing Company, 1997.

Plato. *Gorgias*, translated by Donald J. Zeyl. In *Complete Works*. Indianapolis/Cambridge: Hackett Publishing Company.

Poliakov, Léon. *Auschwitz.* Paris: Gallimard/Juillard, 1973.

Postone, Moishe. *Time, Labor, and Social Domination.* Cambridge: Cambridge University Press, 1993/2003.

Pradeau, Jean-François. "Le sujet ancien d'une éthique moderne." In *Foucault: Le courage de la vérité*, edited by Frédéric Gros. Paris: Presses Universitaires de France, 2002.

Revel, Judith. "Un héritage de Foucault. Entre fidelité et libres usages." *Theory Now* Vol 2, Nᵒ 1 (January–June 2019): http://dx.doi.org/10.30827/TNJ.v2i1.8599.

Ross, Kristin. *Communal Luxury: The Political Imaginary of the Paris Commune.* London/ New York: Verso, 2015.

Rüstow, Wilhelm. *Colloque Walter Lippmann.* Paris: Payot, 1938.

Röpke, Wilhelm. *The Social Crisis of Our Time.* Translated by Annette and Peter Schiffer Jacobsohn. Chicago: The University of Chicago Press, 1950.

Said, Edward. *On Late Style.* New York: Pantheon Books, 2006.

Schmidt, James. "The Words We Have Lost: Translating Kant on Enlightenment." Blog post. May 28, 2013. https://persistentenlightenment.com/2013/05/28/translatingkant1/.

Seneca. *Natural Questions.* Translated by Harry M. Hine. Chicago/London: The University of Chicago Press, 2010.

Serres, Michel. "La géométrie de l'incommuicable: la folie." In *Hermès 1. La communication.* Paris: Éditions de Minuit, 1969.

Sforzini, Arianna. *Les scènes de la vérité: Michel Foucault et théâtre.* Paris: A bord de l'eau, 2017.

Shea, Louisa. *The Cynic Enlightenment: Diogenes in the Salon.* Baltimore: The Johns Hopkins University Press, 2010.

Sloterdijk, Peter. *Critique of Cynical Reason*, Translated by Michael Eldred. Minneapolis/London: University of Minnesota Press, 1987.

Sorel, Georges. *Reflections on Violence.* Translated by T.E. Hulme, revised by Jeremy Jennings. Cambridge: Cambridge University Press, 2004.

Spivak, Gayatri Chakravorty, Sara Danius, and Stefan Jonsson. "An Interview with Gayatri Chakravorty Spivak." *Boundary 2*, vol 20, no. 2 (1993): 24.

Spivak, Gayatry Chakravorty. *A Critique of Postcolonial Reason: Toward a History of the Vanishing Present.* Cambridge, MA: Harvard UP, 1999.

Spivak, Gayatri Chakravorty. "Additional Thoughts." Columbia University. Accessed April 11, 2024. https://blogs.law.columbia.edu/foucault1313/2016/04/14/gayatri-chakravorty-spivak-additional-thoughts/.

Szlezak, Thomas A. *Reading Plato*, translated by Graham Zanker. London: Routledge, 1999/ 2005.

Thucydides. *History of the Peloponnesian War.* London: Penguin Books, 1972.

Treiber, Guilel. "What ought I do?" *materiali foucaultiani*, volume IX numero 17–18, January–December 2020.

Tronti, Mario. *Workers and Capital.* Translated by David Broder. London/New York: Verso, 2019.

Vegetti, Mario. "Foucault et les Anciens." In *Critique* 471–72, no. 42 (August–September 1986).

von Goethe, Johan Wolfgang. *Faust Part One.* Translated by David Luke. Oxford/New York: Oxford UP, 1987/1998.

von Goethe, Johan Wolfgang. *Faust Part Two.* Translated by David Luke. Oxford/New York: Oxford UP, 1994/2008.

Wallenstein, Sven-Olov. "Introduktion." In *Foucault och Antiken,* edited by Sven-Olov Wallenstein and Johan Sehlberg. Hägersten: Tankekraft, 2017.

Wilde, Oscar. "The Critic as Artist." In *The Collected Works of Oscar Wilde.* Ware, Hertfordshire: Wordsworth Editions Limited, 1997.

Zamora, Daniel and Behrent, Michael C., eds. *Foucault and Neoliberalism.* Cambridge, UK: Polity Press, 2015.

Acknowledgments

First of all, I would like to thank my supervisors Sven-Olov Wallenstein and Charlotta Weigelt for their continued confidence in me and their insightful and knowledgeable guidance. Second, I am very sincerely grateful for the readings, comments, remarks, and suggestions made in the seminars of the philosophy department at Södertörn University: Anders Bartonek, Ulrika Björk, Hans Ruin, Marcia Sá Cavalcante Schuback, Nicholas Smith, Gustav Strandberg, and Fanny Söderbäck. My heartfelt thanks also to: Ulrika Björk in the capacity of Director of Graduate Studies in Philosophy; the Head of Department, Anna Victoria Hallberg; Education Administrator Eva Albinsson, and Officer of the Graduate School in Critical and Cultural Theory, Ewa Rogström.

For discussions, conversations, and a sense of community I thank my fellow PhD candidates (current and former): Erik Bryngelsson, Mats Dahllöv, Anna Enström, Mirey Gorgis, Gabriel Itkes Sznap, Emma Kihl, Nicholas Lawrence, Johan Sehlberg, and Anna-Karin Selberg.

For various forms of discussions, remarks, suggestions and assistance, I would like to thank Laurence Le Bras at BnF département des Manuscrits (site Richelieu), Johan Härnsten, Robin Watkins, Michele Masucci, Samo Tomšič, and The Centre for Marxist Social Studies (CMS) research network.

For inviting me to further the work that appears in this thesis, I would like to thank The Foucault Circle, ICI Berlin, Swedish Labour Movement's Archives and Library, Konstfack, Stockholm University of the Arts, Kungl. Konsthögskolan, Palais de Tokyo, ABA Salon Berlin, Göteborgs förening för filosofi och psykoanalys, Tankeverket, and Clandestinoinstitutet. A direct thank you to Avi Alpert and Thomas Hirschhorn, Carla Zaccagnini, AKCG, Michele Masucci, Meriç Algün, Warren Neidich, Jacqueline Hoàng Nguyễn, Tobias Wessely, Rasmus Redemo and Johanna Gustafsson Fürst.

Eternal gratitude to the theory department of the Jan van Eyck Academie, and to the publishing house Tankekraft for publishing my translations of Foucault's lecture courses: I want to acknowledge that some of the work in this thesis already started there.

A special gratitude is reserved for the late Daniel Defert for his kindness and advice, for Erik M Nilsson for letting me catch a glance of Foucault through the perspective of friendship, for Mladen Dolar for his support and suggestions at a crucial moment, for David Payne for his solidarity and support in assisting me with the English language, for Kim West for invaluable readings and suggestions delivered in the best mix of friendship and theoretical affinities, and for Frédéric Gros for his precise and generous reading and response at my final seminar.

Parts of this work have been made possible with grants from *Annika och Gabriel Urwitz Stiftelse, Drakamöllan Nordiskt forum för kultur och vetenskap för stipendievistelse*, and *Vitterhetsakademin*. I will here take the opportunity to express my gratitude to my uncle Lars Rickard Petersson, and to my extended Thor and Thor-Bergman family for their lovely support.

Finally I would like to thank my brother for his love and enthusiasm, and my parents for everything they taught me, their love, and their never failing support. Rebecka Katz Thor, thank you for invaluable advice, suggestions, and support, for being by my side: for everything. To my family for all their love, patience, support, and understanding, I dedicate this work to you, Rebecka, Sam and Isidor.

Södertörn Doctoral Dissertations

1. Jolanta Aidukaite, *The Emergence of the Post-Socialist Welfare State: The case of the Baltic States: Estonia, Latvia and Lithuania*, 2004

2. Xavier Fraudet, *Politique étrangère française en mer Baltique (1871–1914): de l'exclusion à l'affirmation*, 2005

3. Piotr Wawrzeniuk, *Confessional Civilising in Ukraine: The Bishop Iosyf Shumliansky and the Introduction of Reforms in the Diocese of Lviv 1668–1708*, 2005

4. Andrej Kotljarchuk, *In the Shadows of Poland and Russia: The Grand Duchy of Lithuania and Sweden in the European Crisis of the mid-17th Century*, 2006

5. Håkan Blomqvist, *Nation, ras och civilisation i svensk arbetarrörelse före nazismen*, 2006

6. Karin S Lindelöf, *Om vi nu ska bli som Europa: Könsskapande och normalitet bland unga kvinnor i transitionens Polen*, 2006

7. Andrew Stickley. *On Interpersonal Violence in Russia in the Present and the Past: A Sociological Study*, 2006

8. Arne Ek, *Att konstruera en uppslutning kring den enda vägen: Om folkrörelsers modernisering i skuggan av det Östeuropeiska systemskiftet*, 2006

9. Agnes Ers, *I mänsklighetens namn: En etnologisk studie av ett svenskt biståndsprojekt i Rumänien*, 2006

10. Johnny Rodin, *Rethinking Russian Federalism: The Politics of Intergovernmental Relations and Federal Reforms at the Turn of the Millennium*, 2006

11. Kristian Petrov, *Tillbaka till framtiden: Modernitet, postmodernitet och generationsidentitet i Gorbačevs glasnost' och perestrojka*, 2006

12. Sophie Söderholm Werkö, *Patient patients? Achieving Patient Empowerment through Active Participation, Increased Knowledge and Organisation*, 2008

13. Peter Bötker, *Leviatan i arkipelagen: Staten, förvaltningen och samhället. Fallet Estland*, 2007

14. Matilda Dahl, *States under scrutiny: International organizations, transformation and the construction of progress*, 2007

15. Margrethe B. Søvik, *Support, resistance and pragmatism: An examination of motivation in language policy in Kharkiv, Ukraine*, 2007

16. Yulia Gradskova, *Soviet People with female Bodies: Performing beauty and maternity in Soviet Russia in the mid 1930–1960s*, 2007

17. Renata Ingbrant, *From Her Point of View: Woman's Anti-World in the Poetry of Anna Świrszczyńska*, 2007

18. Johan Eellend, *Cultivating the Rural Citizen: Modernity, Agrarianism and Citizenship in Late Tsarist Estonia*, 2007

19. Petra Garberding, *Musik och politik i skuggan av nazismen: Kurt Atterberg och de svensk-tyska musikrelationerna*, 2007

20. Aleksei Semenenko, *Hamlet the Sign: Russian Translations of Hamlet and Literary Canon Formation*, 2007

21. Vytautas Petronis, *Constructing Lithuania: Ethnic Mapping in the Tsarist Russia, ca. 1800–1914*, 2007

22. Akvile Motiejunaite, *Female employment, gender roles, and attitudes: The Baltic countries in a broader context*, 2008

23. Tove Lindén, *Explaining Civil Society Core Activism in Post-Soviet Latvia*, 2008

24. Pelle Åberg, *Translating Popular Education: Civil Society Cooperation between Sweden and Estonia*, 2008

25. Anders Nordström, *The Interactive Dynamics of Regulation: Exploring the Council of Europe's monitoring of Ukraine*, 2008

26. Fredrik Doeser, *In Search of Security After the Collapse of the Soviet Union: Foreign Policy Change in Denmark, Finland and Sweden, 1988–1993*, 2008

27. Zhanna Kravchenko. *Family (versus) Policy: Combining Work and Care in Russia and Sweden*, 2008

28. Rein Jüriado, *Learning within and between public-private partnerships*, 2008

29. Elin Boalt, *Ecology and evolution of tolerance in two cruciferous species*, 2008

30. Lars Forsberg, *Genetic Aspects of Sexual Selection and Mate Choice in Salmonids*, 2008

31. Eglė Rindzevičiūtė, *Constructing Soviet Cultural Policy: Cybernetics and Governance in Lithuania after World War II*, 2008

32. Joakim Philipson, *The Purpose of Evolution: 'struggle for existence' in the Russian-Jewish press 1860–1900*, 2008

33. Sofie Bedford, *Islamic activism in Azerbaijan: Repression and mobilization in a post-Soviet context*, 2009

34. Tommy Larsson Segerlind, *Team Entrepreneurship: A process analysis of the venture team and the venture team roles in relation to the innovation process*, 2009

35. Jenny Svensson, *The Regulation of Rule-Following: Imitation and Soft Regulation in the European Union*, 2009

36. Stefan Hallgren, *Brain Aromatase in the guppy, Poecilia reticulate: Distribution, control and role in behavior*, 2009

37. Karin Ellencrona, *Functional characterization of interactions between the flavivirus NS5 protein and PDZ proteins of the mammalian host*, 2009

38. Makiko Kanematsu, *Saga och verklighet: Barnboksproduktion i det postsovjetiska Lettland*, 2009

39. Daniel Lindvall, *The Limits of the European Vision in Bosnia and Herzegovina: An Analysis of the Police Reform Negotiations*, 2009

40. Charlotta Hillerdal, *People in Between – Ethnicity and Material Identity: A New Approach to Deconstructed Concepts*, 2009

41. Jonna Bornemark, *Kunskapens gräns – gränsens vetande*, 2009

42. Adolphine G. Kateka, *Co-Management Challenges in the Lake Victoria Fisheries: A Context Approach*, 2010

43. René León Rosales, *Vid framtidens hitersta gräns: Om pojkar och elevpositioner i en multietnisk skola*, 2010

44. Simon Larsson, *Intelligensaristokrater och arkivmartyrer: Normerna för vetenskaplig skicklighet i svensk historieforskning 1900–1945*, 2010

45. Håkan Lättman, *Studies on spatial and temporal distributions of epiphytic lichens*, 2010

46. Alia Jaensson, *Pheromonal mediated behaviour and endocrine response in salmonids: The impact of cypermethrin, copper, and glyphosate*, 2010

47. Michael Wigerius, *Roles of mammalian Scribble in polarity signaling, virus offense and cell-fate determination*, 2010

48. Anna Hedtjärn Wester, *Män i kostym: Prinsar, konstnärer och tegelbärare vid sekelskiftet 1900*, 2010

49. Magnus Linnarsson, *Postgång på växlande villkor: Det svenska postväsendets organisation under stormaktstiden*, 2010

50. Barbara Kunz, *Kind words, cruise missiles and everything in between: A neoclassical realist study of the use of power resources in U.S. policies towards Poland, Ukraine and Belarus 1989–2008*, 2010

51. Anders Bartonek, *Philosophie im Konjunktiv: Nichtidentität als Ort der Möglichkeit des Utopischen in der negativen Dialektik Theodor W. Adornos*, 2010

52. Carl Cederberg, *Resaying the Human: Levinas Beyond Humanism and Antihumanism*, 2010

53. Johanna Ringarp, *Professionens problematik: Lärarkårens kommunalisering och välfärdsstatens förvandling*, 2011

54. Sofi Gerber, *Öst är Väst men Väst är bäst: Östtysk identitetsformering i det förenade Tyskland*, 2011

55. Susanna Sjödin Lindenskoug, *Manlighetens bortre gräns: Tidelagsrättegångar i Livland åren 1685–1709*, 2011

56. Dominika Polanska, *The emergence of enclaves of wealth and poverty: A sociological study of residential differentiation in post-communist Poland*, 2011

57. Christina Douglas, *Kärlek per korrespondens: Två förlovade par under andra hälften av 1800-talet*, 2011

58. Fred Saunders, *The Politics of People – Not just Mangroves and Monkeys: A study of the theory and practice of community-based management of natural resources in Zanzibar*, 2011

59. Anna Rosengren, *Åldrandet och språket: En språkhistorisk analys av hög ålder och åldrande i Sverige cirka 1875–1975*, 2011

60. Emelie Lilliefeldt, *European Party Politics and Gender: Configuring Gender-Balanced Parliamentary Presence*, 2011

61. Ola Svenonius, *Sensitising Urban Transport Security: Surveillance and Policing in Berlin, Stockholm, and Warsaw*, 2011

62. Andreas Johansson, *Dissenting Democrats: Nation and Democracy in the Republic of Moldova*, 2011

63. Wessam Melik, *Molecular characterization of the Tick-borne encephalitis virus: Environments and replication*, 2012

64. Steffen Werther, *SS-Vision und Grenzland-Realität: Vom Umgang dänischer und „volksdeutscher" Nationalsozialisten in Sønderjylland mit der „großgermanischen" Ideologie der SS*, 2012

65. Peter Jakobsson, *Öppenhetsindustrin*, 2012

66. Kristin Ilves, *Seaward Landward: Investigations on the archaeological source value of the landing site category in the Baltic Sea region*, 2012

67. Anne Kaun, *Civic Experiences and Public Connection: Media and Young People in Estonia*, 2012

68. Anna Tessmann, *On the Good Faith: A Fourfold Discursive Construction of Zoroastripanism in Contemporary Russia*, 2012

69. Jonas Lindström, *Drömmen om den nya staden: Stadsförnyelse i det postsovjetisk Riga*, 2012

70. Maria Wolrath Söderberg, *Topos som meningsskapare: Retorikens topiska perspektiv på tänkande och lärande genom argumentation*, 2012

71. Linus Andersson, *Alternativ television: Former av kritik i konstnärlig TV-produktion*, 2012

72. Håkan Lättman, *Studies on spatial and temporal distributions of epiphytic lichens*, 2012

73. Fredrik Stiernstedt, Mediearbete i mediehuset: Produktion i förändring på MTG-radio, 2013

74. Jessica Moberg, *Piety, Intimacy and Mobility: A Case Study of Charismatic Christianity in Present-day Stockholm*, 2013

75. Elisabeth Hemby, *Historiemåleri och bilder av vardag: Tatjana Nazarenkos konstnärskap i 1970-talets Sovjet*, 2013

76. Tanya Jukkala, *Suicide in Russia: A macro-sociological study*, 2013

77. Maria Nyman, *Resandets gränser: Svenska resenärers skildringar av Ryssland under 1700-talet*, 2013

78. Beate Feldmann Eellend, *Visionära planer och vardagliga praktiker: Postmilitära landskap i Östersjöområdet*, 2013

79. Emma Lind, *Genetic response to pollution in sticklebacks: Natural selection in the wild*, 2013

80. Anne Ross Solberg, *The Mahdi wears Armani: An analysis of the Harun Yahya enterprise*, 2013

81. Nikolay Zakharov, *Attaining Whiteness: A Sociological Study of Race and Racialization in Russia*, 2013

82. Anna Kharkina, *From Kinship to Global Brand: The Discourse on Culture in Nordic Cooperation after World War II*, 2013

83. Florence Fröhlig, *A painful legacy of World War II: Nazi forced enlistment: Alsatian/Mosellan Prisoners of war and the Soviet Prison Camp of Tambov*, 2013

84. Oskar Henriksson, *Genetic connectivity of fish in the Western Indian Ocean*, 2013

85. Hans Geir Aasmundsen, *Pentecostalism, Globalisation and Society in Contemporary Argentina*, 2013

86. Anna McWilliams, *An Archaeology of the Iron Curtain: Material and Metaphor*, 2013

87. Anna Danielsson, *On the power of informal economies and the informal economies of power: Rethinking informality, resilience and violence in Kosovo*, 2014

88. Carina Guyard, *Kommunikationsarbete på distans*, 2014

89. Sofia Norling, *Mot "väst": Om vetenskap, politik och transformation i Polen 1989–2011*, 2014

90. Markus Huss, *Motståndets akustik: Språk och (o)ljud hos Peter Weiss 1946–1960*, 2014

91. Ann-Christin Randahl, *Strategiska skribenter: Skrivprocesser i fysik och svenska*, 2014

92. Péter Balogh, *Perpetual borders: German-Polish cross-border contacts in the Szczecin area*, 2014

93. Erika Lundell, *Förkroppsligad fiktion och fiktionaliserade kroppar: Levande rollspel i Östersjöregionen*, 2014

94. Henriette Cederlöf, *Alien Places in Late Soviet Science Fiction: The "Unexpected Encounters" of Arkady and Boris Strugatsky as Novels and Films*, 2014

95. Niklas Eriksson, *Urbanism Under Sail: An archaeology of fluit ships in early modern everyday life*, 2014

96. Signe Opermann, *Generational Use of News Media in Estonia: Media Access, Spatial Orientations and Discursive Characteristics of the News Media*, 2014

97. Liudmila Voronova, *Gendering in political journalism: A comparative study of Russia and Sweden*, 2014

98. Ekaterina Kalinina, *Mediated Post-Soviet Nostalgia*, 2014

99. Anders E. B. Blomqvist, *Economic Natonalizing in the Ethnic Borderlands of Hungary and Romania: Inclusion, Exclusion and Annihilation in Szatmár/Satu-Mare, 1867–1944*, 2014

100. Ann-Judith Rabenschlag, *Völkerfreundschaft nach Bedarf: Ausländische Arbeitskräfte in der Wahrnehmung von Staat und Bevölkerung der DDR*, 2014

101. Yuliya Yurchuck, *Ukrainian Nationalists and the Ukrainian Insurgent Army in Post-Soviet Ukraine*, 2014

102. Hanna Sofia Rehnberg, *Organisationer berättar: Narrativitet som resurs i strategisk kommunikation*, 2014

103. Jaakko Turunen, *Semiotics of Politics: Dialogicality of Parliamentary Talk*, 2015

104. Iveta Jurkane Hobein, *I Imagine You Here Now: Relationship Maintenance Strategies in Long-Distance Intimate Relationships*, 2015

105. Katharina Wesolowski, *Maybe baby? Reproductive behaviour, fertility intentions, and family policies in post-communist countries, with a special focus on Ukraine*, 2015

106. Ann af Burén, *Living Simultaneity: On religion among semi-secular Swedes*, 2015

107. Larissa Mickwitz, *En reformerad lärare: Konstruktionen av en professionell och betygssättande lärare i skolpolitik och skolpraktik*, 2015

108. Daniel Wojahn, *Språkaktivism: Diskussioner om feministiska språkförändringar i Sverige från 1960-talet till 2015*, 2015

109. Hélène Edberg, *Kreativt skrivande för kritiskt tänkande: En fallstudie av studenters arbete med kritisk metareflektion*, 2015

110. Kristina Volkova, *Fishy Behavior: Persistent effects of early-life exposure to 17α-ethinylestradiol*, 2015

111. Björn Sjöstrand, *Att tänka det tekniska: En studie i Derridas teknikfilosofi*, 2015

112. Håkan Forsberg, *Kampen om eleverna: Gymnasiefältet och skolmarknadens framväxt i Stockholm, 1987–2011*, 2015

113. Johan Stake, *Essays on quality evaluation and bidding behavior in public procurement auctions*, 2015

114. Martin Gunnarson, *Please Be Patient: A Cultural Phenomenological Study of Haemodialysis and Kidney Transplantation Care*, 2016

115. Nasim Reyhanian Caspillo, *Studies of alterations in behavior and fertility in ethinyl estradiol-exposed zebrafish and search for related biomarkers*, 2016

116. Pernilla Andersson, *The Responsible Business Person: Studies of Business Education for Sustainability*, 2016

117. Kim Silow Kallenberg, *Gränsland: Svensk ungdomsvård mellan vård och straff*, 2016

118. Sari Vuorenpää, *Literacitet genom interaction*, 2016

119. Francesco Zavatti, *Writing History in a Propaganda Institute: Political Power and Network Dynamics in Communist Romania*, 2016

120. Cecilia Annell, *Begärets politiska potential: Feministiska motståndsstrategier i Elin Wägners 'Pennskaftet', Gabriele Reuters 'Aus guter Familie', Hilma Angered-Strandbergs 'Lydia Vik' och Grete Meisel-Hess 'Die Intellektuellen'*, 2016

121. Marco Nase, *Academics and Politics: Northern European Area Studies at Greifswald University, 1917–1992*, 2016

122. Jenni Rinne, *Searching for Authentic Living Through Native Faith – The Maausk movement in Estonia*, 2016

123. Petra Werner, *Ett medialt museum: Lärandets estetik i svensk television 1956–1969*, 2016

124. Ramona Rat, *Un-common Sociality: Thinking sociality with Levinas*, 2016

125. Petter Thureborn, *Microbial ecosystem functions along the steep oxygen gradient of the Landsort Deep, Baltic Sea*, 2016

126. Kajsa-Stina Benulic, *A Beef with Meat Media and audience framings of environmentally unsustainable production and consumption*, 2016

127. Naveed Asghar, *Ticks and Tick-borne Encephalitis Virus – From nature to infection*, 2016

128. Linn Rabe, *Participation and legitimacy: Actor involvement for nature conservation*, 2017

129. Maryam Adjam, *Minnesspår: Hågkomstens rum och rörelse i skuggan av en flykt*, 2017

130. Kim West, *The Exhibitionary Complex: Exhibition, Apparatus and Media from Kulturhuset to the Centre Pompidou, 1963–1977*, 2017

131. Ekaterina Tarasova, *Anti-nuclear Movements in Discursive and Political Contexts: Between expert voices and local protests*, 2017

132. Sanja Obrenović Johansson, *Från kombifeminism till rörelse: Kvinnlig serbisk organisering i förändring*, 2017

133. Michał Salamonik, *In Their Majesties' Service: The Career of Francesco De Gratta (1613–1676) as a Royal Servant and Trader in Gdańsk*, 2017

134. Jenny Ingridsdotter, *The Promises of the Free World: Postsocialist Experience in Argentina and the Making of Migrants, Race, and Coloniality*, 2017

135. Julia Malitska, *Negotiating Imperial Rule: Colonists and Marriage in the Nineteenth century Black Sea Steppe*, 2017

136. Natalya Yakusheva, *Parks, Policies and People: Nature Conservation Governance in Post-Socialist EU Countries*, 2017

137. Martin Kellner, *Selective Serotonin Re-uptake Inhibitors in the Environment: Effects of Citalopram on Fish Behaviour*, 2017

138. Krystof Kasprzak, *Vara – Framträdande – Värld: Fenomenets negativitet hos Martin Heidegger, Jan Patočka och Eugen Fink*, 2017

139. Alberto Frigo, *Life-stowing from a Digital Media Perspective: Past, Present and Future*, 2017

140. Maarja Saar, *The Answers You Seek Will Never Be Found at Home: Reflexivity, biographical narratives and lifestyle migration among highly-skilled Estonians*, 2017

141. Anh Mai, *Organizing for Efficiency: Essay on merger policies, independence of authorities, and technology diffusion*, 2017

142. Gustav Strandberg, *Politikens omskakning: Negativitet, samexistens och frihet i Jan Patočkas tänkande*, 2017

143. Lovisa Andén, *Litteratur och erfarenhet i Merleau-Pontys läsning av Proust, Valéry och Stendhal*, 2017

144. Fredrik Bertilsson, *Frihetstida policyskapande: Uppfostringskommissionen och de akademiska konstitutionerna 1738–1766*, 2017

145. Börjeson, Natasja, *Toxic Textiles – towards responsibility in complex supply chains*, 2017

146. Julia Velkova, *Media Technologies in the Making – User-Driven Software and Infrastructures for computer Graphics Production*, 2017

147. Karin Jonsson, *Fångna i begreppen? Revolution, tid och politik i svensk socialistisk press 1917–1924*, 2017

148. Josefine Larsson, *Genetic Aspects of Environmental Disturbances in Marine Ecosystems – Studies of the Blue Mussel in the Baltic Sea*, 2017

149. Roman Horbyk, *Mediated Europes – Discourse and Power in Ukraine, Russia and Poland during Euromaidan*, 2017

150. Nadezda Petrusenko, *Creating the Revolutionary Heroines: The Case of Female Terrorists of the PSR (Russia, Beginning of the 20th Century)*, 2017

151. Rahel Kuflu, *Bröder emellan: Identitetsformering i det koloniserade Eritrea*, 2018

152. Karin Edberg, *Energilandskap i förändring: Inramningar av kontroversiella lokaliseringar på norra Gotland*, 2018

153. Rebecka Thor, *Beyond the Witness: Holocaust Representation and the Testimony of Images – Three films by Yael Hersonski, Harun Farocki, and Eyal Sivan*, 2018

154. Maria Lönn, *Bruten vithet: Om den ryska femininitetens sinnliga och temporala villkor*, 2018

155. Tove Porseryd, *Endocrine Disruption in Fish: Effects of 17α-ethinylestradiol exposure on non-reproductive behavior, fertility and brain and testis transcriptome*, 2018

156. Marcel Mangold, *Securing the working democracy: Inventive arrangements to guarantee circulation and the emergence of democracy policy*, 2018

157. Matilda Tudor, *Desire Lines: Towards a Queer Digital Media Phenomenology*, 2018

158. Martin Andersson, *Migration i 1600-talets Sverige: Älvsborgs lösen 1613–1618*, 2018

159. Johanna Pettersson, *What's in a Line? Making Sovereignty through Border Policy*, 2018

160. Irina Seits, *Architectures of Life-Building in the Twentieth Century: Russia, Germany, Sweden*, 2018

161. Alexander Stagnell, *The Ambassador's Letter: On the Less Than Nothing of Diplomacy*, 2019

162. Mari Zetterqvist Blokhuis, *Interaction Between Rider, Horse and Equestrian Trainer – A Challenging Puzzle*, 2019

163. Robin Samuelsson, *Play, Culture and Learning: Studies of Second-Language and Conceptual Development in Swedish Preschools*, 2019

164. Ralph Tafon, *Analyzing the "Dark Side" of Marine Spatial Planning – A study of domination, empowerment and freedom (or power in, of and on planning) through theories of discourse and power*, 2019

165. Ingela Visuri, *Varieties of Supernatural Experience: The case of high-functioning autism*, 2019

166. Mathilde Rehnlund, *Getting the transport right – for what? What transport policy can tell us about the construction of sustainability*, 2019

167. Oscar Törnqvist, *Röster från ingenmansland: En identitetsarkeologi i ett maritimt mellanrum*, 2019

168. Elise Remling, *Adaptation, now? Exploring the Politics of Climate Adaptation through Post-structuralist Discourse Theory*, 2019

169. Eva Karlberg, *Organizing the Voice of Women: A study of the Polish and Swedish women's movements' adaptation to international structures*, 2019

170. Maria Pröckl, *Tyngd, sväng och empatisk timing – förskollärares kroppsliga kunskaper*, 2020

171. Adrià Alcoverro, *The University and the Demand for Knowledge-based Growth The hegemonic struggle for the future of Higher Education Institutions in Finland and Estonia*, 2020

172. Ingrid Forsler, *Enabling Media: Infrastructures, imaginaries and cultural techniques in Swedish and Estonian visual arts education*, 2020

173. Johan Sehlberg, *Of Affliction: The Experience of Thought in Gilles Deleuze by way of Marcel Proust*, 2020

174. Renat Bekkin, *People of reliable loyalty...: Muftiates and the State in Modern Russia*, 2020

175. Olena Podolian, *The Challenge of 'Stateness' in Estonia and Ukraine: The international dimension a quarter of a century into independence*, 2020

176. Patrick Seniuk, *Encountering Depression In-Depth: An existential-phenomenological approach to selfhood, depression, and psychiatric practice*, 2020

177. Vasileios Petrogiannis, *European Mobility and Spatial Belongings: Greek and Latvian migrants in Sweden*, 2020

178. Lena Norbäck Ivarsson, *Tracing environmental change and human impact as recorded in sediments from coastal areas of the northwestern Baltic Proper*, 2020

179. Sara Persson, *Corporate Hegemony through Sustainability – A study of sustainability standards and CSR practices as tools to demobilise community resistance in the Albanian oil industry*, 2020

180. Juliana Porsani, *Livelihood Implications of Large-Scale Land Concessions in Mozambique: A case of family farmers' endurance*, 2020

181. Anders Backlund, *Isolating the Radical Right – Coalition Formation and Policy Adaptation in Sweden*, 2020

182. Nina Carlsson, *One Nation, One Language? National minority and Indigenous recognition in the politics of immigrant integration*, 2021

183. Erik Gråd, *Nudges, Prosocial Preferences & Behavior: Essays in Behavioral Economics*, 2021

184. Anna Enström, *Sinnesstämning, skratt och hypokondri: Om estetisk erfarenhet i Kants tredje Kritik*, 2021

185. Michelle Rydback, *Healthcare Service Marketing in Medical Tourism – An Emerging Market Study*, 2021

186. Fredrik Jahnke, *Toleransens altare och undvikandets hänsynsfullhet – Religion och meningsskapande bland svenska grundskoleelever*, 2021

187. Benny Berggren Newton, *Business Basics – A Grounded Theory for Managing Ethical Behavior in Sales Organizations*, 2021

188. Gabriel Itkes-Sznap, *Nollpunkten. Precisionens betydelse hos Witold Gombrowicz, Inger Christensen och Herta Müller*, 2021

189. Oscar Svanelid Medina, *Att forma tillvaron: Konstruktivism som konstnärligt yrkesarbete hos Geraldo de Barros, Lygia Pape och Lygia Clark*, 2021

190. Anna-Karin Selberg, *Politics and Truth: Heidegger, Arendt and The Modern Political Lie*, 2021

191. Camilla Larsson, *Framträdanden: Performativitetsteoretiska tolkningar av Tadeusz Kantors konstnärskap*, 2021

192. Raili Uibo, *"And I don't know who we really are to each other": Queers doing close relationships in Estonia*, 2021

193. Ignė Stalmokaitė, *New Tides in Shipping: Studying incumbent firms in maritime energy transitions*, 2021

194. Mani Shutzberg, *Tricks of the Medical Trade: Cunning in the Age of Bureaucratic Austerity*, 2021

195. Patrik Höglund, *Skeppssamhället: Rang, roller och status på örlogsskepp under 1600-talet*, 2021

196. Philipp Seuferling, *Media and the refugee camp: The historical making of space, time, and politics in the modern refugee regime*, 2021

197. Johan Sandén, *Närbyråkrater och digitaliseringar: Hur lärares arbete formas av tids-strukturer*, 2021

198. Ulrika Nemeth, *Det kritiska uppdraget: Diskurser och praktiker i gymnasieskolans svenskundervisning*, 2021

199. Helena Löfgren, *Det legitima ägandet: Politiska konstruktioner av allmännyttans privatisering i Stockholms stad 1990–2015*, 2021

200. Vasileios Kitsos, *Urban policies for a contemporary periphery: Insights from eastern Russia*, 2022

201. Jenny Gustafsson, *Drömmen om en gränslös fred: Världsmedborgarrörelsens reaktopi, 1949–1968*, 2022

202. Oscar von Seth, *Outsiders and Others: Queer Friendships in Novels by Hermann Hesse*, 2022

203. Kristin Halverson, *Tools of the Trade: Medical Devices and Practice in Sweden and Denmark, 1855–1897*, 2022

204. Henrik Ohlsson, *Facing Nature: Cultivating Experience in the Nature Connection Movement*, 2022

205. Mirey Gorgis, *Allt är våld: En undersökning av det moderna våldsbegreppet*, 2022

206. Mats Dahllöv, *Det absoluta och det gemensamma: Benjamin Höijers konstfilosofi*, 2022

207. Anton Poikolainen Rosén, *Noticing Nature: Exploring More Than Human-Centred Design in Urban Farming*, 2022

208. Sophie Landwehr Sydow, *Makers, Materials and Machines: Understanding Experience and Situated Embodied Practice at the Makerspace*, 2022

209. Simon Magnusson, *Boosting young citizens' deontic status: Interactional allocation of rights-to-decide in participatory democracy meetings*, 2022

210. Marie Jonsson, *Vad vilja vegetarianerna? En undersökning av den svenska vegetarismen 1900–1935*, 2022

211. Birgitta Ekblom, *Härskarhyllning och påverkan: Panegyriken kring tronskiftet 1697 i det svenska Östersjöväldet*, 2022

212. Joanna Mellquist, *Policy Professionals in Civil Society Organizations: Struggling for Influence*, 2022

213. David Birksjö, *Innovative Security Business – Innovation, Standardization and ndustry Dynamics in the Swedish Security Sector, 1992–2012*, 2023

214. Roman Privalov, *After space utopia: Post-Soviet Russia and futures in space*, 2023

215. Martin Johansson, *De nordiska lekarna: Grannlandsrelationen i pressen under olympiska vinterspel*, 2023

216. Anna Bark Persson, *Steel as the Answer? Viking Bodies, Power, and Masculinity in Anglophone Fantasy Literature 2006–2016*, 2023

217. Josefin Hägglund, *Demokratins stridslinjer: Carl Lindhagen och politikens omvandling, 1896–1923*, 2023

218. Lovisa Olsson, *I vinst och förlust: Köpmäns nätverk i 1500-talets Östersjöstäder*, 2023

219. Kateryna Zorya, *The Government Used to Hide the Truth, But Now We Can Speak: Contemporary Esotericism in Ukraine 1986–2014*, 2023

220. Tony Blomqvist Mickelsson, *A Nordic sport social work in the context of refugee reception*, 2023

221. Ola Luthman, *Searching for sustainable aquaculture governance: A focus on ambitions and experience*, 2023

222. Emma Kihl, *Äventyrliga utföranden: En läsning av Agneta Enckells dikter med Isabelle Stengers kosmopolitik*, 2023

223. Cagla Demirel, *Analyzing Competitive Victimhood: Narratives of recognition and non-recognition in the pursuit of reconciliation*, 2023

224. Joel Odebrant, *Spår, kropp, tid: En undersökning av den måleriska gestens materialitet 1952–1965*, 2024

225. Xiaoying Li, *Energy Efficiency in Buildings in the Baltic States and the Nordic Countries*, 2024

226. Thérese Janzén, *Ticks – Ecology, New Hazards, and Relevance for Public Health*, 2024

227. Paul Sherfey, *Cultivating Responsible Citizenship: Collective Gardens at the Periphery of Neoliberal Urban Norms*, 2024

228. Kirill Polkov, *Queering Images of Russia in Sweden: Discursive hegemony and counter-hegemonic articulations 1991–2019*, 2024

229. Karl Katz Lydén, *Critique and the Care of the Self: The Economy of Truth and Government in Michel Foucault's Late Work*, 2024